Also by David LaRocca from Bloomsbury

Estimating Emerson: An Anthology of Criticism from Carlyle to Cavell (2013)

"This is the definitive anthology on America's premier man of letters—Ralph Waldo Emerson." —CORNEL WEST, *Dietrich Bonhoeffer Professor of Philosophy and Christian Practice, Union Theological Seminary, USA*

Emerson's English Traits and the Natural History of Metaphor (2013)

"This immensely learned, deeply thoughtful, and far-ranging book helps re-situate Emerson in his own time, and in ours. More than just a work of scholarship, it rises to the level of philosophical investigation. It is also witty, playful, and, in its own strange way, original." —PHILLIP LOPATE, *Professor of Professional Practice, Writing, Columbia University, USA*

"One of Emerson's most astute interpreters, LaRocca consistently challenges the limits of academic categorization." —ROBERT D. HABICH, *Past President of the Ralph Waldo Emerson Society and Former Editor of the Emerson Society Papers*

The Bloomsbury Anthology of Transcendental Thought (2017)

"This volume is more than an overview of a field of study—it is participating in the creation of one." —TODD MAY, *Class of 1941 Memorial Professor of the Humanities, Clemson University, USA*

The Thought of Stanley Cavell and Cinema (2020)

"A brilliant collection of original essays by major figures in the field. The genius of Cavell's writings on film is in sharp focus throughout." —MICHAEL FRIED, *J. R. Herbert Boone Emeritus Professor of Humanities and the History of Art, Johns Hopkins University, USA*

"The authors in this collection explore what Stanley Cavell might have meant in ways more variegated, thoughtful, original, and illuminating than anything I have seen before. *The Thought of Stanley Cavell and Cinema*, exemplary in its clarity and carefulness, is a watershed both in our understanding of Cavell and of film itself." —ROBERT PIPPIN, *Evelyn Stefansson Nef Distinguished Service Professor, The University of Chicago, USA*

Inheriting Stanley Cavell (2020)

"*Inheriting Stanley Cavell*, beautifully edited by David LaRocca, is so much more than a gathering of reminiscences and testimonials. So many of the pieces in the volume prove gripping, and they cumulatively transformed my sense of what Cavell had accomplished. This volume makes a strong case for the revolution that Cavell's extraordinary philosophic sensibility, powerful presence as a teacher, and wide range of concerns brought about in North American philosophy. The collection is also impressive for its decision to include dissenting voices." —GEORGE TOLES, *Distinguished Professor of English, Theatre, Film & Media, University of Manitoba, Canada*

Movies with Stanley Cavell in Mind (2021)

"All of the contributors to this wonderful, collective enterprise—brought together by David LaRocca—revisit films Cavell loved or take up the invitation to explore new films. In each instance, they reveal the importance of Cavell's writing and method." —SANDRA LAUGIER, *Professor of Philosophy, Université Paris 1 Panthéon-Sorbonne, France*

The *Geschlecht* Complex

*Addressing Untranslatable Aspects
of Gender, Genre, and Ontology*

Edited by

Oscar Jansson and
David LaRocca

BLOOMSBURY ACADEMIC
NEW YORK · LONDON · OXFORD · NEW DELHI · SYDNEY

BLOOMSBURY ACADEMIC
Bloomsbury Publishing Inc
1385 Broadway, New York, NY 10018, USA
50 Bedford Square, London, WC1B 3DP, UK
29 Earlsfort Terrace, Dublin 2, Ireland

BLOOMSBURY, BLOOMSBURY ACADEMIC and the Diana logo are trademarks of Bloomsbury Publishing Plc

First published in the United States of America 2022

Copyright © Oscar Jansson and David LaRocca, 2022
Each chapter copyright © by the contributor, 2022

For legal purposes the Acknowledgments on pp. 329–340 constitute an extension of this copyright page.

Cover design by Eleanor Rose
Cover image: *Birds II*, courtesy of the artist and Document Gallery, Chicago, USA © 2006, John Opera

All rights reserved. No part of this publication may be reproduced or transmitted in any form or by any means, electronic or mechanical, including photocopying, recording, or any information storage or retrieval system, without prior permission in writing from the publishers.

Bloomsbury Publishing Inc does not have any control over, or responsibility for, any third-party websites referred to or in this book. All internet addresses given in this book were correct at the time of going to press. The author and publisher regret any inconvenience caused if addresses have changed or sites have ceased to exist, but can accept no responsibility for any such changes.

A catalog record for this book is available from the Library of Congress.

ISBN: HB: 978-1-5013-8192-8
PB: 978-1-5013-8196-6
ePDF: 978-1-5013-8194-2
eBook: 978-1-5013-8193-5

Typeset by Integra Software Services Pvt. Ltd.

To find out more about our authors and books visit www.bloomsbury.com and sign up for our newsletters.

CONTENTS

1 Contending with Untranslatable Categories; or, Inducing the Nervous Condition of the *Geschlecht* Complex 1
        OSCAR JANSSON AND DAVID LaROCCA

  Appendix I: Unfinished Definitions 35
  Apter, "Lexilalia" | Cassin, "Philosophizing in Languages" | Cavell, "Beginning to Read Barbara Cassin" | Crépon, "*Geschlecht*"

2 Antitheatricality as Critical Idiom 47
        CARO PIRRI

3 The Cruel Beast: Settler Sovereignty and the Crisis of American Zoopolitics 71
        BRIAN W. NAIL

4 Between the Body and Language: Narratives of the Moving Subject in Okwui Okpokwasili's *Bronx Gothic* 101
        LAUREN DIGIULIO

  Appendix II: Indefiniteness, *Geschlechtslosigkeit*, Undoing, Unknowing, Unlearning 127
  Butler, "Gender and Gender Trouble" | Cassin, *Sophistical Practice* | Crépon, "*Geschlecht*" | David-Ménard and Deutscher, "Gender" | Derrida, "*Geschlecht* I: Sexual Difference, Ontological Difference" | Heller-Roazen, "Varieties of Indefiniteness" | Irigaray, *To Be Two* | Malabou, *Changing Difference* | Nancy, *L'Intrus* | Preciado, *Testo Junkie* | Sandford, "'Sex' and 'Sexual Difference'" | Spillers, "Mama's Baby, Papa's Maybe" | Weheliye, *Habeas Viscus*

5   Collapsing the Gender/Genre Distinction:
    On Transgressions of Category in Woolf's *Orlando*   143
    OSCAR JANSSON

6   Gazing at the Untranslatable Subject: From
    Velázquez's *Las Meninas* to Ellison's *Invisible Man*   173
    RICHARD HAJARIZADEH

7   From Lectiocentrism to Gramophonology:
    Listening to Cinema and Writing Sound Criticism   203
    DAVID LAROCCA

    Appendix III: Genre Unlimited/Genre Ungenred   271
    Apter, "Untranslatable? The 'Reading' versus the 'Looking'" | Barthes, *The Pleasure of the Text* | Cavell, "Types; Cycles as Genres"; "*It Happened One Night*"; "The Fact of Television" | Chartier, "Genre between Literature and History" | Crimmins, "Gender, Genre, and the Near Future in Derrida's 'The Law of Genre'" | Croce, "Criticism of the Theory of Artistic and Literary Kinds" | Derrida, "The Law of Genre" | Jauss, "Theory of Genres and Medieval Literature" | Wells, "Genres as Species and Spaces"

Afterword: Trans-Ontology and the *Geschlecht* Complex   293
    EMILY APTER

Bibliography   305
Acknowledgments   331
Contributors   343
Index   346

1

Contending with Untranslatable Categories; or, Inducing the Nervous Condition of the *Geschlecht* Complex

Oscar Jansson and David LaRocca

It's the way of saying things, isn't it, not the things?
—Virginia Woolf, *The Voyage Out*

[...] *for the same thing is for conceiving as is for being.*
—Parmenides, 4ᵀᴴ Fragment

The collective work in this volume has been agitated by what we call the *Geschlecht* complex. Best described as a mode of inquiry—which in time offers a milieu for thinking about the act and art of translation—this complex starts with the recognition of two things. First, the age-old question of the ontological power of naming: of how the words and categories we use not only shape thought and understanding, but affect the possibilities of being in the world; second, the polysemy and multidirectional impact of *Geschlecht* itself. In German, this word denotes not just gender and genre, but kinship, species, kind, sex, race, and more—concepts that may seem too broad, defiantly independent, or even contradictory—thereby unsettling habitual delineations between different taxonomical registers and ontological categories. The effect is particularly apparent in (attempted) translation "out of" German, as the change of linguistic frame to some "foreign" linguistic field—to English, French, Swedish, or whatever the language might be—inevitably entails a conceptual shift, a displacement that discriminates among other possible classifications and excludes their critical implications.[1]

By linking these two points—that is, drawing together questions of ontology and the relationships between different linguistic taxonomies that constitute them—*The Geschlecht Complex* ties philosophy to philology. All of the newly composed long-form essays that follow here examine concrete category problems in art and humanistic thought, and thereby detail the rifts between an expression or an idea and the critical vocabularies at hand for describing them—yet not in the sense of "getting it right," or finding the most appropriate word or near-synonym. Rather, each essay explores how analysis and categorial naming might recognize its own discriminatory nature, and thus its limits, indeed, its failures. How can we denominate sexual, aesthetic, or medial categories—all of which are encompassed by *Geschlecht*—without discounting the interconnections between them? How can we use taxonomies without reproducing the at times violent hierarchies of value and power incumbent in classification? How can we discriminate *among* phenomena without discriminating *against* certain phenomenological classifications? And most importantly: How can we account for the critical implications of what categorization *excludes*—for how the unclassifiable and omitted affects our reasoning, even when barred from conscious thought?

These questions have a particular significance, and genuine resonance for theory, in the context of the contemporary humanities, where calls for transdisciplinary and global perspectives highlight the dilemmas of specialization—not least how the "specialized" inescapably precludes or brackets part of the larger picture (unseen, unheard, and thus unacknowledged). But while *The Geschlecht Complex* can be regarded as a reaction to this shared situation—both as book and as a mode of inquiry—its theoretical foundations have a much older provenance. Whether one looks to ancient metaphysics—going back to Parmenides' discussions of truth and opinion, and Heraclitus' subsequent responses to them—or to modern linguistics and the Sapir–Whorf hypothesis, a central line of reasoning within Western philosophy has to do with prioritizing the relation between language and thought, between word and idea, concept and being.[2] Yet what precisely can we say for the interactivities between *these* realms and linkages—whether language meets or makes experience—when we are not sure of the sufficiency of our linguistic translations of conceptual content? For the commissioned essays gathered in this volume, the most important point-of-reference and immediate inspiration is not Greek antiquity (although it factors heavily), but rather Barbara Cassin's radically contemporary and field-defining work on untranslatability: her brave, nuanced venture in tracing the critical implications of the shifting histories of words, concepts, and ideas—what she calls "philosophizing in languages."[3] Forcefully presented in the massive and collaborative *Vocabulaire européen des philosophies: le dictionnaire des intraduisibles*, Cassin's project is rooted in the fact that certain words in the history of Western philosophy have resisted translation.[4] With examples such as *Geist*, *logos*, *esprit*, and *Pravda*—and to be sure, *Geschlecht*—these philosophical "untranslatables," Cassin argues, illustrate the close connections between the affordances of language and the potentialities of thought; that words provide a vision of the world, and in a sense *become* the world.

In an explanatory note to the background and implications of untranslatability, Cassin recalls the words of Wilhelm von Humboldt, in his *Fragmente der Monographie über die Basken*:

> [...] different languages are not so many designations of a thing: they are different perspectives on that same thing, and when the thing is not an object for the external senses, those perspectives become so many things themselves.[5]

What is highlighted through this linkage between words, perspectives, and "things themselves" is, once again, the power of naming and the ongoing negotiation of nominalism. Cassin's project is not only a captivating recovery and restatement of age-old ontological and nominalist queries, however, but also an active re-inscription of their centrality for critical thought in our contemporary circumstances. Considered through the notion of philosophical untranslatables—the very idea of which is latent in Humboldt's description—the sinuous network of words and things illuminates which philological frames and critical perspectives have come to dominate others; how shifts from Greek to Latin to French or English, for example, have silenced homonyms and expounded polysemy, whether through political strictures, moral preferences, or linguistic displacements. The notion of "philosophizing in languages" thereby calls for a reinvestigation of what the ties between language and thought have meant, and what they continue to mean. In an identitarian age, when everyday words are used as envoys for specialized concepts (and commitments), we are especially in need of extended reflections on the prospects of failing to make the conversion, and in turn, leaving unfilled the realization of genuine conversation.

Cassin's emphasis on a critical *re*investigation of how words affect thought is also central to the method she presents, particularly in the *Vocabulaire*, for placing the work of the translator at center stage (and we might add, the "translator" as critic—that is, one who interprets words monovocally, from within a single language). This method, it should be noted, has close ties to *Begriffsgeschichte* and lexicography, and also exhibits distinctive similarities with modern translation theory. For example, in *The Translator's Invisibility*,

Lawrence Venuti points out that the presumed ideal for linguistic translation in the West has long been "fluency," "transparency," and "invisibility," or more pointedly, an absence of any linguistic peculiarities that would draw attention to the translated text as just that: translated and displaced from an older source, and thereby "*not-original*." In short, the translator should not be recognizable as (an) author. Following this scenario, adjusted as it is from the standard myth of the transparent translator and the object translated-without-loss-or-deviation, Venuti calls attention to texts that instead express their cross-linguistic histories and that harness the critical and cultural effects of *not* conforming to frictionless conventionality.[6] In this revised portrait, the translator—between languages, within a language—is welcomed as a celebrated participant in the shared endeavor to render written thought intelligible, and to remain willing to contend with the unintelligible.

However, both the extent and the implications of Cassin's project are vastly different from Venuti's—and not just in the sense of how the collaborative *Vocabulaire* provides empirical investigations covering two and a half thousand years of philosophical history. In emphasizing how the history of ideas and the outlines of critical thought have been shaped by linguistic strictures, Cassin also presents language as an essentially philosophical crux, rather than a philological predicament. Hence attention to marginalia, footnotes, fragments, extracts, and contested etymologies of critical concepts becomes less a concern with the ideals of translation (as just proffered, and even as revised) than with the history of philosophy itself. In other words, the seemingly minute and marginal, the displaced and excluded, is put at the fore, scaled up to its possibilities of reinterpreting the pregiven and the (apparently) fixed.

A vital and decisive background to Cassin's approach in the *Vocabulaire* is her extensive work on the Sophists and other pre-Socratic thinkers. In *L'Effet sophistique* and *Jacques le Sophiste: Lacan, Logos et Psychoanalyse*, as well as in the *Vocabulaire*, one can readily trace how Cassin's interest in sophistry has affected her methods: in all of these studies, the inquisitive tactic is closely tied to rhetoric, to the argumentative aspects of language, and to the performative underpinnings of any linguistic account of truth.[7] In a more theoretical—and indeed, historiographical—sense, the Sophists also exemplify Cassin's interest in the excluded, the derided, the maligned, and the silenced. Her query is not just a matter of method or what the Sophists *did*, in other words, but also an invitation to consider what the Sophists imply for understanding tradition and history, including the traditions and histories of translation.

One must, in this instance, recall the Sophist's denigration in the popular imagination of Western philosophical discourse, and the predominance of overtly critical reports on their lucrative transformations of falsehoods to half-truths—where commodification is a mark of philosophical compromise, and of moral lapse. Indeed, we can join Cassin in asking ourselves "Who's Afraid of the Sophists?"[8] (Clearly not Cassin.) As suspect ancestors of propaganda, alternative facts, and fake news, and with Plato's call for the banishment of poets from the republic—suffering, as he did, a moral panic over Homer—the Sophists have long been relegated to the margins of respectable Western thought (where Plato, the counter-Sophist par excellence, has not incidentally reigned without interruption for millennia). Not long ago, Alain Badiou noted there are "only three crucial philosophers"—Descartes, Hegel, and "above all, Plato."[9] From this view, which is surely dominant, if not hegemonic, the Sophists function as Philosophy's primordial Other and go-to adversary. But, argues Cassin, this longstanding predicament should also heighten our interest in what the Sophists actually did: what they said, wrote, and claimed. And more to the point, seeing as how the history of the Sophists is "a history of neglected and repressed traditions," actively engaging with a *sophistic* history of philosophy means exploring "the paradigm of what was not only left to the side but transformed and made unintelligible."[10] Oxymoronic as it may seem, considering sophistry as philosophy—despite Plato's, and we should underscore too Aristotle's, fervant contestations and defenses in the other direction—lies at the heart of Cassin's critical project, and as such is a key to understanding the force of philosophical untranslatables in her work and beyond it. Attending to the neglected and cast-off, then, is not just a matter of detailing complicated etymological shifts and defending intellectual commitments, but also of engaging with a critical elaboration of the "tradition" of (Western) philosophy itself. Cassin's orientation supplies a way of examining orthodoxy and of revisiting the past as a means for reimagining the present—and perhaps even setting up the terms for future discussion and debate.

Describing Cassin's engagement with sophistry, in *Logics of Worlds*, Badiou argues that she combines Heideggerian thought and the linguistic turn, thereby synthesizing the idea of a Greek inception of critical thought with an acceptance of everything being language, of a general rhetoric as the closest philosophy might come to the real:

> Convinced that philosophy's inception is fettered by a specific rhetoric (the predicative rhetoric that Aristotle transforms into a general logic, or ontology, in Book I of the *Metaphysics*), Cassin makes Gorgias and his successors into the artisans of another path for philosophy, in which, since "being" is exchangeable with "being said," the function of non-being (ultimately, of silence) is constitutive, in the stead and place of that of being. Ontology is replaced with logology.[11]

While Badiou's take on the Sophists is very different from Cassin's, his outline of the argument just invoked remains sound.[12] For the Untranslatable does not just denote what is *difficult* to translate, but also what *resists* translation, what is *not translated*, or what may never make the passage; the term, then, helpfully designates the excluded and looked-over, that which may be and remain silenced and considered (perpetually) unintelligible. Thus, given the commendations and strictures of Western civilization, the Sophists are "untranslatable" because, in today's youthful argot, they are not "relatable." Given prevailing indoctrination in the Socratic tradition (a cult that stretches from the Greek agora to the present-day amphitheater lecture hall or online classroom), we cannot understand—and are precluded from comprehending—where they are coming from; as such, the Sophists remain largely unintelligible, threatening even, and therefore contest the mainstream, otherwise known as the default mode. In an academic environment that stresses *scientia* and *veritas*, what of ignorance, lapse, and *aporia*?[13]

Furthermore, Badiou's concluding note of a shift from ontology to logology becomes decisive, particularly as "logology" itself exemplifies some of the untranslatable residues Cassin traces throughout the history of philosophy. Technically definable metareferentially as "words about words," the term was coined by Novalis to signify an open-ended philosophical discourse—that is, a mode of expression in some sense aware of itself and of philosophy's linguistic operations. Yet while praising this type of discourse, Novalis also upheld the distinction between Sophists and Philosophers, as in the "Logological Fragments I":

> Sophists are people who, alert to the weaknesses and errors of philosophers, seek to use these to their advantage or generally for certain unphilosophical, unworthy purposes—often philosophy itself. Thus they actually have nothing to do with philosophy. If they are unphilosophical on principle—then they are to be regarded as enemies of philosophy and to be treated as enemies.[14]

Going on to describe the Sophists as "skeptics" (here choosing a cognate that masks the more striking appellation "enemies"), Novalis notes that some of them are worthy of respect, as they have "the genuine philosophical gift of discrimination." However, that capacity matters less than their lack of "spiritual potency"—a lack that he claims ultimately defines them. Novalis' gloss (or is it glossing over?) is expressive of how the Socratic tradition articulates philosophy's tasks, and would have its values emerge endogenously from the righteousness of the tradition's own methods. In doing so, sophistical approaches to the same content or concerns are (almost) automatically defined by their *lack*, and treated as exogenous—that is, as accidental, as deviant, and thus, as suspect and dismissible. Even the term Cassin chooses to describe her critical project, in other words, merges with the key problematic of exclusion: of how the very definition of philosophy has distanced itself from any elaboration of how it has taken form.

Beyond Novalis, logology also joins the fray of two strikingly different disciplinary frameworks. In the 1960s, Dimitri Borgmann popularized the term within the field of recreational linguistics, focusing on things such as lipograms, tautonyms, and acrostics—most successfully in *Language on Vacation*.[15] Around the same time, in *The Rhetoric of Religion*, the renowned theorist Kenneth Burke used "logology" to describe his analyses of symbolic acts and linguistic performatives in the Bible.[16] Seeing as Burke's study concerns itself with how language bridges the sacred and the secular (even the transcendental and the mundane), its difference from Borgmann's musings on metalinguistic word games and self-collapsed poems could hardly be more pronounced. Paradoxically, though, that difference exemplifies the productive force of the term in question: through its contested and contrasting definitions, the rubric of logology in a sense performs what is at stake in Cassin's idea of "philosophizing in languages." We are encouraged to recognize that such a process is not just a matter of observing how language affects thought and defines our perspectives, but that words *become* the world—that linguistic performatives are both acts and artifacts of philosophy. In these senses, the contested and (doubly) self-referential rubric of logology becomes a call for exploring how the words we use are tied to histories of the thinkable. And even more crucially, admitting the etymological charge of translation and the transcendental, how critical vocabularies not only define our reasoning but also determine what is *unthinkable*—what remains excluded, what lies beyond the realm of the acceptable, authorized, pertinent, intelligible, or sensible.

Against the background of logology and philosophical untranslatables, we propose *The Geschlecht Complex* be adopted as both a name for a book and as a mode of inquiry (one that is serially enacted within this volume according to a range of sub-methods and ongoing disciplinary discourses). The project is positioned to address the prevailing connection between the ontological power of naming and the complex histories of analytical vocabularies, and it does so on a case-by-case basis, iterating as it proceeds in a series of crossings—from one media to another, from one discourse to the next, from one discipline to those others that are said to operate under distinct programs and vocabularies. In these contexts, where philosophy is coextensive with philology, we readily acknowledge how prevailing concepts may shift or come apart, paradigms may be displaced or replaced, exchanges made, proxies imposed—and how all of this might, and *should* be unsettling. And yet, the turmoil is also the very point; we are not gathered to reify a counter-program (as if to establish some new school or agenda), but rather to dwell momentarily in the spaces between disciplines, between concepts, between inherited commitments. The chapters, then, do not operate as philosophical *apologia*, but as examinations of the idiopathic. As fellow sufferers of the *Geschlecht* complex, one and all, our shared ambition is to avoid the (mere) rearticulation or even fresh application of dominant ideologies, and instead to roam and range beyond familiar conditions—to ask about what has been left out, obscured, hastily jettisoned, all in the hope of discovering or recovering some orientation toward present and future conditions. In these respects, the essays that follow explore category problems *not* in the sense of finding the most appropriate classifications for particular ideas or works of art, but rather of examining how, when problematic, we can move beyond, displace, or otherwise transform them; how we can account for what our taxonomies and analytical concepts have made unintelligible; and how we might avoid the political, moral, and epistemological violence their hierarchies inevitably entail. To these varied and interconnected ends our critics investigate translations, mergers, and displacements of models, terms, and categories. With these aims the contributing essayists dissect how certain works of art—in film, theater, literature, and other media and elements of experience—portray the boundaries and limitations of disparate critical registers.

The *Geschlecht* complex, at least in the manner we pursue it and respond to it here, does not seek resolution but open-ended debate about inherited and emergent category problems. We aim to study the margins *from the margins*, and not litigate for the margins to become standardized, centralized, or normalized. At last, preserving the potencies of the fringe is itself part of the promising potential of *The Geschlecht Complex*. We do not wish to rid ourselves of the feeling of this agitation but conversely come to consciousness about its necessary and permanent role in our life with language, our contest with the terms and conditions that give shape to philosophical and sophistic expression. Our nervous condition is not a symptom to sedate or eradicate; rather, it is something we wish to cultivate an awareness of so that we might put its energies to productive, illuminating use.

* * * *

Against the background of Cassin's theories of untranslatability and the connections between philosophy and philology, it is hardly surprising that the essays in this volume are coordinated around the notion of *Geschlecht*. Indeed, in many ways the word itself is an ideal example of a "philosophical untranslatable," even if that designation of ideality might seem somewhat paradoxical, and risk a delineation of the productive force in the word's polysemous meanings. But, we hazard to quip, *for lack of a better word*, this designation will do—as it has done for Heidegger, Derrida, and Cassin, among others.

First of all, linguistically speaking, the German word *Geschlecht* at once resists translation into other languages *and*, when pressed, gushes too many possibilities; it appears to operate as a list of synonyms more easily than in a one-to-one ratio. It can be translated "into" so many cognates that one loses track of the "this means that" isomorphism presumed to hold when "moving" words or meanings from one language to another (e.g., coaxing them to "cross over"). In any attempt at making the trip—transferring the senses of *Geschlecht* from German to English, say—one is readily faced with the questions of false equivalency and the mechanics of exclusion that the notion of untranslatability highlights. As has already been pointed out, in English alone *Geschlecht* arrives in translation as gender, genre, kinship, kind, and species, but also sex, race, lineage, community, and generation—among other massive, unruly, and occasional incommensurate categories. Even in the most elementary act of translating this single word, then, dealing with *Geschlecht* means risking that vastly different categories of being are mixed up, made to overlap and obscure one another; the sexual, social, aesthetic, moral, political, philosophical, and historical legacies of each attempted equivalent contend with the others for primacy.

Furthermore, by simply using the word *Geschlecht*, one tests the validity of the law of non-contradiction, either by saying two things at once—X is a gender *and* a genre, Y is a generation *and* a sex—or by not saying what one means. As Marc Crépon has pointed out, this multivocality is heavily dependent on the word's curious compound of vertical descendancy (as in the Greek *genos* [γένος] of race and lineage) with perceptions of horizontal cohesion (as in generation, genre, or gender), where descriptive resemblance overrides communal ancestry.[17] In these senses, the linguistic potentiality of *Geschlecht* can be discriminated ontologically in so far as it marks its belonging to an order or "being of a kind," yet, simultaneously, and thus problematically, it can also remain indiscriminate in the way that it implies both an epistemological and a phenomenological similitude between different orders of belonging. Or put differently, the inherent polysemy of *Geschlecht* constantly reminds us of the outside and the otherwise, for as it delimits a range of different but related categories of being it also draws attention to the act (and art) of categorization itself. The specter of the ancient Sophists comes into view again: instead of diving the depths for essences, they learned to skate on the surface—to notice what appears briefly, then disappears from view; to respond to the variability and endless evolution of language as it interacts and constructs thought.

The effects of troubled and troubling translation are even more pronounced when *Geschlecht* is "moved" to languages other than English. In French, for example, the designations of gender and sex inevitably become the focal points of both politics and ontology (indeed, a politics of ontology and an ontology of politics). For as this distinction between cultural and biological modes of sexual difference—readily apparent in English—is collapsed or absorbed by the single German word, in French it is supplanted by a reference to the distinction itself and expanded by an implicit opening to aesthetics: *Geschlecht* becomes *différence des sexes, identité sexuelle, sexe*, and *genre*. The belated translation of Judith Butler's *Gender Trouble* into French poignantly exemplifies what this polysemy entails, for in considering its French title *Trouble dans le genre*, one inevitably confronts the closeness between gender and genre—and, perhaps, their shared identity. One faces, that is to say, how both aesthetic forms and designations of sexual difference rely on discriminatory acts of definition and categorization; how the powers of naming and taxonomizing affect and codify the ontological potentialities of diverse things, texts, and persons said to occupy the same world. Gender trouble becomes *genre* trouble, and we are prompted to notice the uncanny ways in which people are troubled by their genres as much as texts are troubled by their genders. In related fashion, Ciara Cremin, writing "as a trans woman raised to be a man," proposes that masculinity is a "generic disorder" (especially pronounced in capitalist societies), one that "depends and even thrives upon its very symptoms."[18] These trades and translations advocate on their own behalves for new forms of cognition and recognition, including those moments of incomprehensibility, when we are no longer certain of the categories we are thought to inhabit, or the trouble they may cause.

The exemplary status of *Geschlecht* as a philosophical untranslatable can also be traced by way of its own contested and problematic position in Western thought. In this specific, historic context, its most forceful elaboration is, of course, Jacques Derrida's series of essays about the concept's position and validity in Martin Heidegger's writing—and by necessity, given Derrida's place and time, in post-Heideggerian thought. With an anachronism and asynchrony befitting the disorder and realignments caused by *Geschlecht*, the series of remarks was recently completed, with the third installment being published some twenty-five years *after* the fourth—a publication, one should add, heavily dependent on the editorial efforts of Katie Chenoweth, Geoffrey Bennington, and Rodrigo Therezo.[19] Furthermore, in David Farrell Krell's *Phantoms of the Other: Four Generations of Derrida's Geschlecht*, Derrida's varied and extended analyses of *Geschlecht* are treated at length and with the philosophical rigor they have long undoubtedly deserved.[20] As we have come to more familiar terms with *Geschlecht* as an intellectual phenomenon, we have appreciated how far it is from an arcane subdivision of philosophical and literary theory. Because *Geschlecht* has summoned a veritable library of erudite reaction and output, the *Geschlecht* complex itself involves destabilizing encounters with what might be called the formidable and far-reaching *Geschlecht* scholarly–industrial complex.

As a gloss on the cumulative findings and recommendations at hand, Derrida suggests that what are typically considered ontic categories of being—registers of identity, such as sex, community, or race, for example—connect to the ontological, and thus have implications for Being; in some sense, these classifications constitute the "thereness" of *Dasein*. Much of this intimation is expressed in the subtitle of Derrida's first essay on *Geschlecht*, in which he states the parallel *and* sequential formulation "sexual difference, ontological difference." Without going into lengthy detail on the essay (which, again, Krell has performed with exceptional results), the work deals with the place of the sexual in a course given by Heidegger at Marburg roughly at the time of *Sein und Zeit*. For our purposes here, though, it should be noted how Derrida takes issue with Heidegger's *omission* of *Geschlecht* as a topic worthy of explicit discussion. Calling Heidegger's neglect a "scene of stubborn mutism at the very center of the conversation," Derrida regards Heidegger's emphatic pronouncements on the neutrality of *Dasein* as leading directly to questions of *neutralization* and thus of approaching the metaphysical by way of *subtracting* the differential marks of the ontic, all the while without necessarily arriving at a sense of outright negativity. Rather than issue *Dasein* in its full range of embodied being, *Dasein* is neutered. If this critique is taken up positively—as an omission laden with open-endedness and variability—then the sexual neutrality of *Dasein* opens vistas where it is possible, and indeed unavoidable, to conceive of the pre-differential and pre-dual as not necessarily undifferentiated (homogenous, unitary, un-sexed, etc.), but as an originary positivity (*ursprüngliche Positivität*) imbued with a dynamic multiplicity, because it is geared toward a certain dispersal or "parceling out" of the differentiating marks of sexuality.[21]

To regard *Dasein* as (sexually) neutral and/or neutered, in other words, one has to consider not only what sexual difference *is*, but also the *relation* between being and Being—and especially what happens in that "between," how one becomes the other, or is moved to the outside. Furthermore, casting light on this between-ness also upsets conventional strictures of teleology and intellectual quests for "pure" originarity, thereby mirroring, in a sense, Jack Halberstam's call in *Trans** for opening up analysis to "unfolding categories of being," where the asterisk of the title "modifies the meaning of transitivity by refusing to situate transition in relation to a destination."[22] The gliph operates bivalently: calling us at once to search for its customary marginal annotation and to acknowledge how it exists (independently) as an announcement that no such annotation (definition, destination, etc.) will be on offer. The trans* is an "unfolding" without a crease.

As with Cassin's approaches to untranslatability, and we should add, Emily Apter's elaborations of them, Derrida treats *Geschlecht* as a liminal space for thinking.[23] In each moment of his interpretation, we are made party to a detailing of what happens in the translational shifts between languages, traditions, and analytical taxonomies; and thus, of understanding what happens between words. For Catherine Malabou, another essential voice in the reception of *Geschlecht*, the shifts inherent in the ontic/ontological dimensions of these "betweens" are approachable through the notion of transvestism, as when she states that

> [The] substitutability of Being and the being, understood as the *free circulation* of both, *play*, exchange structure without domination or appropriation of one by the other. [.... T]he transvestism of Being as

the being and the being as Being [then] takes on an entirely different meaning: they point at each other, show one another to each other, lose their identity even as they gain it in this game of the unfamiliar, the strange, the queer.[24]

Although such notes might be further confounding, both the intellectual exploration and the practical mapping of such shifting regions invites a necessary confrontation with the unmooring of discourses and definitions. Even a cumbersome word (in translation, of course) such as "substitutability" provides a useful integration of categories—e.g., not just naming potential surrogates but also nominalizing how they may be exchanged. We need the proxy and the verb to achieve the swap.

In the second essay on *Geschlecht*, Derrida speaks more explicitly of the word itself, signaling the difficulties of its translation. The same basic translational problem remains apparent in his discussion of *genre*—and again, because he is writing in French, the word carries weight as both genre and gender. Similar comments abound in "The Law of Genre," where his emphasis falls on the conceptual disorientation that arises when one tries to classify the very act of generic classification.[25] Such a metaphilosophical puzzle is worth mentioning here because of its closeness to the mode of inquiry we are calling the *Geschlecht* complex. At the heart of its analytical impulse lies both the (ontological) question of the pre-differentiated-though-not-unitary, and the (translational) issues that inevitably arise when one tries to understand or define a given term or concept (of course, including *Geschlecht*). Both concerns connect to the problematic of how supposedly descriptive taxonomies have profound effects on the topographies of possible thought, and conversely, how alterations in categorial practice directly implicate available modes of being. What is this thing? What shall we call it? And how can we be sure we are speaking of the same thing across time and languages?

The *Geschlecht* complex is the name, then, for this constellation of philological and philosophical conditions; for this compounded network of words and ideas that both shape our perspectives on the world and call attention to what we are not seeing seeing (or hearing or perceiving more generally). We live in the complex—are made nervous and strange because of it—and yet aim to point our energies toward it. Again, we do not seek to eradicate or "solve" the complexities we face—that we are—but choose instead to make company with them: being companionable to their indeterminacies, becoming company to ourselves. In these senses, the *Geschlecht* complex is a nervous condition the same way that human physiology presumes a nervous system: they are meant to be recognized, reflected upon, regulated, or recuperated—but in no case repudiated.

* * * *

Apart from the theoretical backgrounds outlined above, sketching the origins and rationale of *The Geschlecht Complex* may arrive as a story of our group's shared intellectual biography. For a stretch of a summer season a few years ago, we found ourselves gathered into a small community of readers—joined only by our interest in doing so.[26] Sharing a table and a diverse set of texts, we roamed vast intellectual terrains and lingered on minute details. We discussed books, films, novels, performance art, anthropological studies, notes on architecture, lexicographical debates, poetry, and much else. We read and re-read independently, in tandem, and together as a group—we hurried ahead and doubled-back, we caught sight of clarity and re-entered the fog line.

In hindsight, the scene of our shared and mutual instruction that summer seems like something out of a campus novel. Equally open to the satirical and the romantic, the set-up was simple: scholars from four continents reading, discussing, and then re-reading texts, each of whom had both time and energy to spare on problems that in daily academic life often lie just out of bounds, beyond the decorum of one's workday responsibilities or disciplinary expectations. (That we are recalling these sessions from deep into the era of the coronavirus pandemic might make for a hybrid genre of the campus novel: where campus crises overlap with epidemiological ones. Moreover, taking our pre-covid freedoms for granted—admitting that they were unseen, unrecognized, underappreciated—the contrast, or contest, between in-person and virtual had not yet fully dawned; that we benefitted from the nuances of sharing the same air have only become more apparent in the time since, and in the isolation we now take as the default, as the normal, and thus as the unremarked upon. Our scholarly nervous condition—already *in medias res*—has, therefore, been affected by the global nervous condition befalling humanity.)

During those sessions, capably lead and consequentially guided by Emily Apter, we not only tracked the undulating etymologies of our shared analytical concepts (genre, gender, media, form, sex, etc.) through our palette of first languages—Spanish, German, English, Swedish, French, Portuguese, Hindi, Chinese—but the disciplinary and epistemological stakes connected to those lexical nuances. Circumventing the shape of the semester and the demands of hard deadlines opened up a space for moving beyond the acutely pressing and immediately solvable. It meant being able to linger with words and concepts stumbled upon through rambling (if decidedly text-based) discussions, devoting energy to translators' footnotes and conceptually rich marginalia. While in a sense a performance of Cassin's call to philosophize in languages, that open-endedness was strange: it lent the possibility of collectively rethinking and then rethinking again those issues whose complexity tends to conceal itself in the workings of disciplinary normalcy—and indeed, to be concealed by it.

Part of the idealized tint of recalling that summer (and surely befitting the campus novel theme) has to do with the setting. The seclusion in Reconstruction-era university buildings in central New York, the calm openness of the summer quad merging with afternoon thunderstorms and heavy waters traversing the downward slope of verdant, fragrant gorges; it all resulted in an atmospheric dynamism almost electric to the senses. However *Sturm und Drang* the image might seem, such voltage does affect one's inner workings—and the way bodies interact in undeniably charged circumstances. The forcefulness of the intellectual exchanges, of course, had less to do with buildings, or weather, or waterfalls, than the fact that we arrived from all over the world, ready, willing, and able to collate a resplendent mix of academic training, disciplinary affiliation, and cultural background. But the allure of the high noon sun and the buzzing of weather warnings on muted phones affected our thinking; they broke the spells of overlong and independent introspection, calling our eyes, one pair at a time, from the dusty tomes and gleaming pdfs to the world outside: to the place that kept being what it is, no matter the words we pondered or which texts we heatedly debated. We were kept aware of the idiosyncrasy of the situation, of the strangeness of that milieu, of the specialness and brevity of "the event." Simplistic as it may sound, the shifting weather upon those edifices of antediluvian rock became an incessant reminder of the things *not that*, the issues and problems and texts we were not engaging. Meteorology went beyond being a cue for coffee breaks and umbrellas; it became a safeguard against deteriorating into navel-gazing and solipsistic dismissals of uncomfortable arguments—a reassuring sign of the obtrusive reality of the outside, the otherwise, and the unfamiliar.

With portable electronic devices in hand, it is easy to forget the monastic legacies impressed upon the landscape of contemporary university campuses. These spaces are designed for cloistering people and their minds, for establishing focus on individual tasks and texts. Simply put, the heavy stone walls are meant to keep the scholar working and safe; to keep the weather, and "the world," outside and at a distance; to diminish interoception. The elective assembly of our shared seminar transformed that otherwise protected space. It provided fulsome opportunities to intermingle and exchange, to analyze collectively and to undertake the work of translation in its many forms—cognitively, somatically, spiritually, linguistically. In these regards, no matter how effectual the weather, and no matter how seemingly synchronized with the heavy afternoon rains, the storms passing through our *inner landscapes* stemmed from the dynamism and inquisitive versatility of collective exploration in our own personal and interpersonal intellectual climates. In place of the run-of-the-mill demand to "focalize" and solve problems individually "through the lens of," we were invited to dwell in them, around them, beside them—in the aggregate. Indeed, we were expected and encouraged to experimentally transpose the problems we face to new registers and translate their analytical impetus to different materials and modes; to attempt approaches by which the problems might not be finally "solved" but could be understood by more than one person, alone in her cloistered room or in her own company during a solitary walk.

There is a vast difference between *solutions* and *understandings*. Allowing an analogy to a purely linguistic point of view (if anything of the sort exists; the notion of *Geschlecht* undoubtedly complicates such perspectives), one could perhaps say on the one hand that such "solutions" would correspond to translating individual words in isolation from meaningful correlates, circumscribing anything that might be deemed a pragmatic context. The "understandings," on the other hand, would instead start with those intangible aspects of language-in-use, their ties to the socio-political, and to historical shifts in semantics. It might seem counterintuitive, but during that summer tracking word-by-word equivalency would be put off to the very end of the examinations, if even attempted at all, and wouldn't be allowed to settle in any case. In the shift from trying to solve to trying to understand, one moves into a space where equivalencies are not at all forthcoming, where the transformative is always present and alive. In that sense, achieving a fixed, final definition or translation would indicate that the ambition to understand had regressed to a drive toward solutions—to what we were appointed to inspect, reconsider, or deconstruct.

The nature of the invitation to understand rather than solve was given form by the copular function of seemingly small questions: the "what if," "what about," "should that," "could this" that provided connections in the varied archipelago of our related but distinct academic disciplines and prevailing topics of interest. That is to say, these questions became roadmaps and logbooks, clarifying where we arrived from conceptually and what we imagined ourselves to be working on. And through this questionnaire, issues of truth claims, category problems, historical divides, and transcultural dissonance became standard; the successive translations and re-phrasings of the problematics at hand allowed for the horizon to shift, steadily opening new perspectives on what we already saw or thought we had secured. And as the *and yet* became a chorus that kept us dwelling in the problems rather than doing away with them, we stepped outside the routinely recognizable patterns familiar to our respective disciplines. The scene helped to mark out the presumptions we inherited, felt comfortable remaining loyal to, or were moved to defend. We pursued a contest with the abundant ready-mades of our minds, our pre-conceived ideas, and more daunting and dangerous still, we tried to stir up the courage to face ideas we had yet to encounter and that we were inexpert at, neophytes fronting the abyss. In these ways, we aimed to address what lay hiding in plain sight "and yet" remained unseen on account of old habits, incommensurate vocabularies, and the limitations inherent in being only one person (gazing out from one perspective).

Despite the fact that texts, talks, and discussions ranged wildly from poetry to anthropology, from philosophy to architecture, from literary theory to contemporary politics, from semiotics to experimental cinema, the central function of that questionnaire—what if, could this, should that, what about, *and yet*—established a strange sense of structure to the chaos. The intellectual roaming, the seemingly free-wheeling approach to traversing vast philosophical and linguistic topographies, was tied to a mode of lingering; of taking in the vistas of disciplines and problematics, considering their charted courses and terra incognita. But most importantly, perhaps, were the examinations of signposts; the traditional monuments of intended directionality and teleological excursus—the cues we are so often given so that we might be encouraged to head in a certain direction and to avoid other routes. Probing pathways and foundations alike, we came to ask who put them there and why. We came to investigate how the words they manifested and the names they spelled out might sound otherwise, might mean differently, and how the borders they drew might run along different lines or abide with no lines at all. Some such signposts, we found, were withered, brittle to the touch. Others had words that seemed immobile, signaling hard-formed patterns ossified in the minds of most. Then there were those words that shifted when we surveyed them, that turned on variable axes—and turned on us, betrayed us, when we sought to secure them.

On a wider scale, then, the method of both roaming and lingering—the mode of inquiry we here anoint the *Geschlecht* complex—draws our attention to boundaries, the periphery, the perimeter, to regions of the mind marked by shifting grounds and less than reliable signposts. By contrast, when we are "in the middle of things," we may have the impression that all is well: in short, that we know where we are (and where the elsewhere remains). But at the edges, coherent identities fray, language and speech sputter. Consider, for instance, how in the coursings of inter-, cross-, and trans-disciplinary studies one often comes upon the phrase "I work at the intersection of x and y." The intersection itself signals a widening of perspective, the possibility of choosing the path forward and exploring new terrain. However, part of the appeal of the phrase has to do with the presumption of knowing what x and y are, and the reassuring thought that if some third, previously unknown domain should appear—at their presumed intersection—one could also, somehow, return to the intersection's preexisting, constituent, and separable parts. While it is tempting to celebrate the new synthesis—a novel *tertium quid*—we should be mindful of what it does to its forebears, *primus* and *secundus*. What is often missed (perhaps *felt*, yet nevertheless left unstated) is the way the proximity of x and y disrupt any otherwise stable account of their status in the wake of their conjugation. And further, when that proximity or contact leads to the assemblage of something new or previously uncharted, the process would inevitably repeat itself (for the *tertium quid* becomes itself a new x). For example, when standards of documentary filmmaking (x) come up against standards of cultural anthropology (y)—as they are, for instance, conjoined in the work of, say, Jean Rouch—we do not merely gain a z (which we do), but the very natures of x and y are transformed. "Ethnographic documentary," the newly assembled z, as practiced (or perhaps even invented) by Rouch, calls for doubling back to foundational notions of both documentary filmmaking (x) and cultural anthropology (y). The Sensory Ethnography Lab, for instance, illustrates the contemporary inheritances of x, y, and z.[27]

The same basic scenario, where x meets y with the effect of both construing z and re-evaluating its precursors, constantly occurs on scenes large and small within modern academia. And as research in one field permeates others, and as philosophies reach across linguistic and cultural boundaries, it has become all the more obvious that interpretive parlances and analytical taxonomies have profound effects not just on communicative patterns, but on methods and configurations of thought. A case in point is how the critical engagements, in recent decades, of comparative literature with other subject areas—fine arts, history, gender studies, media theory, and anthropology, to name a few—have both produced significant theoretical insights and brought to the forefront the epistemic challenges of standardized analytical terminology. Perhaps most forcefully in studies of world literature—among the sociological, historical, and critical varieties—and in connection to the rubric of "the Eurochronology Problem," scholars have investigated the implications of Western historical periodization in descriptions of non-Western art; consider Arjun Appandurai's and Benjamin Conisbee Baer's analyses of colonial modernisms, for example, or the work of Pascale Casanova, Franco Moretti, Alexander Beecroft and others, on the power structures upholding the very notion of international literary history. Furthermore, while emphasizing how critical traditions tend to have set typologies that affect both expectations and analyses, studies have also shown how linguistic differences tend to accentuate dissimilarities between phenomena rather than heighten interpretive sensitivity to resemblance—as in Emily Apter's work on untranslatability, for instance.[28]

Something similar is at stake in the moves within continental philosophy towards its traditional Others (analytical philosophy, the natural sciences), in Alain Badiou's *Being and Event*, for example, or Catherine Malabou's investment in neuroscience—or for that matter, in the vibrant field of medical humanities.[29] On a smaller scale, the pattern repeats itself within historical research of specific periods (when feminist theory meet historiography), or in studies of individual artists or genres (when new methodologies encounter already available source materials). Here the "and yet" meets the "and so on." In each of these instances, it is possible that in one's encounter with the already established—the x and the y—one is less intrigued by the contestation of their ready-made patterns of thought than by what is presented by the newly assembled: the z. Such responses are understandable, given the disorientation caused by the troubling of recognized boundaries and age-old signposts. It is troubling, in short, to face disciplinary self-understanding and ask what if, could this, should that, what about, *and yet*. More to the point, one can ponder what happens in those intellectual intersections and "working definitions" of a given discipline as well as to the boundary conditions of any practiced taxonomy of terms, indeed, to the very cognitive terrain of a field. Among others results, here are several enumerated outcomes:

1. On a conservative line, x cannot inhabit or contribute to y (or vice versa).
2. Both domains (x and y) can coexist in a shared, overlapping zone (z), but cannot fully inhabit one another.
3. There is a failure to connect content between zones (x and y) and i is what we call the impasse.
4. There is a generation of new content between zones (x and y) and s is what we call the surplus.
5. There is a diminution of existing content between zones (x and y) and d is what we call the loss or deficit.
6. Surplus (s) activates awareness of elements that exceed original conditions, deficit (d) of attributes untouched, or left behind; in the first case, we are puzzled by an excess, and in the second case, by an absence.
7. Both domains (x and y) press up against one another in a perpetual contest by virtue of proximity, and generate a productive, if unresolved or irresolvable tension—a result that feels distinct from (3) impasse, (4) surplus, and (5) deficit.

Precluding a shift in paradigm that fully redefines the foundations of x and y (in effect transposing the assemblage of z into a "new" x—perhaps a sibling or variant, an x_1; or, for d, a "new" x, an x_{-1}), each possible result in 1–7 depicts *action* at the border: holding the line, guarding the status quo, or delineating new zones (productive or otherwise). And yet, transcription and translation are not equivalent, so quantification here must remain gestural—and thus, at all times, qualitative (despite the equations suggesting otherwise). Furthermore, such cases of "action" intimate no actual "crossing over" (*trans*), but rather responses to the presumed or potential effects of proposed or attempted transpositions.

In calling attention to intellectual and disciplinary boundaries, it should be noted, the analytical impulse of *The Geschlecht Complex* does not assume the magnitude of paradigmatic shifts. Following the liberatory methods of that summer seminar, situated around a table with a host of texts and temperaments, one should rather say that the opposite is true: *The Geschlecht Complex* assumes the epistemological validity of the *un*paradigmatic. It emphasizes the interest of examining the range of possible actions at the boundaries of disciplines, thoughts, and texts; of lingering at intellectual border-crossings and exploring the translational measure made necessary by that lingering. The method amounts to a sustained call to face the familiar impasse of paradigms, to consider the inability to pass (transfer, traverse, trade places, etc.) and thus a *failure to cross* as important in itself. The metaphor of migration is apt, because the act implies movement and risk—wondering after routes (open, congested, blocked; receptive, polluted, or otherwise infelicitously altered), asking what counts as success; if procreation is the criterion for avian life, can the gifts, grafts, and grifts of language manage a similar fertility and fecundity? Whether the boundaries delimit whole fields of academic inquiry, topographies of political and moral thought, moral epistemologies and semiotic frames of reference, distinct etymologies of analytical concepts, or the reception histories of individual works of art, *The Geschlecht Complex* posits a persistent interest in mapping out what happens at the intersections of x and y, or even, as sometimes happens, before they "meet"; in detailing the epistemological claims of the "between," "after," and "before" from one register to the next; in delineating the ontological implications of the z. Will there be troops sent to defend the borders from all comers? Will there be fences already in place, and intellectual customs officers resting contentedly for their reliance on prominently embanked fortifications? Will the gates be left open, as an invitation or a tease, or never put up in the first place—based on an idea of permeability as its own reward, or a sign of standing power and implied force? Whatever the action at the border is, and whatever the borders themselves delimit—disciplines, conceptual frames, interpretive traditions, historical fore-projections of meaning—exploring those (dis)junctions of thought is of both interest and importance.

These are, of course, somewhat grand claims, despite the precautionary phrasings about highlighting the *un*paradigmatic, or about approaching and attempting to *understand* rather than *solve* a wide range of problems. On a less ostentatious scale, imagining the *Geschlecht* complex as a condition both *of* and *for* thinking, one can delineate some principles—or rather, preoccupations. First, there is the obsessive interest in the work of translation and untranslatability, both literally and figuratively. The latter, which is our true obsession in this volume, simultaneously details the act of transposing texts, subjects, or problems from one catalogue or system to another, and emphasizes the effects of revisiting and reviewing the familiar. Employing "untranslatability" as a virtuous term of art, in other words, leads to an entrenchment and a refinement of a culture of "turning things over," and that spirit is central to our conception of the *Geschlecht* complex as a mode of inquiry. Second, as the "nervous condition" of incessantly (attempted) translation encourages a kind of disciplinary and linguistic attunement that is at once critical and metacritical, the *Geschlecht* complex incites both abstraction *and* theorization. Indeed, untranslatability is a profound idea in its own right; thus, it is neither "post-theory" nor "post-idea," yet somehow, perhaps because of the tractability of the concept, it encounters and courts resistance—such as the proposition that we have arrived, or soon will, in a phase of affairs "post-genre." Third, the linguistic attunement and investment in translational functions motivates an interest in the remainder, the left-behind, and the excluded. We are, in this sense, in the good company of ordinary language philosophy (OLP)—and its progeny ordinary literary criticism (OLC) and ordinary language film studies (OLFS)—although not from the standard-issue interest in "what we say when," but in the complementary act of looking for, and listening after, what is said but remains unseen, unheard—and, even when perceived, unintelligible.[30] To put it bluntly, the analytical impulse of the *Geschlecht* complex hinges on the fact that the words researchers, thinkers, and scholars use not only delineate their epistemological claims—that is, what is considered scientifically knowable—but also circumscribe their ontological commitments: what is taken, simply, *to be*. And equally, that the intermediary regions between words, taxonomies, claims, and commitments are worthy of attention.

* * * *

The most appropriate way of describing the structure of this volume is likely to point, again, to our conception of the *Geschlecht* complex as a mode of inquiry. For as each essay is significant in its own right, providing a detailed analysis of specific material texts or performative incarnations, what aligns the varied parts of the collection to form a whole—consolidates its contribution—is not mere content or contexts, but rather methods and measures of interpretation, as outlined above.

First of all, considering the focus on concrete "category problems" and the untranslatability of *Geschlecht*, the essays gathered here engage in what might be called *conceptual translation* or *categorial untranslatability*. Indicated by the book's subtitle, we are invested in addressing untranslatable aspects of gender, genre, and ontology; that is, committed to remaining sensible to the ways these master terms and parent categories inform any effort to speak "across," or complete a transition from, one point to another, whatever the medium might be: person, text, film, novel, poem, or otherwise. As such, both of these designations—*conceptual translation* and *categorial untranslatability*—can be viewed as attempts to signal the multivocality and "complex" provenance not just of the things and texts considered, but equally in the orders and analytical taxonomies to which they are ascribed to belong. In that sense, the nervous inquisitiveness of dealing with *Geschlecht* expresses itself, symptomatically, as a com*plex* com*plex*.

Furthermore, it should be noted (with knowing repetition) that the conceptual translations explored throughout the volume are not geared toward "solutions" for discrepancies between languages or critical catalogs. In the essays that follow, the distinction between source and target culture is not primarily linguistic, but disciplinary, medial, spatial, and/or temporal. And in employing untranslatability as a methodological keystone, emphasis does not fall on finding equivalencies, but on tackling equivocation; on examining what is *not* appropriate, what is excluded and considered false. By way of overtly metacritical discussions of analytical vocabularies, these examinations also indicate a *why*: a background to understanding what lies out of bonds, or seems to. The same holds true for the essays' extended engagements with how certain works of art (literary texts, films, performances) portray the boundaries between divergent taxonomies and competing chronicles, including related "genres" of expression; consequently, such works—at times incompletely or incoherently defined—can fall short of what history, tradition, or the powers-that-be have deemed "proper." The passive receptions of unarticulated orthodoxies, therefore, come into view— and thus can be addressed by emergent heterodoxies. Authority in its many forms and modes of instantiation vibrates with an uneven force; no petrified monolith, the inherited "dictates" of otherwise finely wrought terms and conditions are suddenly negotiable.

The transpositions of words, texts, and concepts that become the focal points of each essay, in other words, are not characterized by an uninterrupted and turbulence-free transit from one nationally or linguistically defined set to another, but rather along contested lines between analytical domains of inquiry, within transnational taxonomies, and through myriad temporal and geographic philosophical traditions. As such, the conceptual translation of the essays and their materials runs across Roman Jakobson's tripart system (tying "translation proper" both to interpretive "rewordings" and intersemiotic "transmutations"), or, with Paul Ricœur's binary model in mind, simultaneously engage with translation as an exercise of linguistic transposition *and* as a form of hermeneutics.[31] Indeed, in one of the final entries, the notion of "translational hermeneutics" is developed as a method of inquiry, one that can operate independently of consecutive linguistic translation (and perhaps stand as a viable methodology for addressing appeals to inquiry post-genre). In these respects, we are engaged in observing and describing how *influence* makes itself known in works of literature, fine art, and embodied performance.[32] And equally, one might add, in philosophy and criticism.

Speaking of performance, it can be said that the methods as well as the organization of the volume in a sense *perform* their proposals, enact them both as a series of discrete units and as an entity, in that the collection juxtaposes perspectives, trades media types, and undulates between different disciplinary, taxonomical, and historical frameworks. To begin with, this effect is apparent in that the volume primarily consists of six long-form essays tied to different subsets of humanistic disciplines, each principally defined by their traditions and source materials, and each with specific analytical vocabularies: early modern drama, political rhetoric, modernist aesthetics, contemporary performance art, literary theory, film studies, film philosophy, and more. As this diversity is given coherence through a shared focal point in the notion of *Geschlecht*, part of the intellectual impact of the volume as a whole comes from the conceptual connections—and at times productive frisson—*between* the essays.[33] Reading from front to back, the categorial moves between chapters in themselves become an embodiment of the problematics at hand.

Secondly, the effect is enhanced by the way each contributor heeds cues from the thinkers mentioned above (Apter, Cassin, Derrida, et al.), and also draws on a host of further theoretical and conceptual aids—then ties the motley assemblage to the specificities of the materials under consideration. Just as between chapters, in other words, the movements *within* each essay—from philological frames of analysis to taxonomical ones (and then to the metacritical and back again)—also exemplify the interpretive measures of what we call the *Geschlecht* complex. And to be sure, they are necessary for our aims of examining categorial untranslatability and the impact of the unparadigmatic, excluded, and displaced. For while moving between disciplinary and theoretical frames unavoidably leads to some disorientation, that is in itself far from unwanted; rather, we would argue that it is more than welcome—it is sought after, desirable. Because of the undulation, cycling, re-cycling, repetition, recursion, and reflexiveness of ideas, thoughts, and texts—that is, because of the engagement with conceptual translations, both in each essay and throughout the volume as a whole—it is possible to explore mechanisms of categorial naming, translation, and trans functions that remain intangible within varied and distinguishable disciplinary forms.

(Parenthetically, but pertinently, this is precisely where the satirical campus novel of our situation would earn its gravity. Let's give it a title: *Thinking in Untranslatables: An Academic Novel That Should Not Have a Subtitle But Cannot Avoid Parsing Its Varied Contests of Meaning and Signification*. And a back cover description: A group of a dozen or so scholars from what seem like a dozen or so different disciplines gather to make sense of a shared subject, but spends most of its time translating—and perhaps failing to sufficiently translate—ideas from one language, conceptual map, or intellectual record to another.)

The performative aspect of the volume is additionally elaborated by the inclusion of three Appendices with mainly theoretical essays and excerpts written by some of the key inspirations for our thinking on the *Geschlecht* complex—before, during, and after that fecund summer session. Some of these extracts are explicitly called upon in discussions, while others are included in a mode of contrast or contest; images—some mirrored, some distorted—but all slightly shifted through temporal, linguistic, or disciplinary transpositions. Whether originating from critical theory, comparative literature, translation studies, film theory, or philosophy (analytical, continental, American, and otherwise), aligning these seminal texts both with each other and with the newly written essays strengthens the impulse towards re-thinking what we supposedly already understand, as well as exposing what we might think we have misunderstood. Like the shifts and contrasts of critical registers both between and within each of the original essays, the included excerpts function as reminders that we move incrementally in our practice of the *die fröhliche Wissenschaft*—a "gay science" that remains faithful to the spirit of connection *and* contrast imbued in asking, again and again: what if, how about, and yet. In this way, the structure of the volume reflects our perpetual, concentrated interest in cultural and disciplinary translations, the shifts from one analytical schedule to another, and often back again, without end.

(Parenthetically, again, and in a moment of authorial reflexiveness once more befitting the campus novel, we editors can comment on the generation of the present introductory remarks. Namely, that with each of us in our respective academic redoubts—small college towns: one in Sweden and, for a while, in Belgium, the other in America—the writing, reading, and re-writing of these pages have crystalized our com*plex com*plex; performed it, as both act and artifact. With an eye to the shared table and texts recounted above, in our effort to provide orienting remarks to the reader, we undertook to translate across time, tradition, and technique what we gleaned from those summer weeks—as well as from our subsequent, extended editorial engagement with contributors and our selection of excerpts for the volume. As we shared a Google doc—with live, synchronous editing possible across a half-dozen time zones—and later, when we traded marked-up Word files, each intervention of tracking changes and adding comments proved a reminder of the translational negotiations at hand. Such deliberations included the occasionally fraught sense occasioned by attempting to represent the unrepresentable, which often traveled under the question how we could, in fact, arrogate the right to speak cogently for such an explicitly "group experience." In each choice of word, assembly of sentences, and constitution of paragraphs we seem poised to cross over—beyond, out of— individual authorship and into a collective text, a blended brain, a shared voice. Composition thus proposed familiar navigation in the necessary "plagiarism" of existing language [namely, that all sentences feel drawn from some impersonal, pre-existing protocol for written expression, thereby defeating the possibility of, and thus displacing the pressure to, present a distinctive, individuated "voice"]; and joint composition also revealed an uncanny ventriloquism [in which one editor speaks for the other and vice versa]. Does the introduction have two authors or no authors? Which sentences will one editor claim and which will he disown? [Playfully, of course, the favorable ones are mine, the problematical ones are his.] We speak for each other and we do not speak for ourselves. The claims and questions, to our sensibilities, seem of a piece with the recognition and subsequent practice of, or within, the *Geschlecht* complex. We editors are subject to our nervous attempts to make these translations—to repeat, to revise, to retread, to retreat—and to endure the specter that we have, in fact, been stymied in our sincere attempts. The introduction is marked "return to sender"—code unknown, translation untranslatable.)

The inquisitive, experimental, and opened-ended mode of inquiry that we are employing throughout the volume materializes, first of all, in the appendix to these introductory remarks: a collage of short paragraphs and pages, each directed at glosses and explanations of *Geschlecht*, translation, sophism, and "philosophizing in languages." But while certainly central, this collage (and the analyses it connects) should *not* be read as a single, definitive definition. Again, the ambition is not to solve translation debates or do away with interpretive problems, but to understand their nuances, clarify their complexity, appreciate points of overlap and impasse. Our analytical vocabularies—the apparatus of language as such, tuned to the description of linguistic, artistic, and societal expressions—become a de facto means by which to emphasize what appear to be the *ontological* aspects of viewing, listening, reading, translating, and interpreting the various phenomena under our purview. We could call this the "world-creating capacities of the word." The precedent, of course, is biblical; we court Genesis in our thinking of genes, genius, gender, genre, generations, and generativity. So it was written, or rather as it was translated: "In the beginning was the Word (λόγος) ...."[34] The interest infused in and by the words and logic of *The Geschlecht Complex* refract each constituent part of that phrase and its implied "process" as a whole—including, if viewed in reverse, that is, as *The Complex of Geschlecht*.

Following the introductory appendix are three essays concerned with *Geschlecht* through modes of exclusion and negation, as well as theatricality and performances of being or belonging that is not one, or is displaced from "one-ness." In the opening essay, "Antitheatricality as Critical Idiom," Caro Pirri uses *Geschlecht* to closely examine the parageneric status of early modern theater. Reading Stephen Gosson's antitheatrical pamphlet *The Schoole of Abuse*, she details an understanding of theater's generic position by way of negations and mistranslations; of its exclusion, in other words, from the established generic order. Following from this, Pirri also outlines antitheatricality's implications for contemporary criticism, because its "productive negativity" calls attention both to the temporally displaced and the immateriality of historical performance. Moving then to the rhetoric of contemporary American politics, Brian W. Nail explores the language and performance of crisis in "The Cruel Beast: Settler Sovereignty and the Crisis of American Zoopolitics." Specifically, Nail charts the mutations of political discourse on sovereignty in the era of Donald Trump's presidency and its aftermath, using the notions of zoopolitics and *Geschlecht* to describe the intensification of ethno-nationalist perceptions of an inside/outside divide. With numerous examples of utterances where political targets—immigrants, women, ethnic minorities—are attacked, negated, and made unrecognizable as human, Nail describes a Trumpian complex about *Geschlecht*, whose drive toward an inevitably false originary unity can only be properly dispelled through an awareness of *Geschlecht*'s complex polysemy. With this formulation, Nail both displays the successive translations and transmutations of national identity in contemporary political discourse and the possibility of a reversed order.

Both Pirri and Nail, in other words, explore the exclusionary force of negation (historically, generically, politically), while also exemplifying how negations and absences are always inevitably present in any claim to established orders and generic identities. This paradoxical relation is explored further in Lauren DiGiulio's essay, "Between the Body and Language: Narratives of the Moving Subject in Okwui Okpokwasili's *Bronx Gothic*." Focusing on transitions (and translations) between different genres and modes of being, DiGiulio analyzes the "between," the space that persists on either side of a discourse or medium; the space that implies both negation and becoming. What is happening *here*—at this intersection of seemingly foreign phenomena? The body and *language*? The body *as* language? Language *embodied*? Heeding the implied concerns of such questions, DiGiulio examines the intersemiotic translations of narrative patterns in the multimedial performance *Bronx Gothic*, and how that complex structure, in turn, connects with the liminal space of Okpokwasili's position as a Black female subject.

Complementing these three essays—Pirri's, Nail's, and DiGiulio's, both connecting them to each other and opening them up for further thought—is the volume's second appendix of excerpted seminal texts: "Indefiniteness, *Geschlechtslosigkeit*, Undoing, Unknowing, Unlearning." With passages on linguistic negation, political exclusion, sexual and gender differences, as well as ontology, the appendix calls attention to the ties between politics and performance art; between artistic theatricality and "theaters of war." Furthermore, it provides an account of what being-without might mean, whether viewed from generic, sexual, or social perspectives.

Introducing the volume's second group of essays, Oscar Jansson's "Collapsing the Gender/Genre Distinction: On Transgressions of Category in Woolf's *Orlando*" connects the longstanding critical interest in Woolf's elaborations of gender and sexual identity with textual examinations of genre and style in *Orlando: A Biography*. Although in part a performative aspect of the book's central thematic, Jansson argues that its generic structure also translates the social concept of "gender" to the aesthetic concept of "genre," at once linking distinct interpretive registers *and* revisioning the notion of "category" as such. Keeping to our collective interest in genre, but directing focus to other types of text and other arts, Richard Hajarizadeh's essay, "Gazing at the Untranslatable Subject: From Velázquez's *Las Meninas* to Ellison's *Invisible Man*," emphasizes that *Geschlecht* is deeply tied to the ontogenesis of the subject; to "genres of being." With elaborations of Foucault's and Lacan's interpretations of *Las Meninas* and examples from Ralph Ellison's novel *Invisible Man*, Hajarizadeh investigates how the semantic plurality of *Geschlecht* translates to a wider spectrum of societal concerns, where categorial thinking (in one way or another) both affects and is affected by relations of power.

In our final long-form entry, "From Lectiocentrism to Gramophonology: Listening to Cinema and Writing Sound Criticism," David LaRocca investigates how the multilayered medial shift from hearing sounds in cinema to writing about sounds in criticism affects the conceptual frames of genre *and* can be used to elaborate specific notions of translational hermeneutics (all the while anticipating—and responding to—lapses and lacunae, obstructions and dissolutions, in such an interpretive practice). If we have been familiar with the trope of "reading" films (as texts) and "looking" (as an analogue for writing about visual art), what is to be said about our "listening" to cinema (as text, as art)—and in turn, the effort to translate those embodied perceptions into consecutive prose? In this concluding essay, the objective is to discern how listening to cinema might achieve itself as sound criticism. Yet, even when we become attuned to it, can sound, at last, make a satisfying passage—transition, translation—to the page?

Following LaRocca's essay is a third appendix of excerpts from critical texts. Gathered under the rubric of "Genre Unlimited/Genre Ungenred," these selections both individually and collectively explore the limits of genres, and thus complement and contrast the questions raised by LaRocca, Hajarizadeh and Jansson: the boundaries between generic registers; the nature of formal and informal classifications, and genres' relation to other designations of category, type, and name. Concluding the volume, finally, is an Afterword by Emily Apter, where the notions of the unlimited and *Geschlecht* are tied to considerations of the "trans"—of translation, transsexuality, and transpositions of analytical terms.

Moving, then, from film and theater to political discourse and on to performance art, aesthetics, ideological critique, and variations of genre theory (literary, philosophical, cinematic), but maintaining the same principal conceptual target, all of the essays individually engage questions of categorial untranslatability while simultaneously forming a portion of an ongoing discussion of conceptual translation as such. In other words, the volume's mandates and recommendations equally invite reading essays *alongside* as *against* one another, summoning readers to explore what happens in the space between them, quietly imploring hermeneuts to retain an interest in the "and so on" and the "and yet." This rippling, at times even rip-current structure is important, particularly for exploring the ties between untranslatability and the excluded. It pulls one along, no doubt, and threatens time and again to pull one under; and yet, the deep dive only motivates a more spirited search for the surface—for the oxygen, for the light, for the attendant apocalypse (ἀποκάλυψις) of thought.

Equally important, the volume's invitation to read its constituent parts both alongside and against one another is also tied to the perhaps most troubling concern of untranslatability: the question of how far-reaching the validity of the law of non-contradiction can be taken. In a rough and rudimentary sense, we are rebuffed by the incongruency of stating, at once, that A *is* B and that A *is not* B. The implied debate, however, is not with Aristotle and his consolidation and innovation of logic, but rather stems from the fact that when considering any act of translation—whether linguistic, cultural, temporal, disciplinary, or, indeed, logical—one is always contending with multiple, often competing catalogs: where besides the horizontal series of A, B, C there sits the vertical A_1, A_2, A_3. And while still accepting that one cannot claim A to *be* B if one also maintains that A is *not* B, the boundaries of logicality are less distinct if the claim is that A_1 is B_2, and A_2 *is not* B_1. In translation—in *acts* of translation, simply put—something happens even with or to the foundations of logic. Temporality, directionality, rhythm, pace, tone, juxtaposition, and many more factors are formative to any encounter with the "translated"—or its deferment, that is, its "untranslatability."

An untranslatable, in this schema, is a word (or phrase—phoneme, morpheme, or grapheme) that through the history of its use has remained connected to its vertical dimension(s) despite movements along its horizontal axis; where the first, second, or third order of belonging is still marked but inconclusive, is identifiable and yet unmoored. *Geist*, *esprit*, *nous*, *animus*, and *mind*: although one could argue that these words "mean the same thing"—that they all point to the concept of A (mind), that they function as equivalents—their translinguistic usage points in several, opposing directions; however slight their differences, variants present themselves as A_1, A_2, A_3, A_4. And as Cassin would surely argue, in the history of European philosophy, even the most conservative A_1, A_2, A_3, A_4 in fact function as the more radical A, B, C and D—each independent and operating in their own distinctive indexes of semiotic expression (and including both discrete potencies and liabilities). The consequences of Cassin's claim would require a book-length query of their own (another worthy adventure!) and a team of dedicated, diversely situated researchers to parse them out. Not incidentally, just such a sort of inquiry—full of a fitting *esprit du corps*—is precisely what we have hoped to create, to offer here, in this volume.

Through the combined analyses of the essays and excerpts in this collection, attention is drawn to both the horizontal and vertical axes—and as such, to the fringes of the law of non-contradiction. The concept of *genre*, for example, plays a crucial part in all of the essays, but in moving from early modern theater to literary text to performance art to experimental film, the concept's variability is on display as much as its coherence. The same holds true for *gender, race, community*, and all other "derivations" or "definitions" of *Geschlecht* that are dealt with in these inventive, engaging pages. As both empirical and theoretical registers change from one essay to the next, *The Geschlecht Complex* expands and evolves. And yet, the principal problematics remain the unified, despite the intrepid movements from one discipline to another (and back again). Indeed, the principal problematics remain the same *because of* the disciplinary shifts and conceptual translations.

* * * *

As a final remark, ahead of the many to come, we wish to emphasize how the principles and preoccupations of *The Geschlecht Complex* bear on the familiar situation in which one hears much about disciplinary and conceptual boundaries, but far less about how those boundaries are formed, how they are maintained, or who polices them. Throughout this volume, in the spirit of inquiry prompted by our "nervous condition" or intellectual nervous system, by our individual and collective *Geschlecht* complex and in its demeanor of productive curiosity rather than presumed transgression, we will cross boundaries—many of them, and far more than once. As the case may be, on account of such criss-crossing we might get into trouble by the makers, the maintainers, the monitors. Are further investigations into Virginia Woolf's avant-gardist writings really what the world needs, and should those efforts be conducted through blatantly anachronistic conceptual frames? What gains to the discussions of genre and media can be proposed by collapsing one into the other? And do we need any more words about Donald Trump? We propose the answer to such questions is, yes, in so far as *The Geschlecht Complex* provides new or newly revitalized ways of accessing and analyzing familiar topics and entrenched questions. In short, the *Geschlecht* complex may not, in fact, turn out to be a rarefied domain exclusive to this collection (and the inspirations it draws from), but one that, in time, may grow and gain some traction as a shareable, expansive methodology—or, at the very least, remain indicative of a spirit of generous, good-faith inquiry.

While the just-noted questions might amount to initial, skeptical responses to the attempts made in this volume to produce fresh and inquisitive scholarship, there is on our part, of course, a reasonable and unavoidable desire to "get things right"—as the sound argumentative arcs in each of the essays will testify; and yet, we also hasten to suggest, one should not underestimate the potentialities and productivity of the "wrongs." Consider, for instance, Katie Chenoweth's recent examinations of Derrida's "*faute de frappe*"—i.e., the philosophically productive effects of his at times sloppy handling of typewriters; of the insights that might be gleaned from typos, mistakes, and errors.[35] The unexplored remainders and the left-unsaid, the impasses and dead-ends, the circulations and returns to common ground: these are all discoveries worth the time and incident to the cause of conceptual translation. Even the scholarly offenses (not of grammar, say, but of conceptualization or intellectual claim) are more telling than the segments and phrases that fly under the radar; and they speak not only of one's own project, but of its vitality within a given intellectual ecosystem. In these ways, to be called out on offenses—to be charged with transgression, with mistranslation, with a failure to make the connection—would be a continuation of the inquiry into the mechanics of boundaries, of border crossing, and of intellectual in-betweens. After Cassin, we might ask: Who's afraid of untranslatables?

Our collected remarks within this volume, in other words, reflect our projects and processes of analysis, and, in glimpses, our progress. But more importantly, in sharing these thoughts (long gestating and newly updated) we offer reports on the problems we have tried facing these last few years—the "wrongs" we haven't righted, the "solutions" that have kept slipping away in our efforts to understand the matters at hand. And let's be clear: it is not too strong to say that we have willingly faced the turbulence of "wrongs," these churning waters of investigation, in part because that is what we felt during our cloistered summer retreat. Replicating, interpreting, or indeed, *translating* that energy remains a persistent ambition and hope for the collection in hand.

We also share our hope that these remarks will provide a welcome and enduring scene of shared intellectual inquiry. By placing ourselves at the mercy of an incessant intellectual curiosity and fervently attempted experimentation—both made in good faith—we have collectively, and in each of our independently rendered researches, found that our labors were characterized by re-reading, re-translating, re-thinking what we took to be already known. Instead of proffering in this volume a set of solutions for readers (fixed and thus manageable), we endeavor to create an environment suited to further disturbances and thus for further thoughts, that is, a milieu, a method, and a mode for continued engagement rather than merely an inert digest of summarized claims and findings. We both greet and anticipate, that is to say, countering or correcting claims to the propositions put forth; we welcome continued interest in the alternative perspective, the unfamiliar, the otherwise, and the unexpected; we aspire to the situation where someone reads and perhaps re-reads, and then calls out: what if, could this, should that, what about, and so on, *and yet*.

And yet all of this we share with knowing humor, anticipating that our sincere, admittedly romantic, and thus seemingly grandiose ambitions may arrive already antiquated or seem foolhardy—especially in an age given to casually delivered ironic dismissal, a ubiquitous shrug, and a declaration of "meh." Nonetheless, hoping (which is merely another way of describing fear—anticipations of an unknown and unknowable future) might, finally, be yet another sign of our shared and individuated nervous condition, the frame of mind and febrile affliction we all contracted when ensconced among those gorges revealed by the last ice age. In the months and years since, we have begun to find words for our state, internalized its attributes, and integrated them into an approach to "reading" texts—looking at them, listening to them, writing about them, translating and untranslating them. The accumulated actions, the gathered markings, have in time become a distinctive pattern of thought, a mode of inquiry that presents itself whenever one lingers at the border crossings of languages, disciplines, problems, and intellectual environments. We call it, once more, the *Geschlecht* complex. And we hope the following reports will provide a warm and welcome invitation to you, fellow readers, to suffer and enjoy its productive troubling of established boundaries.

Notes

1. The lists of (apparent) synonyms for *Geschlecht* in English noted above (gender, genre, kinship, etc.) should provide initial evidence for the productive questions surrounding successful, complete, or otherwise comprehensible translation. Moreover, the vertiginous effect of such a consideration appears, in our estimation, to activate the complex set of responses we have anointed the *Geschlecht* complex.
2. See A. H. Coxon, *The Fragments of Parmenides: A Critical Text with Introduction and Translation, The Ancient Testimonia and a Commentary*, Revised Edition (Las Vegas: Parmenides Publishing, 2009), and David G. Mandelbaum, ed., *Selected Writings of Edward Sapir in Language, Culture and Personality* (Berkeley: University of California Press, 1963).
3. Barbara Cassin, "Philosophizing in Languages" (2005), *Nottingham French Studies*, vol. 49, no. 2 (2010), 17ff.
4. Let us underscore that Cassin's *Vocabulaire européen des philosophies: le dictionnaire des intraduisibles* (Paris: Seuil, 2004) itself—as a distinctive intellectual project—provides an exemplary case of how the complex situation of the contemporary humanities can be met through collaboration and strength in numbers: impossible for the single mind, in both governing idea and practical outcome, the *Vocabulaire* illustrates the value of interdisciplinary collaboration and dialogue, thereby both mandating the juxtaposition of conflicting thoughts and validating the inquisitive dialectic of mapping unfamiliar intellectual terrains from multiple viewpoints. The case of the *Vocabulaire* can be further supported by the fact that the original French version was later transformed to the equally massive *Dictionary of Untranslatables: A Philosophical Lexicon* (Princeton: Princeton University

Press, 2014), whose translation into English was spearheaded by Emily Apter, Jacques Lezra, and Michael Wood. In the aftermath of translating "untranslatables," Apter wrote the remarkable coda, "Lexilalia: On Translating a Dictionary of Untranslatable Philosophical Terms," *Paragraph*, vol. 48, no. 5 (2015), 159–73.

5 Wilhelm von Humboldt, *Fragmente der Monographie über die Basken*, quoted in Barbara Cassin, "Introduction," in *Dictionary of Untranslatables: A Philosophical Lexicon*, ed. Barbara Cassin, trans. eds. Emily Apter, Jacques Lezra, and Michael Wood (Princeton: Princeton University Press, 2014), xix.

6 Lawrence Venuti, *The Translator's Invisibility: A History of Translation* (New York: Routledge, 2004 [1995]), 1ff, 148ff, 188f.

7 See Barbara Cassin, *L'Effet sophistique* (Paris: Gallimard, 1995) and Barbara Cassin, *Jacques le Sophiste: Lacan, Logos et Psychanalyse* (Paris: EPel, 2012).

8 See Barbara Cassin and Charles T. Wolfe, "'Who's Afraid of the Sophists?' Against Ethical Correctness," *Hypatia*, vol. 15, no. 4 (Autumn 2000), 102–20.

9 See Kenneth Reinhard, "Badiou's Sublime Translation of the *Republic*," in Alain Badiou, *Plato's Republic*, trans. Susan Spitzer (Cambridge: Polity, 2012), vii.

10 Barbara Cassin, *Sophistical Practice: Toward a Consistent Relativism* (New York: Fordham University Press, 2014), 1f.

11 Alain Badiou, *Logics of Worlds: Being and Event II*, trans. Alberto Toscano (New York: Bloomsbury Academic, 2019), 782.

12 One might recall, here, Alain Badiou's entry on the French language in the *Vocabulaire*, and his point about the curious universalism of its particularities and its attendant (apparent?) aptitude for the having or making of rational and analytical discourse. Further commented on by John McKeane—and contrasted with the English language—there arise questions of sophistry, including how different languages reveal, it would seem, different philosophical dispositions, not least exposing how much (specific) words matter, and of how differently words make sense within a given language and between them. See Alain Badiou, "French," *Dictionary of Untranslatables*, 349–54; John McKeane, "Universalism and the (un)translatable," *Translation Studies*, vol. 12, no. 1 (2019), 64–77.

13 See David LaRocca, "Teaching without Explication: Pedagogical Lessons from Rancière's *The Ignorant Schoolmaster* in *The Grand Budapest Hotel* and *The Emperor's Club*," *Journalism, Media and Cultural Studies*, vol. 10 (2016), 10–28 and "The Limits of Instruction: Pedagogical Remarks on Lars von Trier's *The Five Obstructions*," *Film and Philosophy*, vol. 13 (2009), 35–50.

14 Novalis, "Logological Fragments I," in *Novalis: Philosophical Writings*, trans. Margaret Mahony Stoljar (Albany: State University of New York Press, 1997), 50f.

15 See Dimitri Borgmann, *Language on Vacation: an Olio of Orthographical Oddities* (New York: Charles Scribner's Sons, 1965).

16 See Kenneth Burke, *The Rhetoric of Religion: Studies in Logology* (Berkeley: University of California Press, 1970).

17 Marc Crépon, "*Geschlecht*," in Cassin, et al., *Dictionary of Untranslatables: A Philosophical Lexicon*, 394–6.

18 Ciara Cremin, *The Future is Feminine: Capitalism and the Masculine Disorder* (New York: Bloomsbury, 2021).
19 Jacques Derrida, *Geschlecht III: Sex, Race, Nation, Humanity*, eds. Geoffrey Bennington, Katie Chenoweth, and Rodrigo Therezo (Paris: Seuils, 2018).
20 David Farrell Krell, *Phantoms of the Other: Four Generations of Derrida's Geschlecht* (Albany: State University of New York Press, 2015).
21 Jacques Derrida, "*Geschlecht* I: Sexual Difference, Ontological Difference," *Research in Phenomenology*, vol. 13 (1983), 65–83.
22 Jack Halberstam, *Trans* A Quick and Quirky Account of Gender Variability* (Berkeley: University of California Press, 2018), 27.
23 Apart from Apter's contributions to the *Dictionary of Untranslatables*, this context merits a mention of her *Against World Literature: A Politics of Untranslatability* (New York: Verso, 2013), where, among other achievements, she employs philosophical untranslatability to deconstruct the dominant assumption in contemporary World Literature—seen as a disciplinary subset of comparative literature—that everything is translatable.
24 Catherine Malabou, *Changing Difference: The Feminine and the Question of Philosophy*, trans. Carolyn Shread (Cambridge: Polity Press, 2011 [2009]), 38.
25 Jacques Derrida, "*Geschlecht* II: Heidegger's Hand," trans. John P. Leavey, Jr., in *Deconstruction and Philosophy: The Texts of Jacques Derrida*, ed. John Sallis (Chicago: The University of Chicago Press, 1987), 162ff; Jacques Derrida, "The Law of Genre," trans. Avital Ronell, *Critical Inquiry*, vol. 7, no. 1 (1980), 60f.
26 See David LaRocca, "SCT: Summer Camps for Theorists," in *In Theory: The Newsletter of the School of Criticism and Theory*, Cornell University (Winter 2017), 10–11.
27 See details of the Sensory Ethnography Lab at https://sel.fas.harvard.edu/, including descriptions of illustrative projects by such practitioners as Diana Allan, Ilisa Barbash, Lucien Castaing-Taylor, Véréna Paravel, and J. P. Sniadecki.
28 See, for example, Arjun Appadurai, *Modernity at Large: Cultural Dimensions of Globalization* (Minneapolis: University of Minnesota Press, 1996); Alexander Beecroft, *An Ecology of World Literature: From Antiquity to the Present Day* (New York: Verso, 2015); Pascale Casanova, *The World Republic of Letters*, trans. M. D. De Bevoise (Cambridge: Harvard University Press, 2004); Benjamin Conisbee Baer, *Indigenous Vanguards: Education, National Liberation, and the Limits of Modernism* (New York: Columbia University Press, 2019); Franco Moretti, *Modern Epic: The World System from Goethe to García Marquez*, trans. Quintin Hoare (New York: Verso, 1996).
29 See, for example, Alain Badiou, *Being and Event*, trans. Oliver Feltham (New York: Continuum, 2005) and Catherine Malabou, *What Should We Do With Our Brain?*, trans. Sebastian Rand (New York: Fordham University Press, 2008). Beginning principally within the distinct fields of bioethics and narrative medicine, medical humanities developed into a comprehensive exploration of how interdisciplinary modes of thought within the humanities and social sciences can critique and develop medical understanding. For introductions, see, for example, Thomas R. Cole, ed., *Medical Humanities: An Introduction* (Cambridge: Cambridge University Press, 2014) and

Brian Dolan, ed., *Humanitas: Readings in the Development of the Medical Humanities* (San Francisco: University of California Medical Humanities Press, 2015).

30 See Kenneth Dauber and K. L. Evans, "Revisiting Ordinary Language Criticism," in *Inheriting Stanley Cavell: Memories, Dreams, Reflections*, ed. David LaRocca (New York: Bloomsbury, 2020), 141–59; and Andrew Klevan, "Ordinary Language Film Studies," *Aesthetic Investigations*, vol. 3, no. 2 (2021), 387–406. See also Sandra Laugier, *Why We Need Ordinary Language Philosophy*, trans. Daniela Ginsburg (Chicago: The University of Chicago Press, 2013), and Alice Crary and Joel De Lara, "Who's Afraid of Ordinary Language Philosophy? A Plea for Reviving a Wrongly Reviled Philosophical Tradition," *Graduate Faculty Philosophy Journal*, vol. 39, no. 2 (2019), 317–39.

31 Roman Jakobson, "On Linguistic Aspects of Translation," in *On Translation*, ed. Reuben A. Brower (Cambridge: Harvard University Press, 1959), 233; Paul Ricœur, *On Translation*, trans. Eileen Brennan (New York: Routledge, 2007), 11.

32 For a related study of translation as a mode of international influence and transnational communication, see *A Power to Translate the World: New Essays on Emerson and International Culture*, eds. David LaRocca and Ricardo Miguel-Alfonso (Hanover: Dartmouth College Press, 2015), part of the Dartmouth Series in American Studies "Re-Mapping the Transnational" from series editor Donald E. Pease.

33 Drawing on the same lexicon, dictionaries, commentaries, and paratexts, we nevertheless have "defined" *Geschlecht* in relation to our particular projects; a fact that signals the impact of the space between object and parlance in classificatory measures, the (un)translatable residues that linger there, and the obtrusive "transvestism" where either side takes on the appearance of the other. In this way the very notion or nature of *Geschlecht* has shown itself amenable to translation (or, perhaps better, adaptation) while resisting any fixed or monolithic statement. Each contributor here, in other words, appears to be "using" *Geschlecht* in confident, capable ways to illuminate the problematic at hand—the translation of gender and genre in literary texts, for example, an expression of biopolitical governance, or conceptions of race as an horizontal genre of being—without needing to declare, once and for all, that the "working definition" is doing more than that: working.

34 John 1:1 (KJV).

35 Katie Chenoweth, "*Faute de frappe*: Derrida's Typos," *Research in Phenomenology*, vol. 51 (2021), 61–77.

Appendix I
Unfinished Definitions

Apter | Cassin | Cavell | Crépon

ALL OF THE FOLLOWING EXCERPTED PASSAGES have been gathered from seminal theoretical texts that have meaningfully affected our collective work in *The Geschlecht Complex*. By collating these specific lines, paragraphs, and pages as a collage of possible, pertinent, and important definitions, we aim to invite some of the prevailing masters of this discourse—those who have made distinctive and lasting contributions to it—to have a word without interruption, if briefly; and also, as befits our role as makers of a commonplace book, florilegium, macaronicon, or zibaldone, to select a mode of spelling out—that is, to supply sources that underwrite our investigation and provide indications of its *raison d'être*. Although these writers are cited in our chapters—drawn in and depended upon for their orienting expertise and insight—the purpose of this deliberate assembly of fragments is not only to give more room for such airing, but also to study what happens when they are placed in close proximity to one another, and presented consecutively. Commentary emerges from placement and proximity rather than direct address.

Each of the book's three "appendices" provides a service as supplemental (that is, supplying content that helps provide a "more complete" account of our topic and the topography it presumes), and yet we are also intrigued by how the remarks—individually and as a library—remain "unfinished"; how, in effect, each and all solicit us to respond and to add. Moreover, we wished to replicate, or at least agitate, something of the energy of the seminar room: the way, for example, that the recitation of febrile prose in communion— one line after another, one passage after another, mixing and matching—can yield its own generative rewards. Thus, the model of selection, arrangement, and most of all *juxtaposition*—an orientation of contact, complement, and contrast embodied in the collage's design—may transform a simmer into a boil. Energized by the precipitate of such a methodology, a reader may be gratified that the work is incomplete, because, in short, incompleteness and unfinishedness presumes an invitation to further addition. Moving from one excerpt to the next, one segment to another, we ask—what if, could this, what about?—thereby unsettling or deferring any comprehensive, singular, or finalized account. All the while, and with a reader's own mental contributions coming to mind at a remove, unknown to us—each attempted bid for refinement leads to a conclusion that is anything but: and yet, and yet, and yet. The untranslatable definition is, at last, always also an unfinished one.

Oscar Jansson and David LaRocca

* * * *

Geschlecht (German)

English race, kinship, lineage, community, generation, gender, sex

Autrui, *Dasein*, Gender, *Genre*, Humanity, *Leib*, *Menschheit*, People, Sex

> Marc Crépon, "Geschlecht," *Dictionary of Untranslatables: A Philosophical Lexicon*, ed. Barbara Cassin, trans. eds. Emily Apter, Jacques Lezra, and Michael Wood (Princeton: Princeton University Press, 2014), 394.

We start from the primary and unavoidable fact of the plurality of languages. From this follows a second definition: untranslatables are the semantic and/or syntactic symptoms of the differences of languages.

> Barbara Cassin, "Philosophizing in Languages," trans. Yves Gilonne, *Nottingham French Studies*, vol. 49, no. 2 (Summer 2010), 18.

The "Untranslatable"—capitalized here not to reify the intractable properties of select concepts but to indicate a range of nouns, syntactical structures and habits of speech that pose particular translation problems—broadly indicates ways of doing philosophy. In rendering multiple and micropolitical what Félix Guattari would call (following Foucault) "analytic singularity" (such that it no longer allows the statement to function as the "authority of a segment of a universal logos leveling out existential contingencies"), the Untranslatable goes against the grain not only of analytic philosophy, but also of Platonism, medieval scholastic logic, Port-Royal hierarchies of grammar and the universalist language ideologies of the encyclopédistes.[1]

> Emily Apter, "Lexilalia: On Translating a Dictionary of Untranslatable Philosophical Terms," *Paragraph*, vol. 38, no. 2 (2015), 160.

We know that the Greeks blissfully ignored the plurality of languages—they were, to use Momigliano's expression, "proudly monolingual"[2]—so much so that *hellenizein* means "to speak Greek" as well as "to speak correctly" and "to think and act as a civilised man," in contrast with *barbarizein* which violently conflates the stranger, the unintelligible, and the inhuman. How, then, can a work about the Greeks give us any sort of apprehension of the differences of languages? It is very simple—or at least I think I can make it simple; either we start off with things or we start off with words.

On the one hand, we have ontology, as far back as Parmenides' *Poem* and the position of *esti*, "is" and even "there is," "there is being," *es gibt*. In the *Poem*, magnificently interpreted by Heidegger, Being, Thought, and Speech, are intertwined. Man is the "shepherd of being"; he has the responsibility of faithfully and accurately expressing being. And when we leave thought, in order to enter metaphysics—with Plato and Aristotle therefore—we can describe things in this way: language is an *organon*, a tool, a means of communication, and languages, as Socrates says in the *Cratylus*, are simply different materials that can be employed in making this tool,[3] mere costumes of the idea. This is why we must start from things, from what is, and not from words.[4] From this perspective, to translate is to communicate as quickly as possible the thing underlying the words, to reveal the unity of being under the difference of languages, to reduce multiplicity to the singular: translation is then what Schleiermacher calls *dolmetschen*, interpretation, a "go-between."[5]

On the other hand we have "logology,"[6] that is to say, as far back as the *Treatise On Non-Being* by the sophist Gorgias, a critique of ontology which shows how being is nothing more than a result of saying. Being is not always already present. It is rather Parmenides' *Poem*, this time interpreted not by Heidegger but by Gorgias, that creates being as a result of combined semantic and syntactical effects. It produces a series based on the "Word of the path," "is," *esti*, third person singular of the present indicative, in such a way that this series ("is," "to be," "it is in being that it is") culminates in the nomination-creation of the subject, as if secreted by the verb, with the article substantiating the present participle: *l'étant* ["the being"], *to eon*, and its description in a well-rounded sphere—like Ulysses skirting the Sirens, it stays there, firmly planted in the limits of powerful bonds?[7] The world that leads off from words is a completely different world: we are no longer in the realm of onto-logy and phenomeno-logy, which must tell us what is and how it is, but in the realm of the performative, which brings into being what is said. So much so that language is no longer considered in the first instance as a means, but as an end and a force; "Whoever finds language interesting in itself is different from whoever only recognizes in it the means for interesting thoughts,"[8] and as Gorgias observes in his *Encomium of Helene* (§8): "Speech is a great master, which with the smallest and least perceptible of bodies performs the most divine of acts."[9]

Barbara Cassin, "Philosophizing in Languages" (2010), 18–20.

It is Austin and Wittgenstein who have, I believe, most characteristically been felt by their antagonists, at least within analytical philosophy, to practice sophistry (according to a definition of sophistry that Cassin recurs to: "a philosophy of verbal reasoning, lacking any solidity or seriousness"); and at the same time it is characteristic only of them that sophistry is (all but explicitly) a philosophical issue, an issue within philosophy, in which their claims against the establishment of (academic, professional) philosophy imply that those who speak in its name incessantly say what they do not, indeed cannot, actually mean.

Stanley Cavell, "Beginning to Read Barbara Cassin," *Hypatia*, vol. 15, no. 4 (Fall 2000), 100.

In 2006 the literary narratologist Gérard Genette published a book with the inscrutable title *Bardadrac*. It refers to a nickname coined by Genette for a handbag belonging to an early love. " ... [A]s vast as it was shapeless," the bag was "dragged around everywhere, inside and outside, and contained too many things to allow her to find a single one. Yet the false certainty that the thing was there reassured her. The word came to be metonymically applied to the bag's improbable contents; becoming a metaphor for all manner of disorder, fanning out to encompass the world and its cosmic surround. Like a spreading oil stain, it was extensive and comprehensive ...."[10]

"Bardadrac" justly describes what Genette applies it to: a unique kind of dictionary or *systèmeobjet* tending toward manifold disorder; a combination of autobiography, intellectual biography (of the heyday of post-structuralism, containing flash vignettes of his long intellectual partnerships with Barthes and Derrida), translation exercise (especially of idiomatic American expressions), and dictionary (its entries organized from A to Z). The book opens with a prologue situating itself in a line of dictionary-like texts that make it impossible to know what a dictionary is, including Montaigne's *Essais*, in which he writes "*J'ai un dictionnaire tout à part moi*" (I have a dictionary severally and fully to myself), Voltaire's *Dictionnaire philosophique*, Flaubert's *Dictionnaire des idées reçues*, and Barthes' *Roland Barthes par Roland Barthes*. "Bardadrac"—a term for a dictionary as mixed genre as well as a metaphor for the infinitely expansive encyclopedic object—is also an exemplary Untranslatable, a word on the edge of nonsense that exhibits an intractable singularity. As such, it could well have warranted an entry in Barbara Cassin's *Vocabulaire européen des philosophies: le dictionnaire des intraduisibles* (published by Seuil/Le Robert in 2004), which was described in one review as a mad, encyclopedic endeavor that "wears its modest megalomania well" and whose "planet is continental philosophy."[11]

Taking up half a suitcase, weighing in at a million and a half words, its hard white cover cracked at the spine, my copy of the *Vocabulaire* was hauled around with me up flights of subway stairs, over rocky pathways in Corsica and Burgundy, and across airports and train stations. My work on its translation into English between 2007 and 2013, undertaken with co-editors Jacques Lezra and Michael Wood, involved reviewing the work of five translators, revising the bibliography, and reorienting the entire project to an anglophone audience. The *Vocabulaire* presented us with a daunting set of challenges: how to render a work, published in French, yet layered through and through with the world's languages, into something intelligible to anglophone readers; how to communicate the book's performative aspect, its stake in what it means "to philosophize" in translation over and beyond reviewing the history of philosophy with translation problems in mind; and how to translate the untranslatable.

Emily Apter, "Lexilalia" (2015), 159–60.

[...] *Geschlecht* lends itself to a serious task of intralinguistic translation, which consists in finding equivalents for its various significations, in order to better circumscribe its meaning. The stakes of such a task are twofold: it must remove confusion about the different orders of belonging, but also question the constitution and destination of human diversity.

Four meanings of *Geschlecht* must be distinguished.

1 Paternal or maternal lineage (*Geschlecht vom Vater/von der Mutter*). It serves in this sense to assign identity. Thus, in Gotthold E. Lessing's play *Nathan the Wise* [*Nathan der Weise*], Nathan reveals that of his adopted daughter: "Do you not even know of what lineage the mother was [*was für Geschlechts die Mutter war*]?" (IV, 7). But once this identity is specified in the sense of belonging to a lineage, it may become a sign of distinction. This is why *Geschlecht* also refers, in a more restrictive way, to nobility. To belong to a *Geschlecht* also refers, more narrowly to nobility, as is shown in the same play (II, 6) by the exchange between Nathan and the Templar regarding von Stauffen's family: "NATHAN: Von Stauffen, there must be more members of this noble family [*des Geschlechts*],

TEMPLAR: Oh, yes, they were, there are yet many members of this noble family [*des Geschlechts*] rotting here."

2 *Geschlecht* also refers to a larger community, whose extension varies from tribe to humanity in general, by way of a people or a race. Humanity as a whole is thus referred to as *das Menschengeschlecht*, *das sterbliche Geschlecht*, or *das Geschlecht der Sterblichen* (the race of mortals). In a significant displacement of meaning from vertical to horizontal solidarity, *Geschlecht* may also mean a collection of individuals born at the same time: a generation.

3 In a different register *Geschlecht* refers to sexual difference (*der Geschlechtsunterschied*), *Geschlecht* is both sex in general and each sex in particular, male (*das männliche Geschlecht*) and female (*das weibliche Geschlecht*).

4 Finally, in a more abstract register, *Geschlecht* refers to the genus, in the sense of logical category, in the widest sense. It thus refers to the different genera of natural history as well as all sorts of objects and abstractions.

This multivocity, which owes much to the Greek *genos*, is problematic when we must translate *Geschlecht* into other languages. While the last two senses are easily identifiable and do not lead to confusion as long as context reveals when we must think of a sex or genus in a logical sense, translation becomes infinitely more complex once the term refers to a lineage, a generation, or a community or when it intersects with terms referring to people, nation, or race. In such cases the polysemy of *Geschlecht* is compounded by the polysemy of terms like "people," "race," and "nation" that must nonetheless be kept distinct from one another and from *Geschlecht*. What is more, this polysemy turns out to be problematic even in German itself, where *Geschlecht* competes with terms that share aspects of its sense and which, whenever they are introduced or used, raises a theoretical difficulty and entails a polemic.

Marc Crépon, "Geschlecht," *Dictionary of Untranslatables* (2014), 394–5.

[...] The state to which our thinking characteristically leads us—made not numb but voluble—is one of insisting on meaning what we do not quite mean, repeating false necessities to ourselves (for example: if another fails to follow what we say, s/he must be breaking a rule of language). It is a state of what we might call forced insincerity.[12] Or say it is a state of tortured hypocrisy, not to be banished from philosophy. It is exactly philosophy's business, not its other so much as its shadow.

Stanley Cavell, "Beginning to Read Barbara Cassin" (2000), 100.

Because the only "there is" is the humboldtian one of the plurality of languages; "language manifests itself in reality only as multiplicity."[13] Language is and is only the difference between languages. From this perspective, translating is no longer *dolmetschen*, but *übersetzen*, understanding that different languages produce different worlds, making these worlds communicate and enabling languages to trouble each other, in such a way that the reader's language reaches out to the writer's language[14]; our common world is at the most a regulating principle, an aim, and not a starting point. The most apt metaphor is perhaps that of Troubetzkoy, who sees in each language an "iridescent net" so that each, according to the size of his mesh, pulls up other fish.

It is also by starting off with plurality that we philosophers manage to find a trace of the signifier, of the untranslatable "materiality" [*corps*] of languages. What is at stake, then, is not only the plurality of languages, but also each language's internal diversity, the multiplicity of meanings of certain words. It is through equivocation that the signifier enters philosophy, from Aristotle to Freud.

Indeed, Aristotle makes the refusal of homonymy a weapon of mass destruction against sophistry. He bases his refutation of the adversaries of the principle of non-contradiction (the only demonstration of the first principle that is possible without a petition) on the necessity of univocality: in order to speak one must say and signify a single thing, the same for oneself and others. A word cannot simultaneously have and not have the same meaning—"hello" cannot mean "go to hell"—the word is the first encountered entity to satisfy the principle of non-contradiction. The sense of a word, its definition, is the essence of the thing that the word names: "man" signifies a man and means "animal endowed with *logos*." Either one yields to the decision of meaning, or one does not even speak, and as speech is the definition of man, one must be either a plant or a god. Those who speak for the pleasure of speaking, *logou kharin*, find themselves drastically relegated beyond the limits of humanity, and the "sophists" are those who play on homonymy in order to shake the univocality of meaning which the principle of all principles demands.[15] The impossibility of (or ban on) contradiction is, *mutatis mutandis*, as structuring as the prohibition of incest. The commitment of philosophers is to preserve this univocality by dispelling homonymies, if necessary by creating new words.

But what happens when the homonyms, far from being accidental homophones or homographs, are historical signs of the internal fabric and genealogy of a language? Aristotle has great difficulty in finding even one good example of purely accidental homonymy: how can we not see that the shoulder bone resembles the long hooked key of great Greek doors, so much so that its paradigm, *kleis*, "key/clavicle" is not a case of accident, but of image or metaphor just as much as the "foot" of mountains?

So, as good logologists, we have based our argument on Lacan. We have applied to languages what he wrote about the "*lalangues*" of each unconscious in *L'Etourdit*: "a language, amongst others, is nothing more than the integral of equivocations that its history has left in it."[16] Homonymy, equivocation, instead of being—according to Aristotle—the radical evils of language, are not only the condition of witticism but also conditions inherent to a language. On reflection, the Dictionary has never ceased to work on this principle.

I would like to make this perceptible by way of a few examples. Let us take the French word *sens*. More often than not it has several entries in the dictionary: *sens-sensation*, *sens-signification*, and sometimes *sens-direction*. If one thinks as a Hellenist, there is no overlapping zone between the aesthetic family (*aisthaneisthai*, to feel, to sense, to realize) and the semantic family (*semainein*, to signal, signify, to mean), and the French homonymy might be seen to be accidental. But when we consider the problem through the translation of Greek into the Latin of the Fathers of the Church, a different view emerges. The unity of meaning of "sens" operates under the aegis of *sensus* which conveys, especially in the translations of the Bible, the Greek term *nous*. *Nous* firstly denotes the "flair" (Ulysses' dog Argos, having "caught the scent of" his master, dies of joy on a dung heap), then "intuition," "spirit," "intellect," and in harmony with *sensus*, the articulation between man and the world, "signification," and the meaning [*sens*] of the letter. It is the passage from Greek to Latin that helped me to understand that what I took to be mere homonymy was in actual fact a semantic flux, a matter of convergence of meaning.

The choice of these symptoms, or untranslatables, also stems from an awareness of homonyms. For the homonyms of a language are generally only perceived from the viewpoint of, or according to, another language. Thus, in Russian, *pravda*, which we usually render as "truth," means in the first instance "justice" (it is the established translation of the Greek *dikaiosunê*) and is therefore a homonym from the perspective of the French. Conversely, the words "vérité" and "truth" are homonyms from a Slavonic viewpoint because the terms conflate *pravda*, which stems from justice, and *istina*, which stems from being and exactness. The same ambiguity (for us) appears in the root *svet*, light/world, and also in the homonymic problem of *mir*, peace, world, and "peasant commune" on which Tolstoy continually plays in *War and Peace*. We could unravel a good part of the dictionary if we pulled on this thread. Because evidently it is not just a case of isolated terms, but of networks: that which in German is indicated by *Geist* will be sometimes *Mind* and sometimes *Spirit*, and the *Phänomenologie des Geistes* will be translated sometimes as *Phenomenology of Spirit* and sometimes as *Phenomenology of Mind*, making Hegel a religious spiritualist or the ancestor of the philosophy of mind. But this also applies to syntax and grammar, the framework of languages, with syntactic amphibologies or homonymies caused by word order, diglossias (a high and a low language in Russian, which one does not quite know how to convey), the subtleties of tense and aspect that certain languages, and not others, compress, right down to the Spanish couple *ser/estar* which makes the French "être" and the English "to be" even more ambiguous.

Barbara Cassin, "Philosophizing in Languages" (2010), 20–2.

Cassin came to the *Vocabulaire* project less with a precise sense of what an Untranslatable is and more with a sense of how it performs. In the ensemble of her writings on the pre-Socratics and the Sophists she developed the construct to point up the instability of meaning and sense-making, the equivocity of homonymy and amphiboly, the performative dimension of discursive sophistic effects, the risks and rewards of "consistent relativism."[17] The *Vocabulaire* was conceived not as an ensemble of transhistorical concept-histories but as a dynamic system of terms that lay bare their usage and usure, that assimilate actually existing ways of speaking.

Emily Apter, "Lexilalia" (2015), 161.

Hannah Arendt wrote her *Denktagebuch* in several languages, which was a way of dealing with both her exile—"It is after all not the German language that has gone mad!"[18] she said in her interview to Gunter Gauss—and her philosophical culture speaking not only Plato in Greek, Augustine in Latin, Pascal in French, Machiavelli in Italian, Kant, Hegel, Marx or Heidegger in German, but also in the American years, in English, when she only has translations to hand.[19] Significantly, she characterizes this practice of the plurality of languages as a philosophical gesture:

> *Plurality of languages*: if there were only one language, we would perhaps be more assured about the essence of things. What is crucial is that (1) there are many languages and they are distinguished not only by their vocabulary but equally by their grammar, that is to say, essentially by their manner of thinking, and that (2) all languages can be learned.
> Given that the object, which is there to support the presentation of things, can be called "Tisch" as well as "table," this indicates that something of the genuine essence of things that we make and name escapes us. It is not the senses and the possibilities for illusion that they contain that renders the world uncertain, any more than it is the imaginable possibility or lived fear that everything is a dream. It is rather the equivocity of meaning within language and, above all, with languages. At the heart of a homogeneous human community, the essence of the table is unequivocally indicated by the word "table," and yet from the moment that it arrives at the frontier of the community, it falters.
> This wavering equivocity of the world and the insecurity of the human that inhabits it would naturally not exist if it was not possible to learn foreign languages, a possibility which demonstrates that

"correspondences" other than ours exist in view of a common and identical world or even if only one language were to exist. Hence the absurdity of the universal language—against the "human condition," the artificial and all-powerful uniformization of equivocity.[20]

[…] One can well say that the signifier returns in the semantic halo or in the angle of view, like *Brot* and *Bread* according to Benjamin. Equivocity is therefore internal and external; it unsettles the object in its own language, thanks to the tremor of other languages. This "wavering equivocity of the world," linked to the plurality of languages in as much as it is possible for us to learn them, seems to me to be the least violent of human conditions.

Barbara Cassin, "Philosophizing in Languages" (2010), 27–8.

Notes

1. Félix Guattari, "Microphysics of Power/Micropolitics of Desire," *The Guattari Reader*, trans. John Caruana, ed. Gary Genosko (Oxford: Blackwell, 1996), 178.
2. Arnaldo Momigliano, "The Fault of the Greeks" in *Essays in Ancient and Modern Historiography* (Connecticut: Wesleyan University Press, 1977), 11.
3. "If different rule-sellers do not make each name out of the same syllables, we must not forget that different blacksmiths who are making the same tool for the same type of work, don't all make it out of the same iron. But, as long as they give it the same form, even if that form is embodied in different iron, the tool will be correct, whether it is made here or abroad?" Plato, *Cratylus, Complete Works*, eds. J. M. Cooper and D. S. Hutchinson (Indianapolis: Hackett, 1997), 108 (389 e1–390 a2).
4. "It is not from the words that we ought to start, but rather we should seek and learn from the things themselves rather than from the words," Plato, *Cratylus*, 154 (439b). [Translation modified by Gilonne according to Cassin's French version.]
5. Friedrich Schleiermacher, "On the different methods of translating," *The Translation Studies Reader*, trans. Susan Bernovsky, ed. Lawrence Venuti (London: Routledge, 2004), 34–5. Please also refer to C. Berner's glossary in the French version of the text: Friedrich Schleiermacher, *Des differentes méthodes de traduire et autre texte*, trans. A. Berman and C. Berner (Paris: Seuil, 1999), 135–8.
6. This is a term coined by Novalis, who describes the redoubling: "It is amazing, the absurd error people make of imagining that they are speaking for the sake of things; no one knows the essential thing about language; that it is only concerned with itself." Novalis, "Monologue," *German Aesthetic and Literary Criticism: The Romantic Ironists and Goethe*, ed. Kathleen Wheeler (Cambridge: Cambridge University Press, 1984), 92–3.

APPENDIX I

7 On the question of Sophistry as a critique of Ontology, allow me to refer to my book: *L'Effet sophistique* (Paris: Gallimard, 1995), and for this interpretation of Parmenides' poem to my introduction in *Parménide, Sur la nature ou sur l'éant. La langue de l'être* (Paris: Seuil/Points-bilingue, 1998).
8 Friedrich Nietzsche, "Fragments sur le langage" (note de travail pour *Homére el la philologie classique*), translation into French by J-L. Nancy and P. Lacoue-Labarthe in *Poétique 5* (1971), 134. [This note does not appear with the English translation of *Homer and Classical Philology*, translated here from the French by Y. Gilonne.]
9 Gorgias, *Encomium of Helen*. [Translation from Cassin's French version by Y. Gilonne.]
10 Gérard Genette, *Bardadrac* (Paris: Seul, 2006), 25. Translation my own.
11 Ross Perlin, "Philosophers of Babel," *The New Inquiry*, thenewinquiry.com/essays/philosophers-of-babel-2/.
12 "I have seen a person strike himself on the breast and say: 'But surely another person cannot have THIS pain!'" [Ludwig Wittgenstein, *Philosophical Investigations*, trans. G. E. M. Anscombe (Oxford: Blackwell, 1974, 91e].
13 Wilhelm von Humboldt, *Über die Verschiedenheiten des menschlichen Sprachbaues, Gesammelte Schriften*, vol. VI, ed. A. Leitzmann (Berlin: B. Behr, 1907), 240. ["Die Spraehe erscheint in der Wirklichkeit nur als ein Vielfaches."]
14 I am paraphrasing the well-known alternative: "Either the translator leaves the writer in peace as much as possible and moves the reader toward him; or he leaves the reader in peace as much as possible and moves the writer toward him." Friedrich Schleiermacher, "On the different methods of translating", 49. I am choosing with Schleiermacher the uneasiness of the first possibility.
15 Allow me to refer to my introduction in Barbara Cassin, *La Décision du sens, le livre Gamma de la Métaphysique d'Aristote* (Paris: Vrin, 2000).
16 Jacques Lacan, "*L'Etourdit*" in *Scilicet 4* (Paris: Le Seuil, 1973), 47. [translation Y. Gilonne.]
17 For an overview of her writings in English, see Barbara Cassin, *Sophistical Practice: Toward a Consistent Relativism* (New York: Fordham University Press, 2014).
18 Hannah Arendt, "What remains? The language remains: an interview with Günter Gaus," *Hannah Arendt, Essays in Understanding*, ed. Jerome Kohn (New York: Schocken Books, 2005), 13.
19 Cf. Sylvie Courtine-Denamy, "postfacc" in Hannah Arendt, *Journal de pensée: 1950–1973*, vol. II (Paris: Seuil, 2005), 1062–7 [translation Y. Gilonne].
20 Hannah Arendt, *Journal de Pensée*, vol. I, 56–7 [translation Y. Gilonne].

2

Antitheatricality as Critical Idiom

CARO PIRRI

I

WHAT IS THE *GESCHLECHT* OF EARLY ENGLISH THEATER? To inquire about theater's *Geschlecht* would be to ask what early modern theater *was*. It would attempt to demarcate a specific theatrical community or "order of belonging" in which early modern theater as an institution might be placed. But *Geschlecht* might also point to the "community" or "genre" of theater, to the "constitution and destination" of theater's components.[1] In its Greek translation as *theatron*, the word "theater" is not exclusive to institutions. It simply marks a "place from which one sees"—both a thing (a place) and a process (seeing).[2] It invokes both a material proposition, the boundaries of the theater building, and a delimited case for understanding and observation.[3] Theater, much like *Geschlecht*, thus demarcates a category, or an act of translation between categories, without telling us what such categories might contain. It asks us to attend to the parameters of our looking and of our understanding. To inquire about the *Geschlecht* of early modern theater asks us to attend to the conventional historical questions: what theater is or was as an institution, how it fit into established literary or conceptual categories, and what "community" or "lineage[s]" that institution produced.[4] But it also invites us to think about the failure of knowing: states of misperception in which place and process are often at odds with one another, where seeing in that place fails to produce an understanding of its contents or an understanding of the place seen.

While English commercial theater, spanning from the late 1560s to the early 1640s, is often read as a medium (even though it is multimedial) or as a genre (even though it is multigeneric), *Geschlecht* provides a critical vocabulary for thinking theatricality in the space between being and knowing in historical representations and in our own present understanding. *Geschlecht* allows us to reflect on the ways that we understand theater, both in the context of a historical theatrical community (a historical mode of understanding) and understanding of those as a critic looking back upon this community from our own contemporary place of seeing.[5] Understanding, in an early modern English parlance, was, of course, a specifically theatrical term. On the one hand, it referred to knowledge acquisition, "one who has knowledge or comprehension (of something)"; on the other, it accounted for the context of understanding. To be an understander was to be "a spectator standing on the ground or floor in a theater," one who stood *under* the lip of the stage.[6] It marked a specific position within the ambit of theatricality. In Will West's formulation, theatrical understanding captures these two senses, and allows us to reflect on understanding as a "be[ing] present to" theater.[7]

To understand early modern theater's *Geschlecht*, then, is, in a very real sense, to be *in* a place for seeing, to place oneself relative to theater, and to the early modern period more broadly. It is to occupy a place of historical understanding as a contemporary critic and to our conventions of seeing and knowing as modern understanders of early modern theater. Beyond the first doubling, of theater as place and theater as process, is also this second doubling within theatrical practice, between the theatrical occasion and its afterlives: *those* understanders *then* in *their* place for seeing and *we* understanders *now*.

* * * *

This essay draws on *Geschlecht*'s "multivocality" to generate a historically specific vocabulary for intergeneric (mis)translation that was central to the early modern theatrical experience.[8] I do this not only to claim *Geschlecht*'s potential as a critical idiom, but also to think about how early modern theatrical practitioners were articulating their own *Geschlecht* complex in antitheatrical literature: literature that aimed to codify theater by emptying it out of intellectual and generic content, and yet ended up conceptualizing it as an experience, and a way of seeing and thinking, nonetheless. Antitheatricality, as a historical formulation of the anti-conventional qualities of *Geschlecht*, gives us a way of talking about what theater was or did while also talking about what eluded its understanders. It asks how those understanders, under the lip of the stage, also articulated their inability to understand theater: to produce from that place an understanding of category, convention, or kind.

I take on this work with the knowledge of how remote I am from these places and occasions. And yet I do so to emphasize what I have in common with early modern audiences and viewers who reflected on their experience with remoteness, with fragmentary knowledge, and with misunderstanding.

With almost no documentation of eyewitness performance, and with little to no access to even the textual materials of performance work—the scripts (rolls of dialogue used by actors), plots (schematic accounts of entrances and exits kept backstage), and annotated or "company" texts—contemporary scholars of early modern theatricality must rely on our limited knowledge of the historical *mise-en-scène*. Our work is necessarily also an act of reconstruction, both on the theaters themselves, many of which are still being excavated, and on their textual and material remains. In literary theatrical scholarship, the playhouse is often understood to be an affordance of the playtext; it is imagined into being by the reader. What little eyewitness accounts of these spaces and their performances that remain—drawings and diary entries by Simon Forman, Johannes de Witt, and Wencelaus Hollar—are opaque and fragmentary. And yet, as its own place for seeing, the playtext does include us as one of its understanders nevertheless. In metadramatic moments—in stage directions, epilogues, in deictic gestures, in asides—the playtext prompts us to perform these reconstructions, to occupy the position of early modern readers (readers who were also engaged in this work after the theatrical fact). It asks us to see ourselves as co-participants in the construction of the theatrical community, of theater's *Geschlecht*. The audience of theatrical representation is, after all, not only local to the occasion, it also exists in the aftermath: in theatrical criticism, in readings of playscripts, and in the study of theatricality.

Undertaken in the wake of the theatrical turn in early modern studies, "New Theatricality" works to excavate the interpretative assumptions and generic conventions that governed early modern theatrical performance.[9] And it does so through a reading of early English theater's material and textual remains: the cues, hints, stage directions, prop references that the theatrical event leaves behind. The theatrical critic trains their eye on the unspoken or implied conditions of historical performance works to translate these textual remainders into an understanding of conventions at a historical remove. Theatrical critique becomes, to quote Erika Lin, an "act of uncovering," or disclosure of theatrical knowledge, that reveals "the baseline assumptions and expectations" that made early modern theater comprehensible.[10] To work on theatricality is to anticipate that theatrical texts have explanatory and evidentiary power: that they were able to reflect on their own composition and communicate these unspoken conventions to their theatrically literate interpreters. As Jeremy Lopez has noted, it has become a commonplace of the field of theatricality to insist that early modern audiences "were very much aware of the limitations of the early modern stage" and possessed an "equal self-consciousness" to the very drama that they were viewing.[11] However, while studies in theatricality ascribe this self-conscious and authoritative position to theatrical texts and their historical audiences (with a few notable exceptions), they also point out the distance between the critic's position and this historical one. Rather than standing on their contemporary authority, they acknowledge that our understanding of early modern theater is often "disfigured," "fuzzily defined"—based on only "a textual shadow," its provenance "uncertain."[12] They outline the interpretive obstacles between the historical understander and the early modern one and ask us to confront the force of theater's many mediations, the uncertain provenance of the historical reconstruction of its conventions.[13] Through uncovering, there is also the hope of recovering the theatrical literacies that we have lost. There is the possibility for another act of translation between past and present, one that might link the contemporary critic and the historical audience in mutual understanding. But we have only to look closely at historical theatricality (in criticism, indelibly positivistic, materialist, confident about the matter of its own making) to see a dark underside, our own double: the immateriality and inaccessibility of theater, both to us *and its contemporaries*.[14]

II

This essay moves from understanding to misunderstanding and from theatricality to antitheatricality. I read for the thinkable in its most capacious sense, not only as a "decoding of signs," but as a horizon of possibility for what may be seen but is not yet known.[15] In this work, I draw on the critical foundations set by the new theatricality and follow many other scholars, such as Jonas Barish, who have read antitheatricality as a resource for theatrical critique. In Barish's reading, antitheatrical writers viewed theater as a place of ontological and epistemological confusion, where what is known can no longer be inferred from what is seen or shown.[16] This "mingle mangle of fish & flesh, good & bad" (in the words of one antitheatrical pamphleteer) also produces a moral dilemma, the inability to distinguish between good and evil and ultimately, in Daniel Johnston's words, has "distorting effects on the social perception of reality."[17]

Antitheatrical writing, then, is concerned with what theater is by defining what it does, and what it communicates about what it does. Antitheatrical writing is concerned with how audiences respond to theatrical communications, and how forms of perception cultivated in and by the theater, and the conventions of representation native to theatrical experience, can have long-lasting detrimental effects. Theatricality reveals the arbitrary relationship between representation (what is talked about) and presentation (what is presented to view) precisely because it draws attention to the acts of intergeneric translation that move across that gap. In this sense, antitheatrical writing also defines the work of theatricality: the work of identifying and becoming literate in theater's forms and conventions. And it does so precisely because it distinguishes that productive work, the work of learning to read theater, from the experience of being in theater. I show how antitheatrical writers work to separate the theatrical event from the language of theatricality: they translate not only between presentation and representation but also between play and text, between theater and theatricality. They work to extract moral lessons from theatrical experience without claiming that the theater, a place of negativity and moral privation, is the source of those observations. They articulate the conditions of theatrical literacy not by reading theater, but by reading through it, by seeing its ruse. And in the process, they capture the negativity and the anti-conventionality of theatrical experience, an experience that exceeds but is also occasionally antithetical to their understanding, even as they formulate a new theatrical vocabulary for understanding it in and as (anti-)theatrical critique.

By reading the antitheatrical writer as a scholar of theatricality, I work to capture the productive negativity of the word "antitheatrical." The prefix "anti," in early modern representations and in contemporary uses, signals a contrariness, sometimes even "passing into the sense of counterfeit, false."[18] As antitheatricality, the anti has sometimes signaled a refusal to see or to experience theatricality. Rather than a place for seeing, it marks a place for looking away: at times, not only away from theater but away from seeing itself.[19] And yet, in its perverseness (its opposition to its object), the "anti" also dwells in theatricality. Attaching to the objects that it negates, it indicates "a form of art or literature seemingly opposed to the basic conventions or traditions of the form in question or to the form itself"—anti-literature, anti-art, but art and literature nonetheless.[20] Through the force of its opposition it thus preserves the site of a contradiction; both the thing and against the thing, the thing and its double. Antitheater is interested in this conflict, where the form or "visual aspect of a thing" and the genre of that thing (that is, the kind of thing that it is) come up against the codes and categories that appear to govern it.[21] As a subject of critical interest, antitheatricality signals an awareness of theater's oppositions, of its inability to generate genres of knowledge, both about the things that it presents to the eye and (in the context of historical critique) about itself. I use antitheatricality for these reasons as a critical resource, not to mark an opposition to theater, but to identify a signature opposition *within* theatricality. Antitheatricality suggests not an opposition to theater, but an articulation of historical theater's difference from itself. It presents theater as an object of study, of seeing, but one that is entwined with the very thing that it is not. Antitheater is a naming that un-names, a seeing that does not understand, that struggles to articulate what it is, exactly, that is being seen. To read antitheatricality is to move between multiple submerged, opaque, and often illegible remainders of early modern theatrical history.

* * * *

Between the rise of the public theaters in the early 1570s and their closure in 1642, a literature of antitheatricality emerged. Antitheatrical writing, such as Stephen Gosson's *The Schoole of Abuse* (1579), Philip Stubbe's *Anatomy of Abuses* (1583), and William Prynne's *Histrio-mastix* (1633), took aim at theater both as a practice (seeing plays, staging them, playing in them) and as an institution (the newly enclosed theatrical buildings departed from older models that located the theater in the street or in the university). To these antitheatrical writers, the theater was a source of concern and anxiety. The social status of its attendees—apprentices and the illiterate poor—made it suspect, and its proximity to other entertainments such as gambling, dice playing, dueling, bearbaiting, and jigging made it morally and financially ruinous.[22] Theater violated the dictate of the moral artist to "teach and delight."[23] Because it had no inherently moral aim, it tended toward social chaos and debasement.

The antitheatricalist's condemnation of theater as morally corrupt is generally taken, at least in contemporary scholarship, as evidence of its peculiar positionality: on the outskirts of London, outside of the mayor's jurisdiction, it afforded an alternative society, one that had different rules and different possibilities, one that was in London but not *of* it. Or rather, theater was a version of London—itself expansive, turbulent, and increasingly cosmopolitan—that was not sanctioned by public officials.[24] This vision of theater as an alternative society reclaims its *cultural* (rather than formal) negativity as evidence of its popularity as a commercial institution. But the genre of antitheatrical literature offers critics something else as well, moving past the question of what theatricality *was* or might have been, and suggesting instead what it almost was, and even what it wasn't: what knowledges and modes of being it withheld and foreclosed. Antitheatricalists certainly talked about what they saw and understood about the theater, but they were equally invested in what theater withheld from sight and from understanding.

More recent studies of antitheatrical pamphlets have complicated any easy distinction between the democratic popular theater and the authoritarian state. They have noted that plays censored for inciting popular unrest also gained institutional sponsorship—staged in a mildly edited form, they were by no means circumscribed but constituted popular and officially approved entertainments.[25] Even as antitheatrical pamphleteers railed against theater, they were, in some cases, part of the theatrical institution they critiqued. Antitheatrical tracts might share space with playbills and featured similar content, promising to comment on current events and containing elements of role playing and polemic.

In addition, some antitheatrical pamphlets were written by dramatists themselves as an attempt to *reform* the theater (and to speak in a fashionably polemical way about it), rather than eliminate it. As such they can be uniquely valuable texts, for they generate a theatrical vocabulary (a way to talk about theater) at the same time as they struggle with defining exactly what theater is (as a place, a set of practices or behaviors, an assembly, or an institution). These texts can help us to produce a critical vocabulary for how we talk about (or don't talk about) theater and its doubles. Antitheatrical writing attempts to define theater while also accounting for the ways that it disappoints, the ways that it confuses and neglects to constitute a reference point, a set of cues, or a direction. Rather than dwelling on questions of mimesis, of theatrical practice, they instead attempt to come to terms with the value of theatrical evidence, with evidentiariness itself. Antitheatrical writing thus addresses our contemporary critical questions. *What* is or isn't theatricality (the codes, assumptions, and beliefs that we take with us into an understanding of a given performance or reading of a playtext), *where* is theatricality (where is it located in history, in genre, or in space), and *what* can or can't theatricality say or do?

III

The Schoole of Abuse—the pamphlet I will focus on for this essay—was first published in London in 1579, and its author, Stephen Gosson, unfolds his argument across eighty pages of bold gothic type. It was the first and most influential of the antitheatrical pamphlets and was published in multiple editions during its period, "initiating a critical warfare of some proportion."[26] Published when commercial drama was in its early flourishing, and aligning with the careers of playwrights such as William Shakespeare, Christopher Marlowe, and John Lyly, the pamphlet aims not only to anatomize the abuses of the theater, but also to define and outline the audience's experience of being in theaters. As Stephen Hilliard has argued, Gosson's "central fear was that the audiences at the public theaters were true literalists," that they were unable to distinguish between appearance and essence.[27] The pamphlet aims to offer this audience the literacy to understand theater, with the hope that this understanding may breed contempt. Gosson, then, appeals to his readers first as audience members. He professes to be a dramatist and playgoer, and indeed, constructs his pamphlet out of his and his readers' experiences in the theater. In the opening pages, he explains that he has

> [...] seene that which you behold and shun that which you frequent. And that I might the more easier pull your mindes from such studies, drawe your feete from such places, I have sente you a School of those abuses, which I have gathered by observation.[28]

Gosson's text is as much one of classification as it is of condemnation. Simply put, before theater can be universally condemned, it needs to be defined. But as we learn from Gosson, defining theater is no small task. We can see these tensions in the passage above. Gosson first appeals to his readers as fellow theatergoers. *The Schoole of Abuse* emphasizes commercial theater's institutional status. It brings together different occasional modes of playing, grouping them by physical proximity and, in the process, demarcating a community of viewers. Gosson claims to have "seene that which you behold," to draw viewers and readers into a new theatrical community, based on a shared past experience that he now "shun[s]." By creating this new theatrical community of former and present theatergoers, Gosson then distinguishes them based on their evaluation of that experience. And this distinction between his evaluation and theirs hinges on the difference between seeing and beholding. To behold is to also be beholden: it is to exist in a state of absorption. To see is to evaluate, and to evaluate is to "shun." Here, theater is not a space for seeing, although Gosson's pamphlet is. Rather, it is a place of beholding, of absorption. The purpose of the pamphlet is to puncture that absorption even as he draws on the forms of collective experience that popular theater enables. His pamphlet, and its readers who move from being beholders to seers, will "gather [...] by observation" rather than being gathered *by* observation: by the desire to be entertained. Gosson acknowledges the motivating impulses of theatergoers, to gather and to see (fundamental theatrical activities), but he detaches them from their original context within the theatrical occasion and draws on that occasion to produce a new gathering place (his pamphlet) which will "drawe [their] feet." Gosson acknowledges, then, that in order to draw his readers away from theater, he needs to provide them with an alternative.

The Schoole of Abuse provides this alternative by placing these activities of seeing and gathering within a critical frame. Gosson's school is a new theatrical institution that might bracket theater's abuses. It presents the same spectacle as the theater does, but for the purpose of instructing the reader how to read them. What the reader sees and gathers is not a specific theatrical production, but rather the theatrical abuses that are common to all theatrical experience. Gosson's aim is to show what theater is— historically, culturally, generically—by implicating it in a history of abuses that span time (ancient theater) and space (Italian and Spanish theater). Gosson exposes these abuses to sight by "lay[ing] [them] open before your eyes."[29] Theater's abuses may only be seen rightly from within Gosson's school. The theatrical occasion itself is not for seeing but beholding. To be present in a theater is not to watch an action but to be acted upon. By claiming that theater is a place of abuse, Gosson responds to a long tradition of participatory theatricality where audience and actors were not clearly distinguished, as they were in commercial drama, but instead intermingled as co-participants in open air theatrical performances. Gosson's text groups commercial drama with these other forms of participatory theatricality. His title page groups "plaiers" (that is, dramatic actors) in with "pipers [and] jesters" as "caterpillers [*sic*] [i.e., parasites] of a commonwealth."[30] "Their mischievous exercise" is, to Gosson, to abuse theatrical audiences: theater is a device "to wounde the conscience."[31] Here, abuse takes on a literal force through a physical metaphor of wounding. But it is the aimlessness of these wounds, rather than a purposeful intent to wound, that drives Gosson's complaint. In contemporary parlance, the word "abuse" points to an intentional act, but in early modern parlance, abuse would more likely signal "a corrupt practice or custom" (as in "abuses of the court"), and a "misapplication or misuse, especially of words."[32] Theater does not abuse by intent, it abuses by being inhospitable to use, as when something useful—an institution, a rule, a convention—is turned awry in the carnival mirror of theatrical experience. This disordered environment without hierarchy, law, or custom, is precisely what constitutes theater. Theater, in other words, is hostile to theatricality.

If theater, to Gosson, is not a place for seeing, it is also not a place for doing. As Will West has argued in his own work on theatrical understanding, theater was a space of distraction (rather than purposeful action).[33] Gosson captures this difference. To Gosson the point of theater is not to abuse, although it does wound. Instead, the point of theater is to have no point, no proper category, place, or kind. Theatrical poetry is the "lowest forme" of poetry because it fails to perform the point of poetry, which is to move the reader to virtuous action. Good poetry transforms an act of seeing—the reading of poetry—into a doing based on that seeing. It informs the reader: figuratively by educating him, but also literally by impressing upon him the character of "noble men." In Gosson, what makes theatrical poetry the "lowest forme" is not that it has a base form—that it informs the viewer with the character of base men—but that it has little form at all.[34] Theatrical poetry, in Gosson, retains the efficaciousness of poetry, in that it acts upon its viewers—it is a "wounde to the conscience"—but its placement within the *mise-en-scène* makes it impossible for theatrical poetry to produce moral action, or really any action. Any virtuous form that it might possess is mediated away by those "wanton spectacles [...] drawing gods from the heavens, & young men from them selves to shipwrack of honestie." The theater is a place of profusion and diffusion. It "draw[s] [...] from" and not towards. Its action is to turn all actions aside from their proper target. The audience's gaze is turned from seeing to beholding. It is drawn from the virtuous action of the poetic language to a space of raw noise—that "tickle[s] the eare"—and that leads to *inaction*, "from play to pleasure, from pleasure to slouth, from slouth too sleepe" and thus to wounds moral, sexual, and financial: "a generall Market of Bawdrie." The theatrical viewer, here, becomes himself a "shipwrack": an event or occasion (to do vice) rather than a person or thing. He is subsumed and distracted into spectacle, drawn away from himself. One shipwrack begets another.[35]

We can see the complications in Gosson's reckoning of theater as an ungeneric genre, a medium that mediates away meaning. Theater is anti-generic by nature: its only visible structure is the "linkes of abuse" that connect those who frequent it. As Gosson explains, "not that any filthynesse in deede, is committed within the compass of that grounde, as was done in Rome, but that every wanton and his Paramour [...] are there first acquainted." The theater is not a place of action (no filthiness in deed) because it cannot draw its audiences to any purpose—rightful or not. Instead, it is merely a place of juxtaposition and congregation. The "compasse" provides a spatial metaphor for Gosson's claim that theatrical language "tickle[s] the eare."[36] Theater points like the hand of a compass—that is, it does have an effect, but without being grounded in any coherent system of value or assessment, it spins and spins, producing ultimately only congregation and disorientation, and making the audience further susceptible to harm: "so brittle that we break with every fillop; so weake, that wee are drawne with every threade." Gosson's pamphlet gathers these incidental and occasional threads together in a single viewing place, a school, where their "chains" may be seen. "The abuses of plaies," claims Gosson, "cannot be showen, because they passe the degree of the instrument, reach of the Plummet, sight of the minde." Theater does not provide the conditions to even produce knowledge of its own vices, its own assumptions, conventions of laws: in other words, its theatricality. Theater's abuses only become visible when they are "open" to view, not within "open spectacles" but in that other place for seeing that is Gosson's pamphlet.[37]

In the process of gathering together this history of theatrical abuses, of disorientations, and making them constitutive of theater, Gosson's pamphlet gives us a much more capacious theatricality than we're used to. Rather than a process of codification, it instead seeks to anatomize the disorientations and misperceptions inherent in theatrical experience. Gosson's ungeneric approach to theater, his attempt to winnow out theater from theatricality, expands the theatrical occasion to all its generic doublings—including its audience, music, festive entertainment, spectacle, pickpockets, verse and poetry—crushing them together in this space of frenetic juxtaposition. And Gosson's pamphlet becomes the playtext of this occasion, a way of reading it in absentia, of reconstructing it through language. It is not the playtext of any particular play. It is the playtext of theater itself. His pamphlet redoubles theater, making it and its experiences available for observation without the reader having to cross the threshold.

IV

Gosson's view of theatricality is theater without the occasion, theater with a clear subject and object, where theater's audiences, theater's vices, and theater's stage become themselves analytical and conventional content in this new gathering space, this place for seeing theater's abuses. But Gosson's school, his pamphlet, also *restores* the generic content of theater by displacing it from that occasion. What he captures is not only a description of theatrical experience, but also a way of speaking about that experience: another set of conventions for talking about theatrical misperception. We can see this new formal language when Gosson talks about the structure of his school as another gathering place, another potential site of theatrical confusion, confusion that, like the "wanton and his Paramour," follows Gosson out of the theater to become part of this new theatrical occasion. Gosson represents his pamphlet as a second gathering place, a double for the space in which theater happens: "the school which I build, is narrowe, at the first blushe appeareth, but a dogghole; yet smal cloudes carrie water [...] the shortest Pamphlette may shroude matter."[38] By drawing on the rhetoric of "infinite riches in a little room," Gosson represents his school as a second theater in which the first theater is itself presented in a compressed form. The biblical metaphor of the narrow versus the wide gate pits the pamphlet against theater, but only by representing it as a double for the space in which theater happens. Voiding theatricality from theater, it takes its place. Gosson himself acknowledges the admixture of these two theaters—for "where hony and gall are mixed, it will be hard to sever the one from the other."[39]

The potential for his sentiments about theater to be read as sentiments derived by his disordered experiences in theater is a danger that Gosson keeps returning to. Gosson positions himself as still under the influence of an experience that he condemns, one that potentially disorders his impressions: after all, he still "bear[s] the stench of the[se] [experiences] yet in [his] owne nose."[40] Gosson's awareness of his own theatrical indoctrination, the extent to which his time in theaters might have affected his reason, are stated most forcefully on the final page of the pamphlet, which ultimately tapers off into an ambiguous negative: "I will heere ende, desiring pardon for my faulte, because I am rashe; & redresse of abuses, because they ar naught."[41] The coming to naught and being naught, a vision of multiplication and subtraction simultaneously, inscribed within the wooden O of the stage, discloses a realm of sense that is also beyond negativity: the experience of being in theaters that Gosson articulates at the beginning as an *a priori*, and implicitly an inspiration, for his writing. Gosson's theatricality—unclearly disclosed, quickly disavowed—that is, the potential of theater to be more than a collection of trifling experience, but to constitute a mode of thought, a being, a *style*, clouds the manuscript.

* * * *

It is in this admission, this fear of the pamphlet and its author being and coming to "naught" that gives us a chance to reflect again on *anti*theatricality. Gosson's "anti," like his many other grammatical negatives, captures the possibility of "naught-ness" as a style of writing about theater as a *state or genre of negativity*. Theater is a place of "disease", "misrule", with "discommoditie."[42] It has "uncertaine" beginnings and "unworthy" ends.[43] However, like his figural uses of the negative, these grammatical negatives also open a zone of potential being within theater for what Daniel Heller-Roazen has termed the space of the "non." The "non" to Roazen (as in "non-human," "non-amenable," "non-existent") is indefinite because it moves from the space of what is—what can be named and known, even in the absence of certain attributes or virtues—into the space of what "we fail to know."[44] As a grammatical event, the construction of the non articulates an attempt to grasp the untranslatable, the space of that which is excluded from thought. The addition of the non does not precisely negate the word that it is attached to. The meaning of the word is still present, still visible to us. Rather, the non makes visible the processes, the complex, of intergeneric translation:

> [...] every time the particle "not" or "non" is attached to a given word, the same event in speech may be discerned. One term is denied; its denotations are suppressed. Yet in that refusal, a realm of sense is also disclosed: one that has no positive designation, although it is delimited. Something is named, yet the nature of the naming remains opaque.[45]

In the space of the "non" or the "not" the grammatical negative becomes a suppression of meaning, it denies meaning-making or being-making, the very works of fiction. In so doing, however, it points to something else, something that can't quite be articulated. The object is suspended in the balance—a kind of opaque institution that can be marked (has a kind of existence). The "non" marks a refusal to come to a point, to be legible, to enter the material realms of history, of convention, of community. This negation goes beyond the merely "privative," where theater *lacks* something, and into the "indefinite negative," which both is and is not, which "constitutes less the name of a concept than the index of a difficulty which troubles the theory" it is designed to elaborate.[46] The non, like Gosson's pamphlet itself, draws us away from the word that it modifies, but it also asks us to carry over the features of that word, its discursive meanings, with us into that negative interpretive space.

As a philosopher of language, Heller-Roazen fuses the indefinite "non" to a particle of speech: the "non" functions differently than other modes of negation, say an "ex" or a "no" or an "ab", would. But as a literary scholar, one attentive not only to language but also to its uses and inflections, I read the "non" as implicit in the title *The Schoole of Abuse* as it moves through various permutations. Sometimes it seems imbued with the force of the privative, where theater is merely defined by what it lacks. At another moment, it introduces a future possibility, a state of being conjured only in its impossibility, an invocation of theater's impossible futures: a being to come that can, as now, be stated only in the negative. By paying close attention to how Gosson uses his grammatical negatives—not merely as components of syntax but as materials for thought—we can envision a different kind of historical theater than we're used to, one that introduces an additive negativity into what is, grammatically, a seeming subtraction. I read Gosson's "anti," his "abuse," in the space of this indefinite negative.

Drawing from the theater to draw readers away from it, the pamphlet attempts to produce a negative positivity, the space of the nonnegative, out of a pure negative: it attempts to translate theatrical experience into a theatrical vocabulary. Theater, after all, like the world, can be "drawne in a mappe."[47] By filtering his theatricality through the anti, his school also inscribes within itself the "non-sense" of theatricality as a specific style—we might say, the style of (anti)theatricality. Gosson's pamphlet reproduces the theater with a guide, with a structure, and with a "point." In so doing, he lifts the theater from the very context of its own theatricality, giving it a milieu in which it can be *made to mean*, while still articulating it in opposition to itself, as antithetical to the very meaning it makes. In other words, rather than existing as an anti-genre without any form or content, theater takes on a possible (if still negative) shape within the pamphlet itself. His preoccupation with the possibilities (conceptual, grammatical, stylistic, thematic) of negation arise in his critique as an incitement to reflection: a way to decompose his own theatrical responses, his confusion, his illiteracy, his doubt, to reflect them back in the form of the pamphlet. Gosson's conclusion that theater is *not* X (or that it is "non-X") recognizes in theater's naughtiness a lack of recognition, an understanding that theater does not work in accordance with the orders, conventionalities, and hierarchies that Gosson takes as a given: that theater's potential recognizability lies beyond how he would like it to work.

Gosson carefully contrasts the variability of theater to the stability of the pamphlet, but he is continually conferring the pamphlet and the theater with adjacent features and qualities: absorbing them into the pamphlet on one side (these are the positive articulations of the qualities) and in the theater on the other (the negative). Within *The Schoole of Abuse* exists the double, not quite positively articulated negative of that other institution: the theater. This double provides a contrast between the theatricality of theater and the theatricality of his own criticism, where the latter is an account that tries to make theater *mean*, that draws on its negativity to make a point about it, and that inscribes that negativity as the formal residue of a prior theatrical experience. The movement between these two theatricalities, and the deformation of both within the frame of the other, gives us a model for how to talk about antitheatricality as itself the nonnegative of theater's *Geschlecht*.

V

Geschlecht, understood in literary criticism broadly as a question of genre, has often been concerned with identifying those qualities that subject a critical work to a certain understanding of belonging, to a specific context and community, even a specific mode of critique. Genre has stood as a "structure of implication" and "set of formal features" in the text, as something that the text affords but that is activated by prior knowledge and inference.[48] Genre occasions such a hospitality to the critic. It is that in the text that theatricality hinges on, which makes the play of signs, the "semiotic function" of theater, have some purchase in the text, in history, and in early modern theater itself. And this is especially the case in the early modern period, where generic forms have such a defining presence in thought, with, for example, the movement between pastoral and epic being representative of the "grand career" of the poet.[49] Yet genre in the form of *Geschlecht* has different affordances. It is less "hospitable." *Geschlecht*'s "dissemination" of meaning, its categorical corruption, its introduction of nonnegative cues might both repel and embrace the seeing and being of the critic.

What might it mean to subtract negativity from theater's *Geschlecht*? To subtract from it, in other words, its categorical imperative: "*to be or not to be*" in or of a specific genre, for to talk of *Geschlecht* must, definitionally, be to *discriminate*, must be concerned with "order[s] of belonging."[50] In "*Geschlecht* I," Derrida articulates what a neutral *Geschlecht* might look like by driving it into *Dasein*—by moving from genre to ontology. He links *Geschlecht* with a quality of "dispersion," "bestrewal"—in opposition to duality.[51] Derrida's "lexical swarm" of possible translations of genre and kind (here sexual difference) displaces the binary categorical imperative of *Geschlecht* (where it might mean, in our case, to belong or not to belong to a specific category) and produces something akin to *differance*: a dispersal of "transfer[s] and displacements" that often have a "negative sense, yet sometimes have a neutral or nonnegative sense."[52] Derrida's articulation of the neutral is precisely that by which negativity (as opposed to positivity) is itself negated and made to produce something like the nonnegative: a category of sorts, functioning as an "opaque positivity," as a "disseminating" potentiality.[53] And yet within this capacity to "disseminate" pure neutrality, pure positivity, there is always the risk of "a certain contamination," "a mode of inauthenticity."[54] This potential is, by his own admission, hinted at in Derrida's rhetoric, which dwells in "appearances," in "perspective," in the space of the subjunctive and the imagination: in his appeal to "let us imagine then."[55] *Geschlecht*, expressed through the nonnegative, is an imagination of being through an examination of categorical corruption at the very heart of *Dasein*, a dissemination of being beyond itself—"and yet," "and yet."[56]

Even, then, as Derrida translates *Geschlecht* into an ontological position, it also exceeds this position in his own rhetoric and by his own admission. *Geschlecht* can easily move between binary categories and boundlessness, between appearances and to being, or rather, not *between*, which indicates binarity, but more properly *among*; it is the "thrownness"[57] of movement that links concepts in relation, that figures a certain fecundity within the primordial exclusion of *Dasein* (excluded, as it is, from appearances, from sociality, from perception and understanding). Any talk of *Geschlecht* indicates "translation problems that will only get worse for us"; "the thinking of *geschlecht* and the thinking of translation are essentially the same."[58] In "*Geschlecht* I" (an essay nominally about Heideggerian *Dasein*, about ontology and being), *Geschlecht* itself becomes a spectacle. It is rescued from its mundane association with difference as binarity, with category, and instead becomes (for Derrida, possibly for Heidegger) a space of fiction and interpretive possibility.[59]

If we follow Josette Féral in defining theatricality as that which opens a "cleft" in a space for seeing, then something like *Geschlecht* might point us to the movements within a text, the declensions and dispersions, on which this opening, this "cleft" might hinge.[60] The interpretive position that traces these permutations and these mistranslations of *Geschlecht*, that activates *Geschlecht*'s hospitality to mistranslation, to deconstruction, to corruption, is itself theatrical. Or rather it is antitheatrical, for *Geschlecht*'s dissemination of difference also allows one to talk about permutations, about the cue-that-is-not-there or only seems to be there, about the contours and forms of an absence, and allows that absence to "work on discourse."[61] It discloses the space of "play" and "polysemic richness" that is also the space for a slantwise seeing, a mis-seeing, yet not of blindness.[62] This is the space of (anti)theatricality.

* * * *

The forging of theatrical conventions has preoccupied many of theater's critics. Readings of textual cues might allude to long-lost performance conditions or point to assumptions that governed historical reception: Traces of past performance occasions—left for the critic in the play text—create a complex of allusion that goes beyond mere interpretation to an understanding of the structures of perception and implication that make that interpretation possible. Conventions "occur first as anti-conventions or anti-signs [...] meaning that it has taken its place as one of the efficient and invisible chips in the informational circuitry. But how did it get there in the first place if not as an attempt to *break into* the circuit."[63] It is this act of "breaking in" that contains an awareness of theater's opposites, of its oppositions, iterations and citations of form that are not explanatory or generative of a larger pattern or category, that do not "add up" (and yet do not subtract) to what is seen. The conventions or cues that govern theatrical interpretation unite two communities of seers (historical viewers and contemporary critics), but they pose only a hazy outline. Barely understood, they are on their way to understanding, to being seen, but not quite *yet*. These half-conventions, not-quite-crystallized assumptions, or unevenly applied rules for governing performance are still valuable for us, as critics. They encourage us to consider our position as co-participants in the construction of early modern theater and its environs. They also give us a more textured account of what criticism might have looked like in a historical context far different from our own.

Gosson gives us a model for a critical antitheatricality by elaborating the many workings of the nonnegative negative. He provides a premier example of a theater practitioner, someone who contemporary scholars might be inclined to invest in. He is knowledgeable about his craft, but he is also deeply confused about what theater is and does, and what it might be. Gosson's "anti-conventions" attempt to break into the circuit of theatricality, to make it mean differently. They try to fix its meaning as *unmeaning*, as negativity. But in the process of articulating theatrical unmeaning, Gosson also produces a place for seeing the repertoire of partial signs that make it up as an occasion that prefers hesitation, doubt, and unreason, over literacy, durability, and citationality. He refuses to codify theatrical conventions, refuses to grant the theater any conventionality at all. He occupies the space of the "and yet." And in the space of his nonnegative—where theater is not-this but it's also not-not-this—the power to negate, to be definitively negative, has itself been negated. The movement of the double or infinite negative is not a simple disclosure of potentiality; rather, like the nonnegative and disseminating *Geschlecht* of "*Geschlecht* I," it traces a constant movement, a "thrownness" between potential states—a mistranslation and dissemination that sketch out what an antitheatrical criticism might look like.[64] One of the many critical affordances of Gosson's antitheatricality is its ability to position seeing as a counter to certainty (to *understanding*) while still making it central to theatrical critique.

VI

Work on the theatrical literacy of early English audiences has been buoyed by a critical insistence on early modern theatricality's self-reflexiveness, its tendency to reflect on its own composition and make visible its implicit rules. The turn from New Historicism to New Formalism has hinged on the historicity of forms, their placement within a specific interpretive milieu. This has been especially true for early modern drama, where the composition of dramatic texts is often taken to intersect with historical events, and early modern drama is considered to comment knowingly on its own context. This allows critics to attend to the nuances of theatrical staging while also acknowledging the larger horizons of understanding in which it participates. If theater remains an authority on its own making, it then becomes a kind of social commentary, a way of thinking about historical continuities, about obsolete forms or assumptions, about the past. This is a valuable perspective, but it risks, I think, granting theater too *much* authority, especially by restricting the kinds of historical forms that we are prepared to see. A reliance on theater's own metatheatricality, its privileged perspective on its own making, results in an overattentiveness, on the part of critics, to characters who seem to know that they are in a play. Characters like Hamlet and Prospero, for instance, who talk about the operations and functions of theater are taken as authorities, as the mouthpieces for theatrical self-reflexiveness, as guides to audiences. They were privy to the laws of "reality and illusion"—experts in other words, in navigating theater's *Geschlecht* complex.[65]

The idea that early modern popular culture was "knowing," has a longer and far more entrenched critical history.[66] As a counter to medieval unknowing, to superstition, to assumption and belief, the early modern period seems to offer a kind of panacea, a turn to a self-reflexive sensibility. It signals the move from the metatheatricality of the stage to the "self-fashioning" of early modern subjects.[67] The rise of science and epistemology studies within an early modern framework, and a rising interest in rational political formations such as the university, the corporation, the colony, and other figurations of seemingly modern provenance has enhanced the "modern" aspect of the early modern, aligning it more clearly with the position of the critic. From this perspective, our knowingness about early modern drama must reinforce their own historical position, for surely, they must have known what we know about them. Writers such as Katherine Eggert and Julian Yates have articulated critical alternatives to a positive epistemology, conjugating early modern unknowing through "misuse" and "disknowledge."[68] But to claim ignorance as a historical value, especially outside of established parameters such as religious belief or skepticism, would seem to be too much of a critical projection, a confusion of our confusion with theirs. If theater's very form, is bound up in this complex of knowingness, what perspectives, what positions, what formalisms, what histories, are falling out of critique?

Early modern English theater enhances *Geschlecht*'s innate nonnegativity, allows us to trace its thrownness, reading within it a new kind of critical gesture. But the movement of *Geschlecht* also enriches our understanding of early modern theater; it expands the visual field of critique. Instead of relying on the textual "cue" as a pointing gesture, as an indication of something that *was* early modern theater, theater's *Geschlecht* points to a complex of meaning within the theatrical scene, and to the misseeings and misreadings that make up historical and contemporary critique. It recovers a legacy of historical mis/understanding by broadening the critical field to include antitheatricality, to include someone like Gosson as our own critical antecedent, someone interested, as we are, in grappling with theatricality's intersemiotic translations. As Roman Jakobson puts it: "poetry by definition is untranslatable. Only creative transposition is possible: either intralingual transposition [...] or intersemiotic transposition—from one system of signs into another."[69] Theatrical poetry performs this act of virtuosic transposition by insistence that there is *something* to be seen (look here!), and refuses to produce this thing as an object of perception. The "scene" of perception, then, takes priority over and replaces the thing perceived. The theatrical *mise-en-scène* insists on the deictic and gestural component of language, a "mere pointing," that attempts to capture the "nonlinguistic acquaintance" of the "thing itself."[70] But the object of our looking has not yet entered into presence as an object of perception; it is still *en route*, is still being *per*formed in the process of being brought to a state of completion, of translation, but always not *yet* there.

I will conclude here with a brief account of what I think an antitheatrical criticism might look like, or rather how it might inform our understanding of early modern theater. Unlike performativity, which does the work of the coming-into-being or the repertoire, theatricality has receded into the archive, into knowledge, history, and certainty. My project has been a recovery of theatricality, which I take to reside less in the occasion of performance (in what happens on stage) than a threshold of perception—an understanding—marking the place of the critic and the audience. In its articulation of how fraught theatrical understanding can be, and in its interest in triangulating this understanding between theater, audience, and critics, this recovered theatricality, in being sensitive to the nonnegative and indefinite, allows us to perceive the outlines of what early moderns themselves excluded; what they presumed to be unknowable or unknowing.[71]

I offer only one possibility: that antitheatrical critique might shift our emphasis from metadramatic authority to intergeneric confusion, to misreadings, transplantations, and displacements of theatrical knowledge. Which epistemological orders does theatrical unknowing produce? What resonance does an antitheatrical position have within the theatrical scene? By looking for theater's antitheatrical vocabulary, we might add to our list of theatrical negatives, the "dissemination" of early English theater's *Geschlecht* complex. But we might also look precisely to those moments of theatrical mastery, to the presumed totalizing position of Prospero or the "insider's knowledge" of Hamlet, who appears to know more about theatricality than the play's main actors, the "robustious periwig-pated fellows[s]" that "tear a passion to tatters," do.[72] Instead of learning from these moments—that is, instead of following their "cue" and accepting their authority—we might see that they produce only temporary or fleeting forms, ones that are partially translated or mistranslated outright, that aim to be explanatory, and to articulate how theatricality "is [or] hath been" but that ultimately fall short; that are continually undermined, warped back and contorted by their enclosing fictions.[73] These false or partial categories of knowledge articulate the risk attendant in declarations of categorical certainty. By failing to produce genres of knowledge, they also expand the interpretive field, the complex of early modern theatricality.

Notes

1 Marc Crépon, "*Geschlecht*," in *Dictionary of Untranslatables: A Philosophical Lexicon*, ed. Barbara Cassin, trans. eds. Emily Apter, Jacques Lezra, and Michael Wood (Princeton: Princeton University Press, 2014), 394–6.
2 Samuel Weber, *Theatricality as Medium*, 1st edition (New York: Fordham University Press, 2004), 34.
3 Caroline Van Eck and Stijn Bussels, "The Visual Arts and the Theater in Early Modern Europe," *Art History*, vol. 33, no. 2 (April 1, 2010), 208–23, https://doi.org/10.1111/j.1467-8365.2010.00738.x, 212.
4 Crépon, "*Geschlecht*," 395.
5 Crépon, "*Geschlecht*," 395.
6 "Under'stander, N.," *OED Online* (Oxford University Press), www.oed.com/view/Entry/212089.
7 William West, "Understanding in the Elizabethan Theatres," *Renaissance Drama*, vol. 35 (2006), 113–43, 136. West and Stephen Orgel's work on incomprehensibility informs much of the work I do here. See Stephen Orgel, "The Poetics of Incomprehensibility," *Shakespeare Quarterly*, vol. 42, no. 4 (December 1, 1991), 431–7, https://doi.org/10.2307/2870462.
8 Crépon, "*Geschlecht*," 395.
9 Henry S. Turner, "Toward a New Theatricality?," *Renaissance Drama* 40 (January 1, 2012): 29–35, https://doi.org/10.1086/rd.40.41917496.
10 Erika T. Lin, *Shakespeare and the Materiality of Performance* (Basingstoke: Palgrave Macmillan, 2012), 8.
11 Jeremy Lopez, *Theatrical Convention and Audience Response in Early Modern Drama* (Cambridge: Cambridge University Press, 2007), 2.
12 Henry S. Turner, "Toward a New Theatricality?," *Renaissance Drama*, 40 (January 1, 2012), 29–35, https://doi.org/10.1086/rd.40.41917496; see also Barbara Hodgdon and W. B. Worthen, "Renaissance and/or Early Modern Drama and/or Theater and/or Performance: A Dialogue," *Renaissance Drama*, 40 (January 1, 2012), 19–28, https://doi.org/10.1086/rd.40.41917495. Robert Weimann, *Author's Pen and Actor's Voice: Playing and Writing in Shakespeare's Theatre*, eds. Helen Higbee and William West (Cambridge, UK; New York: Cambridge University Press, 2000), 87; William West, "Intertheatricality," in *Early Modern Theatricality*, ed. Henry S. Turner, Oxford 21st Century Approaches to Literature (Oxford University Press, 2013), 151–72, 156; Jeremy Lopez, "Dumb Show," in *Early Modern*

Theatricality, ed. Henry S. Turner, Oxford 21st Century Approaches to Literature (Oxford University Press, 2013), 291–305, 301; Mary Thomas Crane, "Optics," in *Early Modern Theatricality*, ed. Henry S. Turner, Oxford 21st Century Approaches to Literature (Oxford University Press, 2013), 250–69, 269.

13 For the older historicist model of theatrical criticism see Glynne Wickham, Herbert Berry, and William Ingram, *English Professional Theatre, 1530–1660* (Cambridge: Cambridge University Press, 2009). See also the work of W. W. Greg on theatrical ephemera and the problems of editing playtexts. On the textual model of criticism, see Harry Berger, Jr., *Imaginary Audition: Shakespeare on Stage and Page* (Berkeley: University of California Press, 1990).

14 Antonin Artaud, *The Theater and Its Double*, trans. Mary Caroline Richards (New York: Grove Press, 1958).

15 Josette Féral, "Foreword," *SubStance*, vol. 31, no. 2 (2002), 3–13, https://doi.org/10.1353/sub.2002.0025, 8.

16 Jonas A. Barish, *The Antitheatrical Prejudice*, first edition (Berkeley: University of California Press, 1981), 89.

17 Daniel Johnston, "Ontological Queasiness: Antitheatricality and the History of Being," *About Performance*, no. 14/15 (2017), 195–211, 196. Quote from the antitheatrical pamphlet cites Stephen Gosson, 1554–1624. *Plays Confuted in Fiue Actions Prouing that they are Not to be Suffred in a Christian Common Weale, by the Waye both the Cauils of Thomas Lodge, and the Play of Playes, Written in their Defence, and Other Obiections of Players Frendes, are Truely Set Downe and Directlye Aunsweared. by Steph. Gosson, Stud. Oxon London, Imprinted for Thomas Gosson dwelling in Pater noster row at the signe of the Sunne, 1582*: Image 28 http://pitt.idm.oclc.org/login?url=https://www-proquest-com.pitt.idm.oclc.org/books/playes-confuted-fiue-actions-prouing-that-they/docview/2248575472/se-2?accountid=14709.

18 "Anti-, Prefix 1," *OED Online* (Oxford University Press), www.oed.com/view/Entry/8501.

19 On antitheatricality as an anti-visuality see Michael Fried, "Barthes's Punctum," *Critical Inquiry*, vol. 31, no. 3 (March 1, 2005).

20 "Anti-, Prefix 1," *OED Online*.

21 "Form, n," *OED Online* (Oxford University Press), www.oed.com/view/Entry/73421.

22 On the social milieu of the popular commercial theaters see Andrew Gurr, *Playgoing in Shakespeare's London*, third edition (Cambridge; New York: Cambridge University Press, 2004).

23 Philip Sidney, "The Defense of Poesy," in *English Renaissance Literary Criticism* (Oxford: Clarendon Press; New York: Oxford University Press, 1999), 336–91, 345.

24 On the early modern theater and criminality see Bryan Reynolds, *Becoming Criminal: Transversal Performance and Cultural Dissidence in Early Modern England* (Baltimore: Johns Hopkins University Press, 2002).

25 See, for example, the critical conversation involving the censor's contribution to Shakespeare's collaborative play *The Book of Sir Thomas Moore*. Gillian Woods, "'Strange Discourse': The Controversial Subject of 'Sir Thomas More,'" *Renaissance Drama*, New Series, 39 (January 1, 2011), 3–35; Nina S. Levine, "Citizens' Games: Differentiating Collaboration and Sir Thomas

More," *Shakespeare Quarterly*, vol. 58, no. 1 (2007), 31–64, https://doi.org/10.1353/shq.2007.0014; John Jowett, "Introduction," in *Sir Thomas More*, third edition (London: Bloomsbury Arden Shakespeare, 2011), 1–129; Tracey Hill, "'The Cittie Is in an Uproare': Staging London in *The Booke of Sir Thomas More*," *Early Modern Literary Studies*, vol. 11, no. 1 (May 2005), 2–19.

26 Arthur F. Kinney, "Stephen Gosson's Art of Argumentation in *The Schoole of Abuse*," *Studies in English Literature, 1500–1900*, vol. 7, no.1 (1967), 41–54, 41.

27 Stephen S. Hilliard, "Stephen Gosson and the Elizabethan Distrust of the Effects of Drama," *English Literary Renaissance*, vol. 9, no. 2 (1979), 225–39, 234.

28 This reference to Gosson's *Schoole of Abuse* cites the 1587 edition, which contains pages printed with, but now missing from, the publicly available first edition of 1579. Stephen Gosson, 1554–1624. *The Schoole of Abuse Contayning a Pleasant Inuectiue Against Poets, Pipers, Players, Iesters, and such Like Caterpillers of a Common Wealth; Setting Vp the Flagge of Defiance to their Mischiuous Exercise, and Ouerthrowing their Bulwarkes, by Prophane Writers, Naturall Reason and Common Experience. … by Stephan Gosson Stud. Oxon London, By Thomas Dawson for Thomas Woodcocke, 1587.* http://pitt.idm.oclc.org/login?url=https://www-proquest-com.pitt.idm.oclc.org/books/schoole-abuse-contayning-pleasaunt-inuectiue/docview/2240873793/se-2?accountid=14709. All further references to the main text are from the 1579 edition and will be cited using the page numbers of the TCP full text transcription. When page numbers are not available, I will refer to the heading and page number of the section. Stephen Gosson, 1554–1624. *The Schoole of Abuse Conteining a Pleasant [Sic] Inuectiue Against Poets, Pipers, Plaiers, Iesters, and such Like Caterpillers of a Co[m]Monwelth; Setting Vp the Hagge of Defiance to their Mischieuous Exercise, [and] Ouerthrowing their Bulwarkes, by Prophane Writers, Naturall Reason, and Common Experience: A Discourse as Pleasaunt for Gentlemen that Fauour Learning, as Profitable for all that Wyll Follow Virtue. by Stephan Gosson. Stud. Oxon London, for Thomas VVoodcocke, 1579.* http://pitt.idm.oclc.org/login?url=https://www-proquest-com.pitt.idm.oclc.org/books/schoole-abuse-conteining-plesaunt-sic-inuectiue/docview/2264173271/se-2?accountid=14709.

29 Gosson, *The Schoole of Abuse*, 6.
30 Gosson, *The Schoole of Abuse*, Title.
31 Gosson, *The Schoole of Abuse*, 15v.
32 "abuse, n," *OeD Online* (Oxford University Press), www-oed-com.pitt.idm.oclc.org/view/Entry/821?isAdvanced=false&result=1&rskey=3DaybE&.
33 Will West has talked about antitheatrical pamphlets represent the theater as a space of visual distraction where playing speaking, dancing, and musical performance would produce overlapping and competing sensory experiences. William West, "State of the Field" talk at Rutgers University, 2017.
34 Gosson, *The Schoole of Abuse*, 6, 8.
35 Gosson, *The Schoole of Abuse*, 27, 12, 6–7, 18.
36 Gosson, *The Schoole of Abuse*, 11, 18, 7.
37 Gosson, *The Schoole of Abuse*, 26, 21, 42.
38 Gosson, *The Schoole of Abuse* (1587), Aiv.v.

39 Gosson, *The Schoole of Abuse*, "The Epistle Dedicatoire," 4, 3.
40 Gosson, *The Schoole of Abuse* (1587), Aiv.r.
41 Gosson, *The Schoole of Abuse*, "The Epistle Dedicatoire," 5, 41.
42 Gosson, *The Schoole of Abuse*, 21, 19, 42
43 Gosson, *The Schoole of Abuse*, 1, 21.
44 Daniel Heller-Roazen, *No One's Ways: An Essay on Infinite Naming* (New York: Zone Books, 2017), 255.
45 Heller-Roazen, *No One's Ways*, 10.
46 Heller-Roazen, *No One's Ways*, 32.
47 Gosson, *The Schoole of Abuse*, "The Epistle Dedicatoire," 4.
48 John Frow, *Genre*, first edition (London; New York: Routledge, 2005), 9–10.
49 Richard Helgerson, *Self-Crowned Laureates: Spenser, Jonson, Milton, and the Literary System*, first edition (Berkeley: University of California Press, 1983).
50 Crépon, "Geschlecht," 396.
51 Jacques Derrida, "Geschlecht I: Sexual Difference, Ontological Difference," *Research in Phenomenology*, vol. 13 (1983), 19.
52 Derrida, "Geschlecht I," 17-18.
53 I borrow "opaque positivity" from Richard Doyle, *On beyond Living: Rhetorical Transformations of the Life Sciences* (Stanford, CA: Stanford University Press, 1997), 10.
54 Derrida, "Geschlecht I," 17–8, 21, 25.
55 Derrida, "Geschlecht I," 10-11, 9.
56 Derrida, "Geschlecht I," 8–11.
57 Derrida, "Geschlecht I," 21.
58 Derrida, "Geschlecht I," 17.
59 Derrida, "Geschlecht I," 21, 17.
60 Josette Féral and Ronald P. Bermingham, "Theatricality: The Specificity of Theatrical Language," *SubStance*, vol. 31, no. 2 (2002), 94–108, https://doi.org/10.1353/sub.2002.0026, 97.
61 Derrida, "Geschlecht I," 9.
62 Derrida, "Geschlecht I," 9, 12.
63 Bert O. States, *Great Reckonings in Little Rooms: On the Phenomenology of the Theater* (Berkeley: University of California Press, 1985), 12.
64 Derrida, "Geschlecht I," 21.
65 As Jeremy Lopez has recently argued, such characters "were very much aware of the limitations of the early modern stage" and possessed an "equal self-consciousness" to the very drama they were viewing. They were, in other words, understanders in both senses: they attended plays as spectators and thus were part of the theatrical community, while also aware of theater's laws of "reality and illusion." See Jeremy Lopez, *Theatrical Convention and Audience Response in Early Modern Drama* (Cambridge: Cambridge University Press, 2007), 2.
66 Lin, *Shakespeare and the Materiality of Performance*, 24 discusses the concept of theatrical privilege whereby "knowing" characters demonstrate their knowingness through an understanding of theatrical conventions rather than by occupying a specific place on stage, usually close to the audience, as had previously been articulated by Robert Weimann.

67 On self-fashioning, see Stephen Greenblatt, *Renaissance Self-Fashioning: From More to Shakespeare* (Chicago: The University of Chicago Press, 2005).
68 Julian Yates, *Error, Misuse, Failure: Object Lessons From The English Renaissance*, first edition (Minneapolis: University of Minnesota Press, 2002); Katherine Eggert, *Disknowledge: Literature, Alchemy, and the End of Humanism in Renaissance England* (Philadelphia: University of Pennsylvania Press, 2015).
69 Roman Jakobson. "On Linguistic Aspects of Translation," in *On Translation*, ed. Reuben Arthur Brower, 232–9 (Harvard University Press, 1959), 238.
70 Jakobson, "On Linguistic Aspects of Translation," 232.
71 Jakobson. "On Linguistic Aspects of Translation," 232.
72 William Shakespeare, *Hamlet*, ed. G. R. Hibbard (Oxford, UK; New York: Oxford University Press, 2008).
73 Sidney, "The Defense of Poesy," 346.

3

The Cruel Beast: Settler Sovereignty and the Crisis of American Zoopolitics

Brian W. Nail

"Trump is a beast," Bannon was cackling, practically giddy over what he had just witnessed.
—JOSHUA GREEN, *DEVIL'S BARGAIN*

"You've called women you don't like 'fat pigs,' 'dogs,' 'slobs,' and 'disgusting animals' ... Does that sound like the temperament of a man we should elect as president?"
—BILL PRESS, "DONALD TRUMP COMES COMPLETELY UNHINGED"

"Unhinged. You wouldn't believe how bad these people are. These aren't people. These are animals."
—PRESIDENT DONALD J. TRUMP

"Who is that, the beast and the sovereign? Who are the beast and the sovereign? What are they, elle *and* lui*?"*
—JACQUES DERRIDA, *THE BEAST AND THE SOVEREIGN*

I

For his supporters, Trump's election in November 2016 signaled the emergence of a new political order, one focused explicitly upon the reassertion of America's sovereignty and pre-eminence as an economic superpower. In his speech to the United Nations General Assembly in September 2018, Trump, with no apparent sense of irony, dogmatically rejected what he termed "the ideology of globalism." And following his critique of the legitimacy of the UN Human Rights Council and the International Criminal Court, he asserted that "We will never surrender America's sovereignty to an unelected, unaccountable, global bureaucracy."[1] As promised on the campaign trail, the Trump Administration then pursued a range of foreign and domestic policy initiatives representative of a turn to "hard power"—internationally, this turn was clearly demonstrated through the administration's efforts to cut funding and staffing for the State Department as well as the U.S. Agency for International Development and to increase the Defense Department's budget authority.[2] Domestically, five days after his inauguration, Trump signed an executive order that provided U.S. Immigration and Customs Enforcement (ICE) the mandate to hire ten thousand additional agents. This expansion of ICE was followed by the adoption of a "zero tolerance" policy for illegal immigration, and the introduction of the administration's family separation policy. These and other similar policy moves in the first half of Trump's term in office, such as America's departure from the Paris Climate Agreement, its dissolution of the Iran nuclear deal, and the escalating trade war with China, were part of an explicit reassertion of America's sovereign power in response to its perceived weakening during Barack Obama's eight years in office. At the center of these various domestic and foreign policy shifts, Trump's utilization of racist tropes to legitimate his unrealized plan to construct a wall along the border with Mexico illustrated the administration's explicit commitment to a nativist ideology of white supremacy.[3]

American politics has long been steered by a bipartisan commitment to neoliberalism. But in recent years, the crisis tendencies of capitalism have steadily undermined this neoliberal status quo, beginning most notably with the 2008 financial crisis. As Nancy Fraser observes, the emergence of Trumpism and other similar anti-immigrant movements of economic nationalism throughout Europe are the result of a widespread distrust in the neoliberal status quo: "It is as if masses of people throughout the world had stopped believing in the reigning common sense that has underpinned political domination of the last several decades."[4] In short, neoliberalism is undergoing what Fraser terms a "crisis of hegemony," and Trump "is the poster child for this hegemonic crisis."[5] With the political left ill-equipped to respond to this crisis of hegemony, the stage was set for a counterhegemonic assertion of nativist discourse that has long sustained settler hegemony in the United States.

Despite Trump's own financial investment in globalization, Nikhil Pal Singh argues that his political discourse surprisingly departed from the neoliberal status quo: "Trump dared to venture beyond the neoliberal and imperial terrain, wielding a populism that invoked an abandoned generation of virtuous heartland producers to a foreign policy that emphasized hitting hard and unilaterally, but only against clearly marked enemies."[6] Furthermore, Trump's turn to hard power and the explicit reassertion of American sovereignty was mirrored by a rhetorical attack on the "inclusionary niceties of neoliberal diversity talk," characterized by Trump's explicit use of racist, sexist, and otherwise derogatory language.[7] Playing the part of the "feisty business genius," Joan Wallach Scott asserts, "[t]he rage singled out enemies—domestic and foreign—as the cause of disappointment and decline: Mexican rapists and drug dealers; Muslim immigrant terrorists; feminists, gays, lesbians, trans people, D/democrats (with both capital and lowercase d), Hillary Clinton, elites, academics, journalists, the politically correct, and especially African Americans, with Barack Obama at the head of the list."[8] This political discourse represented a revival of the nativist ideology that has persistently plagued American politics. The rise of the America First ideology that propelled Trump to victory in 2016 may be understood as an intensification of nationalist imperialism that has long underscored the nation's efforts to secure its future, domestically and internationally, at the expense of the well-being of those beyond its national and cultural borders. Trump's presidency did constitute a crisis for American politics, but not merely the crisis of liberalism or political civility that so many mainstream progressives bemoaned.

The notion of a crisis, as Janet Roitman suggests, is misleading if it is interpreted as signifying something unique or without historical precedent; the language of crisis is often employed as a way of interrupting or breaking free of a causal chain of events in the hope of overcoming the problematic continuity that exists within a political or economic order between the past and the present.[9] The recent crisis of American politics, if one may provisionally designate it as such, draws into question the violence of its present as well its past. The election of Donald Trump may be regarded as a revolutionary moment of America's refounding. This refounding is a repetition as well as a modification of the inclusive–exclusive violence that has been there from the beginning. The "Make America Great Again" (MAGA) mantra is, of course, a literal repetition of the spirit of Reaganism, but it is also a reification of that vision of America made possible by the legacy of neoliberalism bequeathed to it from that era. As Joan Wallach Scott suggests,

> It is the making "explicit," not only rhetorically, but in fact, of the wish for white supremacy—the elevation of it to a national goal—that distinguishes "trumpism" from its neoliberal aspects and from other

forms of racism. "Make America Great Again" conceptualizes the nation not just as a firm, but as an exclusively *white* firm. There is no question of extending the bounties of capitalism to anyone else.[10]

If the ascendancy of global finance brought about the "wilding" of American society, as Charles Derber famously argues, then the rise of Trump signaled a renewed commitment to America's settler mythos—America as a perennial frontier land, where primitive accumulation is once more the telos of the citizen-soldier.[11]

The recent so-called "crisis of political liberalism," or what has been termed the rise of "illiberal" politics, is an overt manifestation of the zoopolitical logic of settler sovereignty. If the US has experienced a crisis, it is one that is simultaneously a breakdown of an existing hegemonic order as well as a configuration or reassertion of a counterhegemonic order still in the making. In this essay, I argue that the emergence of Trumpism signals a crisis of American zoopolitics that was precipitated by a growing distrust in the neoliberal status quo. Through an examination of the various semantic registers of the word *Geschlecht*, this chapter will provide a theoretical framework for interpreting the discursive characteristic of this crisis of American zoopolitics. When the various concepts that may be declined from the word *Geschlecht*—such as "people," "race," "nation," and "animal"— become closely aligned within a polemical discourse that deploys these various terms according to an exclusionary logic designed to legitimate state-sponsored violence, it may be argued that a given polity, namely the United States, is in the grip of a complex on, of, and about *Geschlecht*. Further, the origins of Trump's expression of this complex are to be found within the zoopolitical logic of settler sovereignty and the violent solipsism of its founding myths.

The semantic plurality of the word *Geschlecht* reflects the diversity that necessarily characterizes a viable political community. In order for a political community to survive, it must simultaneously create a space for diverse identities to exist in concert with one another while also unifying those differences into a coherent expression of political sociality. Roberto Esposito describes this paradoxical dynamic in immunological terms. In reference to the biopolitical meaning of the "body politic" metaphor, Esposito suggests that "[b]y placing the body at the center of politics and the potential for disease at the center of the body, it makes sickness, on the one hand the outer margin from which life itself must continually distance itself, and, on the other, the internal fold which dialectically brings it back to itself."[12] Thus, the survival of political community according to Esposito's account requires the persistence of a "constitutive antinomy" that results from an effort to define that community in opposition to borders, nations, cultures, or ideologies which are perceived to threaten the autonomy of the body politic, yet it is that very conflict which unifies the body politic as a coherent form.[13]

Esposito utilizes the immunitary relationship between a mother and a fetus or "[t]he figure of the implant, whether an artificial prothesis or a natural implant like fertilized eggs in the mother's womb," to posit a model for political community that foregrounds how this community transforms its immunitary responses, so that rather than excluding what is marked as foreign, it can include what it now marks as similar. He concludes that "once its negative power has been removed, the immune is not the enemy of the common, but rather something more complex that implicates and stimulates the common."[14] Failure to neutralize the exclusionary force of the body politic's immunitary response may result in a crisis of autoimmunity, when the "warring potential of the immune system is so great that at a certain point it turns against itself as a real and symbolic catastrophe leading to the implosion of the entire organism."[15]

Trump's rhetorical commitment to racist nativism, or what I will term his complex about *Geschlecht*, may be understood as a crisis of autoimmunity in American political discourse. This crisis has taken place at the complex point of convergence between neoliberal economic precarity and the rapid diversification of America's socio-political and cultural landscape. As a particular expression of zoopolitical discourse, the complex about *Geschlecht* manifests itself as an overdetermined drive to secure heteropatriarchal governance and authority through the assertion of ethno-racial and sexual hierarchalization. The nativist discourse that has recently come into focus is part of a much longer history of exclusionary politics. Nevertheless, Lindsay Pérez Huber asserts that "the effects of the articulatory practices of racist nativism, as performed by Trump, can be understood as the creation of a space that affords the opportunity for a virulent adherence to white supremacy."[16] Huber notes that using the concept of racist nativism as a framework for understanding Trump's immigration discourse elucidates the ways that "perceived racial differences construct false perceptions of people of color as 'non-native,' and not belonging to the monolithic 'American' identity—an identity that has historically been tied to perceptions of and constructions of whiteness."[17] Crucially, Huber also observes that historically this racist nativism, through its focus on immigrants, fails to acknowledge the ethno-racial diversity of "those already residing in the U.S."[18]

Trump's racist nativism consolidates as well as disavows the plurality of *Geschlecht* in the name of safeguarding a narrow conception of political community. But in doing so, the language of *Geschlecht*, and its various declensions, paradoxically signals the presentment of a condition of plurality that, in the parlance of deconstruction, is "always already" implicated by the conditions which occasion its use. Trump's America First agenda emerged in the face of increasing racial and cultural diversification that he and his followers regard as a threat to a "traditional America" that has privileged the power and status of wealthy white people through the subordination of people of color as well the white working class.[19] Alongside this demographic shift, the global economy that has emerged in recent decades with the advent of neoliberalism has led to greater economic uncertainty in majority white regions of America's heartland.

The convergence of America's demographic and cultural diversification with a neoliberal expansion of economic and social precarity has created a political landscape hospitable to the rise of right wing populism. While these socio-economic factors, and particularly the reality of white working-class poverty, are often invoked to explain the unlikely election of Donald Trump, the cultural logic of racist nativism stretches back to the very origins of the United States, a nation whose very existence is founded upon the exclusionary violence of settler colonialism.[20] Trump's discourse of racist nativism, which I theorize in this essay according to the inclusive–exclusive dynamics of his complex about *Geschlecht*—which, in turn, is made visible by the analytical force of the *Geschlecht* complex—is not, as some would have it, a recent development within the otherwise racially neutral culture of American political liberalism. Rather, it is a demonstration of the ways that American democracy continues to operate as a primitive form of zoopolitics, which defines political community in terms of a shared national and cultural identity. American democracy remains primitive not simply as a result of its relative historical youth, and not only because it remains bound up with the cultural logic of settler colonialism, but perhaps most importantly because it continues to persuade itself through the myth of American exceptionalism that its form of government is a democracy par excellence. Consequently, it is incapable of embracing what Derrida describes as the messianic logic of democracy—according to which the ideals of reciprocity, equality, and ethical responsibility that give meaning to the very concept remain unrealized. Believing that democracy has indeed arrived, America fails to embrace the promise of democracy, which Derrida describes as

> Awaiting without horizon of the wait, awaiting what one does not expect yet or any longer, hospitality without reserve, welcoming salutation accorded in advance to the absolute surprise of the *arrivant* from whom or which one will not ask anything in return and who or which will not be asked to commit to the domestic contracts of any welcoming power (family, State, nation, territory, native soil or blood, language, culture in general, even humanity)[...].[21]

No matter how far America's pursuit of liberal democracy appears to take it away from its own "illiberal" past, its intransigent nationalism will persistently threaten to draw it back into the throes of a complex about *Geschlecht*. As Derrida suggests, "Like those of the blood, nationalisms of native soil not only sow hatred, not only commit crimes, they have no future, they promise nothing even if, like stupidity or the unconscious, they hold fast to life."²² This effort to cling to its own settler mythos, even at the expense of the future, leads us into the domain of America's zoopolitical crisis.

II

In May 2018, the Trump administration hosted a roundtable discussion of California's status as a so-called "sanctuary state."²³ In this meeting with a selection of politically sympathetic sheriffs and local politicians, Trump called into question the actions of cities and local law enforcement agencies who opt not to detain undocumented immigrants at the time of arrest in order to hand them over to ICE agents for deportation. Deploying a turn of phrase that became idiomatic within his border security discourse, he proclaimed, "Catch and release—think of it. We catch somebody, we find out they're criminals. We end up having to release them, and they go into our society."²⁴ After these remarks, Sheriff Margaret Mims of Fresno cited the supposed threat of the criminal organization known as MS-13 as an example of a group of undocumented criminals who are potentially protected due to the Supreme Court's ruling in *Arizona v. United States*. In this case, the Court determined that it is unconstitutional for local law enforcement agents to arrest a person residing in the United States simply on the suspicion that they may be undocumented or in violation of federal immigration law, even if an individual indeed turns out to be undocumented.

In response to Mims' invocation of the perceived danger posed by the presence of MS-13 gang members, Trump argued, "We have people coming into the country or trying to come in, we're stopping a lot of them, but we're taking people out of the country. You wouldn't believe how bad these people are. These aren't people. These are animals."²⁵ The phrase "Catch and release" is, of course, an idiomatic expression specific to the sport of fishing. Through his use of this metaphor of hunter and prey, Trump reveals the zoopolitical nature of his efforts to "secure the border" from the perceived threat of undocumented immigrants and asylum seekers. His turn of phrase reveals the predatory dynamics that frame his understanding of border security by positioning America's law enforcement and border patrol agents as human-hunters in pursuit of what he presents as immigrant-animal-prey.²⁶ The very designation of the MS-13 gang members as animals in conjunction with the idiom of "catch and release" provides the necessary linkage for examining what Derrida describes as "this becoming-beast, this becoming animal of a sovereign who is above all a war chief, and is determined as sovereign or as animal faced with the enemy."²⁷ It is this contest with the "enemy" *as animal* that frames the logic of settler zoopolitics.

Within the expansive body of scholarship focused on biopolitics, the principle of zoopolitics occasionally emerges as a term analogous to biopolitics, but its meaning is often unclear. In *The Beast and the Sovereign*, Derrida establishes that there is no essential difference between biopolitics and zoopolitics. In contrast to Giorgio Agamben, who attempts to define human political and ethical life apart from animal life through his distinction between *bios* and *zoē*, Derrida argues that

> [...] man is that living being who is taken by politics: he is a political living being, and essentially so. In other words, he is zoo-political, that's his definition, that's what is proper to him, *idion*; what is proper to man is politics; what is proper to this living being that man is, is politics [...].[28]

After many characteristic twists, turns, and aporias that circulate throughout Derrida's seminars, he concludes this session with a reference to *The Gift of Death*, another of his key works on the problem of ethical responsibility, one which sheds some light on what is at stake in challenging Agamben's effort to ascribe ethical and political existence to humans alone. Through his close examination of Kierkegaard's reading of the *akedeah* in *Fear and Trembling*, in *The Gift of Death* Derrida reflects upon the impossibility of being ethically responsible to the irreducible singularity of every individual within a given community while also simultaneously acting in the interest of the common good of that very same community. Derrida asks, "How would you ever justify the fact that you sacrifice all the cats in the world to the cat that you feed at home every morning for years, whereas other cats die of hunger at every instant? Not to mention other people?"[29]

In this rather dark but seemingly trivial aside, it is possible to observe the ontobiological demands that give rise to the ethical and political challenges of human existence. By invoking the ethical dilemma that is posed by the seemingly commonplace responsibility that a pet owner holds to their cat, to feed them, Derrida highlights the sacrificial economy that subverts even this ethical demand. Through the apparently ethical decision to feed one's *own* cat, one fails to feed all of the *other* cats that one does not claim ownership of and therefore responsibility for. But of course, the seemingly feral nature of these *other* cats, their shear lack of domestication, typically places them beyond the scope of the average pet owner's ethical concerns. Lacking any given name, these feral cats are deprived of the linguistic signifier through which they might otherwise be permitted into the privileged but nonetheless highly restricted realm of animal domesticity.

By designating so-called MS-13 gang members as animals, and deploying them as a virtual synecdoche of all immigrants who come to the border, Trump classifies all who seek to cross the border as some sort of migratory creature, incapable of language, reason, culture, etc. He renders them illegible and unnamable by denying them a voice, thus undermining their varied and numerous legal claims for refuge. "Finding oneself deprived of language," Derrida observes, "one loses the power to name, to name oneself, indeed to answer for one's name. The sentiment of this deprivation, of this impoverishment, of this lack would thus be the great sorrow of nature. It is the hope of requiting that, of redemption from that suffering, that humans live and speak in nature—humans in general not just poets."[30] The opposition between the human and the animal forms an ontological and epistemological basis for the elaboration of various regimes of apartheid. In his essay "Racism's Last Word," Derrida contemplates the peculiar power of the word "apartheid" as a neologism masquerading as an idiom. He notes that

> [...] there is no racism without language. The point is not that acts of racial violence are only words, but rather that they have to have a word. Even though it offers the excuse of blood, color, birth—or, rather, *because* it uses naturalist and sometimes creationist discourse—racism always betrays the perversion of a man, the talking animal.[31]

In this reference to the "talking animal," Derrida is invoking the Western theological and philosophical conception of the defining characteristic of the human species as the animal with language, *zōon logon ekon*, as opposed to *zōon alogon*, "a living being without *logos*," a distinction that Derrida discusses in detail in his reading of Heidegger in the *The Beast and the Sovereign*, in which he uncovers the largely unremarked relation between the concept of sovereignty and the figure of the animal.[32]

From the very outset of the seminars, Derrida elucidates what he terms "a profound and essential ontological copula" that characterizes the relationship between "the beast [feminine *la bête*] and the sovereign [masculine: *le souverain*]. *La, le*."[33] As the bracketed comments on translation indicate, the feminine and masculine designation of the terms not only signals difference but also more importantly a certain form of heterogeneous copulation. Throughout the seminars, Derrida is preoccupied with demonstrating how the discourse of sovereignty and the discourse of animality are not only interwoven with one another, but also how this "onto-zoo-anthropo-theologico-political copulation" gives rise to, or engenders the entire lexicon of human sociality—a sociality that is itself constituted in and through its relationship to the so-called "animal."[34]

In his reading of La Fontaine's fable of *The Wolf and the Lamb*, a reading which owes much to Louis Marin's earlier study of the fable,[35] Derrida examines what might be regarded as a zoopolitical struggle for property, sustenance, and juridical authority, all of which are presented as the legitimate domain of the sovereign, that is the wolf, in this tale created for the instruction and edification of Louis, *Le Dauphin*, the son of Louis XIV. La Fontaine's fable portrays a violent encounter between a lamb and a hungry wolf (*bête cruelle*) on the banks of a river. The fable reveals to its reader the moral that "the reason of the strongest is best" thematizes the self-authenticating logic of sovereignty through its portrayal of the wolf. The wolf, driven by hunger, arrives at a stream to find a young lamb drinking its water. After accusing the lamb of muddying his drinking water, the wolf also claims that the lamb has slandered him. When the lamb points out that he was only recently born, the wolf replies that it must have been one of his family members (*ton frère*). Finally, the wolf takes the lamb into the woods and eats him, without due process—"*Sans une autre forme de procès.*" Derrida asserts that "in La Fontaine's fable revenge has to unleash itself blindly against all those who are presumed to be related, allied, socially or by blood, by a link of fraternity, with the presumed guilty party, be it a child, a powerless lamb that is basically accused of being guilty before even being born."[36] The wolf indicts the lamb on the basis of mere guilt by association or rather speciation, and therefore Derrida concludes that the wolf's proclamation, "If not you, your brother then" consolidates "all the perversions of collective, transgenerational, familial or national, nationalistic and fraternalistic accusation[.]"[37] Therefore, as I have argued so far, the wolf who is sovereign, the cruel beast, embodies and consolidates the multiple meanings of *Geschlecht*, albeit in another language. And like the children of undocumented immigrants, who, by virtue of their infancy, are detained without due process at America's border, in the name of securing that which is perceived to be the natural birthright of all "native-born" Americans, as well as all the children of undocumented immigrants currently residing in the United States, in a perpetual state of inclusive-exclusion, the cruel beast of American zoopolitics pronounces, "You are therefore guilty at birth, by your birth, guilty for being born what you were born."[38]

This logic of guilt, not simply by association but rather speciation, according to the logic of American zoopolitics, is what is at work in Trump's now infamous proclamation that "We have people coming into the country or trying to come in, we're stopping a lot of them, but we're taking people out of the country. You wouldn't believe how bad these people are. *These aren't people. These are animals.*"[39] In order to grasp the zoopolitical dynamics at stake in such designations of animality, it is necessary to discern the operative presence of the complex about *Geschlecht* which provides the psycho-rhetorical basis for Trump's racist nativist discourse.[40]

III

An exploration of the semantic range of the word *Geschlecht* reveals a deep and irreducible tension that is at stake when the term is used to define the internal and external boundaries of human sociality and subsequently political community. Heidegger's essay on the poetic language of Georg Trakl remains one of the most important expositions of the various meanings of

Geschlecht, and in his own efforts to define the word, Marc Crépon draws on Heidegger to expand upon the term's connotative range. He suggests that "It refers to race but also to kinship, generation, and gender, as well as the notion of sex, which divides all the former[.]"[41] The notion of *Geschlecht* may be regarded as a kind of watchword, signaling the presence of what may be termed zooplitical discourse.

In a November 2018 speech addressing what his administration presented as the impending arrival of a so-called "migrant caravan" at the southern border, Trump summed up his administration's opposition to undocumented immigrants as follows: "Illegal immigration hurts American workers, burdens American taxpayers, and undermines public safety, and places enormous strain on our local schools, hospitals, and communities in general, taking precious resources away from the poorest Americans who need them most."[42] He described the so-called "caravan" as an "invasion," suggesting that "[t]hese are tough people in many cases; a lot of young men, strong men and a lot of men that maybe we don't want in our country[.]"[43] Later in the speech, Trump suggested that rather than allow asylum seekers to leave detention centers after submitting legal claims for asylum, the administration's new policy would be to detain them: "We're going to catch; we're not going to release. They're going to stay with us until the deportation hearing or the asylum hearing takes place. So we're not releasing them into the community."[44] Repeating the hunting and fishing idiom that he deployed during his cabinet meeting with law enforcement agents earlier in May, Trump once more utilizes the language of animality to designate undocumented people as non-human. Through his repeated references to undocumented immigrants and asylum seekers as "aliens" whose efforts to reside in the United States poses a specific threat to the security of women and children, Trump portrays them as a kind of invasive species whose very existence threatens the supposed security of native-born Americans.

Through his zoopolitical discourse, Trump sought to establish political community through appeals to shared expressions of ethno-national identity and invocations of the shared humanity of those "native" to such a community, a humanity that he constituted over and against the racially othered category of the non-native whose existence he portrayed as a threat to the cultural hegemony and socio-economic well-being of so-called "American taxpayers." Trump's rhetoric evokes the zoopolitical lexicon of *Geschlecht* in all of its various declensions, through his racially coded stigmatization of immigrants as prey for America's military and border patrol agents. Despite the overt appeals to racial stereotypes within Trump's speech, a crucial paradox emerges whose logic may be understood through a close reading of the deconstructive dynamics of *Geschlecht*. Even in his efforts to consolidate America's national and cultural identity over and against the perceived threat of an alien invasion, he nevertheless acknowledged that America's existing population consists of a significant number of immigrants, stating that "We've issued 40 million green cards since 1970, which means the permanent residency and a path to citizenship for many, many people,"[45] thus demonstrating Walt Whitman's famous assertion in his preface to *Leaves of Grass* that America is indeed "not merely a nation but a teeming nation of nations."[46]

While the term is often deployed in a unitary manner, as a way of defining cultural, political, or even inter-species differences, the semantic indeterminacy of *Geschlecht* is derived from the logic of inclusive–exclusion that either explicitly or implicitly governs its use. However, the duality that appears implicit to the term is neither semantically nor ontologically determinative. In Derrida's series of essays and lectures on *Geschlecht*, he examines Heidegger's use of the term in relation to the question of philosophical nationalism, and the problematics of nationalism in general. Concluding his first essay on Heidegger and sexual difference, Derrida asks, "How is difference deposited among two? Or again if one kept to consigning difference within dual opposition, how can multiplication be stopped in difference? Or in sexual difference?"[47] Like so many other terms within Derrida's deconstructive lexicon—such as trace, mark, and sign, concepts whose polysemy is mystified or obscured through the binary logic of Western metaphysics—the concept of *Geschlecht* invokes the ontological and epistemological contradictions involved in rhetorical pronouncements of a collective "we" that constitutes a sense of shared identity through the logic of inclusive-exclusion. Derrida suggests in his reading of Heidegger's lecture on Trakl that "the word '*Geschlecht*' has in German, 'in our tongue' (it is always a question of 'we'), a multitude of significations. But this singular multitude must gather itself together in some manner."[48] Heidegger, according to Derrida, sought to configure the meaning of *Geschlecht* in relation to the generality of *Dasein*, which transcends the binary logic of sexual difference. Thus, within the metaphysics of *Dasein*, Derrida considers Heidegger's conceptualization of sexuality as pointing the way toward a non-binary schematization that is characterized by multiplicity, plurality, and dispersion.[49] Although Heidegger seeks to free *Geschlecht* from the binary logic of sexual difference, another opposition emerges which serves to stabilize the term's semantic indeterminacy.

In "*Geschlecht* II: Heidegger's Hand," which has attracted tremendous scholarly attention in recent years, Derrida calls attention to the distinction that Heidegger draws between human hands and those of apes. He suggests that "In its very content, this proposition marks the text's essential scene, marks it with a humanism that wanted certainly not to be nonmetaphysical ... but with a humanism that, between a human *Geschlecht* one wants to withdraw from the biologistic determination ... and an animality one encloses in its organico-biologic programs, inscribes not *some* differences but an absolute oppositional limit."[50] This oppositional limit, and its consequences for a range of critiques of existing biopolitical regimes, has been widely discussed by scholars. Further in this essay, Derrida explores how the seemingly impassable opposition between the animal and the human frames the logic of other semantic variations of *Geschlecht*. Analyzing Heidegger's reading of Trakl's two poems on "the decline of the Occident, *as* Occident," Derrida focuses in on the opening line of "Occidental Song," which begins, "O the soul's nocturnal wingbeat (*Flügelschlag*)." Heidegger's reading of this line takes the root word of *Geschlecht*, which is *Schlagen*, meaning "to strike, beat, stroke,"[51] as the interpretive key to Trakl's poem: "The striking (*Der schlag*) whose imprint gathers together such a splitting in two in a simplicity of the *one* race (*der sie in die Einfalt des 'Einen Geschlechts' prägt*) and thus restores the stocks of the species (*die Sippen des Menschengeschlechts*) and the species itself in the sweetness of more serene infancy[.]"[52] Consequently, Derrida concludes that Heidegger

> thematizes at once the polysemy and the focal simplicity of "*Geschlecht*," in "our tongue." This tongue, which is ours, German, is also the tongue of "our *Geschlecht*," [...] if *Geschlecht* also means family, generation, stock.[53]

The relation between *Schlag* and *Geschlecht* as it is revealed in Derrida's analysis of Heidegger's reading of Trakl demonstrates the extent to which the polysemic character of *Geschlecht* may be consolidated through an ideological frame which seeks to align the meanings of race, sex, nation, and species from the standpoint of a performative articulation of a politically and culturally designated conception of an inclusive–exclusive "we."[54]

While Heidegger conceptualizes *Geschlecht* according to the uniquely human experience of *Dasein*, Freud conceives of *Geschlecht* as an expression of a procreative drive that is an ontological feature of human as well as animal life. In his early work, *Three Essays on the Theory of Sexuality*, Freud utilizes a form of the word *Geschlecht* to develop his libidinal theory of sexuality. While translator Ulrike Kistner suggests that "the terminological distinction between 'sex' and 'gender' was not historically, conceptually, or discursively available to Freud at the time," she argues that Freud nevertheless "problematizes any correlation between biological markers, the determination of 'sex', and psychical attributions."[55] Freud deploys the term *Geschlecht* to "distinguish between two different sexual regimes in humans"; Kistner translates *Sexualtrieb* as "sexual drive," which Freud uses to describe various non-procreative expressions of sexuality; and then there is *Geschlechtstrieb*, translated as "genital drive," which Freud uses to describe "the object-related, genitally organized drive of adult sexuality."[56] Kistner points out that despite the practice of translating the word *Trieb* as "instinct" in James Strachey's popular translation of *Drei Abhandlungen*, in fact, the German cognate *Instinkt* does not appear in Freud's original text.[57] Instead, Freud uses the word *Trieb* to describes the genital drives of humans as well as animals.[58] *Geschlechtstrieb* is a feature that indeed unites humans and animals according to Freud. Thus, Kistner argues that Freud does not seek to define the differences between the sexual regimes of humans and animals "as the older discussions on the difference between *Instinkt* and *Trieb* seemed to imply."[59] Freud falls victim to the hierarchical and exclusionary force of *Geschlecht* in the *Three Essays*, arguing that during puberty the genital drive overtakes the non-procreative, infantile sexual drive, and the procreative, heterosexual *Geschlechtstrieb* constitutes the "final, normal shape" of human sexuality.[60]

In *Beyond the Pleasure Principle* and *Civilization and Its Discontents*, Freud elaborates upon his libidinal theory of sexuality to express two related but also contradictory drives, which have been termed by Freudian scholars as *Eros*, associated with the procreative and pro-social dynamics that typify *Geschlechtstrieb*, and *Thanatos*, which may be associated with what Freud refers to as the death drive, characterized not only by a sadistic urge to destroy the object of sexual desire but also with other indirect forms of violence, such as profanity, offensive jokes, and racial slurs.[61] Like the constitutive antinomy that Esposito theorizes in terms of the immunitary logic that sustains political community, *Eros* and *Thanatos* operate in dialectical tension with one another. Far from being an aberrant feature of human psychology, Freud maintains that the death drive is fundamental to the pursuit of human survival. In *Civilization and Its Discontents*, he observes that humans "are not gentle creatures who want to be loved, and who at the most defend themselves if they are attacked[.]"[62] On the contrary, he argues that aggression is one of humankind's most prominent "instinctual endowments."

> As a result, their neighbor is for them not only a potential helper or sexual object, but also someone who tempts them to satisfy their aggressiveness on him, to exploit his capacity for work without compensation, to use him sexually without his consent, to seize his possessions, to humiliate him, to cause him pain, to torture and to kill him. *Homo homini lupus* [Man is a wolf to man]. Who, in the face of all his experience of life and history, will have the courage to dispute this assertion?[63]

This propensity for aggression that may be associated with the death drive is not for Freud something anterior to human nature. As his invocation of the wolf–man copula evinces, the death drive reveals the constitutive relation that humans share with the so-called animal. In his own analysis of the classical figure of *homo homini lupus* in the work of modern political philosophers such as Thomas Hobbes and Michel de Montaigne, Derrida remarks the curious alliance that persistently arises "between all these claimants to sovereignty who thus assemble and so resemble each other: the wolf, man, God. The one *for* the other."[64] Like the procreative drive *Geschlechtstrieb*, which humans and animals must each possess in order to survive, the inclination of humans to prey upon other human indicates to Freud the extent to which human sociality is sustained by finding opportunities to deflect this aggression, which might otherwise threaten to destroy a community, elsewhere onto victims who do not belong to a given social or political group: "It is always possible to bind together a considerable number of people in love, so long as there are other people left over to receive the manifestations of their aggressiveness."[65] Freud cites the historical antagonisms between neighboring European political communities such as Scotland and England, among others, as evidence for his theory of that it is "precisely communities with adjoining territories, and related to each other in other ways as well, who are engaged in constant feuds and in ridiculing each other[.]"[66] Consequently, the philosophical anthropology that emerges from Freud's elucidation of the dialectic relation between sexual procreation and the death drive gives rise to the constitutive elements of the complex about *Geschlecht*. The aporetic tensions that typify the unstable boundaries between the human and the animal, neighbors and enemies, the beast and the sovereign, and finally rival nations, all begin to appear within the semantic range of *Geschlecht*.

Crépon notes that German scholars, from Kant to Herder, sought to cope with the term's indeterminacy by substituting more univocal terms such as *Stamm* and *Rasse*. Nevertheless, he suggests that the multivocity of *Geschlecht* remains problematic when it is used to refer to "a lineage, a generation, or a community or when it intersects with terms referring to people, nation, or race."[67] The problem is not only that the terms "people," "race," and "nation" are also themselves abstractions, but that the definition of these terms also "raises a theoretical difficulty and entails a polemic." The metaphysical–ontotheological nature of these terms is betrayed by an awareness of their socio-cultural constructedness. And just as cultural and political communities themselves are delimited through the elaboration of founding myths, definitions of race, ethnicity, and nationality are the constitutive elements of exclusionary as well as inclusionary mythmaking.[68]

It is fitting, then, that Crépon turns to an examination first of Martin Luther's and then Martin Buber and Franz Rosenzweig's translation of Genesis, in which the human species is represented as Noah's divinely chosen descendants, the progeny of a cataclysmic sifting of the wicked and the redeemed. The book of Genesis explicitly thematizes the fulfillment of God's promises to promulgate "a sanctified genealogical futurity," promises which according to A. Samuel Kimball "establish not only the social and political but nothing less than the metaphysical center post of the Israelite nation to come."[69] The expropriation of this promise from the Jewish people and its transferal to Christianity was an essential tenet of Luther's supersessionism, which maintained that God had abandoned the covenant with the Jewish people due to their rejection of Jesus Christ as the messiah, thus transferring the status of "chosen people" to Christians.[70] In Genesis 10:32, Luther translates the Hebrew word *toledot* (begettings or generations) using the word *Geschlechtern*, "These are the families of the sons of Noah, after their generations, in their nations [*in ihren Geschlectern und Leuten*]."[71] However, in their translation, Buber and Rosenzweig elide *Geschlecht*, and instead introduce the phrase "*nach ihren Zeugungen, in ihren Stämmen*," with the implication that *Zeugungen* signifies "vertical begetting" and the word *Stämmen* connotes "horizontal division."[72] Buber and Rosenzweig's translation attempts to draw a subtle but crucial distinction between the procreative connotations of the word *Zeugungen*, while also resisting what appears to be the more unitary and potentially ethno-nationalistic concept *Leuten* through the introduction of the term *Stämmen*, which nevertheless also evokes the notion of tribalism, albeit in the plural rather than singular sense implied by Luther's term *Leuten*. Consequently, Crépon concludes that, more explicitly than its English counterparts,

> *Geschlecht* concentrates [...] the risks involved with any designation of community: that of being led back to an order of belonging deriving primarily from generation and ascendancy (thus from sexuality as well)—that is, the risk of a contamination of politics by genealogy.[73]

These efforts to restrict or contend with the polysemic and nonetheless totalizing force of *Geschlecht* thus reveal a key dynamic at work in the practice of zoopolitics—namely, the linguistic construction of human sociality, and therefore political community, through the designation of terms that on the one hand imply a shared ethnic, religious, or political identity, while also excluding other competing forms of human sociality. The practice of zoopolitics, as it is manifested within Trump's idiom of racist nativism, seeks to suppress the heterogeneity resident to the term *Geschlecht*—and equally, the critical force of acknowledging this heterogeneity that the *Geschlecht* complex reveals as a mode of inquiry. Trump's zoopolitical discourse suggests the possibility of singular, totalistic narratives of peoples, nations, races, and expressions of sovereignty in an effort to refound America as a seemingly unified political community, that in fact has never nor ever shall exist. In short, the emergence of the complex about *Geschlecht* is occasioned by the recognition that the homogeneity of the nation is always already in the midst of its dissolution.

IV

According to Derrida, it is a remarkable paradox that throughout the history of modernity it has been "the most powerful sovereign states, which, making international right and bending it to their interests, propose and in fact produce limitations on the sovereignty of the weaker states, sometimes [...] going so far as to violate or not respect the international right they have helped institute[.]"⁷⁴ In both its geo-economic and military activities, the United States has embodied both the fragility and rage of the wolf who seeks to justify its appetites through aspersions of human rights violations, and more recently unfair trade policies. As Derrida explains:

> Those powerful states that always give, and give themselves, reasons to justify themselves, but are not necessarily right, have the reason of the less powerful; they then unleash themselves like cruel, savage, beasts, or beast full of rage.⁷⁵

The fragility and rage of the wolf has long characterized America's foreign policy; it is detectable in the nation's longstanding commitment to an endless War on Terror as well the escalating militarization of its border security efforts. Moreover, the fragility and rage of the wolf has now emerged as a prominent dynamic within its domestic politics as well. Joan Wallach Scott argues that the agenda of

> "Make America Great Again" is about a fantasized nostalgia for a time (in antebellum American) when, as Roy Moore recently put it, "our families were strong, our country had a direction"; it is about the good times of slavery, not about restoring corrupted principles of liberty and justice.⁷⁶

The future of the white, hetero-familial citizen, and by extension the future of America, is thus predicated, as in the practice of chattel slavery, upon the sacrificial expropriation of resources away from the general citizenry and to an elite, ruling class. The legitimation of this sacrificial expropriation is one of the primary functions of the complex about *Geschlecht*. When terms such as nation, family, race, and species are employed in the name of a racial and political hierarchization, signaling the structuring influence of this complex, the internal dissolution of the prevailing class is already at stake.

Reflecting upon the historical specificity of the Holocaust,⁷⁷ Roberto Esposito suggests that Nazism constituted a radicalization of biopolitical sovereignty:

> Nazi politics wasn't even a proper biopolitics, but more literally a *zoopolitics*, one expressly directed to human animals. Consequently, the correct term for their massacre—anything but the sacred "holocaust"—is "extermination": exactly the term used for insects, rats, and lice.⁷⁸

Esposito's analysis simultaneously points to the ways that the practice of zoopolitics entails a rigid and linguistically determined opposition between the "animal" and the "human," a binary opposition that structures and legitimates violence against all life that is designated as sub-human, and he also reveals the extent to which zoopolitical sovereignty demonstrates a *perceived* radicalization of the inclusive–exclusive logic that typifies biopolitics. While biopower may be theorized as an inclusive–exclusive force that "can achieve an effective command over the entire life of the population only when it becomes an integral, vital function that every individual embraces and reactivates of his or her own accord,"[79] the practice of zoopolitics is characterized by an intensification of the exclusionary dynamic of biopolitics that, in its most explicit form, may be regarded as genocidal. Esposito notes the Nazi genocidal agenda was termed *Soziale Desinfektion*, a phrase that reflects the immunitary paradigm that elsewhere he theorizes as the operative logic that governs political and juridical order. The logic of immunity can sustain the life of a political body "but only by continuously giving it a taste of death."[80] By finding ways to incorporate elements of its constitutive other, the political body might strike a balance between its inclusive and exclusive dynamics; however, when the exclusionary logic of immunity grows too strong, "at a certain point it turns against itself as a real and symbolic catastrophe leading to the implosion of the entire organism."[81] The work of sovereignty is to institute and regulate the legal and political systems that keep this immunitary logic in play. But when the exclusionary force of sovereignty surpasses its inclusive dynamics, the ensuing crisis of autoimmunity leads to an inevitable crisis of political hegemony, as the organizing logic of the body politic seeks to configure itself anew. This process is often, although not necessarily, a violent one.

Trump's turn away from so-called "politically correct" language and towards a more "muscular" rhetorical style has been characterized by an unapologetic embrace of a nativist, ethnocentric, and sexist political discourse. Under the Trump Administration, the hostility towards women's health and reproductive rights that has long characterized the anti-abortion agenda of American conservatism was expressed in the form of a hostile and predatory attitude toward women in general. Elaborating on Ian Haney Lopez's elucidation of "dog whistle politics," in which politicians rhetorically encode racist ideas into their discourse in ways that appeal to those who are already initiated into its vernacular, former state Senator Wendy Davis argues that Trump's sexist discourse is best described as a "wolf whistle politics" that aggressively frames women politicians and women's issues in demeaning, sexualized terms. But unlike the dog whistle politics of the past, which stopped short of overt racism, today's practitioners of "wolf whistle politics" disempower women by divesting them of political agency while also appealing to heteropatriarchal values and norms that reduce women to sexualized and primarily procreative agents in the service of the traditional heteronormative family unit.

This designation of politics designed to disempower women as "wolf whistle politics" is appropriate because, as Derrida suggests, "[s]exuality is most often held to be bestial in itself; sexual desire is the beast in man, the most boisterous and most avid, and the most voracious beast."[82] Therefore, it is no mere coincidence that while Trump's propensity for sexual predation is well-known, he has been enthusiastically embraced by counter-feminist movements who see him as a sovereign capable of re-establishing (as if it were ever truly lost) the ascendancy of male political and economic power. Such appeals to heteropatriarchal norms, in particular the concern for securing "hetero-familial citizenship," have been historically linked to conceptualizations of the viability of the national future. When the "modal form of the citizen" begins to shift away from "a straight, white, reproductively inclined heterosexual" and toward an increasingly diverse demography, "the logic of the national future comes into crisis."[83]

For those committed to the project of nationalistic heteronormativity, the coherence of America's national narrative is called into question when political challenges to white heteropatriarchal hegemony converge with growing economic and social inequality, exacerbated by growth of transnational corporations, whose values reflect a superficial but nonetheless divergent commitment to multiculturalism and gender equality.[84] Trump's "wolf whistle politics," like his racist nativism, were yet another symptom of the complex about *Geschlecht*, the overdetermined drive to secure heteropatriarchal governance and authority through the assertion of ethno-racial and sexual hierarchalization.

V

In the final year of Trump's presidency, the United States experienced the "real and symbolic catastrophe" of self-implosion that Esposito defines as a crisis autoimmunity. The administration's disastrous handling of the coronavirus pandemic and Trump's (mainly) failed effort to undermine the results of the 2020 presidential election culminated in his personal incitement of a riot at the U.S. Capitol in January 2021—perhaps, a final effort to secure his political position or merely a final symbolic act of spite for a political establishment he persistently referred to as "the swamp." In either case, the riot embodied the conceptual antinomies and violent paradoxes of the MAGA movement. The "law and order" president inspired his followers to violently breach the Capitol, the heart of the country's legislative branch, smearing feces on the walls, vandalizing the building, and stealing various public and personal items; in the process one member of the Capitol Police Force was killed and many others were injured.

On the surface, the riot may be understood as the inevitable outcome of Trump's disinformation campaign and persistent assertions that the presidential election was illegally stolen from him. Many of his followers suggested they were merely acting on the orders of the president to "take back their country." However, one iconic figure effectively elucidates the logic of settler-colonial violence that inspired the attack on the Capitol—various photographs of Jacob Chansley (a.k.a. Jack Angeli), a well-known Trump supporter and self-described "QAnon shaman," appeared in social media posts and news stories covering the riot; he was shirtless, face painted red, white, and blue, carrying a spear with an American flag attached, and wearing a faux bison headdress.

In an interview published by *Arizona Republic*, Chansley openly acknowledged his costume's connection to Native American culture and the feeling of masculine power that he associated with the bison's horns. In her detailed analysis of his choice of clothing, Anna Gawboy asserts, "Angeli's appropriation of First Nation ceremonial attire to participate in an insurrection intended to overturn the outcome of the 2021 presidential election is particularly twisted considering that tribal members across the U.S. overwhelmingly voted for Biden, and increased voter turnout on Navajo and Hopi nations is one of the factors that turned Arizona blue."[85] Gawboy goes on to explain that this appropriation of Native American culture within the context of explicit acts of settler-colonial dispossession was not unique. In 1773, the self-described Sons of Liberty, "put on Mohawk ceremonial garb, boarded three British East India trading ships, and dumped 342 chests of tea into Boston Harbor. The Boston Tea Party was just one of many protests in which white colonists assumed First Nation identities[.]"[86] For the Sons of Liberty and for Chansley, the decision to wear traditional Native American ritual attire was deliberate and symbolic: "By donning Indigenous dress, white colonial figures laid their claim to the continent and transferred imaginary Native qualities such as unfettered freedom and noble heroic savagery to themselves."[87] As a synecdoche for the MAGA movement in particular, and for the inclusive–exclusive violence of US settler colonialism in general, Chansley's alter-ego, Jack Angeli, embodies the overdetermined dynamics ethno-racial and heteropatriarchal hierarchization that typify the discursive operations of the complex about *Geschlecht*.

Likewise, the complex about *Geschlecht* was on full display in the speech Trump delivered to his supporters at the Ellipse on January 6th. In this speech, the various connotations of *Geschlecht*—"people," "race," "nation," and "animal"—were deployed and consolidated according to Trump's America First ideology. After addressing the crowd as "American patriots" and running through his usual complaints about the "fake news media" and its supposed unwillingness to accurately report the number of people in attendance at the event, Trump asserted, "We're gathered together in the heart of our nation's capital for one very, very basic and simple reason: To save our democracy."[88] Claiming that the election was being stolen by Democrats and "weak Republicans," and that a Biden Administration would destroy the country, he offered his supporters the following exhortation: "You're *stronger*, you're *smarter*, you've got more going than anybody. And they try and demean everybody having to do with us. And you're *the real people*, you're the people that built this nation. You're not the people that tore down our nation."[89] Returning again to his critique of so-called "weak Republicans," he claimed, "[t]hey've turned a blind eye, even as Democrats enacted policies that chipped away our jobs, weakened our military, threw open our borders and put America last."[90] His speech then careened through a litany of complaints about the press, criticism of establishment Republicans, xenophobic scapegoating, and racist attacks on his political opponents; he identified Oprah Winfrey, Stacey Abrams, as well as Michelle Obama and Barack Obama as rivals to his presidential campaign, employing the racist dog whistle "Barack *Hussein* Obama" when referring to the former president.[91]

Suggesting the pandemic provided Democrats with an opportunity to "steal the election," Trump described the disease as the "China virus," and blamed China for the nation's failing economy and the need for an economic stimulus plan: "*China destroyed these people*. We didn't destroy. China destroyed them, totally destroyed them."[92] He concluded the speech with a brief allusion to the border wall, the largely mythical project that nevertheless defined his political identity, complete with the zoopolitical trope of predation: "Remember, the wall, they said it could never be done. One of the largest infrastructure projects we've ever had in this country, and it's had a tremendous impact, that we got rid of *catch and release*."[93] Despite, or perhaps as a result of, his failed efforts to undermine the results of the election, Trump's zoopolitical rhetoric reached its zenith on January 6th. The various declensions of *Geschlecht*—"people," "race," "nation," and "animal"—were all deployed, implicitly or explicitly, in an effort to catalyze his supporters. The Capitol riot was a critical moment in the crisis of American zoopolitics as I have defined it in this essay; it was a rupture of the neoliberal status quo that was also simultaneously a kind of riotous celebration of America's zoopolitical identity.

Emboldened by his exhortations to "fight like hell," Trump's supporters breached the security infrastructure of the Capitol, and at times, it appeared their efforts faced little resistance from Capitol Police. Trump's supporters were persuaded that it was their right, as citizens, to assert ownership over the Capitol. Moments before forcing their way into the building, some of rioters exclaimed, "[t]ime to take back what's ours! A new 1776 has just begun!"[94] The ensuing violence was not merely a causal effect of Trump's so-called populist brand of rhetorical violence. It was a reassertion of the acquisitive violence that founded America's settler democracy. As he stood in front of the vice president's chair in the Senate, Chansley prayed, "Thank you for filling this chamber with patriots that love you and that love Christ. [...] Thank you for allowing the United States of America to be reborn."[95]

After his arrest, Chansley explained in an interview from jail that "it was my intention to bring divinity, and to bring God back into the Senate."⁹⁶ These tropes of renewal, rebirth, and re-divination along with calls to violently reappropriate the nation in order to putatively restore its former strength are indicative of a deep and abiding weakness that lies at the heart of American zoopolitical discourse.

The Trumpian complex on, of, and about *Geschlecht*, as an exaggerated and intensified mode of American zoopolitical discourse, embodies the fundamental weakness of all expressions of settler monolingualism and by extension settler sovereignty. In his effort to consolidate the various semantic evocations of *Geschlecht*, Trump displays what Derrida describes as the "inexhaustible solipsism" of settler colonial notions of linguistic, cultural, and ethnic purity:

> For contrary to what one is often tempted to believe, the master is nothing. And he does not have exclusive possession of anything. Because the master does not possess exclusively, and *naturally*, what he calls his language, because, whatever he wants or does, he cannot maintain any relations of property or identity that are natural, national, congenital, or ontological, with it because he can give substance to and articulate [*dire*] this appropriation only in the course of an unnatural process of politico-phantasmatic constructions, because language is not his natural possession, he can [...] thanks to that very fact, pretend historically, through the rape of a cultural usurpation, which means always essentially colonial, to appropriate it in order to impose it as "his own."⁹⁷

The first trick of settler sovereignty is first to lay claim by force to that which does not and cannot ever rightfully belong to it, and then to persuade others of its legitimacy, "to make others believe it, as they do a miracle, through rhetoric, the school, or the army."⁹⁸ According to Derrida, "Liberation, emancipation, and revolution" is its second trick, "It will provide freedom from the first while confirming a heritage by internalizing it, by reappropriating it—but only up to a certain point, for [...] there is never any such thing as absolute appropriation or reappropriation."⁹⁹

Because its appropriation can never be complete, because its sovereignty is always indeed predicated upon an appropriation and dispossession of Indigenous land that is *unnatural*, the US must re-enact its own revolutionary and nonetheless "politico-phantasmatic" founding. Endlessly disturbed by its own incomplete and unjustifiable appropriation, the Trumpian complex about *Geschlecht* is a predictable, indeed inevitable, by-product of the violent solipsism of settler sovereignty: "Mad about itself. Raving mad."¹⁰⁰ Through his "wolf whistle" politics, his racist nativism, and his impolitic rhetoric, Trump became the "cruel beast" of American zoopolitics, upsetting settler liberalism's appearance of civility, revealing the ideological roots of the complex in the founding myths of a nation constituted by its predation of *fellow* people. "Not the *bestiality* of the beast—and the sovereign. Not the *bêtise* of the beast—and the sovereign. But the beast *itself* and the sovereign."[101] As his former political adviser and campaign strategist once observed, "Trump is a beast," a distinctly American one.

Trump's quest to "Make America Great Again" added exponentially to the nation's longstanding legacy of "regeneration through violence."[102] In deconstructive terms, every act of unification is also, at the same time, an act of dispersion. Likewise, if the complex on, of, and about *Geschlecht*, as I have defined it in this essay, may be regarded as an overdetermined drive to assert ethno-racial and hetero-patriarchal authority, it is also therefore caught up in a desire to establish unity through violent and fragmentary exclusion. In October 2020, the US House Judiciary Committee published an over-five-hundred-page report on its investigation of the Trump Administration's Family Separation Policy. The authors of the report suggest that the trauma migrants suffered due to this policy was compounded by the Administration's "carelessness in tracking separations."[103] Several hundred children who were separated from their families may never be reunited. The committee's report concludes that the policy was enforced by "an Administration that was willfully blind to its *cruelty* and determined to go to unthinkable extremes to deliver on political promises and stop migrants fleeing violence from seeking protection in the United States."[104] Already, even among his political adversaries, the rhetorical inflection of American zoopolitics begins to pull the "veil of reason" over the eyes of the sovereign.[105]

In providing a brief exculpatory flourish, "*willfully* blind to its *cruelty*," his political adversaries pass judgment but defer justice. At the time of writing, the Biden Administration continues to detain migrants, mostly unaccompanied minors and families, in overcrowded facilities. Meanwhile, it has maintained a policy enacted by the Centers for Disease Control and Prevention under Trump that enables border patrol to circumvent existing immigration and refugee laws under the auspices of the 1944 Public Health Services Act, which empowers the US Surgeon General to expel migrants if they may be considered a threat to public health.[106] The border remains a site of immunological conflict, where the US acts out its own real and symbolic crisis of autoimmunity.

Consequently, Trumpism is not an aberration of the fundamental logic of American political liberalism but rather an explicit manifestation of the violent and exclusionary logic that it relies upon as an extension of settler sovereignty. Some writers have characterized the emergence of Donald Trump and other populist leaders as part of a growing movement of "illiberal" politics, which they often frame as a kind of breakdown of a political liberalism.[107] However, such efforts obscure the exclusionary violence that is inherent to forms of liberalism that remain firmly rooted in the institutions of settler sovereignty. Focusing in particular on the historical development of liberal democracy in the United States, Adam Dahl has demonstrated that American democratic thought is founded upon, and remains complicit in, the colonial dispossession of Indigenous people. He argues that "[i]n the process of constructing the sovereign people as an imperial constituency, ideologies of democratic empire embraced the constituent power of the people as the authorizing force of territorial expansion."[108]

Crucially, Dahl traces the origins of American democratic thought back to its roots in the ideology of settler colonialism, and he argues that "[g]rappling with the foundational role of colonial dispossession in shaping modern democratic thought must lead to a reimagining of the democratic tradition and democratic identity."[109] In his efforts to decolonize the democratic tradition, Dahl draws upon Indigenous critical theory, in particular the work of Joan Cocks and Taiaiake Alfred, both of whom draw into question political liberalism's individualistic conception of popular sovereignty. Instead of subscribing to a notion of popular sovereignty that aspires to "self-insulation and self-mastery," Dahl suggests that a non-sovereign conception of democracy would emphasize the interdependency and harmony in the name of "sustaining collective life."[110] The question of whether or not such "non-sovereign conception of democracy" is indeed operable within America's constitutional order remains the crucial question.

Derrida speculates on an alternative form of sovereignty, one which contends with the rage and fragility of the wolf, the sovereign dove: "What the dove's footsteps and the wolf's footsteps have in common is that one scarcely hears them. But the one announces war, the war chief, the sovereign who orders war, the other silently orders peace."[111] An expression of sovereignty that might be capable of counteracting the thanatic rage intrinsic to the complex about *Geschlecht* must embrace its own fragility. All expressions of sovereignty, even those intent on peace, risk a certain identitarian politics that establishes community through appeals to shared ideology, morality, and culture; a political community oriented toward what Derrida describes as the "promise of democracy" would be one that is always, already in the midst of its own unrealized becoming. In this context, the notion of *Geschlecht* might operate not as a unitary concept, but rather as one freed to embrace its own polysemic character. That is to say, in contrast to the Trumpian complex on, of, and about *Geschlecht*, one might signal to the critical force of the *Geschlecht* complex as a mode of inquiry; as a method for delegitimizing the nativist projection of *Geschlecht* as unitary.

While upholding the ideal of pursuing a community that makes possible the arrival of equality and absolute hospitality, such a democracy would hesitate to announce its own arrival in light of the realization that "never have violence, inequality, exclusion, famine, and thus economic oppression affected as many human beings in the history of the earth and humanity."[112] The hesitancy and provisionality of this political community that embraces the promise of democracy may despair at the recognition of its own fragility and inadequacy, but it does not seek to *master* this despair. Derrida suggests that "[s]ome, and I do not exclude myself, will find this despairing 'messianism' has a curious taste, a taste of death."[113] But this death that Derrida finds on the very tip of his tongue does not possess the same logic and force as the self-destructive death drive that motivates the failed state to implode as a result of its own fragile rage. This is rather the much longer and more measured death that occurs as one generation gives birth to and then gives way to another. It is the taste of death that comes when one beholds the face of a newly arrived infant and recognizes in the promise of their eyes one's own fortuitous mortality. This "gift of death" that is also the gift of the arrivant does not readily lend itself to settler sovereignty's obsession with borders: "The gift, if there is any, will always be *without* border."[114] Like *Geschlecht*, the gift is migratory, and must remain so, if it is to be a source of hope.

Notes

1. "Remarks by President Trump to the 73rd Session of the United Nations General Assembly," U.S. Mission to the Organization of the American States, September 25, 2018, https://usoas.usmission.gov/remarks-by-president-trump-to-the-73rd-session-of-the-united-nations-general-assembly-new-york-ny/.
2. Hal Brands, *American Grand Strategy in the Age of Trump* (Washington, DC: Brookings Institution Press, 2018), 176.
3. Lindsay Pérez Huber, "Make America Great Again: Donald Trump, Racist Nativism and the Virulent Adherence to White Supremacy Amid U.S. Demographic Change," *Charleston Law Review*, vol. 10 (2016), 215–50.
4. Nancy Fraser, *The Old Is Dying and the New Cannot Be Born: From Progressive Neoliberalism to Trump and Beyond* (New York: Verso Books, 2019), 8.
5. Fraser, *The Old Is Dying*, 9.
6. Nikhil Pal Singh, *Race and America's Long War* (Berkeley: University of California Press, 2017), 165.
7. Singh, *Race and America's Long War*, 165.
8. Joan Wallach Scott, "Trump," *Political Concepts: A Critical Lexicon*, vol. 1, no. 5 (2018), 1.
9. Janet Roitman, "Crisis," *Political Concepts: A Critical Lexicon*, no. 1 (2012).
10. Scott, "Trump," *Political Concepts*.
11. For a detailed historical account of the persistence of the concept of the frontier as mythical space of endless accumulation and dispossession that remains constitutive America's national identity, see Greg Grandin, *The End of the Myth: From the Frontier to the Border Wall in the Mind of America* (New York: Metropolitan Books, 2019).
12. Roberto Esposito, *Immunitas: The Protection and Negation of Life* (Cambridge: Polity, 2011), 15.

13 Esposito, *Immunitas*, 17.
14 Esposito, *Immunitas*, 18.
15 Esposito, *Immunitas*, 17.
16 Huber, "Make America Great Again," 231.
17 Huber, "Make America Great Again," 220–1.
18 Huber, "Make America Great Again," 220–1.
19 Huber, "Make America Great Again," 232–9.
20 Roxanne Dunbar-Ortiz, *Loaded: A Disarming History of the Second Amendment* (San Francisco: City Lights Books, 2018. eBook); Adam Dahl, *Empire of the People: Settler Colonialism and the Foundations of Modern Democratic Thought* (Lawrence: University Press of Kansas, 2018).
21 Jacques Derrida, *Specters of Marx: The State of the Debt, the Work of Mourning and the New International*, trans. Peggy Kamuf, Routledge Classics (New York, London: Routledge, 1994), 81–2.
22 Derrida, *Specters of Marx*, 213.
23 "Remarks by President Trump at a California Sanctuary State Roundtable."
24 "Remarks by President Trump at a California Sanctuary State Roundtable."
25 "Remarks by President Trump at a California Sanctuary State Roundtable."
26 Jacques Derrida, *The Animal That Therefore I Am*, trans. David Willis, ed. Marie-Louise Mallet (New York: Fordham University Press, 2009), 41–2.
27 Jacques Derrida, *The Beast and the Sovereign*, vol. I, trans. Geoffrey Bennington, eds. Michel Lisse, Marie-Louise Mallet, and Ginette Michaud (Chicago: The University of Chicago Press, 2010), 10.
28 Derrida, *The Beast and the Sovereign*, 1:348–9.
29 Jacques Derrida, *The Gift of Death*, trans. David Wills (Chicago: The University of Chicago Press, 1996), 69.
30 Derrida, *The Animal That Therefore I Am*, 19.
31 Jacques Derrida, "Racism's Last Word," trans. Peggy Kamuf, *Critical Inquiry*, vol. 12. no. 1 (1985), 292.
32 Jacques Derrida, *The Beast and the Sovereign*, vol. II, trans. Geoffrey Bennington, eds. Michel Lisse, Marie-Louise Mallet, and Ginette Michaud (Chicago: The University of Chicago Press, 2010), 218–46.
33 Derrida, *The Beast and the Sovereign*, 1:1.
34 Derrida, *The Beast and the Sovereign*, 1:18.
35 Louis Marin, *Food for Thought*, trans. Mette Hjort (Baltimore: Johns Hopkins University Press, 1997)
36 Derrida, *The Beast and the Sovereign* 1:209.
37 Derrida, *The Beast and the Sovereign* 1:209.
38 Derrida, *The Beast and the Sovereign* 1:209.
39 "Remarks by President Trump at a California Sanctuary State Roundtable," italics added.
40 In this essay, my argument takes a broadly Freudian psychoanalytic approach to rhetorical analysis, that is perhaps best summed up by Derrida's observation that "Freud said as early as 1897 that there was no difference in the unconscious between reality and a fiction loaded with affect." "No Apocalypse, Not Now (Full Speed Ahead, Seven Missiles, Seven Missives)," *diacritics*, vol. 14, no. 2 (1984), 23.

41 Marc Crépon, "*Geschlecht*," in *Dictionary of Untranslatables: A Philosophical Lexicon*, ed. Barbara Cassin, trans. eds. Emily Apter, Jacques Lezra, and Michael Wood (Princeton: Princeton University Press 2014), 394.
42 Ian Schwartz, "Trump Addresses Illegal Immigration Crisis: 'We Will Not Allow Our Generosity To Be Abused,'" *RealClear Politics*, November 1, 2018.
43 Schwartz, "Trump Addresses Illegal Immigration Crisis."
44 Schwartz, "Trump Addresses Illegal Immigration Crisis."
45 Schwartz, "Trump Addresses Illegal Immigration Crisis."
46 Walt Whitman, "Whitman's Preface," in *Walt Whitman: Selected Poems 1855–1892*, ed. Gary Schmidgall (New York: St. Martin's Press, 1999), 3.
47 Jacques Derrida, "*Geschlecht* I: Sexual Difference, Ontological Difference," *Research in Phenomenology*, vol. 13 (1983), 83.
48 Jacques Derrida, "*Geschlecht* II: Heidegger's Hand" (1987), trans. John P. Leavey, Jr., in *Deconstruction and Philosophy: The Texts of Jacques Derrida*, ed. John Sallis (Chicago: The University of Chicago Press, 1987), 184
49 Derrida, "*Geschlecht* I: Sexual Difference, Ontological Difference," 83–4.
50 Derrida, "*Geschlecht* II: Heidegger's Hand," 173–4.
51 James F. Ward, *Heidegger's Political Thinking* (Amherst: University of Massachusetts Press, 1995), 244.
52 Trakl quoted in Derrida, "*Geschlecht* II: Heidegger's Hand," 187–8.
53 Derrida, "*Geschlecht* II: Heidegger's Hand," 188.
54 Derrida, "*Geschlecht* II: Heidegger's Hand," 162ff.
55 Ulrike Kistner, "Translating the First Edition of Freud's *Drei Abhandlungen Zur Sexualtheorie*," in *Sigmund Freud, Three Essays on the Theory of Sexuality: The 1905 Edition*, trans. Ulrike Kistner (London and New York: Verso Books, 2017), lxxxii–lxxxiii.
56 Kistner, "Translating the First Edition of Freud's *Drei Abhandlungen Zur Sexualtheorie*," lxxxi.
57 Kistner, "Translating the First Edition of Freud's *Drei Abhandlungen Zur Sexualtheorie*," lxxix.
58 Kistner, "Translating the First Edition of Freud's *Drei Abhandlungen Zur Sexualtheorie*," lxxx.
59 Kistner, "Translating the First Edition of Freud's *Drei Abhandlungen Zur Sexualtheorie*," lxxxi.
60 Herman Westerink, "Freud's Discussion with Psychiatry on Sexuality, Drives and Object in Three Essays," in *Deconstructing Normativity?: Re-Reading Freud's 1905 Three Essays*, eds. Philippe Van Haute and Herman Westerink (London and New York: Routledge, 2017), 32.
61 Eric Shiraev, *Personality Theories: A Global View* (London: SAGE Publications, 2016), 109.
62 Sigmund Freud, *Civilization and Its Discontents*, trans. James Strachey (New York: W.W. Norton, 1962), 58.
63 Freud, *Civilization and Its Discontents*, 58.
64 Derrida, *The Beast and the Sovereign*, 1:57.
65 Freud, *Civilization and Its Discontents*, 61.
66 Freud, *Civilization and Its Discontents*, 61.
67 Crépon, "*Geschlecht*," 395.
68 Maria Pía Lara, *The Disclosure of Politics: Struggles Over the Semantics of Secularization* (New York: Columbia University Press, 2013), 84.

69 A. Samuel Kimball, *The Infanticidal Logic of Evolution and Culture* (Newark: University of Delaware Press, 2007), 123.
70 Michael J. Vlach, "Various Forms of Replacement Theology," *The Master's Seminary*, vol. 20, no. 1 (2009).
71 Luther quoted in Crépon, "*Geschlecht*," 395.
72 Luther quoted in Crépon, "*Geschlecht*," 396.
73 Luther quoted in Crépon, "*Geschlecht*," 396.
74 Derrida, *The Beast and the Sovereign*, 1:208.
75 Derrida, *The Beast and the Sovereign*, 1:209.
76 Scott, "Trump," *Political Concepts*.
77 Michael Rothberg, "Power," in *The Routledge Handbook of Contemporary Jewish Cultures*, eds. Nadia Valman and Laurence Roth (London: Routledge, 2017), 129.
78 Roberto Esposito, *Bíos: Biopolitics and Philosophy*, trans. Timothy Campbell (Minneapolis: University of Minnesota Press, 2008), 117.
79 Michael Hardt and Antonio Negri, *Empire* (Cambridge: Harvard University Press, 2000), 23.
80 Esposito, *Immunitas*, 9.
81 Esposito, *Immunitas*, 17.
82 Derrida, *The Beast and the Sovereign*, 1:86.
83 Lauren Gail Berlant, *The Queen of America Goes to Washington City: Essays on Sex and Citizenship* (Durham, NC and London: Duke University Press, 1997), 18.
84 Berlant, *The Queen of America Goes to Washington City*, 18.
85 Anna Gawboy, "Horned Headdress Guy Is Not A Viking: White Supremacy's Native American Thefts," *Medium* (blog), January 17, 2021, https://medium.com/perceive-more/horned-headdress-guy-is-not-a-viking-392777632215.
86 Gawboy, "Horned Headdress Guy Is Not A Viking: White Supremacy's Native American Thefts."
87 Gawboy, "Horned Headdress Guy Is Not A Viking: White Supremacy's Native American Thefts."
88 Brian Naylor, "Read Trump's Jan. 6 Speech, A Key Part Of Impeachment Trial," *NPR*, www.npr.org/2021/02/10/966396848/read-trumps-jan-6-speech-a-key-part-of-impeachment-trial.
89 Naylor. "Read Trump's Jan. 6 Speech, A Key Part Of Impeachment Trial."
90 Naylor. "Read Trump's Jan. 6 Speech, A Key Part Of Impeachment Trial."
91 Naylor. "Read Trump's Jan. 6 Speech, A Key Part Of Impeachment Trial."
92 Naylor. "Read Trump's Jan. 6 Speech, A Key Part Of Impeachment Trial."
93 Naylor. "Read Trump's Jan. 6 Speech, A Key Part Of Impeachment Trial."
94 Marc Fisher et al., "The Four-Hour Insurrection: How a Trump Mob Halted American Democracy," *Washington Post*, January 7, 2021, www.washingtonpost.com/graphics/2021/politics/trump-insurrection-capitol/.
95 Luke Mogelson, "Among the Insurrectionists," *The New Yorker*, January 25, 2021.
96 "QAnon Shaman claims he wasn't attacking the country in first interview since Capitol riot arrest," CBS News, March 5, 2021, https://www.cbsnews.com/news/qanon-shaman-capitol-riot-interview-60-minutes-plus-2021-03-04/.
97 Jacques Derrida, *Monolingualism of the Other: Or, The Prosthesis of Origin*, trans. Patrick Mensah, first edition (Stanford, CA: Stanford University Press, 1998), 23.

98   Derrida, *Monolingualism of the Other*, 23.
99   Derrida, *Monolingualism of the Other*, 24.
100 Derrida, *Monolingualism of the Other*, 24.
101 Derrida, *The Beast and the Sovereign*, 1:138.
102 Richard Slotkin, *Regeneration Through Violence: The Mythology of the American Frontier, 1600–1860* (Norman: University of Oklahoma Press, 2000).
103 David Shahoulian et al., *The Trump Administration's Family Separation Policy: Trauma, Destruction, and Chaos* (Washington, DC: Subcommittee on Immigration and Citizenship. US House of Representatives, 2020), https://judiciary.house.gov/uploadedfiles/the_trump_administration_family_separation_policy_trauma_destruction_and_chaos.pdf?utm_campaign=4526-519.
104 Shahoulian et al., *The Trump Administration's Family Separation Policy: Trauma, Destruction, and Chaos*.
105 Sheila Foster, "Race and Ethnicity, Rawls, Race, and Reason," *Fordham Law Review*, vol. 72, no. 5 (January 1, 2004), 1718.
106 Lucas Guttentag, "Coronavirus Border Expulsions: CDC's Assault on Asylum Seekers and Unaccompanied Minors," *Stanford Law School* (blog), https://law.stanford.edu/2020/04/15/coronavirus-border-expulsions-cdcs-assault-on-asylum-seekers-and-unaccompanied-minors/.
107 Yascha Mounk, *The People Vs. Democracy: Why Our Freedom Is in Danger and How to Save It* (Cambridge, MA: Harvard University Press, 2018).
108 Adam Dahl, *Empire of the People: Settler Colonialism and the Foundations of Modern Democratic Thought* (Lawrence: University Press of Kansas, 2018), 10.
109 Dahl, *Empire of the People*, 184.
110 Dahl, *Empire of the People*, 189.
111 Derrida, *The Beast and the Sovereign*, 1:4.
112 Derrida, *Specters of Marx*, 106.
113 Derrida, *Specters of Marx*, 212.
114 Jacques Derrida, *Given Time: I. Counterfeit Money*, trans. Peggy Kamuf (Chicago: The University of Chicago Press, 1991), 91.

4

Between the Body and Language: Narratives of the Moving Subject in Okwui Okpokwasili's *Bronx Gothic*

Lauren DiGiulio

I

THE PERFORMANCE WORK OF CONTEMPORARY Nigerian-American writer, performer, and choreographer Okwui Okpokwasili is concerned with representations of the Black female body in relation to language. Using text, movement, sound, and visual design, her work aims, as she has said, to "generate a kind of radical intimacy, an empathic feedback loop."[1] Throughout her multidisciplinary practice, she explores how the body enacts and departs from its role as a bearer of discourse, employing the body as a vehicle for communicating narratives that carry linguistic meaning and present abstract movement. These narratives operate beyond semantic function in order to create an immersive relationship with the viewer. Okpokwasili describes the movement in her performance practice as evoking "multiple breaks—energy breaking through the body; the body breaking down; the body rupturing as it encounters unbearable memories, but then rebuilding, finding grace and stillness in the echoing breach."[2] In 2014, Okpokwasili created a solo performance titled *Bronx Gothic* in collaboration with her husband, visual artist and filmmaker Peter Born. Throughout this work, she uses her performing body as a vehicle to create emotional intimacy with the audience through choreographic and textual means. Literary elements of epistolary narrative, Victorian *Bildungsroman*, and West African griot storytelling are interwoven to explore themes of feminine adolescence, friendship, and intimacy.

Performance is interdisciplinary by nature, as of course it incorporates elements of sound, visual imagery, choreography, and spoken text. *Bronx Gothic* pushes into the ruptures between genres that performance often blends together by emphasizing transitions between the body's movements and dialogue. Over the course of the performance, which lasts just over an hour, Okpokwasili reads a series of fictionalized "reconstructed notes" that, as she tells it, she and a childhood girlfriend passed back and forth during their adolescence. At transitional moments throughout the narrative, she sings, falls to the floor, and rolls across it, executing movements that both mirror the emotion that her story describes, and depart from it to create multiple layers of recounting. After opening the performance with a dance, she recites a poem (about running to a boiling ocean) before moving to the dance floor, and singing a song: "I am alike those broken wings. Particles of dust and radiant air." The new narratives that she employs shift between spoken dialogue and physical performance, as she offers translations from verbal to corporal representation, and back again. These moments of transition between forms offer us new ways of thinking about how dance can mobilize the subject to push against historical narratives of trauma. In the space that is created by these retellings, Okpokwasili can trace individual, collective, and historical memories.

Like much contemporary dance work being produced now, *Bronx Gothic* was born from a network of commissioning organizations, and developed over the course of several years in a variety of residencies and presenting venues, both throughout the United States and internationally. Co-commissioned and co-presented by Danspace Project and P.S. 122 in New York City (now Performance Space New York), it was shown in process at various points in its four-year development, and premiered in New York at Danspace Project as part of the 2014 COIL Festival. *Bronx Gothic*, therefore, has a complex production history, and my approach to writing about this work necessitated a choice as to which iteration would best serve my own engagement with its layered forms. Ultimately, the recording of a live performance at Portland Institute for Contemporary Art, which was presented and filmed in conjunction with On the Boards in Seattle on September 12th, 2015, proved to be the clearest and most direct engagement with the live work that was available at the time of this writing.

* * *

In this essay, I consider the ways that embodied performance informs our conception of *Geschlecht*, and likewise, how the account we provide for

Geschlecht informs our notions of embodied performance. By slipping between registers of form and eliciting a reciprocal, critical gaze on the notions they carry with them, Okpokwasili traces collective and personal memory within her own body through her relationship to language and explores the way these can be linked to—and depart from—traditional literary genres. Okpokwasili uses her subject position as a Black woman to explore how language disintegrates—how she pulls away to create meaning through movement—and returns to language later on. Literary and choreographic forms are explored and discarded as she moves in a choreographic rhythm among physical, linguistic, image-based, and sonic modes of knowledge production. Her body's movement among these multiple forms creates an intimate space both with the audience, who bear witness to these movements within and outside of linguistic expression, and with various aspects of the self, as she contends with personal and collective traumas. By using her body as a site of emotional excavation that consistently moves between modes of visibility and form, *Bronx Gothic* disrupts the perceived stability of individual subject positions to create space for Black female subjectivity to move among these forms. It explores the movement between adherence to narrative structure and the process of both textual and physical disintegration. What kind of relation between past memories and the experience of the present can emerge from representations of the body as visible and obscure, in turn? Where can the subject reside among embodied representations of different aspects of the individual self?

Okpokwasili opens our thinking toward a new kind of genre—one that takes the individuality of her voice and pushes against the contours of established narrative modes to find space for more fluid means of communication. Her work combines the forms of many existing literary and choreographic genres, and expands each by integrating her speech and movement in order to create her own. *Bronx Gothic* engages the literary traditions of epistolary narrative, Victorian *Bildungsroman* and its adaptation by African-American women writers of the twentieth century, as well as a variety of performance traditions, including Japanese Butoh, West African griot storytelling, and American postmodern dance. As such, even through the most basic descriptions of *Bronx Gothic*, one is faced both with the transitional aspects of its structure, and the clashes between differing generic categories. Following this, I draw upon a range of critical methodologies throughout this essay to address the varied literary genre forms that Okpokwasili employs as she layers and expands each through speech and movement. How does *Bronx Gothic*'s use of epistolary narrative help us think through the constitution of Black feminine subjectivity? How does the figuring of abjection toward the end of the work extend its psychoanalytic engagement with nineteenth-century Gothic literature and the *Bildungsroman*? To what extent does Okpokwasili's use of the performing body to physicalize historical, personal, and collective trauma prompt a closer reading of performance theory and the conception of narrative entanglement? And how do the elements of exhaustion and distintegration of her moving and speaking body connect to discourses around the historically subjugated position of Black women's performance?

II

In *Bronx Gothic*, Okpokwasili stages herself as a subject in between positions of address. Departing from the convention in which narrators speak from the point of view of a single character or with a passive voice, Okpokwasili speaks in the voices of two Black adolescent girls who communicate through written correspondence. *Bronx Gothic*'s narrative takes an epistolary form that allows Okpokwasili to explore the evolving identities of her two writing subjects as she moves between their voices. By moving fluidly between their two narrative positions, she explores the liminal space constituted by the pubescent Black female adolescence through her use of both language-based narrative and abstract movement. As her position of address moves between these forms, we see each mode—text and movement—disintegrate and reconstitute as she inhabits each mode and returns to form.

At regular intervals throughout *Bronx Gothic*, Okpokwasili stands at the downstage microphone and reads from a stack of handwritten notes on lined yellow and white legal paper. The first time we hear her voice, she says, "I want to share something with you. It's a note that was passed between two girls at the tender age of eleven, one of which was me."[3] As her first utterance, Okpokwasili acknowledges her physical presence onstage and initiates engagement with three different interlocutors: the audience, her girlhood friend, and her younger self. She then proceeds to "read" the notes, investing each girl's voice with a distinctive characterization. The girl we hear first—the one who we at first assume to be Okpokwasili's younger self—has a higher timbre and a sheltered outlook. She hasn't gone through puberty yet, and asks her more physically developed friend, who speaks in a lower, more sultry tone, about sexual pleasure, male anatomy, and the mechanics of physical intimacy. This spoken narrative unfolds as a series of dialogues that occur between sections of dance and song-based performance. The more mature girl shares her dream of running to the beach, and the more innocent one teaches her how to practice lucid dreaming. Eventually, the two girls get into a physical fight, and Okpokwasili, inhabiting the role of older narrator, describes how her younger self lost contact with her friend after the girl got pregnant and left school. She tries to track her down, years later, and ends up at an apartment flooded with blood, only to discover what we as audience have already begun to realize: that her friend is in fact an aspect of her younger self. It is also revealed that her friend was abused at the hands of her mother's boyfriend during the time of the two girls' correspondence, creating a doubled climax that integrates aspects of the ruptured self that has been broken by various forms of trauma.

By using physical performance to move between aspects of speech and movement, Okpokwasili gathers disparate aspects of her embodied self while allowing the gaps between them to remain open, creating a space where a new form of subjectivity can reside. The multiple elements of her subject position remain distinct, but communicate with each other throughout the beginning of the performance. *Bronx Gothic* uses an epistolary narrative form to distinguish the voices of the two aspects of Okpokwasili's younger self. Their correspondence creates a sense of intimacy between the voices of the two girls, and between the performer and the viewing audience. This close relationship is engendered by the element of first-person direct address and description of subjective expression constituted by the letter's form. Historically, the epistolary form has been central both to the development of aesthetic forms and in the constitution of the modern subject.[4] Indeed, the rise of the epistolary novel in eighteenth-century England represents a formative time in the history of English literature. Samuel Richardson's 1740 novel *Pamela; or, Virtue Rewarded*, which is generally considered to be a crucial text in the development of the novel's form, recounts the story of a young woman who is physically abused and sexually harassed at the hands of her male employer before he eventually repents, and they marry.[5]

Comprised as a series of letters written by the virtuous protagonist to her parents, *Pamela* departs from the classical dramatic plot convention dictated by Aristotle, in which characters' actions are privileged over the description of internal emotions.[6] In his canonical book on the development of the novel's form titled *The Rise of the Novel*, Ian Watt describes Richardson's narrative mode as reflective of a change in aesthetic outlook in the late eighteenth century: "The transition from the objective, social and public orientation of the classical world to the subjective, individualist and private orientation of the life and literature of the last two hundred years."[7] As Watt describes it, the development of the epistolary novel corresponds to a greater sense of individualism and secularization of thought that arose in response to the process of modernity and increased urbanization in and around London.[8] This element of individualism was represented in the form of "private experience" that epistolary form describes. As leisure time for the middle classes increased, and literacy among women became more common, letter-writing emerged as a popular pastime, which ensured contemporary readership of new literature even as it reflected the familiar form of correspondence.[9] The shift from the form of the epic tale to the epistolary novel therefore signals the transition of narrative emphasis from public action to private experience, which is of course then made public again in the form of the novel.

The transition from public objectivity to individual subjectivity constitutes a key moment in the development of the modern writing subject. As

Elizabeth Heckendorn Cook describes in her work on gender in eighteenth-century epistolary literature, the predominant ideology for the construction of subjectivity in early modern Europe centered around the conception of the conjugal family as the space where the "authentic" self could evolve. The form of the letter-narrative is, therefore,

> [...] formally and thematically concerned with competing definitions of subjectivity: it puts into play the tension between the private individual, identified with a specifically gendered, classed body that necessarily commits it to specific forms of self-interest, and the public person, divested of self-interest, discursively constituted, and functionally disembodied.[10]

This tension between the public and private spheres is present in Okpokwasili's delivery of letters that are emblematic of her childhood friendship. By publicly reading the private letters of an intimate correspondence to the audience, she brings the personal into the realm of the public, and creates a relationship between "herself" as narrator, the audience, and the two girl correspondents.

Epistolary narrative further explores this realm of the private through the immediacy of its expression and ability to convey compelling descriptions of subjective emotion. Watts describes Richardson's "conviction that epistolary converse gave him the emotional satisfaction which ordinary life denied."[11] By describing narrative events in first person more or less as they occur, the letter-writing form places the audience in the position of the narrator's correspondent, and allows us to feel close to her. When Okpokwasili reads the letters from her legal pad, this is just what happens: the audience is included in what is essentially a private sphere, despite its being made public by way of the performance. Indeed, as the private nature of the epistolary form opens its purview to affective description, emotions are conveyed in the space of such intimacy. Cook argues that this private realm, "found its discursive mode in the familiar letter and its epistemological model in the idea of a universal, transparent language of the expressive body, which offers a window onto the heart."[12] By communicating in an epistolary mode, the two girls describe their growing sense of emotional intimacy in affective terms, and bring the audience into the space of this private sphere.

* * * *

Apart from the elaboration of public and private elicited through *Bronx Gothic*'s use of epistolary forms, Okpokwasili's spoken words also connect to corporal aspects of the performance. The core ability of language to describe the expression of emotion is explored throughout, as the work uses the naming of different body parts to transition between moments of pure "narration" and moments of embodied movement. Toward the beginning of her performance, after the second section of letter-reading, Okpokwasili falls to the floor, creating jerky, abstract movements in which she attempts to get up, but the weight of her body repeatedly pulls her back to the ground. She lies still, then stands, and walks toward the microphone to pick up the fallen letters from the ground. The character of the naïve girl then explains to the more mature one how she achieves lucid dreaming. "Ask yourself, 'Am I awake?'" the girl says, as she steps away from the microphone and begins to walk slowly toward stage right, repeating this phrase after naming a different part of her body. "Look at your hand ... now ask yourself, 'Am I awake?'" The act of looking then elides into the act of touching: "Touch your thigh [...] now ask yourself, 'Am I awake?'" The verbal evocation of these different elements, followed by the question as to whether the character, and by extension the audience, is truly "awake" or "sleeping" draws our attention into the present moment and evokes a meditative focus on the embodied performance in real time. Further, the slippage of linguistic description from "looking" to "touching" collapses the distance between the narrator's viewing of her own body, which supposes a separation between herself as a viewing subject and her body as a viewed object, and the physical feeling of touching her body, which more immediately figures the touching subject as closer to the touched object.[13] By focusing our attention on elements of her body, these spoken words ask us to engage with Okpokwasili in a phenomenological manner, thereby collapsing the distance between the audience as viewing subjects and Okpokwasili as a viewed object. The description of these emotional elements coupled with her physical movement furthers *Bronx Gothic*'s model of epistolarity. As the sensual modes of looking and touching are brought into correspondence, the viewer enters into an emotionally intimate exchange with Okpokwasili as a performer.

Okpokwasili's linguistic evocation of her performing body leads into a movement-based sequence in which the mature girl guides herself through a lucid dream. She touches her face while repeating the lines about touching the different parts of herself and sings, "I'm in your shadow, in your shade. Don't go on, disintegrate. Be dispersing. Spread away. Be alike night and day," before dropping to the floor. Physically sprawled out, she recounts what she would dream about: "Can we be bound together right now [...] universal-bound, boundariless." As the lights dim, she arises and places a plastic bag, which has been hanging from the ceiling, on her head before the lights go to Black. Here, the spoken description allows her to transition into song, which leads to movement-based expression on the floor and the physical gesture made with the bag. As she vocally calls out for the disintegration of her body into a "boundariless" state, her words also dissolve, and her performing body takes over to express what it might feel like to "disperse." Her gesture of placing the bag over her head suggests a desire for the kind of dispersal found in death. In this moment, Okpokwasili calls not only for the dissolution of the body itself, but also for the space between bodies. As she begs to be "bound together" with her friend, she communicates her desire to collapse the distance between the two halves of what we come later to realize in the performance is her split subjectivity. The stakes of her desperation become apparent as she moves toward annihilation, which she can achieve either in merging with another body or in death. Okpokwasili's desire to integrate these two aspects of herself recalls Luce Irigaray's figuration of the structure of intimacy, which operates as an approach to intersubjectivity. In Irigaray's account, physical intimacy inaugurates a transgression of the self into "an awakening of intersubjectivity."[14] However, according to this model of intimacy, connection is made possible only by settling into a subject position within language.[15] As the mature girl calls for the emergence of a more intersubjective position, she also begins to take up her own subject position within language as she narrates her experience of Black girlhood.

These transitions between speech and movement are constructed through the form of epistolary narrative, which evokes a more direct relationship between the narrator as a writing subject and her emotions. In *Bronx Gothic*, the letters that the narrator writes to her friend become metonymically linked to her yearning for self-integration. After all, writing a letter requires both distance between the writer and the addressee, and desire for communication. Gerald MacLean asserts that reading such correspondence requires a careful consideration of the site of both subjects: "Letters require places. More precisely, what is required are the spaces separating the places between which the letter travels. Letters are directed from here to there, across a space in between, the abode of the never entirely absent other."[16] Okpokwasili's epistolary narrative is only viable to the extent that it is predicated on a distance between the two girl characters.

Although we never learn the girls' names, we recognize them by the difference in their voices, personalities, and experiences. One is naïve, thoughtful, and inquisitive; the other is more mature and defensive, carrying pain as well as desire. In his famous seminar on Edgar Allan Poe's story "The Purloined Letter," Jacques Lacan figures the letter as a symbol of the linguistic signifier whose message always remains empty.[17] The letter is unlike other objects because, "it will be *and* not be where it is, wherever it goes."[18] To the extent that the letter is a vehicle for communication, it perpetually exists in the gap between correspondents. However, to claim that the letter is both sited *and* not sited is not to assert that the writing subject has no significance beyond the circulation of the empty signifier. On the contrary: Okpokwasili uses the gaps between the two aspects of self to find rupture within language that she amplifies with choreographic movement to find space outside of it, where movement can create meaning alongside the process of signification. She expresses desire to integrate the two aspects of self throughout the narrative and "find" her friend whom she lost, just after the letters were written, and by phenomenological means eventually locates her friend inside her own body.

Okpokwasili's use of epistolary narrative begins to inscribe the self in writing, while attempting to close the distance between the self and the other. She consciously draws upon the literary tradition of the epistolary novel's use of female narrators, who often serve as the protagonists of such forms.[19] Anne Bower describes the female protagonists' use of the letter form, "not only to affirm herself, not only to bridge the gap between self and other, but often to *rewrite* the self, presenting a personal self-definition that contradicts, supersedes, or supplements the identity others have assumed her to have."[20] Given its focus on self-writing, epistolary form functions as an apt means by which female writers, and particularly female writers of color, revise the narratives that have historically circulated around the categories of their identities. *Bronx Gothic* furthers this tradition by extending the mode of epistolarity in multiple directions. Here, Okpokwasili enters into correspondence with multiple aspects of herself, with the audience, and with a complex combination of literary and choreographic genres.

III

The writing of African-American feminist authors serves as an important precursor to *Bronx Gothic* thematically and politically, but also in the sense of exploring and mixing forms where Okpokwasili can express an experience of Black adolescent girlhood. Such writing often creates its own network of correspondence between current works, and those of earlier generations. Alice Walker's 1982 epistolary novel *The Color Purple*, for example, has been considered as an incorporation and revision of Zora Neale Hurston's 1937 novel *Their Eyes Were Watching God*. Henry Louis Gates, Jr. argues that Walker's novel effectively functions as a "letter" to Hurston.[21] Celie, the protagonist of *The Color Purple*, who is mute and suffers abuse at the hands of her sadistic husband, "*writes* herself into being, before our very eyes," through the use of her pen."[22] By writing letters, Celie enters into discursive exchange, from which she has previously been excluded by condition of her muteness. Through the act of writing, she constitutes herself as a subject. Gates further links the epistolary form of Walker's novel to the tradition of slave narratives, asserting that the plot details Celie's "life and times, her bondage and her freedom."[23] Here, epistolarity functions as a mode of writing by which the Black female subject creates a space for her own subjective voice to reside, on her own terms. To the extent that *Bronx Gothic* engages in this conscious mode of metacritical epistolarity, it actively corresponds with the constellation of writings around female adolescence and the formation of the African-American female subject in literature.

The notion of "coming into being" for many Black feminist writers can also be considered through the transitional moment portrayed in *Bronx*

Gothic as a moment of adolescence. Okpokwasili positions adolescence as a space wherein multiple aspects of her identity are negotiated. The movement between elements of her subjectivity is figured as a movement among a myriad of discursive registers: between speech and movement, between the past and the present, and between aspects of self. She also positions herself as a subject in between bodies. Okpokwasili explores the subtleties of the corporal and emotional terrain of the pubescent experience as she shifts between two distinct subjectivities, each with its own embodied voice and sensibility. The two girl characters, one at the beginning of her development and the other farther along in her pubescence, share stories about the discovery of their sexuality and its attendant experiences. "What is an orgasm?" the naïve girl asks the mature one as the opening phrase of dialogue between the two characters. "An orgasm is what you get when you have sex," answers the mature girl, to which the childlike girl answers that she thinks she has already had one with her Frisbee.[24]

These instances of emotional intimacy are juxtaposed by moments of anger between the two friends, in which the vulnerability that the mature girl feels as a result of her developing body is displaced into animosity toward the naïve girl (although we later come to realize these two characters are separate aspects of the same girl, they are presented as two distinct characters at this point in the performance). After the moment of lucid dreaming, in which the naïve girl guides the mature girl into recognizing herself in her dreams, the mature girl tells her how she buys cigarettes for her mother's boyfriend, and that he "lets her smoke his cigarettes" while he looks after her. After the naïve girl asks her if her mother knows, she answers, "Hell no!" The next letter we hear is a verbal diatribe against the naïve girl, who is accused of being selfish because she is reticent about sharing her jump rope. Later in the monologue, we realize that she is upset because she thinks the naïve girl told a classmate about her sexual activity, and her boyfriend is upset with her because he doesn't think she is a virgin. "Do you know what love is?" she asks, aggression in her voice. She then begins to describe her self-doubt, and switches her narrative position from first to third person while maintaining the same voice of the mature girl character: "I am in pain right now. [...] How does she survive the blackness inside of her? Who got the key?"[25]

In the scene just described, the conception of blackness as a dark, painful interior becomes externalized as an expression of violent anger, as the figure of "blackness" slips between internal and external characteristics. By physically voicing the "pain" of "blackness inside of her," she externalizes its description—the characteristic of "blackness" slips from the inside of her body onto her skin, and we understand it as both an interior, emotional condition and as an exterior, visible characteristic of racial difference. She articulates her inner emotions around the conception of her difference as she attempts to negotiate her place in relation to herself and to her environment.

The exploration of her emotional interior as dark, painful, and full of secrets extends *Bronx Gothic*'s engagement with the tradition of African American women's epistolary writing into the genre of nineteenth-century Gothic literature, wherein the exploration of sexuality often coincided with themes of transgression and fright, with a focus on emotion rather than rational thought.[26] In nineteenth-century postbellum American literature, the question of racial difference became a more prominent theme, as the United States was "ghosted by the past of slavery."[27] By taking up the themes of interiority, nascent sexuality, and abjection, *Bronx Gothic*—as its title suggests—signals its commitment to this genre, even as Okpokwasili challenges its borders by moving between registers of form.

* * * *

Okpokwasili's work further engages the tradition of the minority women's *Bildungsroman* in American literature, which stages questions around the politics of remembering in relation to the emotional and physical development of young women of color. *Bronx Gothic*'s narrative slippage between the embodied voices of the two girls at different stages of puberty reframes the traditional genre of the *Bildungsroman*. Rather than presenting a story of how a young boy becomes a mature man (as in Goethe's *Wilhelm Meister's Apprenticeship*, or Dickens' *Great Expectations*, or the feminized aspect of this form in Brontë's *Jane Eyre*), Okpokwasili stages the narrative as a dialogue between two aspects of the Black feminine self.[28]

The genre of the "coming of age" novel emerged in the eighteenth century as a German humanist adaptation of the heroic epic, most principally defined by a teleological progression toward the attainment of knowledge by a young male protagonist, that results in his attainment of spiritual fulfillment and integration into bourgeois society after a series of moral challenges.[29] In the twentieth century, women writers of color have taken up this form as a way of engaging the dialogue associated with W. E. B. DuBois' notion of "double consciousness," and to extend the complexity of doubled voicing into the matrix of feminine subjectivity. In his landmark 1903 work *The Souls of Black Folk*, DuBois describes Black subjectivity as always already doubled, as its structural position within white discourse creates the condition of seeing oneself from the dual positions of both one's own proper subjectivity and of the position of whiteness, in which subjective difference is made visible.[30] This conception of split subjectivity is extended by Black feminist critics who assert that Black women's writing complicates this doubling by engaging in a dialogue not only with external discourse, but also within the internal space of the subject herself. For Black women, consciousness is further riven by the multiple aspects of "othering" that occur within the self, as both "Black" and "woman." Mae G. Henderson describes Black women's writing as characteristically dialogic, to the extent that it stages conversations within the self as a means of engaging the doubled and redoubled nature of Black female subjectivity:

> What is at once characteristic and suggestive of Black women's writing is its interlocutory, or dialogic, character, reflecting not only a relationship with the "other(s)," but an internal dialogue with the plural aspects of self that constitute the matrix of black female subjectivity. The interlocutory character of black women's writing is, thus, not only a consequence of a dialogic relationship with an imaginary or "generalized Other," but a dialogue with the aspects of "otherness" within the self.[31]

In the case of the female *Bildungsroman*, the conversations between these aspects of self come to the fore, as the protagonist struggles to negotiate her multiple internal subjectivities as well as the task of finding her social place as she matures to adulthood. This internal conversation among aspects of the Black female subject leads to what Henderson describes as the condition of "speaking in tongues."[32] Glossolalia, or the act of speaking in unknown languages, is a practice associated with Black women in the Pentecostal church, in which speaking in unfamiliar ways to the Holy Spirit is a means of finding grace. Henderson posits that Black women must speak not only in a variety of voices, but also in "competing and complementary discourses— discourses that seek both to adjudicate competing claims and witness common concerns."[33] Thus, "speaking in tongues" requires fluency both in communicating by means of extraordinary modes of speech that operate outside symbolic discourse, and via the diverse elements of languages already known to shared communities.

This tactic of finding multiple modes of communication is formulated in response to the subjugation of Black women's bodies perpetuated by the signifying process. In her germinal 1987 essay "Mama's Baby, Papa's Maybe: An American Grammar Book," scholar Hortense J. Spillers describes the ways that signification maintains the legacy of transatlantic slavery in the Americas. Terms used as "markers" to confine Black women within delineated identity categories are:

> [...] so loaded with mythical prepossession that there is no easy way for the agents buried beneath them to come clean. In that regard, the names by which I am called in the public place render an example of signifying property *plus*. In order for me to speak a truer word concerning myself, I must strip down through layers of attenuated meanings, made an excess in time, over time, assigned by a particular historical order, and there await whatever marvels of my own inventiveness.[34]

For Black women, the articulation of the self requires undoing layers of violent and oppressive terminological structures that have built up over time. To the extent that Okpokwasili uses movement and language together to extend meaning beyond the purview of the spoken word, she works at breaking down hegemonic narratives surrounding Black women's bodies. She uses the literary forms of epistolarity and *Bildungsroman* with Gothic themes and overtones to explore how these genres circumscribe the iterative experiences of Black female adolescence, but then moves beyond these categorical forms to articulate an embodied sense of self. This circumscription also marks her transition from linguistic to embodied expression.

The extension of language into corporeal meaning occurs at key moments throughout *Bronx Gothic*, in which the dialogue between the two girls breaks down and movement is employed as a way of continuing the subject's desired expression. It is in the moments where language disintegrates—the two girls misunderstand each other, become angry, or are emotionally triggered by speech—that Okpokwasili pushes against the formal boundaries of these literary genres to move her performance more fully into a movement-based register. At three distinct moments throughout the performance, Okpokwasili falls suddenly to the floor and executes jerky movements in which she attempts to lift herself up using first her legs and then her arms, only to have her limbs slammed back to the floor as they exhibit a sense of exhaustion. Elbows and knees knock against the ground as her limbs are articulated in parts. Her movement gives the effect of a body that is trying to stand but cannot be controlled, as if she is desperately willing herself to stand. Yet in these moments, her body resists the requisite response, collapsing awkwardly in a state of inertia. These broken movements extend the feeling of the fragmented self that her epistolary text begins to express. As audience, we see Okpokwasili's performing body in a desperate state of desire, panicked and frustrated that the body's limbs are not receiving the messages being sent by the conscious brain. In these moments, Okpokwasili inhabits the mature girl's feeling of disconnection between the way she sees herself and the way that others— her friend, and other men she describes at the corner bodega—see her. Her feelings of ugliness toward herself are turned inward, causing language to break down and become expressed through the body's motion. In much the same way that writing in an epistolary mode communicates an interior emotional state, Okpokwasili's movements serve as an exterior, physical manifestation of her emotional relationship to herself.

IV

Okpokwasili uses physical motion to disrupt the separation of fixed media categories within *Bronx Gothic*. Her movement eventually evokes narrative language, and then provides a means for her to disrupt its signifying process when her spoken text is unable to function as a vehicle for her experience. The rhythm of Okpokwasili moving toward and away from the production of language throughout *Bronx Gothic* is deeply connected to the thematic exploration of subjectivity, but no less remarkable is how the metacritical register inherent in the composition of the performance—in the moves between narrative forms, in the embodied shifts between different generic domains—becomes its own kind of choreography.

The performance begins with Okpokwasili already in motion before transitioning into language-based narrative as her body becomes exhausted, and slips back into movement at points of narrative rupture. As the audience enters the theater at the Portland Institute for Contemporary Art, they encounter Okpokwasili in a state of motion. She stands in an upstage corner of the space, facing away from the audience toward the voluminous white scrims that curtain the back and sides of stage. Small incandescent domestic table lamps lie about the floor, clustered with long grasses and flowers in patches around the edges of the playing space. A low-level drone noise hums as Okpokwasili's hips and legs move in a subtle but consistent vibrating twerking motion that ripples up into her arms, shoulders, and neck. Lit from below, her body casts a blurry shadow onto the white scrim behind her. She appears as a doubled image, outlined starkly against the wall and projected as a loosely formed shadow as it sways in motion. This is an intense and durational movement that slowly becomes larger as the audience take their seats.

The shivering twerk at Okpokwasili's hips and legs becomes a twitching as it moves throughout her body, extending into her arms and head. She raises her arms horizontally as the dance becomes more expressive. The drone sound that accompanies her movement grows into a cacophony of voices whose speech is indecipherable before exploding into a pounding electronic bass rhythm that repeats as Okpokwasili's motions become more extreme. The durational quality of the movement that emanates from her hips and legs creates an insistence that already feels exhaustive by the time her movement begins to spread. Yet it persists—and as audience, it feels as if the movement is both coming from within and also as if it is compelled from the outside.

At this moment, the performer is visibly exhausted. Sweat drips down her back as the movement of her arms and knees becomes jerky. Okpokwasili's motion continues for a full twenty-five minutes into the performance before she turns around. The music ends abruptly as we are confronted with the vulnerable image of her dancing body glistening with sweat, and still moving. She looks out at the audience and pulls the top of her burgundy dress away from her body with the thumb and index fingers of her hands. Drenched in sweat, the dress peels away from her body as she continues to shudder. The sound of her moving body becomes foregrounded as her heavily labored breathing extends the abiding accompaniment of the drone music, which has now fallen away. Exhausted, she seems on the verge of physically collapsing. We watch her watching us, as the sound again intensifies for another five minutes or so, and she moves to the microphone in the center of the space. Once positioned in front of it, she gesticulates wildly with her arms and thrusts her chin out in extreme motion. At the edge of physical collapse, she conjures the function of speech through the enactment of gesture that evokes a stylized version of animated conversation. The lights go to Black, and we finally hear Okpokwasili's voice in the darkness as the light on the microphone shines down at her hands as she clutches the letters from which she reads. Having summoned the production of language from an interior space, she physically relaxes, and begins her narration. The performance's text emerges only at the point where her movement breaks down, and assumes the primary meaning-making function of the work as her physical motion recedes.

Okpokwasili's attenuated movement sequence at the beginning of *Bronx Gothic* establishes the pattern of movement between registers of visual, textual, and choreographic form, between aspects of her own subjectivity, and between the way she negotiates her relation to herself and how others see her. As the lights shine brighter and she intensifies her movements, we recognize her watching us, as audience. We become implicated in her consistent motion as radical emotional intimacy is created between performer and audience. Operating separately from linguistic expression, this movement establishes Okpokwasili's subjectivity in a public—although very intimate—setting. Literally moving against generic conventions, she rejects the kinds of framing that limit her self-articulation. By starting the performance with this movement, she sets up *Bronx Gothic*'s rhetorical shifts between literary and choreographic form, anticipating the turns among genres and modes of dance that her narration follows. It also signals the tenuous relationship among her character's modes of self. Her movement physicalizes the model of epistolary narrative, in which communication moves back and forth between subjects, while also emphasizing the aspect of embodiment that serves to distinguish the two girls.

Later, after the younger girl teaches the older girl how to lucid dream, Okpokwasili's movement returns as linguistic communication between the two girls disintegrates, and the force of the naïve girl's emotion becomes too laden for text to bear. Toward the middle of the performance, the mature girl begins to berate her friend, directing racial slurs at her, and telling her that she's ugly. "Am I awake?" the naïve girl answers meekly. After the girls agree to meet at the corner store to buy cigarettes for the boyfriend of the mature girl's mother, the naïve girl stands up to her oppressive doppelgänger. She describes how she lights a cigarette for her friend, as her knees and hips begin to move in real time. The droning sound that accompanies movement throughout the work begins to build slowly as the girl describes her mounting frustration:

> You keep saying that you telling me the truth, 'cause you my best friend. And the truth is, you so fine and I'm so ugly. You fucking boys, and I'm

fucking stupid. I know. I know 'cause you make sure I know. And I'm standing here and I'm trying to see myself, and you blocking me. Get off me. Get off me.

Her voice becomes deeper as it connects with her anger, and the pulsing electronic music from the opening sequence starts to play. She describes fighting back her friend's words: "Am I standing here with you? Am I guiding you? I want to slap you. I want to slap your face. [...] I sucker slap you. I sucker slap you so hard. Cocksucker. Motherfucker."[35] With legs bent and arms straightened outward, her body begins to pulsate with the force of her newfound anger, which she directs outward in order to finally break free of her friend's verbal abuse and establish her own sense of identity.

In order to create this rupture, the naïve girl must turn to physical means, which Okpokwasili expresses through movement. As communication between the two girls becomes untenable in light of the naïve girl's mounting frustration, choreography assumes the responsibility for the production of meaning. The shift from linguistic narrative to dance gradually disrupts the separation of media categories, as the boundaries between language and her moving body dissolve. The naïve girl evokes images of the phallus in order to draw her boundaries, and uses it as a weapon: "Do you feel that? That's my dick. It's spitting in your face [...] it's tearing your head off. I'm ugly. I'm Medusa, motherfucker." She pulses her shoulders, circles her head, and pumps her arms outward to express the force of her defensive stature as she takes on the position of the abject, ugly subjectivity that her friend describes, in order to vanquish her abuser. As her words fall away and her movement is foregrounded, we see flashes of the more reticent, tiptoeing naïve girl still present under the assertive performance of her newfound aggression. Finally, she falls to her knees and leans back on her hips, hovering above the ground and looking around in awe before falling face first onto the floor. She attempts to rise several times and collapses. When she finally stands, she looks around and opens her mouth in a motion to speak. Her voice expresses itself as a song: "I do love you like a long, warm walk on a big Sunday. [...] I feel a clear hum, I feel a clear hum, and a low pulse when you're near." As language disintegrates, Okpokwasili's movement operates beyond any clear signifying system in order to communicate the complexity of the character's multi-layered feelings about her simultaneous love and anger at her best friend. And again, after her body becomes exhausted, language returns.

* * * *

At a moment when the mature girl's words fail to articulate anything, Okpokwasili moves away from textual expression, and physical movement is necessary in order to communicate outside of what is contained within language. As the naïve girl, Okpokwasili strains against the confines of her friend's name-calling. The slurs used against her seek to reduce her subjectivity to single traits that are based on her gender and racial identity, in debased terms. These are truly "empty" signifiers, wholly devoid of content and used here only in the service of labeling another in order to degrade. The naïve girl responds to these epithets by first wresting control of the dialogue, and then pushing out and beyond linguistic expression with physical means.

After receiving these verbal abuses, the naïve girl begins her note at the start of this episode with a threat: "Dear you back: My heart is a jagged rock. Don't make me take it out and cut you." The metaphor of the girl's heart as a jagged rock is placed alongside the use of the heart as a metonym for her damaged feelings. Eventually, she does take out her "jagged heart," which is now transformed into a "dick" that she wields as a weapon with which to slap her friend. Taken at symbolic value, this "dick" functions as a phallic object that stands in for the use of the empty signifier slurs deployed by her friend. In the language of Lacanian psychoanalysis, the phallus occupies a structural position within the symbolic order.[36] It does not function as a real object, or even as the object that it may symbolize. Rather, the phallus functions as a signifier that operates within the economy of desire.[37] By taking up her "dick" and using it to virtually destroy her friend, she appropriates the tools of signification that have been employed against her to articulate space for her subjective position through violence. She turns the empty signifier of the phallus back on itself, using movement and sound to support her process.

We feel the emotional force of the young girl struggling for self-definition, the physical impact of her energy as her developing body yields to anger at those who seek to denigrate her, and the strength of her resolve to thrive. Once she has vanquished her friend, her spoken text falls away, and she continues her choreographic movement in rhythm with the pulsating electronic accompaniment. After taking control of the linguistic process by which she has been abused, she pushes beyond it to further delineate her newly articulated subjectivity. Pumping her shoulders, hips, and knees with the vibrating movement that she employs throughout the performance, Okpokwasili pushes her hands forward and loosens her neck so that her limbs become more elastic. She becomes absorbed into the choreographic motion of her body's vibration. No longer affiliated with words, she communicates with the audience through movement to create an intensive, intimate space between performer and viewers. We become keenly aware of Okpokwasili's consistent, repeated motion, and are held in a moment that words do not seem to reach.

V

Okpokwasili uses physical movement to push through the borders of derivative language in order to create space for the specificity of her voice to emerge. The presence of her exhaustion in the beginning sequence of the work, indexed by both the visible sweat that drips from her face and torso at moments of physical exertion in her dancing, and her collapsing motions at the end of these intense episodes, brings the performance into a mode of exertion that goes beyond the realm of symbols. Here, we are confronted not with a performative representation of Black suffering, but with the physical presence of Okpokwasili at the point of exhaustion, on the threshold of collapse. We recognize the presence of pain in the proliferation of her sweat, which darkens her red dress in large patches as her movement attenuates. The duration of her movement further invokes this pain as we see her looking around, seemingly aware of her incessant motion but unable to control it. Indeed, we recognize throughout this sequence that Okpokwasili is performing with "restored behaviour": she is invoking the memories of pain felt collectively and personally by Black women and interpreting this material through her individual body.[38] The impact of her performance here lies partly in the way that it repeats the physical impact of those memories. She invites this pain into her bodily figure, mastering it by letting it overwhelm her through her movement. Within the framed space of her performance, her body seems to be moved by a compulsory force, and her conscious mind is separated from its pulsing, watching her own movement and also watching the audience as we look at her. We see her shape this performance of exhaustion as both "real"—to the extent that her sweat is real and her breath quickened—and also "restored," as we recognize that she is performing, and therefore ultimately in control. It is through her body's performance of physical expressions that this pain is communicated.

In her work on the nature of expressibility, Elaine Scarry asserts that pain is inherently unshareable because it resides exclusively within the body of the sufferer. Thus, "whatever pain achieves, it achieves in part through its unsharability, and it ensures this unsharability through its resistance to language."[39] The pain that is evoked by Okpokwasili's performance does indeed resist language. However, this resistance to language stems not from its inherent unsharability, as Scarry suggests, but rather its capacity to create meaning that defies linguistic expression. Okpokwasili communicates bodily pain and endurance through her physical performance in connection with the audience. This performance of pain works outside of language because it also operates ambiguously. As audience, we can read her performance of "exhaustion" and "endurance" by the signals of the presence of sweat and breath that she produces, but the designation of these linguistic descriptions is far from the complete picture. We could also say, perhaps, that the difficulty of her movement opens out into a more ecstatic release. Or that it conjures anxiety due to her performed loss of self-control. Her physical performance cannot be fully described by language because it evokes a host of complex reactions that are communicated directly by Okpokwasili's masterful shaping of her dance.

At *Bronx Gothic*'s climax, Okpokwasili's narrator brings the audience on her emotional journey inward as she confronts a foundational moment of trauma. In this moment, she witnesses her younger self in pain, and brings her two selves into contact. Now a grown woman, the narrator seeks to find her childhood friend—the mature girl who left school after she became pregnant. She describes the process of taking on her friend's identity to obtain her address from municipal authorities, and speaking to her friend's old boyfriend at the corner bodega before going to the apartment where she resides. She is waylaid by a memory of her mother's boyfriend asking her to blow smoke rings out of her mouth, and we realize that it is her mother's boyfriend who was responsible for her pregnancy. As she prepares to enter the building, her words evoke images of birth:

> Feel the water rolling in on top of you, and rolling away. You're like a newborn baby. And even with the blood and the shit and all the white stuff that comes out with the baby, you're clean. Cause the water keeps coming in. And you know what comes in with the water? Light.[40]

Despite the presence of abject fluids that attend the bodily processes of birth—shit, blood, and placenta—she remains cleansed by the water that pours over her. Upon entering the building, she encounters pools of blood that lead to the door of the apartment, and instead of finding her friend inside, the narrator witnesses a young girl having a miscarriage:

> I see the little girl bleeding in the middle of the living room. No one showed her where the pads are [...] and I'm looking at that ugly girl and I have no pads and no tampons, and I'm looking at her still as stone, 'cause it's like I'm looking in a mirror. It's like I'm looking in a mirror. And I'm so ashamed that I want to vomit. And that's not her period—it's a big bloody lump. And it's more than blood and uterine lining underneath her legs. It's not easy to clean all that shit up. How am I supposed to clean all that shit up?[41]

Okpokwasili stands in relative stillness throughout this monologue, delivering the narrative with a subdued yet intense emotional vocality that rises in intensity. At the moment of her entry into the apartment hallway, she drops to her knees, and her voice elevates to a throbbing yet controlled wail. She crawls toward the letters that have dropped to the floor and gathers them, repeating a line we have heard now at several points throughout the performance, in a singsong tone, "You'd better gather your skin, girl. Pull it together." Throughout this episode, we move with the narrator through her confrontation with her doubled subjectivity. First, as she enters the apartment building, she bears witness to her own birth and is washed clean. Moments later, she recognizes herself in the place of her best friend as she approaches her friend's apartment. By recognizing an aspect of herself as the mature girl, whom she now confronts in the living room, the two subjectivities that she has articulated throughout the performance are brought together, yet still maintain a doubled relationship. She beholds her younger self as a separate image and tries to help her as she witnesses her suffering. As she seeks the source of the blood she encounters at the doorway of the apartment building, she finds herself constituted in her own doubled image—at the site of trauma, and in pain.

VI

Okpokwasili's figuration of the Black female body in pain engages established discourses within critical race theory on the relationship between Black subjectivity and the experience of trauma. In *Bronx Gothic*, the process of discovering the self is figured as a fraught journey into the past, into the unconscious, and into communal memories that are as-yet unknown to the narrator. Her figuration of pain explores the historical link between Black female subjectivity and the experience of trauma. Historian Saidiya Hartman describes pleasure associated with the Black female body as inherently entwined with pain, because the expression of Black pleasure always already operates under threat of violence. This violence is figured within the history of social, physical, and economic oppression experienced by Black people under slavery, and is expressed as abiding pain: "Pain must be recognized in its historicity and as the articulation of a social condition of brutal constraint, extreme need, and constant violence; in other words, it is the perpetual condition of ravishment."[42]

Because pain is inextricably bound up with pleasure, bodily enjoyment is also inseparable from the ravishment and destruction of the body. Thus, the "breakdown" of the Black body as it is engaged in performance, "also illuminates the dilemma of pleasure and possession since the body broken by dance insinuates its other, its double, the body broken by the regiment of labor and (dis)possessed by the chattel principle."[43] Okpokwasili's performance of pain's expression opens from her visible and emotional breakdown as she is "debilitated" by her dance. In the epistolary narrative, her words communicate an emotional breakdown at the points where her split subjectivity, rendered as a disintegration of correspondence between the two girls, exhausts language. In these moments, Okpokwasili finds the contours of each mode of expression, pushing against the forms of both choreography and text in order to find space for her subjective voice.

These moments of rupture—in which the performer's body becomes physically fatigued and the language of friendship becomes too much to bear—serve as triggers of memory. According to Hartman, the collective trauma of domination enables performative repetition in ritual, which both facilitates the recognition of the self and acknowledges that which can never be fully recovered.[44] These breaches, which *Bronx Gothic* enacts in the physical breakdown of both Okpokwasili's body and spoken text, point to the layers of embodied memory that lie beneath the specificity of the characters' actions.

In his influential book on the relationship between memory and history, Joseph Roach describes the ways that the body enacts collective memory through performance: "The voices of the dead may speak freely now only through the bodies of the living."[45] Living bodies stage collective memory by means of performance, and these memories can serve as alternative counterparts to narrative histories produced through cultural practices. For Roach, the practice of exploring what he terms "genealogies of performance" attend to the ways that memory abides in the body and can be traced through its gesture and expression:

> Performance genealogies draw on the idea of expressive movements as mnemonic reserves, including patterned movements made and remembered by bodies, residual movements retained implicitly in images or words (or in the silences between them), and imaginary movements dreamed in minds, not prior to language but constitutive of it, a psychic rehearsal for physical actions drawn from a repertoire that culture provides.[46]

Genealogies of performance reside in *Bronx Gothic*'s expressions of physical and textual breakdown. As Okpokwasili's narrator enacts the relationship between the two versions of her younger self, she uncovers the complex layers of emotion that reside within her personal history. The various traumas that are unearthed throughout the course of the performance resonate with intensity as Okpokwasili literally stages their excavation in real time, and it is by means of performance that this residual pain and complexity is excavated.

To the extent that Okpokwasili uses dance, spoken text, and song to communicate the narrative of her embodied storytelling, she performs in the tradition of the West African griot. The word "griot" is typically translated as "praise-singer," and griots fulfill a myriad of civic and ritual duties within traditional West African societies, including genealogist, historian, diplomat, interpreter, teacher, and musician.[47] Griots hold knowledge of the past and are responsible for perpetuating cultural histories through the performance of stories, songs, and poetry of a specific culture. As master communicators, they usher both individuals and groups through ritual ceremonies that serve as transitions between phases of life, and into death: namings, initiations, courtships, marriages, civic installations, and funerals. In *Bronx Gothic*, Okpokwasili draws on the griot storytelling form to communicate the tale of a Black girl's adolescence and survival of trauma. Her narrator serves as the griot of both her own story, told through movement, song, and spoken word to the audience, and of the transition from her split subjectivity in adolescence toward the recuperation of the lost aspect of self that was injured by traumatic events. The forms of both epistolary narrative and *Bildsungsroman* are integrated within this aspect of griot storytelling. She inhabits multiple aspects of herself, told through the voices of the two girls, as a master narrator who bears herself through adolescence, and between multiple modes of discourse. After witnessing the miscarriage of her younger self, she stands at the microphone and addresses her friend—this doubled aspect of her subjectivity—as an intimate element of herself: "You are a curve in my back. You're the rough skin on my tongue. So of course I found you, even if you were hidden."[48] She then repeats the thematic dialogue that asks her interlocutor to focus on different points on her body, and to ask herself if she is awake. Okpokwasili steps slowly away from the microphone and backs into the curtain, facing the audience, as the stage lights come up gradually behind her and she eventually leaves the space. By locating this "lost" aspect of self within her own body, the narrator finally confronts the rupture induced by the traumatic events of the past, and recuperates her younger self at the site of such trauma.

In this moment, *Bronx Gothic* works against what Orlando Patterson has termed "natal alienation," the condition of relations produced by slavery that denies the slave access to his or her own cultural heritage.[49] Okpokwasili's search and eventual finding of her younger self, which was ruptured through trauma, actively creates a network of relationships among multiple aspects of her ego, as well as her identity across time. These historical entanglements are difficult to unravel, as genealogies of Black cultural heritage are obscured by natal alienation. Indeed, the tenuous relationship between obscurity and visibility is staged throughout *Bronx Gothic* as a condition of trauma structured by the subjectivity of contemporary Black girlhood. The process of discovering the self is figured as a fraught journey into the past, into the unconscious, and into communal memories that are as-yet unknown to the narrator. As the narrator revisits her past and witnesses the site of trauma, she navigates her way into the unconscious, tracing the contours of the unknowable as she abandons movement for linguistic expression, and eventually returns to the physical. In contrast to the act of viewing, which presupposes the possibility of knowing, and requires illumination, the act of feeling is predicated on the body's sense of touch, which can be carried out in darkness.

Just as Okpokwasili moves between the production of spoken language and movement, so too does she slip in and out of visibility. Here, darkness becomes the condition by which Okpokwasili can move. Navigating her way among aspects of her identity allows her to create a network of relations across her emotional and cultural history, in embodied terms. By means of her consistent temporal, physical, and formal movement, she resists any fixed position on which she can rest. Through the persistent displacement of both speech and movement in turn, Okpokwasili pushes against discursive and choreographic forms in order to create a space that permits complete freedom of movement, where body and text mingle, and roam unbound.

Notes

1. Okwui Okpokwasili, Artist in Residence talk for Artists at the Crossroads, Times Square, New York City. February 1, 2016, https://youtu.be/DkmY1BF4eZI.
2. Okwui Okpokwasili, "Artist Statement" for *Bronx Gothic*. http://mappinternational.org/blocks/view/477/.
3. Okwui Okpokwasili, *Bronx Gothic*, video, ontheboards.tv, 2014.
4. Concerning the constitution of the modern subject, the letter inhabits a curious position of the "in-between," in that it's a central aspect of the modernized forms of communication that in early modern times, but especially in the eighteenth century, reshaped the relationship between public and private spheres and formed part of eliciting the rise of bourgeois subjectivity. For more on this, see for example the chapter on social structures of the public sphere in Jürgen Habermas, *The Structural Transformation of the Public Sphere: An Inquiry into a Category of Bourgeois Society*, trans. Thomas Burger (Cambridge: MIT Press, 1989).
5. Nancy Armstrong argues that this novel further represents an important shift in the formation of the female subject within English literature, because the object of erotic desire is transferred from Pamela's body to her words. *Desire and Domestic Fiction: A Political History of the Novel* (Oxford: Oxford University Press, 1990), 13–14.
6. "Tragedy is essentially an imitation not of persons but of action and life, of happiness and misery." Aristotle, "Poetics" in *Aristotle on the Art of Poetry*, trans. Ingram Bywater (Oxford: Clarendon Press, 1920), 13a.
7. Ian Watt, *The Rise of the Novel: Studies in Defoe, Richardson and Fielding* (Berkeley: University of California Press, 1959), 176.
8. Watt, *The Rise of the Novel*, 177.
9. Watt, *The Rise of the Novel*, 189.
10. Elizabeth Heckendorn Cook, *Epistolary Bodies: Gender and Genre in the Eighteenth-Century Republic of Letters* (Stanford: Stanford University Press, 1996), 8–9.
11. Watt, *The Rise of the Novel*, 191.
12. Cook, *Epistolary Bodies*, 93.
13. Eve Kosofsky Sedgwick conceives of the act of touching as a strategic method of eschewing the dichotomy between subject and object, because touching is inherently phenomenological. "Attending to psychology and materiality at the level of affect and texture is also to enter a conceptual realm that is not shaped by lack nor by commonsensical dualities of subject versus object or of means versus ends." Eve Kosofsky Sedgwick, *Touching Feeling* (Durham: Duke University Press, 2003), 21.

14. Luce Irigaray, *To Be Two*, trans. Monique M. Rhodes and Marco F. Cocito-Monoc (New York: Routledge, 2001), 25.
15. Irigaray, *To Be Two*, 26: "Each must have the opportunity to be a concrete, corporeal and sexuate subject, rather than an abstract, neutral, fabricated, and fictitious one."
16. Gerald MacLean, "Re-siting the Subject," in *Epistolary Histories: Letters, Fiction, Culture*, eds. Amanda Gilroy and W. M. Verhoeven (Charlottesville and London: University Press of Virginia, 2000), 177.
17. "For the signifier is a unit in its very uniqueness, being by nature symbol only of an absence." Jacques Lacan, "The Seminar on 'The Purloined Letter,'" in *Yale French Studies*, vol. 48 (1972), 54.
18. Lacan, "The Seminar on 'The Purloined Letter,'" 54.
19. The protagonists in Samuel Richardson's first two epistolary novels, *Pamela* and *Clarissa*, were both the eponymous female characters. In the mid-twentieth century, the epistolary mode experienced resurgence in experimental, feminist, and collectively written texts. Janet Altman asserts that the letter form lends itself particularly well to experimental modes of writing because it encourages, "elliptical narration, subjectivity and multiplicity of points of view, interior monologue, superimposition of time levels [and] presentation of simultaneous action." Janet Altman, *Epistolarity: Approaches to a Form* (Columbus: Ohio State University Press, 1982), 25.
20. Anne Bower, *Epistolary Responses: The Letter in 20th-Century American Fiction and Criticism* (Tuscaloosa and London: The University of Alabama Press, 1997), 14.
21. Henry Louis Gates, Jr., *Signifying Monkey: A Theory of African-American Literary Criticism* (Oxford: Oxford University Press, 2011), 253. eBook.
22. Gates Jr., *Signifying Monkey*, 253.
23. Gates Jr., *Signifying Monkey*, 255.
24. Okpokwasili, *Bronx Gothic*.
25. Okwui Opokwasili, *Bronx Gothic*, video, ontheboards.tv, 2014.
26. Andrew Smith, *Gothic Literature* (Edinburgh: Edinburgh University Press, 2013) and David Punter, *The Literature of Terror: A History of Gothic Fictions from 1765 to the Present Day, Vol. 1: The Gothic Tradition* (New York: Routledge, 2013).
27. Smith, *Gothic Literature*, 102.
28. This generic refashioning has long historical underpinnings that concern the reworking of the initial narrative of the development of the white German male by African-American and feminist writers of color to assert modes of anti-hegemonic subjectivity.
29. G. B. Tennyson, "The *Bildungsroman* in Nineteenth-Century English Literature," in *Medieval Epic to the Epic Theater of Brecht: Essays in Comparative Literature*, eds. Rosario Armato and John M. Spalek (Los Angeles: University of Southern California Press, 1968), 136.
30. W. E. B. DuBois, *The Souls of Black Folk*, ed. Brent Hayes Edwards (Oxford: Oxford University Press, 2007), 8.
31. Mae G. Henderson, "Speaking in Tongues: Dialogics, Dialectics, and the Black Woman Writer's Literary Tradition," in *African American Literary Theory: A Reader*, ed. Winston Napier (New York: New York University Press, 2000), 350.

32 Henderson, "Speaking in Tongues," 354.
33 Henderson, "Speaking in Tongues," 356.
34 Hortense J. Spillers, "Mama's Baby, Papa's Maybe: An American Grammar Book," *diacritics*, vol. 17, no. 2, Culture and Countermemory: The "American" Connection (Summer, 1987), 65.
35 Okpokwasili, *Bronx Gothic*.
36 Dylan Evans, *An Introductory Dictionary of Lacanian Psychoanalysis* (London: Routledge, 1996), 142–3.
37 Jacques Lacan articulates his formulation of the phallus as signifier in a 1958 lecture at the Max-Planck Institute in Munich titled "The Signification of the Phallus." Here, he develops Freud's figuration of the penis as an object of desire into a structural position, which operates symbolically as a linguistic signifier. "The phallus is a privileged signifier of that mark in which the role of the logos is joined with the advent of desire." Jacques Lacan, "The Signification of the Phallus," in *Ecrits: A Selection*, trans. Alan Sheridan (London: Routledge, 1977), 318.
38 Richard Schechner describes "restored behavior" as a defining characteristic of performance. By enacting restored behavior, the performer acts "in/as other." "Restored behavior is 'out there,' distant from 'me.' It is separate and therefore can be 'worked on', changed, even though it has 'already happened.'" Richard Schechner, *Between Theater and Anthropology* (Philadelphia: University of Pennsylvania Press, 1985), 51, https://search.alexanderstreet.com/view/work/bibliographic_entity%7Cdocument%7C1829120?account_id=13567&usage_group_id=98342.
39 Elaine Scarry, *The Body in Pain: The Making and Unmaking of the World* (Oxford: Oxford University Press, 1985), 4.
40 Opokwasili, *Bronx Gothic*.
41 Okwui Opokwasili, *Bronx Gothic*, video, ontheboards.tv, 2014.
42 Saidiya V. Hartman, *Scenes of Subjection: Terror, Slavery, and Self-Making in Nineteenth-Century America* (New York: Oxford University Press, 1997), 51.
43 Hartman, *Scenes of Subjection*, 78.
44 Hartman, *Scenes of Subjection*, 76.
45 Joseph Roach, *Cities of the Dead: Circum-Atlantic Performance* (New York: Columbia University Press, 1996), xiii.
46 Roach, 26.
47 Thomas A. Hale, *Griots and Griottes: Master of Words and Music* (Bloomington: Indiana University Press, 1998), 18–25.
48 Okpokwasili, *Bronx Gothic*.
49 Orlando Patterson, *Slavery and Social Death: A Comparative Study* (Cambridge, MA: Harvard University Press, 1982), 5.

Appendix II
Indefiniteness, *Geschlechtslosigkeit,* Undoing, Unknowing, Unlearning

Butler | Cassin | Crépon | David-Ménard | Derrida | Deutscher | Heller-Roazen | Irigaray | Malabou | Nancy | Preciado | Sandford | Spillers | Weheliye

AUTHORS IN THIS BOOK, AS ELSEWHERE, have attempt to speak of *Geschlecht*, and in large measure struggled to define "it" across time and translation. The "having" of *Geschlecht* thus also arrives as a kind of dispossession or lack: we are assigned it, but cannot say precisely what it is. Each person feels implicated by the many entries *Geschlecht* allows or invites or demands (race, sex, kinship, kind, gender, genre, and so on), but where we belong, are suited, is left unstated, undefined.

If we have spent time addressing the potentiality of *Geschlecht* as identifiable, what about turning the discourse inside out to ask what it means to be *without Geschlecht*—to be *Geschlechtslos*? For instance, what is it to be asexual, without kin, without country, without genre; to be outside of category, or negated by what dominant classifications allow? What is it to be Black in a white society? To be a woman in patriarchy—or to be a woman *within* patriarchy: is that the same? What of the trans function for people who "cross over" from one category to another, or choose to *remain* in the crossing? What of texts and artworks that have no genre, either because they transgress established orders or because established orders allow them insufficient definition? How does negation and undoing connect to the having or discharging of power? What bindings and disjunctions exist between taxonomies of *Geschlecht* and the case-by-case, the separate being, the individual body?

All of these questions, these familiar problems of philosophy, politics, and art, have been explored at length for millennia—and yet satisfying responses remain elusive, just out of reach—or well beyond; how could we tell the difference? In the following extracts and excerpts, we may be surprised anew how, in many ways, that gap—that *Geschlechtslosigkeit*—is the reply we seek: that the indefinite, category-less, and open-ended must be part of, if not central to, our understanding of the world. We shall skirt calling such lacunae "answers," yet they do present themselves as grounds for understanding what remains problematic, and in some ways provocative about living beyond category or (comprehensive) comprehension. The proposal of the *Geschlechtslos*—or the perpetual state of *Geschlechtslosigkeit*—upsets the logic of the quest for clarity and completeness by giving an unfinished "non-answer," or an "undoing" of an answer where there might otherwise be (according to a different system of assessment and value) a clear, succinct statement of facts. By acts of undoing, we arrive in the realms of unknowing and unlearning.

Appendix II pursues *Geschlechtslosigkeit* along at least two prominent analytical registers: where languages are unsettled and undone by their movement across (*trans*) zones of difference (e.g., dwelling in the impasses between language, and the indefiniteness of meaning that follows); and the way human bodies affect their own translations—confirming once again that *homo sapiens* is not a thing but a process, an interminable "becoming" that yields only a perpetual transition, and thus an existence constrained by endless translation (whether of DNA or dictionary, logic or lexicon, family or pharmacopeia). In these passages, as elsewhere in the volume, we pause at the border crossing, at the margin, at those liminal spaces that declare their "in between." Line by line, we are summoned to acknowledge how the *Geschlechtslos* entails a life lived in ellipsis.

OSCAR JANSSON AND DAVID LAROCCA

* * *

The place of indefinite names and verbs in Aristotle's doctrine of language is modest, yet it is precisely defined. When the philosopher calls to mind such expressions as "non-man" and "non-just," it is to clarify related logical matters, such as the theory of contradiction and the types of contrariety, and to account for the relations among well-formed statements [...] Behind the systematic inquiry into the regularities of logical form, however, there lurked a persistent question: what does it mean for a term to be "indefinite"?

Daniel Heller-Roazen, "Varieties of Indefiniteness," *No One's Ways: An Essay on Infinite Naming* (New York: Zone Books, 2017), 33.

APPENDIX II

> [...] the universal is a strategy rather than a value per se, definitive and ultimate; or, even, the best universal is complex, many sided, and relative.
>
> Barbara Cassin, *Sophistical Practice: Toward a Consistent Relativism* (New York: Fordham University Press, 2014), 237.

Of sex, one can readily remark, yes, Heidegger speaks as little as possible, perhaps he has never spoken of it. Perhaps he has never said anything, by that name or the names under which we recognize it, about the "sexual-relation," "sexual-difference," or indeed about "man-and-woman." This silence, therefore, is easily remarked. [...] A transitive and significant silence (he has silenced sex), one that belongs, as he says about a certain *Schweigen* ("*hier in der transitiven Bedeutung gesagt*"), to the path of a speech he seems to interrupt. But what are the places of this interruption? Where does the silence work on that discourse? And what are the forms and determinable contours of that non-said?

> Jacques Derrida, "Geschlecht I: Sexual Difference, Ontological Difference," trans. Ruben Bevezdivin and Elizabeth Rottenberg, *Psyche: Inventions of the Other*, Vol. II, eds. Peggy Kamuf and Elizabeth Rottenberg (Stanford: Stanford University Press, 2008), 7, 9.

Long ago, H. A. Wolfson proposed a luminous reconstruction of the Aristotelian typology of absent things.[1] He showed that one may distinguish among three types of logical terms in the philosopher's works, which would seem to imply three conditions of non-being. There are, first, the expressions employed in "negation" (*apophasis*), in the sense that Aristotle gives to this term. This is the denial that a certain predicate may be attributed to some subject, or, metaphysically stated, that a certain property belongs to some substance. To evoke an Aristotelian sentence discussed in detail by Aristotle's greatest early commentator, Alexander of Aphrodisias, in the late second or early third century, one may take the following utterance as exemplary of such "negation": "The wall does not see [*oukh' horai*]." In this case, the verbal predicate, "seeing," is denied to the nominal subject, "the wall," and the sign of the negation is the word "not" (*oukh*), placed before the predicate.[2]

Such statements of negation may be distinguished from assertions including terms that express a "privation" (*sterēsis*). A corresponding example of such a statement may be simply given: "The blind man does not see [*oukh' horai*]."[3] In its grammatical shape, such a predicate is indistinguishable from that attributed to the wall; but for Aristotle, a fundamental logical and metaphysical difference separates them. The not seeing of the wall is "negative" in structure; the not seeing of the blind man, by contrast, is "privative." The negative term signifies the absence of a certain property in a subject, even where that subject would never be expected to possess it.

It is in this sense that one may assert that the wall "does not see," without suggesting that the situation might be otherwise. The privative term does more; it suggests that the subject has been "deprived" of some attribute that it might also have possessed.[4] In this case, one asserts, in other words, that a property is positively "lacking."[5]

> Daniel Heller Roazen, "Varieties of Indefiniteness," *No One's Ways* (2017), 34.

From the moment that I was told that I must have a heart transplant, every sign could have vacillated, every marker changed: without reflection, of course, and even without identifying the slightest action or permutation. There is simply the physical sensation of a void already open [*déjà ouvert*] in my chest, along with a kind of apnea wherein nothing, strictly nothing, even today, would allow me to disentangle the organic, the symbolic, and the imaginary, or the continuous from the interrupted—the sensation was something like one breath, now pushed across a cavern, already imperceptibly half-open and strange; and, as though within a single representation, the sensation of passing over a bridge, while still remaining on it.

If my heart was giving up and going to drop me, to what degree was it an organ of "mine," my "own"? Was it even an organ? For several years already, I'd been acquainted with my heart's arrhythmia and palpitations—nothing really that significant (these were the measurements [*chiffres*] of machines, like the "ejection fraction," whose name I liked): not an organ, not a deep red, muscular mass with pipes sticking out of it, which I now suddenly had to picture to myself [*me figurer*]. Not "my heart" endlessly beating, as absent to me till now as the soles of my feet walking.

It was becoming a stranger to me, intruding through its defection—almost through rejection, if not dejection.

> Jean-Luc Nancy, *L'intrus*, trans. Susan Hanson (East Lansing: Michigan State University, 2002 [2000]), 3.

Let's face it. I am a marked woman, but not everybody knows my name.

> Hortense J. Spillers, "Mama's Baby, Papa's Maybe: An American Grammar Book," *diacritics*, vol. 17.2 (Summer 1987), 65.

The English term "sex" can reasonably be translated by *sexe* in French, as both languages define sexuality as "the collection of psychological and physiological notions" that characterize it. However, it is sometimes inaccurate to translate "sex" by *sexe*, given that in English "sex" is in many circumstances contrasted with "gender," which is not the case in French.

> Monique David-Ménard and Penelope Deutscher, "Gender," *Dictionary of Untranslatables: A Philosophical Lexicon*, ed. Barbara Cassin, trans. eds. Emily

Apter, Jacques Lezra, and Michael Wood (Princeton: Princeton University Press, 2014), 375.

The translation of "gender" into German was more difficult, since the word *Geschlecht* operates as both biological sex and social gender. This term enforced a strong cultural presumption that the various cultural expressions of gender not only followed causally and necessarily from an original sex, but that gender was in some ways mired in sex, indissociable from it, bound up with it as a single unity. [...] Like *genus* in Swedish, which implies species-being, so *Geschlecht* in German implied not only a natural kind, but a mode of natural ordering that served the purposes of the reproduction of the species.

Judith Butler, "Gender and Gender Trouble," *Dictionary of Untranslatables* (2014), 377.

[... Each] language constitutes an autonomous geography, a net for understanding the world in its own way, a net to catch the world, create its world (something like logology again).

Barbara Cassin, *Sophistical Practice* (2014), 10.

W. E. B. DuBois predicted as early as 1903 that the twentieth century would be the century of the "color line." We could add to this spatiotemporal configuration another thematic of analogously terrible weight: if the "black woman" can be seen as a particular figuration of the split subject that psychoanalytic theory posits, then this century marks the site of "its" profoundest revelation. The problem before us is deceptively simple: the terms enclosed in quotation marks in the preceding paragraph isolate overdetermined nominative properties. Embedded in bizarre axiological ground, they demonstrate a sort of telegraphic coding; they are markers so loaded with mythical prepossession that there is no easy way for the agents buried beneath them to come clean. In that regard, the names by which I am called in the public place render an example of signifying property plus. In order for me to speak a truer word concerning myself, I must strip down through layers of attenuated meanings, made an excess in time, over time, assigned by a particular historical order, and there await whatever marvels of my own inventiveness. The personal pronouns are offered in the service of a collective function.

Hortense J. Spillers, "Mama's Baby, Papa's Maybe" (1987), 65.

As Heidegger reminds us, in a text that Derrida has commented upon at length, *Geschlecht* is impressively multivocal. It refers to race but also to kinship, generation, and gender, as well as the notion of sex, which divides all of the former: "The word equally means the human species [*das Menschengeschlecht*], in the sense of humanity [*Menschheit*], and species in the sense of tribe, stock, or family [*Stamme, Sippen, und Familien*], all of which is further intersected by the generic duality of the sexes [*das Zweifache der Geschlechter*]."

> Marc Crépon, "Geschlecht," *Dictionary of Untranslatables* (2014), 394.

The distinction between "sex" and "gender," which was laid out by Stoller in 1968 and adopted by feminist thought in the early 1970s, represents for this movement a political and sociological argument in the name of which we must distinguish the physiological and the psychological aspects of sex, without which we would land in a biological essentialism with normative import regarding sexual identity.

> Monique David-Ménard and Penelope Deutscher, "Gender," *Dictionary of Untranslatables* (2014), 375.

The idea of racializing assemblages, in contrast, construes race not as a biological or cultural classification but as a set of sociopolitical processes that discipline humanity into full humans, not-quite-humans, and nonhumans.

> Alexander G. Weheliye, *Habeas Viscus: Racializing Assemblages, Biopolitics, and Black Feminist Theories of the Human* (Durham: Duke University Press, 2014), 12.

Aristotle makes no mention of indefinite terms, either by name or by example. One can only wonder where exactly he would situate their specific variety of non-determination. What is lacking to the "non-man"? What may one deny to his imaginable non-qualities?

> Daniel Heller-Roazen, "Varieties of Indefiniteness," *No One's Ways* (2017), 36.

"Sex" is not so much the fact of the exclusive division of the human species into male and female as the *presumption* of this fact, and, importantly, the presumption of the *efficacy* of this fact. That is, the popular concept of "sex"—casually employed by most modern European philosophers at one time or another (consider, for example, Rousseau's remark in *A Discourse on the Origin of Inequality*, "Aimables et vertueuses citoyennes, le sort de vorte sexe sera toujours de gouverner le nôtre," or Locke in *Some Thoughts Concerning Education*, "The principal aim of my Discourse is, how a young Gentleman should be brought up from his Infancy [...] where the difference of Sex requires different treatment, 'twill be no hard matter to distinguish")—is constituted by the presumption that there just is a naturally determined sex duality (the exclusive division into male and female) and that this duality is also naturally determining.

> Stella Sandford, "'Sex' and 'Sexual Difference,'" *Dictionary of Untranslatables* (2014), 972.

There is nothing to discover in nature; there is no hidden secret. We live in a punk hypermodernity: it is no longer about discovering the hidden truth in nature; it is about the necessity to specify the cultural, political, and technological processes through which the body as artifact acquires natural status.

> Paul Beatriz Preciado, *Testo Junkie: Sex, Drugs, and Biopolitics in the Pharmacopornographic Era*, trans. Bruce Benderson (New York: The Feminist Press at the City University of New York, 2013 [2008]), 35.

First there was "sex" understood as a biological given, and then came "gender," which interpreted or constructed that biological given into a social category. This story was, at least, the one that held sway as feminist anthropologists (Ortner, Rubin) sought to distinguish between an order of nature and an order of culture. Nature was understood to come first, even though no one thought one could identify the scene of nature apart from its cultural articulation. Its "firstness" was then ambiguously temporal and logical. The formulation helped to make sense of important feminist propositions such as the one made by Beauvoir in *The Second Sex*: "One is not born, but rather becomes a woman." If one is not born a woman, then one is born something else, and "sex" is the name for that something else we are prior to what we become.

> Judith Butler, "Gender and Gender Trouble," *Dictionary of Untranslatables* (2014), 377.

The concept of neutrality seems very general at first. It is a matter of reducing or subtracting, by means of that neutralization, every anthropological, ethical, or metaphysical predetermination so as to keep nothing but a relation to itself, a bare relation, to the Being of its being. This is the minimal relation to itself as relation to Being, the relation that the being which we are, as questioning, maintains with itself and with its own proper essence. This relation to self is not a relation to an "ego" or to an individual, of course. Thus *Dasein* designates the being that, "in a definite sense," is not "indifferent" to its own essence, or to whom its own being is not indifferent. Neutrality, therefore, is first of all the neutralization of everything but the naked trait of this relation to self, of this interest for its own being in the widest sense of the word "interest." The latter implies an interest or a precomprehensive opening in the meaning of Being and in the questions organized around it. And yet!

And yet this neutrality will be rendered explicit by a leap, without transition and in the very next item (second guiding principle) in the direction of *sexual* neutrality, and even of a certain *sexlessness* (*Geschlechtslosigkeit*) of being-there. The leap is surprising. If Heidegger wanted to offer examples of determinations to be left out of the analytic of *Dasein*, especially of anthropological traits to be neutralized, he had many to choose from. Yet he begins with, and in fact never gets beyond, sexuality, or more precisely sexual difference. Sexual difference thus holds a privilege and seems to belong in the first place—if one follows the statements according to their logical connections—to that "factual concretion" that the analytic of *Dasein* should begin by neutralizing. If the neutrality of the term *Dasein* is essential, it is precisely because the interpretation of this being—which *we* are—must be carried out *prior to* and *outside of* a concretion of this kind. The *first* example of "concretion" would then be the belonging to one or the other of the sexes. Heidegger does not doubt that they are two: "This neutrality *also* indicates that *Dasein* is neither of the two sexes [*keines von beiden Geschlechtern ist*]."

Jacques Derrida, "*Geschlecht* I: Sexual Difference, Ontological Difference" (2008), 11–12.

There is nothing to discover in sex or in sexual identity; there is no *inside*. The truth about sex is not a disclosure.

Paul Beatriz Preciado, *Testo Junkie* (2013), 35.

[... If] one only understood gender as the cultural meanings that sex acquires in any given social context, then gender was still linked with sex, and could not be conceptualized without it. Some feminists such as Elizabeth Grosz argued that if gender is the cultural interpretation of sex, then sex is treated as a given, and there is no way then to ask how "sex" is made or what various cultural forms "sex" may assume in different contexts. Indeed, if one started to talk about the cultural meanings of "sex," it appeared that one was talking rather about gender.

Judith Butler, "Gender and Gender Trouble," *Dictionary of Untranslatables* (2014), 377.

We now know that to speak of "genders" is no longer to speak of "sexes." Consequently we must accept the idea that feminism can now be understood as a *féminisme sans femme*, a feminism without women. Woman as a predicate is no longer an obvious given, if in fact it ever was. So if the feminine has a "meaning," it is in as much as the permission to question the identity of woman follows from the deconstruction and displacement of this identity.

This situation also impacts the supposed integrity of the concept of "sexual difference," for to say that gender is constructed is to question difference understood as binary. There are not just two genders; there is a multiplicity of genders. Masculine and feminine can refer to several of these gender identities at once, without referring to originary anatomical or social givens.

> Catherine Malabou, *Changing Difference: The Feminine and the Question of Philosophy*, trans. Carolyn Shread (Cambridge: Polity Press, 2011 [2009]), 5–6.

Whether one speaks of neutrality or sexlessness (*Neutralität, Geschlechtslosigkeit*), the words strongly emphasize a negativity that manifestly runs counter to what Heidegger is trying thus to mark. It is not a matter here of linguistic or grammatical signs at the surface of a meaning that, for its part, remains untouched. By means of such manifestly negative predicates, one must be able to read what Heidegger does not hesitate to call a "positivity [*Positivität*]," a richness, and even, in a heavily charged code, a "potency [*Mächtigkeit*]." This clarification suggests that the sexless neutrality does not desexualize; on the contrary, its *ontological* negativity is not deployed with respect to *sexuality itself* (which it would instead liberate), but with respect to the marks of difference, or more precisely to *sexual duality*. There would be no *Geschlechtslosigkeit* except with respect to the "two"; sexlessness would be determined as such only to the degree that sexuality is immediately understood as binarity or sexual division.

> Jacques Derrida, "*Geschlecht* I: Sexual Difference, Ontological Difference" (2008), 14.

Emphasizing the difference between man and woman leads to a new consideration of their carnal approach and union.

If both become by linking themselves to a vertical transcendence appropriate to their gender, there is another transcendence between them. For those who are faithful to their own gender, this horizontal transcendence cannot be overcome. The conflict which arises from the appropriation of the freedom of the other no longer makes sense between those who love each other: desire grows from an irreducible alterity.

The other is and remains transcendent to me through a body, through intentions and words foreign to me: "you who are not and will never be me or mine" are transcendent to me in body and in words, in so far as you are an incarnation that cannot be appropriated by me, lest I should suffer the alienation of my freedom. The will to possess you corresponds to a solitary and solipsistic dream which forgets that your consciousness and mine do not obey the same necessities.

[...] It is not necessary to bestow upon the other a capital letter, an excessively quantitative valuation, in order to make this other's transcendence appear. Such a valuation places transcendence beyond you, where it annuls and repudiates you as *you*, you-other for I-me. This capitalization of the Other paralyzes us by means of a fictitious freedom, by means of an absence from ourselves, extasies from our incarnation. In fact, the consciousness represented by this "O" remains exterior to a language which is made flesh in you, in me, in us. Before being law or truth exterior to us, "consciousness outside of us", as Sartre writes, language should make our body and our history into a single subjectivity, possibly in relationship with the subjectivity of the other. Does language not exceed its own power, truth, ethicality, as long as it is not the way for being I in me and I with you?

Luce Irigaray, *To Be Two*, trans. Monique M. Rhodes and Marco F. Cocito-Monoc (New York: Routledge and The Athlone Press, 2001), 18–19.

I have—Who?—this "I" is precisely the question, the old question: what is this enunciating subject? Always foreign to the subject of its own utterance; necessarily intruding upon it, yet ineluctably its motor, shifter, or heart—I, therefore, received the heart of another, now nearly ten years ago. It was a transplant, grafted on. My own heart (as you've gathered, it is entirely a matter of the "proper," of being one, or one's "own"—or else it is not in the least and, properly speaking, there is nothing to understand, no mystery, not even a question: rather, as the doctors prefer to say, there is the simple necessity [*la simple évidence*] of a transplantation)—my own heart in fact was worn out, for reasons that have never been clear. Thus to live, it was necessary to receive another's, an other, heart.

Jean-Luc Nancy, *L'Intrus* (2002), 2.

Wonder is the passion of difference; this difference is neither undetermined nor asexual. Irigaray's analyses push the Cartesian view further by viewing wonder precisely as the opening to gender difference. Even if we never wonder at anything other than difference and even if wonder is the ontological and theoretical passion *par excellence*—Being is the wonder of all beings—in order for this difference to touch us, it must be inscribed within bodies since it is bodies that initially differentiate beings. The inscription of difference in bodies bears a certain mark, namely, gender. The other strikes us first through gender. Or rather, what is other in all others is gender, which is neither determined nor judged, since wonder suspends predication. Gender can only appear through its difference from another gender. Consequently, wonder, "the point of passage,"[6] allows the sexes to maintain a degree of autonomy grounded in their difference; it thus offers a space of freedom and desire, a possibility of separation or alliance. Considering the other with admiring wonder, in the Cartesian sense, it is impossible to assimilate them: in wonder, the other is "not yet assimilated or disassimilated as known," he or she is not absorbed, incorporated, or appropriated. "Wonder is a mourning for the self as an autarchic entity; whether this mourning is triumphant or melancholy. Wonder must be the advent or the event of the other. The beginning of a new story?"[7]

Genders cannot substitute for one another nor be assimilated to each other; they keep their secret. Since wonder does not have an opposite, it remains open, as an infinite difference that generosity extends: "Wonder constitutes an opening prior to and following that which surrounds, enlaces."[8] In this non-reductive apprehension of the sexes, Irigaray sees a way to clear an ethical space of recognition of the feminine: the feminine as the affective union between Being and sex(es).

The admiration of wonder is in fact structurally linked to the feminine in so far as it reveals the ontological opening as a *maternity*. Because it is the *first* of all passions, it is the mother of all desire. Thus Descartes "situates woman in the place of the first and last passion."[9] The mother-passion, the first woman and last passion (last because it is the most complete, the most accomplished), conditions all meetings between genders, whether they are different or the same. And so, because all subjects are able to wonder, all subjects are feminine.

Catherine Malabou, *Changing Difference* (2011), 12–13.

In other words, in the historic outline of dominance, the respective subject-positions of "female" and "male" adhere to no symbolic integrity.

Hortense J. Spillers, "Mama's Baby, Papa's Maybe" (1987), 66.

Modern humanity, at least since the era of Descartes, has made the wish for survival and immortality an element of a general program of "mastery and possession of nature." In this way, humanity has programmed an increasing strangeness of "nature." It has revived the absolute strangeness of the double enigma of mortality and immortality. What religions used to represent, modern humanity has exposed to the power [*puissances*] of a technology that postpones the end in all the senses of the word. In prolonging the end, technology displays an absence of ends: which life should be prolonged, and to what end? To defer death is thus also to exhibit and underscore it.

Only it must be said that humanity has never been ready for any form of this question, and that humanity's non-preparation for death is but the blow and injustice of death itself.

Jean-Luc Nancy, *L'Intrus* (2002), 6–7.

Ammonius teaches that, for the purposes of logic, a term such as "non-man" cannot be viewed as a name, at least in the primary sense that philosophers attribute to that type of expression:

> A name signifies one nature, that of the thing named. Yet each such vocal sound [as an indefinite name] destroys one thing, namely, what is signified by the name said without the negative <particle>, and also introduces all the other things beside that, both those which are and those which are not. For non-man is not just said of a man, but also of a horse or dog, or of a goat-stag or centaur, and of absolutely all things which are or are not. For this reason he [Aristotle] bids us call them, this whole class, "indefinite names": "names," on the one hand, because ... they signify one thing in a way, namely everything beside the definite thing considered as one, e.g. "non-man" signifies everything besides man as being one in just this respect, that all have in common their not being just what a man is; but "indefinite" because what is signified by them does not signify the particular existence of any thing, which is the rule among names, but rather a non-existence which applies equally to things which are and which are not [*aorista de, dioti to hyp'autōn sēmainomenon oukh' hyparxin tina pragmatos sēmainei, hoper tois onomasin ethos, all'anuparxian ousi te homoiōs kai mē ousin epharmozousan*].[10]

Aristotle himself had not explicitly treated the question of whether a term such as non-man signifies "the particular existence of any thing" or a "non-existence." Yet it is the Aristotelian terminology that allows this metaphysical distinction to be drawn. Ammonius reasons in terms of negation and privation. He supposes that there are certain negative expressions that may be truly predicated, even when they signify properties that do not exist; the example is the wall that "does not see." Then, as he knows well, there are terms signifying privations, such as that of which one makes use in stating that the blind man "does not see"; in this case, the validity of the term depends on a state of virtual possession.[11] Recalling the distinction between the implications of negation and privation, Ammonius resolves an old problem by a single gesture: he sets indefinite names among negations. He then introduces a new specification. Whereas an ordinary negative term merely denies a certain quality, a "transposed" designation, as he defines it, has a double function. By its "non-," it first "destroys one thing." Then, from that initial elimination, it "introduces" a panoply of non-existences: "everything beside the definite thing" that has been evoked. For Ammonius, an indefinite name thus un-names and names at once. The term "non-man" indicates that the subject of which it is predicated is "not man", even as it conjures up the indistinct nature that is common to horse and dog, goat-stag and centaur.

Ammonius appears to have drawn the elements for his argument from a remark made by Aristotle concerning indefinite verbs, rather than names. Discussing such predicates as "non-ails [or 'does-not-ail']" and "non-recovers [or 'does-not-recover']," Aristotle had stated that such verbs "hold indifferently of anything, whether existent or non-existent" (*homoiōs eph' hotououn hyparkhei, kai ontos kai mē ontos*).[12] If "non-recovers" can signify both something existent and something non-existent, the commentator seems to have reasoned, so, too, may "non-man" signify both a real and an imaginary animal; it can, then, designate "absolutely all things," with the exception of "man." The examples Ammonius offers of such an unlimited range of things, however, belie his claim. Despite their real and imaginary diversity, horse, dog, goat-stag, and centaur, although admittedly both existent and non-existent, share a common trait. They belong to the same genus of which "man" is a species. They are all, quite simply, animals. "Absolutely all things" might well have included a stranger collection; its members could have contained among them such things as plants, numbers, Athens, and propositions. The excess of Ammonius' "deflected" name seems, therefore, less than absolute. "Non-man" may "destroy" the signification of "man," but it nevertheless appears to preserve the unity of a single genus. As R. Petrilli has remarked, the Greek commentator has, perhaps unwillingly, introduced a "restriction" on the rule that he proposes.[13] His semantic "non-determination," however vast its potential field of reference, remains obstinately, if tacitly, determinate.

In this respect, Ammonius' treatment concords with the two monuments of the late antique philosophy of language that are Boethius' *Commentaries on On Interpretation*.[14] Completed in the second decade of the sixth century, these works were to become vastly influential in the parts of Europe in which Latin remained in use. For centuries, they accompanied Boethius' own translation of Aristotle's first books on the rules of reasoning, which every student pupil of philosophy, from the Middle Ages through the Renaissance, would study. Like Ammonius, who was his contemporary, Boethius explains that, according to Aristotle, an indefinite name signifies by effecting a process of semantic "removal." As Boethius writes in his first commentary on the Aristotelian treatise, "He who says non-man" removes 'man' [*Qui vero dicit non-homo hominem tollit*]."[15] In his more extended second interpretation, he likewise declares: "What is meant by 'non-man' is whatever is outside 'man,' once 'man' has been annulled [*Sublatio enim homine quidquid praeter hominem est. hoc significat non-homo*]."[16] Boethius' remarks make clear that he would accept Ammonius' thesis that an indefinite name possesses a status close to that of the negative term, which siginifies "a non-existence which applies equally to things which are not." As if to illustrate this point, Boethius offers, as a first example of such a name of a "non-man," "Sulla," the designation of the historic Roman dictator; a "man," one might reason, who, being long dead, is "no man" now.[17] Yet

Boethius also takes a further step, for he suggests that an indefinite term's meaning points beyond the genus to which its correspondingly definite name pertains. For Boethius, *non-homo* can be said not only of a dead man, or an animal, real or imaginary, but also "of a stone, or of a log of wood, or of other things [*de lapide vel de ligno vel de aliis*]."[18]

For this reason, Boethius explains, there was once a debate "among the ancients," as to whether such a term could be called a "name" (*nomen*) in any sense. One party maintained that, to be a name, an expression must possess a "well-delimited meaning" (*est circumscriptivae significationis*), "definitely" (*definite*) signifying whatever it is that it designates. It is certain that, by such standards, *non-homo* cannot be called a *nomen*. A second party, however, stretched the linguistic and logical category of the name, distinguishing between the *nomen* in this primary and simple sense (*simpliciter*) and the *nomen* in a secondary acceptation. This group reasoned that, when grasped in an attenuated form, the category of name applies to any term that signifies without reference to time (or tense), even if such signification occurs "indefinitely" (*indefinite*).[19] Boethius' own doctrine combines these two positions. He holds fast to the classical theory that, strictly speaking, "every name definitely signifies the thing it names."[20] For the philosopher, if not the grammarian, therefore, "non-man" cannot be considered a real name. Yet Boethius admits that, in a secondary meaning, one may also speak of names when evoking expressions that signify "indefinitely," by means of an act of "removal" and "annulment."

Daniel Heller-Roazen, "Varieties of Indefiniteness," *No One's Ways* (2017), 38–41.

Notes

1 Harry Austryn Wolfson, "Infinite and Privative Judgments in Aristotle, Averroes and Kant," *Philosophy and Phenomenological Research*, vol. 8, no. 2 (1947), 173–87, reprinted in *Studies in the History of Philosophy and Religion*, eds. Isadore Twersky and George H. Williams (Cambridge: Harvard University Press, 1973–7), vol. 2, 542. For a more recent study of Aristotle's theory of "negations," see Allan T. Bäck, *Aristotle's Theory of Predication* (Leiden/Boston/Cologne: E.J. Brill, 2000), 199–227.
2 For Alexander's commentary, see *Alexandri Aphrodiensis in Aristotelis Metaphysica Commentaria* (= *Commentaria in Aristotelem graeca I*), ed. Michael Hayduck (Berlin: Reimer, 1891), 327, 18–20; English in Alexander of Aphrodisias, *On Aristotle's Metaphysics IV*, trans. Arthur Madigan (Ithaca: Cornell University Press, 1993), 122. The commentary refers to *Metaphysics IV*, 2, 1004a 10–16.
3 See Aristotle, *Categories* X, 10a 26–12b 5.

4 See Aristotle's discussion of privation in *Metaphysics* V, 1022b22–1022b32.
5 In this sense, privation is, as Aristotle famously remarks, like an "idea": see *Physics* B 183 b18–20. Cf. Heidegger, "Vom Wesen und Begriff der Φυσις," in *Gemsatausgabe* I, vol. 9: *Wegmarken* (Frankfurt am Main: V. Klostermann, 1976), 294–5.
6 Irigaray, *Ethics of Sexual Difference*, 75.
7 Irigaray, *Ethics of Sexual Difference*, 75.
8 Irigaray, 81–2. Irigaray connects the first passion of the *Treatise*, wonder (*admiration*), to the last, generosity. Wonder is the passion of difference, while generosity is the passion of the same. But generosity is not, for all that, a reduction to the identical, since it involves seeing in the other the universality of the opening to difference: "Those who have this understanding and this feeling about themselves [generous self-esteem] are easily convinced that every other man can also have them about himself, because there is nothing therein that depends on others." Descartes, *Passions of the Soul*, art. 54, 104.
9 See Irigaray, *Ethics of Sexual Experience*, 80.
10 *Ammonius*, 42.1–8; English in *On Atistotle's "On Interpretation"*, 1–8, 50.
11 The qualification is important, for it allows one to avoid the fallacious conclusion that, by virtue of the law of the excluded middle, if it is false that "The wall is blind," it must be true that "The wall is not blind." Such an inference would be valid only if "blind" could be predicated of anything whatsoever; but to field of application of such a predicate is limited to such subjects as could, by nature, be said to possess the corresponding positive predicate ("seeing").
12 *De interpretatione* 3, 16b 15–16; English in Barnes, *The Complete Works of Aristotle*, vol. 1, 3. See L. M. De Rijk, "The Logic of Indefinite Names in Boethius, Abelard, Duns Scotus and Radulphus Brito," in *Aristotle's Peri hermeneias in the Latin Middle Ages: Essays on the Commentary Tradition*, eds. H. A. G. Braakhuis and C. H. Kneepkens (Groningen: Ingenium Publishers, 2003), 207–33, esp. 213–16.
13 Raffaella Petrilli, *Temps et détermination dans la grammaire et la philosophie anciennes* (Munster: Nodus Publikationen, 1997), 26.
14 On the commentaries, see James Shiel, "Boethius's Commentaries on Aristotle," *Mediaeval and Renaissance Studies*, vol. 4 (1958): 217–44, esp. 228–34.
15 Anicius Manlius Severinus Boethius, *Commentarii in librum Aristotelis Peri hermeneias*, ed. Karl Meiser (Leipzig: Teubner, 1887–80), vol. I, 52.15.
16 Boethius, *Commentarii in librum Aristotelis Peri hermeneias*, vol. 2, 62, 14–16.
17 This translation follows Migne's edition, rather than Meiser's, as confirmed by a reading of the manuscript proposed by H. A. G. Braakhuis: see De Rijk "The Logic of Indefinite Names," 212.
18 Boethius, *Commentarii*, 62, 11.
19 Boethius, *Commentarii*, 62, 21–9.
20 Boethius, *Commentarii*, 62, 16–18: *omne enim nomen ... definite id significant quod nominatur.*

5

Collapsing the Gender/Genre Distinction: On Transgressions of Category in Woolf's *Orlando*

Oscar Jansson

I

WRITING IN HER DIARY on November 7, 1928, Virginia Woolf confessed to have grown "two inches and a half in the public view." The reason was that her new book, *Orlando: A Biography*, had quickly become a popular success and far out-sold her previous work. By Quentin Bell's account, *To the Lighthouse* had sold less than four thousand copies since its publication in May the previous year. *Orlando* sold more than eight thousand in the first six months, causing an economic and popular breakthrough for Woolf—and, as she wrote, a noticeably increased public stature.[1] In early fall, however, all that seemed impossible. In September she complained that orders for the new book were scarce—mainly due to the obtrusive generic marker of the subtitle. "No one wants biography," the booksellers said. It didn't much matter that Miss Ritchie, the Hogarth Press market liaison, interjected that it was a novel.[2]

To be sure, *Orlando* is no standard biography. It is based on Vita Sackville-West, Woolf's friend and lover, and is "life writing" in the sense of being intended as a portrait of her.[3] One could even argue the subtitle should read "writing Vita," through a tongue-in-cheek etymology between the Greek "βιογραφια" (*biographia*), the Latin meaning of her name, and plain English. But as Orlando lives for more than three hundred years while aging only twenty, and as s/he experiences a seemingly magical sex change halfway through the story, it is far from out of bounds to say that the book takes some liberties regarding factualness and reality. From a formal and generic view, it is *more* than a written life.

Neither were Miss Ritchie's claims entirely true, however, for while *Orlando* dislocates the conventional strictures of biography, it also disqualifies established notions of the novel. Given the variability often ascribed to the latter this might seem too bold a claim. But if measured against "the most hybrid of literary forms" (as Terry Eagleton calls the novel), or when positioned between History and Poetry (as E. M. Forster thought it to be), or even when considered as the sole literary form that can envelope the rift between Man and the World in Modernity (as Lukàcs would have it do), *Orlando* both *is* and *does* something more.[4] This curious fact is evident in Woolf's critical reception, where the book is often found to be the odd one out among her works, and not least found distinctly different from Erich Auerbach's canonical exegesis of perspective and time in *To the Lighthouse*.[5] The book has even been omitted from a number of major studies. John Batchelor, for example, precludes *Orlando* from consideration in *Virginia Woolf: The Major Novels*, as does Mitchell A. Leaska in *The Novels of Virginia Woolf*; the latter with the motivation that "its scope, direction, and texture are aesthetically so different from the novels themselves."[6] There is something quite telling in that phrase, *the novels themselves*, and the proclamation that *Orlando* is different, somehow.

Illustrating the same fact, Nigel Nicolson has famously pointed out that *Orlando*'s background in the personal, highly emotional affair between Woolf and Sackville-West means that it is not just a novel-biography, but "the longest and most charming love letter in literature."[7] Equally important are the critical readings where the book is seen as a palpably intellectual and impersonal pamphlet on gender roles and sexuality. Then there is the book's partly elegiac, partly satirical function as cultural and literary history, rendered through Orlando's own poetical exploits, his/her encounters with the canonical figures of English Literature, and the elaborate emulations of the literary conventions of the historical times the story moves through. And in each case—the biographical, the political, and the historical—there are signals of a metapoetical register that underlines a self-referential concern in the story as such; of how the formal matters in presenting the facts of Orlando's life are interesting in themselves. This latter aspect explicitly ties the book as a whole to a problematic of the divide between Fiction and Truth, Life and Literature—well beyond the confines of "novel" or "biography." And in doing so, the metapoetical also suggests that all of it be viewed from a critical distance, with a sizeable pinch of salt.

Given this complex mixture of literary conventions—or, perhaps, the complicated disregard of their interrelations—it is unsurprising that upon finishing the book, Woolf took a mockingly ironic stance about its generic identity. "Anyhow I'm glad to be quit this time of writing 'a novel,'" she wrote in her diary, "and hope never to be accused of it again."[8] In November 1925, while still working on *To the Lighthouse*, she wrote Sackville-West in a similar vein and asked her to invent a new name for her writings: "Thinking it over, I see I cannot, never could, never shall write a novel. What then, to call it?"[9] And in the short essay "What is a Novel?", first published in 1927, Woolf called for the destruction of the "imaginary but still highly potent bogey" of the seemingly hegemonic generic rubric; *the novel*. Significantly, in that text she also asked that writers themselves should define their work and specify them as chronicles, documents, rhapsodies, fantasies, or dreams.[10]

Or as biography, one might add, but it's already been pointed out that it doesn't really do more to cover *Orlando* than "novel" does. One could perhaps use Alistair Fowler's distinction between genre, subgenre, and mode, and call it a "satirical *Künstlerroman*," hinting at the artistic ambitions of both the actual Vita, the fictional Orlando, and Woolf herself, not least as exemplified by the book's metapoetical digressions.[11] The problem with that type of generic hierarchy, however, is firstly that it actualizes a narrow set of narrative conventions whose bounds *Orlando* readily transgresses. Trying to delineate the book's plot or kernel events in connection to novelistic genre conventions, for example, one would soon be out of luck, as the narrative's emphasis is rather on the transmutation of any such structures. Secondly, the precision of a modulated subgenre diminishes the curious fact that *Orlando: A Biography* is *both* a love letter and political pamphlet, that it *does* function as literary history, and equally, that it actually elaborates a form of poetics. Just as the standard claim from pragmatic semantics—that *Orlando* is a novel, or biography, if considered as such—what the Fowlerian distinction gains in terms of categorization, it loses in descriptive accuracy.

Arguably the same holds true for Mikhail Bakhtin's notion of the novel. The genre's most foundational characteristic, he contends, is that it is "uncompleted" and defined by its ability to appropriate other literary forms and conventions.[12] But while the Bakhtinian perspective is apt for historical investigations of generic evolution, the allowance of nearly everything explains little of the present complexity: what it lays bare within a dynamic system of genres, it disguises in the structural particularities of the singular case. Even J. J. Wilson's suggestion, in the suitably titled essay "Why is *Orlando* Difficult?", that the book should be considered an "anti-novel" is problematic. For while the association to Laurence Sterne and *Tristram Shandy*—the archetypical anti-novel—is valid in terms of how *Orlando* reads within the novel's generic conventions, the ruling negation of the rubric also suggests that those conventions are and must be *Orlando*'s primary frame of reference.[13] This needn't be the case. Indeed, this simply *isn't* the case. Whether in terms of how the book thematically critiques dualistic thinking, or of how it moves between and beyond different formal registers, the binary structure of the "anti" is far too reductive of what *Orlando* actually does. As with "novel," "biography," or "love letter," the descriptive ambition of "anti-novel" relies on a much narrower interpretive frame than the book itself suggests. Rather than a single designation, one must concede that standard formulations of generic identity fail to encapsulate *Orlando*; that it is of a different register than most text. It eludes categorization. One could even claim that it not only transgresses categories, but presents an uncategorizable view of category itself. But what, then, to call it?

* * * *

From a critical viewpoint, the complexities of *Orlando*'s generic make-up have attracted far less attention than its thematic explorations of gender, often in connection to Woolf's personal life. Simply put, the explicit links to Sackville-West have encouraged cross-referencing readings to Woolf's diaries, letters, and essays, eliciting analyses of how *Orlando* not only mirror's their relationship but also elaborates the writer's views on gender and sex. This largely exemplifies what Jane Goldman writes of how Woolf's reception has turned on two axes—modernism and feminism—and that considerations of *Orlando* have tended towards the latter, especially in connection to queer and lesbian criticism.[14] In recent years, studies have also begun to include transgender perspectives—though crucially not to *transgenre*.[15] As in many queer and lesbian investigations, this turn to transsexuality preserves a reliance on biographical and contextual backgrounds. It also highlights a conception of *Orlando* as curiously *avant la lettre*—particularly in terms of how it can be seen as expressive of post-structuralist critique, even in the late 1920s.[16]

A key reference point for many biographical readings of *Orlando* is Woolf's elaboration of androgyny in *A Room of One's Own*, her celebrated essay on gender and art written at roughly the same time. A central passage is where she sketches "a plan of the soul" as consisting of one male and one female part, and, referencing Coleridge, ties the coexistence of the two to creativity and art—and then asks whether "the androgynous mind is less apt" to keep them apart than "the single-sexed mind."[17] Elaine Showalter famously criticized this idea in *A Literature of Their Own*, calling it "utopian" and lacking of "zest and energy."[18] From the point of view of a social, feminist critique of literary history that makes sense, particularly as Woolf's idea suggests that bodily sex is less important than the sexuality of the artist's mind. And as any outline of literary history will show, the opposite is true: the patriarchy has privileged men, not "androgynous minds." However, as Toril Moi has pointed out, Showalter's view is perhaps too limited. Rather than confined to historiography, she contends, Woolf's elaboration of gender in *Orlando, A Room of One's Own*, and other texts are best understood by way of Julia Kristeva's three-part description of feminist action. More specifically, Moi sees Woolf's writing as suggestive of Kristeva's third position, where the masculine–feminine binary is laid bare as metaphysical and deconstructed.[19] This is particularly interesting when considering that Kristeva's model is theoretical rather than empirical. Further, as Moi's view positions Woolf's texts significantly before their time, it also implies that Woolf herself confounds both temporal and physical delineations. It is not only *what she wrote* but *what she seems to have been* that falls outside the regular orders of belonging, outside the logically and temporally categorizable. In that sense, even the Kristevan, post-structuralist perspective invites the biographical and contextual as a key for understanding Woolf's writings on gender, sex, and being.

Both Showalter and Moi exemplify studies where the thematic of gender and sexuality are explicitly conceived as more important than the formal particularities of Woolf's writing. Interestingly, in the case of *Orlando* the same hierarchy applies even in essays where generic or formal aspects are explicitly considered. For example, anticipatory glances at *A Room of One's Own* have prompted examinations of how the modes of characterization in *Orlando* predict the essay's discussions of androgyny and the "man-womanly."[20] Alongside conventions of biography, other studies hinge on Woolf's relationship with Sackville-West, and how it elucidates a conflict between societal norms and Woolf's complex thinking on gender and sexuality. The details of their love affair became public knowledge in the early 1970s, through a series of biographies and letter collections—especially Quentin Bell's *Virginia Woolf: A Biography* and Nigel Nicolson's *Portrait of a Marriage*.[21] Referencing this, Leslie Kathleen Hankins simply states that "*Orlando* came out of the closet as a lesbian text in the 1970s," later specifying that the text is "a lesbian *feminist* one." She then contextualizes *Orlando*'s text within Woolf and Sackville-West's private correspondence, and describes their elaborately premeditated ways of avoiding both domestic and public censorship. With analytical rigor, Hankins thereby lays bare *Orlando*'s "subversive, pervasive and persuasive lesbian strategies."[22]

Hankins also notes, however, that the biographical context is not only an interpretive correlate, but an outline for the book's formal structure: the limits of the sexual politics that shaped Woolf and Sackville-West's letters, she argues, also shaped the aesthetics of *Orlando*. Similarly, Laura Marcus portrays the book's background in Woolf's personal and social life, pointing out, for example, that "some of the central historical and biographical images that animate *Orlando*" have their roots in her visits to Knole, the Sackville-West ancestral estate. Marcus illustrates how this impulse to life-writing turns around on itself, particularly through Woolf's conceptions of Victorian biography (and, one could note, the fact that her father was a prominent biographer).[23] But again, while this undoubtedly explains certain aspects of the book, the tendency is that *Orlando*'s complicated form is subsumed by its complex thematic; that the ideas expressed overrule the particularities of the expression.[24] One might even say that its depiction of sexual difference is taken to be ideal, a metaphysical portrait of a Sackville-West as "Being," whereas the minutiae of this ideal as being, in fact, practical, formal, and textual, is displaced or overlooked.

To be clear, the fact that *Orlando* circulates the feminist node of Woolf's reception isn't problematic in itself: concerns of gender and sexuality are emphatically central to the book.[25] But through this dominant framework questions of its formal complexities are put out of bounds. From the biographical frame, this means that Woolf's reflections on androgyny are given precedence over her ideas about the novel as a literary form—as well as over the actual text as writing practice. Thematically, it means that the considerations of how categories mix and intertwine are located in interrogations of gender—but excluded from examinations of genre. And this, I hazard to contend, actually *is* problematic. For what happens in *Orlando*, both thematically and formally, is that one bleeds into the other: the exploration of generic boundaries is tied to laying bare of the limits of gender, and the examination of sexual fluidity is connected to the attempts at writing in a mode of formal mutability. Pamela Caughie has pointed to this fact in stating that "[t]he text of *Orlando* is as unstable as the sex of Orlando."[26] Put more bluntly, in conjoining its formal and thematic materials, *Orlando* collapses the distinction between gender and genre; it turns one into the other, and depicts both as something not recognized by the pregiven categories of either sexual or literary life.

And yet, this seems to be exactly what is precluded from *Orlando*'s critical record, for in the distinction Goldman indicates in separating modernism and feminism, there is also an estrangement between the aesthetic and the political.[27] So what happens, then, to the conception of *Orlando*'s generic stature if it is allowed to blend with the story's portrayal of gender? How would it affect the accepted orthodoxies of the two axes of Woolf's reception, with the dominant distinction that has been upheld between formal and thematic concerns, and its inherent separation of the biographical, historical, political, and aesthetic registers of *Orlando*? How does the importance of calling out Orlando's sex—and through that, the meaning of the androgynous—affect the act of designating the book as novel, biography or love letter? Can the idea of the "man-womanly" or of the performative and shifting aspects of gender explain the book's generic refashioning? Does the examination of transgender differ from the exploration of transgenre? And finally, in what ways can Woolf's question of what to call her writings be taken into account when considering what to call Orlando's (and Vita's) way of being, sexually, politically, and aesthetically?

All of these questions are tied to *Orlando*'s collapsed distinction between the social and political orders of "gender," and the formal and poetical registers of "genre." Thereby they also point to a more central concern of how *Orlando* portrays category itself; how it works through the categories of "genos" rather than the supposedly isolated facts of gender and genre. And again, the questions also point to what I would hypothesize as the book's conjunction of the thematic and the formal—to how "What, then, to call it?" is always at once a political and poetical question.

In the passages that follow, I'll explore possible routes of answering these questions. As method, material, and mode of inquiry, apart from the text of *Orlando* itself this exploration takes hold of the notion of *Geschlecht*. The simple reason is, firstly, that it means both "gender" and "genre" (alongside a host of other categorizing concepts), and thereby points to the semantic relevance of *not* always distinguishing between different orders of belonging. Second, and more importantly, the notion of *Geschlecht* also highlights the discriminatory aspects of any act of categorization—whether in terms of how Leaska precludes *Orlando* from considerations of "the novels themselves," or how Marcus subsumes its formal particularities in biographical backgrounds.[28] In the simplest of terms, *Geschlecht* provides a means of resistance to these hierarchizations.[29]

Three aspects of *Orlando* are given particular attention: the configurations of the book's paratexts; the uses of metaleptic narratorial comments; and the text's successive transformation of style. In each of these there is either an expressed moment of contrast, of emphasis on the border between two seemingly opposing things, or a stress on sequential transformation. Each of these aspects also highlight how the book's shifting and contested gestures toward generic identity can be viewed in terms of its deconstruction of gender binaries. And each of these aspects play a part in illuminating how the complex structure of *Orlando* combines and contests biographical, political, historical, and metapoetical registers in what amounts, ultimately, not only to an investigation of the categories of gender and genre, but of category itself.

II

The booksellers telling Miss Ritchie that no one wanted biographies primarily reacted to the seemingly clear generic signal of the subtitle. It does say "A Biography," after all. Fully in line with Genette's standard formulation on paratexts as gestures toward interpretive schemata, they took the subtitle to mean something fairly straightforward: a generic marker, indicating the book's background, form, and content.[30] They were wrong, of course, both in the sense that *Orlando* soon became a popular success and in the way that the generic marker isn't straightforward at all. Rather, it is one of many examples of how *Orlando* places contesting signals side by side, and of how the text's structure is made of differing generic markers that compete for the reader's attention.

Apart from the subtitle, the book's paratexts also include a dedication ("to v sackville-west"), a preface by the author, numerous illustrations, and an index. Of course, paratextual features vary between editions (the design of dust jackets change, reprints can include quotes from critics or scholarly introductions, etc.), but these provide the baseline for what Woolf herself included.[31] In a contemporary review Arnold Bennett—a famous Bloombury antagonist—commented on the paratexts: calling *Orlando* "a very odd volume," he allowed "some justification" for the preface but saw none for the index, clearly indicating that the book did not match available genre categories.[32] Given a closer look, this seems to be exactly the point. Rather than provide a clear interpretive framework, the paratexts lay out contradictory snares and nooses, pointing the reader in one direction and then another.

The preface, to start, is replete with ironies and contradicting assertions. While giving thanks to a list of fifty-odd names of friends, family, and public intellectuals (a few of them long dead), the preface says nothing of Orlando, the book's background, or of its personal significance for Woolf.[33] Helen Southworth has argued that this wellspring of circumstantial information is "undoubtedly meant to amuse and to challenge," thereby indicating the preface's status as a complexly ironic formal experiment. But she also argues that it functions as a document on Woolf's "cultural, financial and social networks" of the late 1920s, and stress the evidence it gives to the sociopolitical realities of *Orlando*'s historical moment.[34] In other words, the preface at once performs and discredits the conventions of its own genre, mapping different and contesting interpretive modes in the dual move of claiming and counter-claiming their validity.

The illustrations follow a similarly multidirectional pattern. Most of them are staged photographs of Sackville-West, others are photographic reprints of paintings hanging at Knole, and a few are pictures of Woolf's family members.[35] In her letters to Sackville-West, Woolf proposes different castings for the characters and comments on the selections of reprints from Knole, indicating both that she thought them artistically important and that they were meant to connect to the biographical ambition of the book.[36] None of the illustrations are factually described, however, but given names and titles of imagined characters. While biographically and historically evidentiary, in other words, the portraits are fictionalized and transposed from referential reality to an aesthetic register. As such, the portraits can be considered part of *Orlando*'s extended investigation of the divide between Fiction and Truth, between Life and Literature—and essentially of the book's attempt to move beyond the generic confines of both "novel" and "biography." The early eighteenth-century photograph of Orlando on her return to England, for example, is technically impossible as it predates Niépce's early photographic experiments by a few generations. Further, it should be showing an Orlando more than a hundred years old, but it is a picture of Sackville-West in her prime.[37] Then again, it is also just that: a picture of Sackville-West, the actual living person the character of Orlando is meant to portray. And this is very much the point. While being a truthful rendition of the biographical subject, the formal presentation draws attention to the impossibility of it actually being biographical; to the necessarily transformative function it has over both the depicted and the depiction. Apart from highlighting the conventions of life-writing and portraiture, it thereby adds a critical and metapoetical register to the portrait of Vita/Orlando—and underscores the fact that the categories at hand for describing what occurs are faulted.

Orlando's index continues this multidirectional pattern of the paratexts' gestures to different categories and interpretive frames. Three-pages long and printed in double columns, it mainly lists the story's *dramatis personae*. And as with the preface and the illustrations, the index retains a crucial criterion of its form: it is organized alphabetically. However, again as with the other paratexts, the index also transgresses its generic confines, as it is a hopscotch of the large and the small, of the living and the inanimate, of person, beast, and thing. Thereby—and in utter disregard of the genre's established hierarchies—it is expressive of a forceful critique of the distinctions between different categories of being.[38] Accordingly, Westminster Abbey (personified and listed as "Abbey, Westminster") is placed alongside Queen Anne, Sir Thomas Browne, Cicero, and Dryden. "Canute, the elk-hound" directly precedes Thomas Carlyle, just as "Pippin, the spaniel" does Alexander Pope.[39] The effect this entails of categories bleeding into one another, is not lessened by the fact that Canute and Pippin were Sackville-West's dogs. For while it is worth noting that at the moment of Woolf's writing they were just as real as Westminster Abbey, it more crucial that the dogs are written into a taxonomy where buildings, animals, and poets both coexist and are made to merge; turn into each other.

The index's overturn of categories—and of its own function as a logically organized arrangement of facts—can also be seen in the posts for "Archduchess Harriet of Finster-Aarhorn" and "Archduke, Harry, the." First, the former is cross-referenced to the latter, by way of a note to "*see Archduke Harry*". While this speaks to the two characters being one and the same (although at different stages in Orlando's life), in formal terms it nevertheless indicates their complex separability: the posts skirt each other on the page, highlighting their closeness and visually collapsing their differences. Second, the formal *jouissance* of the conjoined-yet-split index posts points to a directly political statement on the categorizability of gender. The female Harriet is given one long name of indistinguishable parts, while for the male Harry even the determinant particle is distinguished by a comma and given a section for itself. The conventional thinness of female characters, in other words, is contrasted with the supposedly complex strata of the male. And in doing so, the posts for Harriet and

Harry direct the formal experiment with the index as genre to *Orlando*'s thematic inquiry. Genre ties in with gender; collapses into it.

The generic code-breaking of the index—and its thematic impact—is even more pronounced in the post for Orlando. By far the longest and the only item with subdivisions, it essentially reads as a synopsis of the book itself, from Orlando's "appearance as a boy" to the "birth of her first son." The shift in grammatical gender between those events is central, of course, signaling the impact of Orlando's sex change. Equally important is the fact that both his becoming a woman and being publicly declared one (in the legal considerations of his/her inheritance) are separated, as it emphasizes the dislocation of physical, social, and judicial sex. However, the thematic centrality of the portrayal of Orlando's sex change is complicated by the post's overall structure, as no regard is given to the significance of its recounted events. Breaking an ankle is presented as equal to marriage, buying elk hounds to being judicially proclaimed a woman, and Orlando's love of reading to being confused with her cousin or writing her *magnum opus*. Further, as each event relies on "Orlando" as its grammatical subject and is rendered without particles or auxiliary verbs, the collapsed hierarchies within the index post is mirrored in its form. For as this bare grammar could be seen as a signal towards factualness and objectivity, the produced effect is directly opposite: in adopting the straightforward structure of the index, the post for Orlando actually adapts its conventions for other, highly subjective and idiosyncratic ends. Fully in line with the index's more extensive disregard for the hierarchies of categorization, in the other words, its portrayal of Orlando hinges on collapsed rather than upheld distinctions.

In more technical terms, the index directly parodies the conventions of Victorian biography—thereby adding a generic critique to its ironic examination of gender and other social orders of belonging. Given Woolf's interest in biography, this is hardly surprising. In "The New Biography," for example, an essay from 1927, she coined the often-quoted phrase of the "marriage of granite and rainbow," concerning how biography should aim at intertwining actualities and facts with more elusive expressions of personality. In doing so she also argued against the strictures of Victorian biographers, who sought "truth as truth is to be found in the British Museum" and to whom life "was a series of exploits."[40] Undeniably, this argument shares common ground with *Orlando*. And as Laura Marcus has outlined, at various junctures of Orlando's story Woolf openly critiques the biographical genre—not least in her disregard for the narrative kernel points of birth and death (wholly excluded from the book) and in the transgressive impact of writing about women.[41]

Using "The New Biography" as a template for *Orlando* is not as straightforward as it might seem, however. First of all, it was initially published in the *New York Herald Tribune* as a review of Harold Nicolson's

Some People, a writer Woolf knew well. It is a review of the book of a biographer-friend, in other words, who also happened to be Vita Sackville-West's husband. Further, although Nicolson is portrayed as representing a certain brand of twentieth-century biography, the *exemplum* for Woolf is Boswell's writing on Samuel Johnson, somewhat widening the scope of the word "New." Finally, in the essay Woolf also expresses serious reservations about the possibility of actually melding fact with fiction in any biography, new or otherwise. "Truth of fact and truth of fiction are incompatible," she writes, and bluntly states that although Nicolson points in the right direction "the biographer whose art is subtle and bold enough to present that queer amalgamation of dream and reality" has yet to present herself.[42]

"The New Biography" does not, in other words, provide a clear categorical scheme for *Orlando*, or do away with the question of the book's generic identity. Rather, the interpretive valence the essay holds lies in the outline of the *artistic act of merger*, in the gesture towards transgressing dichotomies and rethinking categorical delineations. Through the ironic inversions of convention (which, again, in the index hinge on the contrast between the bare factualness of the presentation and the idiosyncratic disregard for established hierarchies of events), a heightened awareness is directed to a wider spectrum of problems. It is not only that a particular Victorian biography of a typically masculine register is parodied, or that the evaluative conventions for determining "significant life events" are overturned. What's relevant is how even the paratexts of *Orlando* call attention to an inquiry of more fundamental distinctions—between life and literature, masculine and feminine, animal and human, as well as between the living and the inanimate. To put it simply, it is not just the genre of biography that gets what's coming to it, but also the seemingly innate categorizations of modern society. That also means that the preface, the index and the illustrations do more than play with gender and genre: they investigate *genos* and *Geschlecht*, and provide an invitation to critically rethink conceptions of category. From such a view one first has to dispute Mr. Bennett's aforementioned review—there is plenty of justification for the index—and then simply agree. A very odd volume, indeed.

III

The first chapter of *Orlando* instantly raises questions of how both the character of Orlando and the text itself should be categorized, principally by way of mockingly ironic narratorial comments. Establishing a structural scheme that runs through the entire book, a key to these comments is the collapsed distinction between gender and genre, where both are portrayed through a dissolution of dichotomies, and in a manner that implies the integration of expressive form with thematic content. Consider the contrast between textual levels and modes of description in the opening paragraph, for example:

> He—for there could be no doubt about his sex, though the fashion of the time did something to disguise it—was in the act of slicing at the head of a Moor which hung from the rafters. It was the colour of an old football, and more or less the shape of one, save for the sunken cheeks and a strand or two of coarse dry hair, like the hair of a cocoanut. Orlando's father, or perhaps his grandfather, had struck it from the shoulders of a vast Pagan who started up under the moon in the barbarian fields of Africa; and now it swung, gently, perpetually, in the breeze which never ceased blowing through the attic rooms of the gigantic house of the lord who had slain him.[43]

It has been pointed out that the opening sets off with an allusion to the Italian poet Ariosto's *Orlando Furioso*, from 1532—and not least the Renaissance *romanza*'s treatment of gender and the androgynous.[44] Pauline Scott, for example, maintains that there are distinct similarities between the love triangles in the two books and their ties to the protagonists' bouts of madness. In Ariosto's version, the triangle is made up of Orlando, Angelica, and Medoro, with Orlando losing his wits when he discovers that Angelica has married a man well below his own societal stature. In Woolf's rendition, this equates to (the male) Orlando, Sasha, and the unnamed sailor who Orlando finds entangled with his Russian Princess during the Great Frost—a sighting that both sets off an immediate rage and starts a series of events that leaves him a recluse.[45] Maureen M. Melita is equally certain of *Orlando Furioso*'s importance for Woolf's narrative. She argues that part of the innovative force in Ariosto lies in the androgynous natures of two characters: Marfisa and Bradamante. At different stages of Woolf's book, the personality traits and virtues that these two characters embody find their way into Orlando, ultimately producing a protagonist that in Melita's words "is capable of appeasing the desire for a feminist heroine who is also an epic heroine."[46]

These remarks exemplify, once again, how questions of gender have dominated *Orlando*'s reception, while its genre is less explored. However, the allusion to *Orlando Furioso* is also important in formal terms. First, apart from the name and the fact that fighting Moors was a favorite pastime for Ariosto's protagonist—which affects the whole outline of the scene—the reference itself functions as a time stamp for the narrative, putting a seal of the Renaissance on Orlando's situation. In an extended sense, the temporal grounding also foregrounds the formal inventiveness of both works: Ariosto wrote when Aristotle's *Poetics* was the theoretical baseline for literary form, and the *romanza* simply allowed for more intricate narrative and stylistic blends than either drama, epic, or lyric—similarly, that is, to how the novel functioned during the 1920s. One should not pretend that the *romanza* and Woolf's book hold equivalent positions in their respective genre systems, but one could allow that both works relate to their respective genre histories in a similarly complex manner.

Second, the text's dialogue with Ariosto foregrounds and juxtaposits its different textual levels in a way that upsets the reliance on any single critical register. Rather, what is important is mutability and indefiniteness— what Woolf called the "queer amalgamation of dream and reality."[47] The narratorial comment on Orlando's gender in the very first sentence, for example, significantly presented within dashes, is central to the entire book: "He—for there could be no doubt of his sex, though the fashion of the time did something to disguise it—was in the act of slicing at the head of a Moor which hung from the rafters."[48] Both the descriptive certainty of the *in medias res* opening and the immersive links to *Orlando Furioso* are instantly halted by this statement, as it immediately establishes a divide between the text's intra- and extradiegetic dimensions. For while it describes Orlando, the sentence also introduces the narrator as a presence to be reckoned with, particularly as it signals a distance between Orlando and the narrator, and thereby inscribes a dual or split critical register to the story itself.

The temporal aspect of this distance is marked by the reference to "the fashion of the time"—a reference that implicitly suggests a certain commonality between narrator and reader. To put it simply, Orlando's time is not theirs; if it were, they could not recognize the otherness of its dress codes. As the narratorial comment is discursively marked by dashes, separating the narrative description from the metaleptic comment, the temporal distance is inscribed within the textual structure. As Melba Cuddy-Keane argues, this type of dialectic is central to Woolf's approach to historicism, both in terms of historical reading and representations of historical pasts.[49] The same effect is enhanced in the subsequent likening of the Moor's head to a football in both color and shape, "save for the sunken cheeks and a strand or two of coarse, dry hair". The juxtaposition of images—one commonplace and contemporary with the reader, the other macabre and descendant from medieval times—both emphasizes the historical registers of Orlando's story and suggests the readers affinity to the narrator's rendition of them.[50]

Soon thereafter, however, a distance is also inscribed in the relation between narrator and reader. In the first description of Orlando's physical appearance, where he is depicted standing in the "heraldic light" of a window at his ancestral home, the narrator proclaims that:

> [...] those who like symbols, and have a turn for deciphering of them, might observe that though the shapely legs, the handsome body, and

the well-set shoulders were all of them decorated with various tints of heraldic light, Orlando's face, as he threw the window open, was lit solely by the sun itself. A more candid, sullen face it would be impossible to find. Happy the mother who bears, happier the biographer who records the life of such a one! Never need she vex herself, nor he invoke the help of novelist or poet.[51]

The narratorial metalepsis—here in the mentioning of "those who like symbols" and in the latter note on the biographer's happiness—hinders the reader's immersion with the scene. But unlike the opening lines, what is at stake here is not an historical register but the truthfulness of the narrator. Both the presuppositions about the reader's interpretive leanings and the claims to facticity perform an elaborate play with generic category and authorial position.[52] On the one hand the heraldic light of the ancestral home and the descriptions of Orlando have direct referents in Knole and Sackville-West (Woolf was especially enamored by her shapely legs).[53] This points to a biographical function, and a sincerity of feeling in the last two sentences: it is, simply, Virginia describing Vita, in an honest attempt at writing her portrait. In this view, the "fantasy" of Vita being a boy is nullified by the fact that as a child, she felt like one.[54] But on the other hand, the passage also does the opposite, and highlights a central problematic of "writing portraits." In gendering the biographer as male ("nor *he* invoke") Woolf actualizes the conventional "maleness" of the Victorian biography she was so skeptical about, and suggests the impossibility of the entire genre. More significantly, Woolf thereby distances herself from the text in a way that diminishes the referential quality of the passage; as marked in the discourse, this is *not* Virginia describing Vita, but a fictional biographer describing Orlando, the Elizabethan nobleman.

The opening paragraphs, then, use a complex intertextual backdrop to establish both a temporal frame and a thematic acuity, while simultaneously interjecting a narratorial presence that emphasizes the rift between different textual elements, as well as between the reader and the text's contesting generic signals. The same effect is produced later in the story, in the section on Orlando's adventures of June 1712. At that point, Orlando has become a woman and lives in a London on the verge of Enlightenment, where society under Queen Anne "was of unparalleled brilliance." Although sick of the incongruities and complex mannerisms of social life, Orlando hastily accepts when invited to the rooms of the Countess of R., "a certain great Lady." Her principal drive is the desire to meet prominent writers—Addison, Dryden, and Pope—but the narrator is clearly skeptical; apart from numerous digressions on the nature of wit, the narrator also makes room for comments on Orlando's obtrusive infatuation with Poets. These comments are most obvious the third time Orlando goes to Lady R. First, the narrator clarifies that she "was still under the illusion that she was listening to the most brilliant epigrams in the world," while it is mainly high-society gossip.[55] Later, Mr. Pope, described as "the little gentleman," makes an entrance, in a passage that reads:

> Then the little gentleman said,
> He said next,
> He said finally,[*]
> Here, it cannot be denied, was true wit, true wisdom, true profundity. The company was thrown into complete dismay. One such saying was bad enough; but three, one after another, on the same evening! No society could survive it.
>
> [*]These sayings are too well known to require repetition, and besides, they are all to be found in his published works.[56]

The section as a whole (and the subsequent passages where Addison and Swift are introduced by way of lengthy quotes from their texts) clearly exemplifies Cuddy-Keane's definition of Woolf's three-parted historical critical praxis: first Woolf locates the text "in a discrete historical period known by its unlikeness to the present," then she uses the comparison to interrogate the present, and finally attempts to meld them into a "continuous now."[57] The critical phase of this historical dialogism is produced by the omissions: the blank spaces highlight both the temporal and cultural distance between Orlando and the reader, inquiring about the actual relation between present and past. But apart from that, the narratorial comment—principally the one discursively separated to a footnote—also stresses the contemporaneity of the text itself, and again emphasizes the relation between narrator and reader. As in the early description of Orlando standing in the heraldic light, the reader is made aware of what he or she should read into things; how his/her perception is meant to be transformed by the text itself, by what s/he is perceiving. And while hinting at conventions of reading, the narrator simultaneously translates them to a register of writing; giving a glimpse into the process of textual construction, thus underlining a metapoetical dimension of the book's historical register.

The same pattern holds a few pages later, when Orlando meets Nell. Rife with metaleptic nitbits in parentheses or between dashes (especially concerned with how they view each other's sex and the nature of Nell's profession; she is a prostitute), the scene's climax takes the form of a long narratorial comment. Following a series of quotes from "gentlemen" who have analyzed the desires of women and their dependency on men, the narrator simply states that Orlando *did* find enjoyment in the company of her own sex and leaves it "to the gentlemen to prove, as they are so fond of doing, that this is impossible."[58] Although more attuned to politics than history—the scene with Nell can be viewed as a sort of political pamphlet on the women's question—the primary effect is to distance the reader from the text and invite a critical interpretive stance.

These types of narratorial comments run rife through the entire book, and their function remains the same: rather than suspension of disbelief, they call for scrutiny and fine-sheared analysis—perhaps even a critique of belief itself. An indication of this is that there are 243 parentheses marks in *Orlando*. Many of them contain narratorial comments, but not all narratorial comments are found in parenthetical remarks (there are some, for example, in the quotes above that are marked by other means). Suffice to say that it is hard finding a page of *Orlando* that doesn't have one, whether its function is metaleptic or descriptive.

One of the more pointed examples is when the narrator relates Orlando's seclusion after the thawing of the Great Frost. First comes an assertion that "probably the reader can imagine" the types of description needed to portray that life went on but nothing really changed (shifting moon phases, leaves that change color, cobwebs gathering in a corner), highlighting the supposed commonality between reader and narrator-as-biographer. But then a reverse comment states that all of it might have been told "more quickly by the simple statement that 'Time passed' (here the exact amount could be indicated in brackets) and nothing whatever happened."[59] This not only heightens awareness of the metapoetical scrutiny of historical and biographical writing. The hint towards the "Time passes" section of *To the Lighthouse* also ironically inscribes a simultaneously *auto*biographical and *auto*poetical register, emphasizing the collapse of *Orlando*'s generic boundaries.

In short, the narratorial comments—whatever their form—are part of Woolf's strategies for crossing between and moving beyond different critical registers; for exploring the divide between Life and Literature, gender and genre, reader and writer, and for translating one into the other (and then back again). The form of the narrator's presence, in other words, is collapsed into the themes it continually brings to the fore, on the relationships between biographical, historical, political, and metapoetical categories.

IV

Jane de Gay has argued that *Orlando*'s narrative structure connects to traditional periodizations of literary history, as the Renaissance, the Restoration, the Enlightenment, the Romantic era, the Victorian period, and the present (i.e., the 1920s) each roughly correspond to a chapter in the book. This means, according to de Gay, that the book's structure lays the ground for a critique of historiography and historical consciousness, literary or otherwise.[60] One could add that the historical eras also affect *Orlando*'s different gestures at generic identity, particularly as each chapter emulates the dominant literary style of the period depicted. Or put in slightly different terms, both Orlando's own poetical exploits—what s/he writes, mainly through revisions of "The Oak Tree"—and the main narrative is rendered in connection to the literary conventions of the time periods s/he inhabits, with the result that differing interpretive and evaluative frames are merged and collapsed into each other.

Sometimes these performative translations of historical convention are directly connected to metaleptic narratorial comments. One such example is when the narrator echoes a Richardsonian formal realism and seizes the opportunity to talk of more pressing matters as Orlando rides from her estate to London. Another is when the narrator is forced to recite the calendar, because Orlando's life at that point is spent sitting in a chair thinking, and Life (more specifically, life-writing) "has nothing whatever to do with sitting still in a chair and thinking."[61]

Interestingly, however, some of the more elaborate instances of stylistic emulation are less explicitly metapoetical, than thematically oriented to gender. The first one is found in the opening chapter, and immediately follows the narrator/biographer's initial claim of being free from the fantasies of both novelists and poets. Contrary to that claim, the text initiates an intimate imitation of Elizabethan poetry and drama. First, there are the descriptions of Orlando himself. Rife with romantic imagery, these "catalogues of youthful beauty," as the narrator calls them, are reminiscent of love sonnets: the "peach down" of his red cheeks, the "arrowy nose," the teeth of "an exquisite and almond whiteness," the "eyes like drenched violets." Second, there are the descriptions of what Orlando (then a would-be Elizabethan poet) writes: dramas of Kings and Queens confounded by "horrid plots," pervaded with abstract personages and "noble sentiments." In his texts there is "never a word said as he himself would have said it," but still, the narrator contends, they have a remarkable "fluency and sweetness."[62]

In both of these descriptive forays, the text uses historical literary conventions to simultaneously characterize Orlando and to comment on dominant views of the cultural moment he inhabits. Because the scene is one of the more obviously biographical—attempting, as it does, a portrait of Sackville-West in the heraldic light of Knole—those conventions are also connected to the genre of life writing (and, through the typically male Victorian biography, highlights the thematic of gender). Following this, one could argue that the characterizing function the passage is direct and sincere: Orlando/Sackville-West really is the spitting image of a love sonnet—at least to the narrator/Woolf. However, despite the appropriation of Elizabethan poetic imagery not being explicitly marked by inversions or ironies, the scene is arguably reliant on an ironic distance *within* the conventions themselves. Shakespeare's "Sonnet 130," for example, that opens with the line "My mistress' eyes are nothing like the sun," parodically foregrounds the ready-made phrases of Renaissance poetry, begging the question if *anyone* can (and ever could) look like that. In *Orlando* this irony is doubled in the sense of being marked as conventional—or rather, conventionalized. It connects what could be called a performance of the history of poetry with both gendered visual stereotypes and the limits of biographical portraiture.

Because the successions of emulated styles are founded in Orlando's conceptions of and reactions to the spirit of the ages s/he lives through, they also have an impact on the portrayal of subplots. Simply put, the style not only relates to the times Orlando inhabits, but the various problems and intrigues s/he faces. As such, the book's stylistic mutability connects to what Michael R. Olin-Hitt defines as *Orlando*'s play with narrative desire, and Woolf's subversion of the teleological plot structures of classical realism: rather than a fixed end, it constantly points to an incessant and mutable "now."[63] An indication thereof is found when a female Orlando living in Victorian times takes a walk on the moors close to her estate. She is out there in an attempt to dispel questions of why she is alone when everyone else has a mate; the spirit of the Victorian age, it seems, is all about partnership and marriage, all about finding a husband. What sets off her lamentations is the simple fact that when asked to see the wedding ring of her housekeeper, the latter responds that "not the Archbishop nor the Pope nor Queen Victoria on her throne" could get her to take off her ring.[64] When after eight full pages the passage ends, Orlando is engaged to Maramaduke Bonthrop Shelmerdine, Esquire.

The passage is modeled on a Brontëan archetype of the Victorian novel, and is structurally reminiscent of the book's opening paragraph, where *Orlando Furioso* sets the thematic tone on androgyny. Here, focus is directed to considerations of more traditional gender roles arguably inscribed in the Brontëan narrative. In sharp contrast with the majority of the book, however, the passage is almost completely free of narratorial comments. The reason is, quite simply, that the emulated style precludes them. On the one hand the narratorial presence is an ostensibly natural occurrence that bars metaleptic segments. On the other, the internal focalization positions Orlando herself as the primary inquirer, and those opacities that in other sections of the book would invite commentary she clarifies herself. For example, when Orlando finds a steel-blue rook's feather one reads that "[s]he loved birds' feathers. She had used to collect them as a boy."[65] Rather than relegated to parentheses or a footnote, the emulated style allows both the thematic of gender and the invitation to view it from a critical distance to be integrated in the main text.

In the final chapter, the literary conventions of Orlando's life catch up with Woolf. Calendar-wise it ends, quite literally, at the present moment of the book's publication (which would have been the future, seen from the moment of writing), and the last illustration, titled "Orlando at the present moment," is actually of Sackville-West as she anticipates a meeting with

Woolf.⁶⁶ Further, stylistically the final section embodies the de-centered time frames and perspectives of high modernism. Woolf emulates herself, to put it bluntly: the narrative becomes at once cohesive and poetically rambling, combining long-lost thoughts with sensory perceptions, cut-up phrases with self-referential quotes. In a singularly Proustian passage, where a handbag becomes the equivalent of a madeleine, it says:

> "Time has passed over me," she thought, trying to collect herself; "this is the oncome of middle age. How strange it is! Nothing is any longer one thing. I take up a handbag and I think of an old bumboat woman frozen in the ice. Someone lights a pink candle and I see a girl in Russian trousers."⁶⁷

Over the consecutive pages, Orlando's memorial reveries turn into an open contestation with identity viewed as a centered self. "I'm sick to death of this particular self" she says, "I want another." And later: "'What then? Who then?' she said. 'Thirty-six; in a motor-car; a woman. Yes, but a million other things as well.'"⁶⁸

The passage lures one to consider it an end point, not just to the final chapter, but to the intellectual enterprise of the book as a whole. One is enticed to think that finally, with Modernity and modernism, the Truth of Life is made available, expressionable. But as Olin-Hitt points out, the twentieth-century rendition of Orlando's identity is in no way privileged over the preceding ones.⁶⁹ Arguably the opposite is more accurate. In the final chapter, as Woolf performs an act of historical dialogism with her own time, the call to critical distance is louder than ever. Or put differently, the paradoxical undercurrents of parodying herself, of metapoetically emulating the literary conventions she herself has participated in molding, signals an outright collapse of generic stability. Consider the final time stamp: "And the twelfth stroke of midnight sounded; the twelfth stroke of midnight, Thursday, the eleventh of October, Nineteen Hundred and Twenty Eight." If anything, as the book literally attempts to write through the distinction between text and reality, it underscores how it from the very first line—and even the paratexts—has contrasted and collapsed different critical registers and interpretive categories.

V

What can one make of all this? A political novel-biography with historiographical ambitions and metapoetical underpinnings, where the latter continually puts a halt to any attempt at generic categorization? Is it *without* genre—a notion hardly conceivable? Does it *move beyond* genre? As has already been pointed out, no single designation seems to fit. For example, even if limited to the very first pages, what happens in *Orlando* makes the potentially wide-ranging and complex notion of "satirical *Künstlerroman*" seem narrow and straightforward. Or put in more general terms: whether one looks at how the paratexts ironically elude stable generic categorization, how narratorial comments juxtapose textual levels and interpretive modes, or how the successive emulations of historical literary styles portray and problematize different formal conventions, the deconstructive impulse of *Orlando* signals a critical stance to any type of categorial conformism. As Orlando herself puts it, "Nothing is any longer one thing." But what, then, to call it?

There is an important parallel between *Orlando*'s formal reluctance to fixed generic categories and those thematic explorations of gender, androgyny, and transsexuality that have long been emphasized in the book's critical reception. Simply put, Moi's view of the *avant la lettre* poststructuralist frames for Woolf's writing practices (via Kristeva's critical approach to the dominion of ideological language) directly connects to the book's performance of collapsed categorial stability in both sexual politics and genre poetics. This connection is principally a mode of resistance, characterized by a denial of the unavoidability of the given—whether in generic taxonomies, matters of style or designations of sexual being. The book portrays a drive beyond conventional definitions of conceptual categories. Thereby it details a question on how one could categorize the uncategorizable, as different critical registers are contrasted and collapsed into each other.

Seen through the axes of modernism and feminism that has ordered Woolf's reception, *Orlando*'s elaborate resistance to categorization can thus be considered exemplary of an *avant la lettre*, feminist and poststructuralist critique—much as Moi has pointed out, in the designation of Woolf in Kristevan terms. But in a sense, that makes it all the more confounding that the formal and generic aspects of *Orlando* have largely been displaced for its exploration of gender and androgyny. Both aspects, for one, are readily apparent in Kristeva's thoughts on literature and poetic language. Discussing the thetic she notes that mimesis and poetic language are "corruptions of the symbolic," emphasizing especially how modern poetic language "attacks not only denotation (the positing of the object) but meaning (the positing of the enunciating subject)."[70] In the *Tel Quel* essay "A New Type of Intellectual: The Dissident," published a few years after the French edition of *La Révolution du langage poétique*, she maintains this generatively revolutionary power of the poetic. After recounting the possibility of dissidence with political rebels and psychoanalysts, she moves to describing "the experimental writer" as one who can undermine the law of symbolic language:

> [...] the writer who experiments with the limits of identity, producing texts where the law does not exist outside language. A playful language therefore gives rise to a law that is overturned, violated and pluralized, a

law upheld only to allow a polyvalent, polylogical sense of play that set the being of the law ablaze in a peaceful, relaxing void.[71]

Both "the law" and "the symbolic" are, of course, grounded in (capitalist) patriarchy, in the dominance and suppressing impulse of ideological language; of words and names for things and categories. Within the framework of Kristeva's thought, then, the collapse of the gender/genre distinction is already there: the deconstruction of the male–female binary has everything to do with forms of language. The spark that sets "the being of the law ablaze" comes from textual "experiments with the limits of identity," from the violating and pluralizing overturn of the law.

Kristeva's argument gives a certain clarity to the relevance and importance of including *genre* in the problematics of *gender*, and vice versa. However, it does little to solve the problem of *genos* or *Geschlecht* in Woolf's novel-biography–love letter. For while the theory might detail the text's potentially transformative dissidence to ideological categorizations, it doesn't actually clarify the categories it presents as an alternative—or rather, how it presents categories differently. In other words, while Kristeva's theories might help explain what *Orlando* does, they give no answer to what it is, or presents itself as being.

The problem persists, in other words, of *what, then, to call it*. This has less to do with establishing a functional interpretive frame (the formal and thematic exploration of liminality is tied to both aesthetics and ideology and can be discerned without finalizing categorial rubrics) than with meeting the text's demand for a different sort of categorization. In a sense, where *Orlando*'s critical elaboration of "gender" can be enunciated by triangulating "androgyny," "queer," and "the man-womanly," the formal underpinnings of that critique seem to be out of bounds of generic designations: there simply aren't any appropriate categories for the book's form. Or rather, where the transformative portrayal of "gender" is met with both neologism and reinterpretation of classical concepts, the transformation of "genre" is tied back to the everyday use of the seemingly best concept at hand: *the novel*.

In Hankins' investigation of Woolf's and Sackville-West's textual strategies for avoiding censorship, for example, even the most complex maneuvers are subsumed by rather simple rubrics. Thus, when she suggests that "[t]he complex text of *Orlando* is a letter with multiple dueling addressees," she also states that the tension between those addressees "provides much of the wit, delight and power of the novel."[72] She is likely right—especially about the dueling part; in *Orlando*, everything is claimed, contested, and counter-claimed—and yet that significant slip of the tongue of calling the book both a letter and *a novel*. With that single designation, the room for considering the formal or generic aspects of *Orlando*'s thematic and political explorations of gender are drastically reduced. It displaces the dissident practice of formal experimentation to the stable (even if contested) category of an established form.

In a similarly everyday-sounding parapraxis, Pamela Caughie lets in the notion of "the novel" when she argues that *Orlando* functions as a critical analysis of the symbolic order. Again, Kristeva's ideas provide an important background, not least in terms of how assuming sexual identity is a prerequisite for admittance to language: "Woolf brings out the arbitrariness of that identity, the arbitrariness of language itself, through Orlando's switching from one sex to another, and from one poetic language to another, as well as through the shifting of her own rhetoric in this novel."[73]

For both Hankins and Caughie, the formal complexity of *Orlando* has everything to do with gender, and with criticizing the ideological strictures of gender categories. More pointedly, the portrayal of the otherwise of sexual identity has everything to do with textual flexibility—with collapsing and transgressing the categorical impulse of categorial frames. And yet that imaginary bogey, *the novel*, persists—despite the generative power of the transgression ultimately being one of language, and of form. Still potent, it seems, long after Woolf herself called for its destruction. The simple explanation for this is of course that neither Hankins nor Caughie deem "the novel" as reductive of what *Orlando* is. Implicitly, they take "novel" to mean something along the lines of what Bakhtin, Eagleton, and Lukács did—as the pinnacle of formal flexibility, allowing for anything. But again, the problem is that it also means something much less inventive, something that connotes the same type of generic stability and conventionality that biography does, and did for Woolf.

But what, then, to call it? And more importantly, what names and categories and critical registers does *Orlando* project into being? A possible answer presents itself in Catherine Malabou's discussions of "plasticity." Elaborated over a series of texts, moving from Hegel to neuroscience by way of the conditions of women philosophers, the main principle of plasticity is the dual ability to receive and produce form; to be both susceptible to outside influence and to retain, in that process, something unchanged, something unchangeable by external pressures.[74] From such a view the critique of the categorial fixity in ideologically marked dualities—male/female, gender/genre, Life/Literature, perhaps also novel/biography—results less in the "relaxing void" Kristeva mentions, than in a distinct but liminal space of being-in-transformation.[75]

In *Changing Difference*, for instance, Malabou presents this transformative mode of being through a rigorous examination of the relation between sexual and ontological difference, particularly with regard to hierarchies of categorization and what she calls the status of "the feminine" in philosophy. Traces of this problematic, one should stress, are more directly available in the French *le féminin*—that is, in how the feminine takes the masculine article, explicitly subordinating it to male structures. Furthermore, as

Malabou points out the same problem is even imbued in gender theory, as "we must accept the idea that feminism can now be understood as a *féminisme sans femme*."[76] The genre of feminism, in other words, as a category of thought, criticism, and practice, has been strangely stripped of the feminine gender.

Moving through a series of questions, Malabou contends that this curious state in post-feminism where "woman" is negated and deprived of her being is less liberating than a status quo: although given new vocabularies, the practice of letting "woman" define herself only in terms of the violence done to her (whether of domestic, social, or theoretical orders) is as ancient as philosophy.[77] Despite the insistence of this violence, however, women persist, in both social reality and philosophical discourse; and equally, the "feminine" persists. That seemingly simple fact, in turn, becomes the basis for Malabou's argument about "the feminine" as an empty form of essence; distinguished by its plastic ability to withstand and adapt to external force (an argument, one could mention, tied to Descartes' view of the passions, Levinas' notion of hospitality, Irigaray's discussions of sexual difference, and Derrida's analyses of auto-eroticism). And that argument, I hazard to claim, is deeply relevant to the question of what to call *Orlando*; to the question of what it is and projects as possible modes or categories of being—whether sexual or textual, whether as gender, genre, or *Geschlecht*.

On the relationship between sexual and ontological difference (given in terms of the reliance of Being on the transformability of being), Malabou writes:

> If it is true that its structural potential is part and parcel of the meaning of being, then the feminine is both one of the possible modes of this being or one of the ontic substitutes of being in the exchange process. This point brings us back to the shared etymological origin of *genus* and *gender*: *genos*, genre as essence. If this essence is thought of as "changing," if transformability defines its ontological status, the problem is no longer that the "feminine" can be "reduced" to woman (once again, I find the cautions against this sort of "reduction" just as suspect as the supposed reduction itself). The question is that while the feminine or woman (we can use the terms interchangeably now), remains one of the unavoidable modes of ontological change, they themselves become passing, metabolic points of identity, which like others show the passing inscribed at the heart of gender.[78]

A lengthy quote for exercising an idea already presented; that in *Orlando* the acts of merger and the processes of transformation ultimately posit both gender and genre as malleable, that the text projects a category that is essentially plastic.

While the impact of this idea on the concept of "genre" might be tolerated (indeed, it could be inscribed in both the established tradition of the theorization of the novel, and dominant histories of modernist literary form),[79] the essentialist approach to "gender" is adamantly at odds with Moi's and others' approach to Woolf's portrayals of the feminine as a performance. Recall, for example, how at the one place where the word "gender" occurs in *Orlando*, it details how Orlando at the close of the eighteenth century changes clothes to navigate various social environments, switching from breeches to petticoats to "a China robe of ambiguous gender" and enjoying "the love of both sexes equally."[80] Although the empirical set consists of this one sample (marking the dramatic evolution of the word "gender" in the twentieth century) the case seems clear: for Woolf, it is a construct, something socially performed, signaled by exterior distinctions. But in certain respects, equally at odds with those readings, is the incessant emphasis in *Orlando* that things remain the same, despite constant change: it is an unsurprising effect of Woolf's curiously *avant la lettre* position, tending, as it does, to an anachronous middle ground both between and beyond theoretical frameworks. As Cuddy-Keane puts it, *Orlando* is "the narrative of radically different selves who are nevertheless the same self."[81] Essentialist, but changing; essentially changing. In the transformation scene, where Orlando lays to rest as a man and wakes up as a woman, this fact of permanence despite drastic change is famously emphasized: "Orlando had become a woman—there is no denying it" the narrator states, and continues: "But in every other respect, Orlando remained precisely as he had been. The change of sex, though it altered their future, did nothing whatever to alter their identity."[82]

Viewed through the optics of Malabouian plasticity, then, the question of *what, then, to call it* takes on a different tone. It is fundamentally *not* a question of what genres booksellers thought marketable or what rubrics Woolf herself saw as appropriate for her writings, but the central yet elusive point of the entire text of *Orlando*. Its both thematic and formal insistence on the artistic act of merger, on "nothing any longer being one thing," and the clashes in generic designation that arise from *Orlando*'s incessant play with liminality—in the ironies of the paratextual structure, in the metaleptic calls for critical distance, in the successive shifts of aesthetic convention—becomes less a matter of particular names (novel, biography, literary history) than a depiction of what the generic *is*. Just as the re-inscribed essence of *le féminin* does away the reduction of "feminine" to "woman" because the mode of ontological change suffuses both, the reduction of *Orlando: A Biography* to the anarchic yet conventional strictures of "the novel" is diminished by forceful transformations occurring in and between the lexical field those names depict: Orlando—Biography—Novel.

In the final analysis, perhaps that is all one can hope to describe. How in *Orlando*, Woolf curiously manages to translate an abundance of categories into something much more, how the text continually emphasizes the aesthetic act of merger and uses the pressures of both social and generic conventionality in the attempt at truthful portraiture, full of all the change that occurs in social reality. Perhaps all one can claim is that *Orlando* circumscribes the concepts of "novel" and "biography"—and even "literature." That one turns into the other, and both change; that both Being and being are transformed in Woolf's attempt to mold life into text; in her attempt at writing Vita.

Notes

1 Quentin Bell, *Virginia Woolf: A Biography.* vol. II (London: The Hogarth Press, 1990 [1972]), 140.
2 Virginia Woolf, *A Writer's Diary* (London: The Hogarth Press, 1959 [1953]), 133–5.
3 Woolf, *A Writer's Diary*, 117.
4 Terry Eagleton, *The English Novel* (Malden: Blackwell Publishing, 2005), 5f; E. M. Forster, *Aspects of the Novel* (London: Edward Arnold & Co., 1928), 15; Georg Lukács, *The Theory of the Novel*, (London: Merlin Press, 2006 [1920]), 88.
5 Erich Auerbach, *Mimesis: the Representation of Reality in Western Literature*, trans. Willard R. Trask (Princeton: Princeton University Press, 1971 [1946]), 525ff.
6 Mitchell A. Leaska, *The Novels of Virginia Woolf: From Beginning to End* (London: Weidenfeld and Nicolson, 1977), xxi; John Batchelor, *Virginia Woolf: The Major Novels* (Cambridge: Cambridge University Press, 1991).
7 Nigel Nicolson, *A Portrait of a Marriage: V. Sackville-West and Harold Nicolson* (New York: Atheneum, 1974), 202.
8 Woolf, *A Writer's Diary*, 128.
9 Virginia Woolf, *The Letters of Virginia Woolf; Volume 3: 1923–1928. A Change of Perspective*, eds. Nigel Nicolson and Joanne Trautmann (London: The Hogarth Press, 1977), 221.
10 Virginia Woolf, "What is a Novel?" (1927), in *The Essays of Virginia Woolf; Volume IV: 1925–1928*, ed. Andrews McNeillie (London: The Hogarth Press, 1994), 415.
11 Alastair Fowler, *Kinds of Literature: Introduction to the Theory of Genres and Modes* (Oxford: Clarendon Press, 2002 [1982]), 40ff, 56ff, 107ff.
12 Mikhail Bakhtin, "Epic and Novel," in *The Dialogic Imagination: Four Essays*, ed. Michael Holquist, trans. Caryl Emerson and Michael Holquist (Austin: University of Texas Press, 1981), 3ff.
13 J. J. Wilson, "Why is *Orlando* Difficult?," in *New Feminist Essays on Virginia Woolf*, ed. Jane Marcus (London: MacMillan, 1981), 173.
14 Jane Goldman, *The Cambridge Introduction to Virginia Woolf* (New York: Cambridge University Press, 2006), 135, 68.
15 Lucas Crawford points out that because its depiction of gender-crossing is based on a personally imbued notion of empathy rather than dysphoria,

Orlando provides a counter-narrative to common parlance of transsexuality in sexology and psychiatry. Lucas Crawford, "Woolf's *Einfühlung*: An Alternative Theory of Transgender Affect," *Mosaic*, vol. 48, no.1 (2015), 165–81; Pamela L. Caughie puts the book in a framework of modernist notions of the transsexual, arguing that it both reconceives contemporary views of transsexualism and refigures the temporal structure of modernist life writing. Pamela L. Caughie, "The Temporality of Modernist Life Writing in the Ear of Transsexualism: Virginia Woolf's *Orlando* and Einar Wegener's *Man Into Woman*," *Modern Fiction Studies*, vol. 59, no. 3 (2013), 502–3.

16 See M. Keith Booker, "What's the Difference? Carnivalization of Gender in Virginia Woolf's *Orlando*," in *Techniques of Subversion in Modern Literature: Transgression, Abjection and the Carnivalesque* (Gainsville: University of Florida Press, 1991); György Kalmár, "Parler-Entre-Elles: Possibilities of a Less Phallocentric Symbolic Economy in Virginia Woolf's *Orlando*," *The AnaChronisT*, vol. 16 (2011), 57–79.

17 Virginia Woolf, *A Room of One's Own* (London: The Hogarth Press, 1959 [1929]), 148.

18 Elaine Showalter, *A Literature of their Own: From Charlotte Brontë to Doris Lessing* (London: Virago, 2011 [1977]), 216.

19 Toril Moi, *Sexual/Textual Politics: Feminist Literary Theory*, second edition (London and New York: Routledge, 2002), 12–14.

20 See Jane de Gay, "Virginia Woolf's Feminist Historiography in *Orlando*," *Critical Survey*, vol. 19, no. 1 (2007), 62–72; Esther Sánchez-Pardo González, "'What Phantasmagoria the Mind is': Reading Virginia Woolf's Parody of Gender," *Atlantis*, vol. 26, no. 2 (2004), 75–86.

21 Bell calls *Orlando* "interesting biographically," and enumerates a series of scenes that allude to Woolf's life at the time, often but not only connected to Sackville-West (*Virginia Woolf: A Biography*, vol. II, 135); Nicolson succinctly states that "[t]he effect of Vita on Virginia is all contained in *Orlando*," emphasizing that it is Virginia's "exploration" of the other (*Portrait of a Marriage*, 202–03); George Spater and Ian Parsons make short and toned-down references to the relationship between Woolf and Sackville-West in *A Marriage of True Minds: An Intimate Portrait of Leonard and Virginia Woolf* (London: Jonathan Cape & Hogarth Press, 1977), 116–17, 135, 143. Suzanne Riatt sees a more forceful biographical dynamic in *Orlando*, e.g., in pointing out how Woolf established her own claim to Sackville-West's life by writing it. See *Vita and Virginia: The Work and Friendship of V. Sackville-West and Virginia Woolf* (Oxford: Clarendon Press, 1993), 34–40.

22 Leslie Kathleen Hankins, "Orlando: 'A Precipice Marked V' Between 'A Miracle of Discretion' and 'Lovemaking Unbelievable: Indiscretions Incredible,'" in *Virginia Woolf: Lesbian Readings*, eds. Eileen Barrett and Patricia Cramer (New York and London: New York University Press, 1997), 181f, 185ff.

23 Laura Marcus, *Virginia Woolf* (Plymouth: Northcote House Publishers, 1997), 115–16, 117ff.

24 Sandra Gilbert makes related conclusions, equally stressing Woolf's desire to write about Sackville-West and her ability to comment and critique both biography as a genre and contemporary conceptions of gender and sexuality. Sandra Gilbert, "*Orlando*: Introduction," in *Virginia Woolf: Introduction*

to the Major Works, ed. Julia Briggs (London: Virago Press, 1994), 188–91, 195–9. Melanie Micir argues along the same lines, claiming that the temporal structure of *Orlando* undermines the normative force of conventional biography, and that Woolf "is modeling an alternative—feminist, modernist, queer—biographical structure." Melanie Micir, "The Queer Timing of *Orlando: A Biography*," *Virginia Woolf Miscellany*, vol. 82 (2012), 12.

25 Interestingly, the same appears to hold true for Sally Potter's 1992 film adaptation of *Orlando*. Comments on the film's generic and formal innovations have taken as a baseline the exploratory portrayals of English history and of gender roles. See Floriane Reviron-Piégay, "Translating Generic Liberties: *Orlando* on Page and Screen," *Biography*, vol. 32, no. 2 (2009), 316–39; Anne Ciecko, "Transgender, Transgenre, and the Transnational: Sally Potter's *Orlando*," *The Velvet Light Trap*, vol. 41 (1998), 19–34.

26 Pamela Caughie, "Virginia Woolf's Double Discourse," in *Discontented Discourses: Feminism/Textual Intervention/Psychoanalysis*, eds. Marleen S. Barr and Richard Feldstein (Urbana: University of Illinois Press, 1989), 42.

27 Jane Goldman, *The Cambridge Introduction to Virginia Woolf* (New York: Cambridge University Press, 2006), 135, 68.

28 Leaska, *The Novels of Virginia Woolf*, xxi; Marcus, *Virginia Woolf*, 115–16, 117ff.

29 Viewed from the perspective of linguistic translation, and more specifically of translation as a decision process, it is as if *Geschlecht* removes all the instances where one must choose between synonyms. Instead, it points to some language, register, or semotic system where the choice itself is precluded. Take, for example, Jiří Levý's "trivial example" of rendering the title of Bertolt Brecht's play *Der gute Mensch von Sezuan* in English, and how it requires a decision on whether the good person in Sechuan is a man or a woman. That decision is upended by *Geschlecht*. Instead of the progressive circumscription inherent to the transactional measure of reducing "der Mensch" to "man" or "woman" in order to acquire new readerships, *Geschlecht* functions as an invitation to stay in the field of indecision where contested meanings persist. Cf. Jiří Levý, "Translation as a Decision Process" (1967), in *The Translation Studies Reader*, ed. Lawrence Venuti (London and New York: Routledge, 2004), 148f.

30 Gérard Genette, *Paratexts: Thresholds of Interpretation* (New York: Cambridge University Press, 2001 [1987]), 1f. Note that Genette introduced the notion of paratexts in *Palimpsestes* (1981).

31 Virginia Woolf, *Orlando: A Biography* (London: Vintage Classics, 2016 [1928]). The edition here cited does include an introduction by Helen Dunmore, but is otherwise stripped of citations from critics or notes on awards etc., which are common paratextual features.

32 Arnold Bennett, "A Woman's High-Brow Lark," *Evening Standard*, November 8, 1928, 7. Reprinted in Robin Madjumdar and Allen McLaurin, eds., *Virginia Woolf: The Critical Heritage* (London: Routledge & Hegan Paul, 1975), 232–3.

33 Woolf, *Orlando*, 3–4.

34 Helen Southworth, "Virginia Woolf's *Orlando* Preface, the Modernist Writer, and Networks of Cultural, Financial and Social Capital," *Woolf Studies Annual*, vol. 18 (2012), 79–80.

35 Gilbert, "*Orlando*: Introduction," in Briggs, *Virginia Woolf*, 205; Nicolson, *Portrait of a Marriage*, 203.
36 Woolf, *The Letters of Virginia Woolf; Volume 3: 1923–1928*, 434, 435, 442.
37 Woolf, *Orlando*, 111.
38 Derek Ryan, "*Orlando*'s Queer Animals," in *A Companion to Virginia Woolf*, ed. Jessica Berman (Chichester: John Wiley & Sons, 2016), 111.
39 Woolf, *Orlando*, 237–9.
40 Virginia Woolf, "The New Biography" (1927), in *The Essays of Virginia Woolf; Volume IV: 1925–1928*, ed. Andrew McNeillie (London: The Hogarth Press, 1994), 473ff.
41 Marcus, *Virginia Woolf*, 117.
42 Woolf, "The New Biography," 478, 474.
43 Woolf, *Orlando*, 5.
44 The reference to Ariosto is somewhat camouflaged, to be sure, and one could note that while Woolf's diary states her ambition of "satirizing everything" in *Orlando*, she makes no explicit references to the *romanza*. Woolf, *A Writer's Diary*, 105, 117.
45 Pauline Scott, "The Modernist Orlando: Virginia Woolf's Refashioning of Ariosto's *Orlando Furioso*," in *Modern Retellings of Chivalric Texts*, ed. Gloria Allaire (Burlington: Ashgate, 1999), 92ff.
46 Maureen M. Melita, "Gender Identity and Androgyny in Ludovico Ariosto's *Orlando Furioso* and Virginia Woolf's *Orlando: A Biography*," *Romance Notes*, vol. 2 (2013), 123f, 131.
47 Woolf, "The New Biography," 478.
48 Woolf, *Orlando*, 5.
49 Melba Cuddy-Keane, *Virginia Woolf, The Intellectual, and The Public Sphere* (Cambridge: Cambridge University Press, 2003), 157f.
50 Woolf, *Orlando*, 5.
51 Woolf, *Orlando*, 6.
52 Sherron E. Knopp argues the book's "central relationhip between Orlando and the Biographer," and though she doesn't go into formal detail, the narrator's metaleptic comments speak in her favor. See Knopp, "'If I Saw You Would You Kiss Me?': Sapphism and the Subversiveness of Viriginia Woolf's *Orlando*," *PMLA*, vol. 103, no. 1 (1988), 28–9.
53 Woolf, *The Letters of Virginia Woolf; Volume 3: 1923–1928*, 412.
54 Gilbert, "*Orlando*: Introduction," in Briggs, *Virginia Woolf*, 205f.
55 Woolf, *Orlando*, 137ff.
56 Woolf, *Orlando*, 142.
57 Cuddy-Keane, *Virginia Woolf, The Intellectual, and The Public Sphere*, 156.
58 Woolf, *Orlando*, 152–5.
59 Woolf, *Orlando*, 65–6.
60 de Gay, "Virginia Woolf's Feminist Historiography in *Orlando*," 63f.
61 Woolf, *Orlando*, 131, 190–1.
62 Woolf, *Orlando*, 6–7.
63 Michael R. Olin-Hitt, "Desire, Death, and Plot: The Subversive Play of *Orlando*," *Women's Studies*, vol. 24 (1995), 483–4.
64 Woolf, *Orlando*, 171.
65 Woolf, *Orlando*, 175.

66 Nicolson, *Portrait of a Marriage*, 203.
67 Woolf, *Orlando*, 217.
68 Woolf, *Orlando*, 217, 219.
69 Olin-Hitt, "Desire, Death, and Plot: The Subversive Play of *Orlando*," 486–7.
70 Julia Kristeva, *Revolution in Poetic Language* (1974), trans. Margaret Waller (New York: Columbia University Press, 1984), 57ff.
71 Julia Kristeva, "A New Type of Intellectual: The Dissident" (1977) trans. Seán Hand, in Toril Moi, *The Kristeva Reader* (Oxford: Basil Blackwell, 1986), 295.
72 Hankins, "Orlando: 'A Precipice Marked V' Between 'A Miracle of Discretion' and 'Lovemaking Unbelievable: Indiscretions Incredible,'" in Barrett and Cramer, *Virginia Woolf: Lesbian Readings* (1997), 182.
73 Caughie, "Virginia Woolf's Double Discourse," in Barr and Feldstein, *Discontented Discourses* (1989), 47.
74 Catherine Malabou, "Plasticity," in *Dictionary of Untraslatables: A Philosophical Lexicon*, ed. Barbara Cassin, trans. eds. Emily Apter, Jaqcues Lezra, and Michael Wood (Princeton: Princeton University Press, 2014), 786ff.
75 Kristeva, "A New Type of Intellectual: The Dissident," 295.
76 Catherine Malabou, *Changing Difference: The Feminine and the Question of Philosophy*, trans. Carolyn Shread (Cambridge: Polity Press, 2011 [2009]), 5f.
77 Malabou, *Changing Difference*, 2ff, 7f, 14, 26ff.
78 Malabou, *Changing Difference*, 39f.
79 See Guido Mazzoni, *Theory of the Novel*, trans. Zakhia Hanafi (Cambridge: Harvard University Press, 2017); Fredric Jameson, *Antinomies of Realism* (New York: Verso, 2013); Douglas Mao and Rebecca Walkowitz, eds., *Bad Modernisms* (Durham: Duke University Press, 2006).
80 Woolf, *Orlando*, 156.
81 Cuddy-Keane, *Virginia Woolf, The Intellectual, and The Public Sphere*, 156.
82 Woolf, *Orlando*, 96.

6

Gazing at the Untranslatable Subject: From Velázquez's *Las Meninas* to Ellison's *Invisible Man*

Richard Hajarizadeh

The mirror provides a metathesis of visibility that affects both the space represented in the picture and its nature as representation; it allows us to see, in the centre of the canvas, what in the painting is of necessity doubly invisible
—MICHEL FOUCAULT, THE ORDER OF THINGS

Everything in the picture is manifested as no longer being representation but representative of representation.
—JACQUES LACAN, THE OBJECT OF PSYCHOANALYSIS

Lacan: "Je ne déforme pas ce que vous dites? Quoi?"
Foucault: "Vous reformez."
—JACQUES LACAN, LE SÉMINAIRE, LIVRE XIII

I

IN HIS ESSAY "*Geschlecht* I," Jacques Derrida examines the German term *Geschlecht* in connection with Martin Heidegger's usage of the word in theorizing varying categories, inflections, and moods of being-there

[*Da-sein*]. With possible English translations ranging from "genre," "gender," and "sex," to "race," "species," and "kind," *Geschlecht* remains a porous term whose semantic plurality demands translation while resisting clear-cut translational logics of equivalency and reference. Derrida observes that critical inquiry into Heidegger's use of *Geschlecht* has tended, in the case of "sex" and "gender," to render the term as pertinent solely to ontic dimensions of being—that is, to particular instances of subjective experience rather than to the ontological inscription of symbolic meaning *as* experience for the subject who lives out identity categories. For this reason, Derrida argues, critics have identified an ostensible reticence to address sexual difference in Heidegger's writings, insofar as categories of sex and gender remain *a posteriori* to matters of ontology.[1] Under such critical interpretation, sex, gender, race, or any other *Geschlecht* synonym would remain within the intellectual domain of scientific, anthropological, and biological *épistèmes*, a condition necessitating the elision of Being through analysis of particular modes of existence.

Against this notion of sex, gender, or race as of purely ontic concern, Derrida would read *Geschlecht* as not merely naming a subject's particular experience of identity categories, but also as naming a subject's ongoing interface with language *vis-à-vis* identity, and thus with power. As content, *Geschlecht* designates the substance of identity constructions, and specifically power's inscription in the subject through lived experience. Simultaneously as form, however, *Geschlecht* also designates the ongoing directive towards inscription that power demands of its subjects: that bodies must furnish identity categories with their own flesh and blood.

In this essay, I explore certain potentialities opened through Derrida's analysis of *Geschlecht* in relation to power, identity, and bodies. I connect the particular distributions of identity, *qua* content, to the injunction to identify within language, *qua* form, broaching an analytic of "embodiment" that branches out from historical analyses of "the subject." If, as Derrida suggests, particular identity categories, and power's mandate for subjects to identify within them, can be read as simultaneous functions of power, then the term "embodiment" here gestures towards the ongoing relationship that power insists upon between knowledge categories and the bodies made to represent them. I begin by theorizing the ontogenesis of the subject, juxtaposing contrapuntal readings of the Diego Velázquez painting *Las Meninas* as performed by Michel Foucault and Jacques Lacan. I go on to explore a function Derrida identifies with *Geschlecht*, that of "dispersion," to read race at once as a horizontal Genre of being—i.e., as the *possibility* of identity—and as denoting a set of distinct genres—concrete effects of power—that the subject dwells in. Reading race as embodiment, I situate my argument through an analysis of Ralph Ellison's *Invisible Man*, arguing that racial identity, insofar as it relates to knowledge categories, ultimately entails material subjugation to biopolitical regimes of control.

Considering *Geschlecht* to name a singular multiplicity of potential meaning, I argue, one can observe not only how power regulates subjects through identity, but one can also critique active racial genres as always contingent, partial, and therefore open to perennial reinterpretation. Here I employ the term "genre" over "category" to describe race, as the term "genre" enacts the untranslatable antagonism of forces internal to the symbolic parameters conditioning the emergence of the racialized subject through institutional power. Race and its relationship to power, I conclude, is given multilateral possibilities for interpretation, and therefore for critique, when viewed as a genre embodied by the subject.

II

On May 18, 1966, Michel Foucault sat in attendance at the eighteenth weekly session of Jacques Lacan's annual seminar.[2] Lacan had devoted the previous week to developing the psychoanalytic concept of the partial object, and Foucault heard that his analysis of Diego Velázquez's *Las Meninas* in the newly published *Les mots et les choses* [*The Order of Things*] had informed the discussion.[3] During the session, Lacan made several allusions to Foucault's presence in the room, directly addressing him only once: "I am not deforming what you say? Am I?" Foucault's response to Lacan was no less brusque: "You are reforming."[4]

In his article "The Other Side of the Canvas: Lacan Flips Foucault over Velázquez," Thomas Brockelman asserts the above minimal exchange intimates more than a merely professional dispute between the two thinkers. For Brockelman, the disparities between the Foucaultian and Lacanian analyses of *Las Meninas* signal entirely "contrasting approaches to subjectivity and history." Foucault cites the subject of the painting as the "un-presented" sovereigns, King Philip IV and his wife, who appear only in secondary, specular representation. Arguing the painting entails a series of mediatory relations between painted characters allows Foucault to nominate the specular, principally instantiated in the sovereign gaze, as originative of meaning. Foucault extends his claim beyond Velázquez's work, arguing in *The Order of Things* that *Las Meninas* embodies a larger classical-era epistemological turn, one that would install representation over essence as the *ratio cognoscendi* permitting conceptual regimes to arise. As Brockelman specifies, "the mirror at the back of the depicted room, in which the King and Queen are reflected, tips the viewer of *Las Meninas* off to what's on the other side of the reversed canvas."[5] That the sovereign figures emerge only through a mirror image in *Las Meninas* indicates the primacy of absence for representation. Using this insight, Foucault implicates various historical and modern *épistèmes* in mistaking representation *qua* absence for presence in the construction of the human as an object of knowledge.

Lacan begins the May 18th session by acknowledging the function of the gaze in *Las Meninas* as a "relevant point of intersection" between Foucault's critical field, philosophy, and his own, psychoanalysis.[6] As the session proceeds, however, Lacan argues that Foucault's predominant focus upon the relations between the depicted figures—relations which simulate the drama of subject constitution—results in an analytical myopia. Despite a particular interest in the represented content of the painting, Foucault omits to examine the "reversed" canvas portrayed in the picture's left-hand side. The canvas, whose content remains unavailable to the spectatorial position, forms for Lacan the major site of resistance to Foucault's reading, and by extension to Foucault's concept of the subject.[7] Velázquez obscures the canvas from the spectator's view, Lacan contends, so as to stage the ultimate inaccessibility that conditions viewer engagement with the painting's represented content. More precisely, in dissimulating the surface upon which the subject of representation would appear, Velázquez allows us to gaze upon the representative field itself and thereby to affront the absence undergirding representation, an absence of which Foucault writes in *The Order of Things*. Lacan here shifts the register of spectatorial engagement with *Las Meninas* from "mirror" to "window." Foucault emphasizes painting-as-mirror in order to suggest that *Las Meninas* reflects the relational gazing, produced of absence over presence, between its depicted figures. As a result, Foucault consigns himself to analyzing *Las Meninas* only at the level of its represented content. Alternatively, Lacan argues for painting-as-window in order to theorize *Las Meninas* as an object in excess of its represented content, and therefore as a *window into* representative functionality. As Brockelman puts it, Lacan calls the spectatorial position into question by arguing that *Las Meninas* refuses to seduce the viewer into "imaginary identification" with its narrative content.[8] Whereas Foucault asserts that *Las Meninas* bears witness to historical relations of power in and through representation, Lacan maintains that the painting is "representative of representation"—that it calls attention to itself as a representation.[9] In so doing, *Las Meninas* visibly rehearses the absence allowing for but vitiating representational meaning in art; an absence that, for Lacan, originarily enables meaning, representation, and identity in the subject.

Foucault's larger methodological reliance on a historicist analytic embroils him in two problematic commitments. Firstly, Foucault's historicism compels him to duplicate the same system-building logic that, according to him, precipitated erecting the human as an object of knowledge in classical and post-classical eras. By beginning and concluding *The Order of Things* with differing yet complementary analyses of *Las Meninas*, Foucault exchanges one history—the positivistic, scientific account of the world—with another history, the history Foucault himself details in order "to challenge the reassurance offered by smooth historical narrative."[10] The second of Foucault's commitments involves his notions of infinite finitude and origin. Imagined to result from specific historical causalities, infinite finitude, which permits a perpetual open-endedness in conceptual systems, and origin, which persistently obscures its own historicity, remain shielded from the absence conditioning historical narrative. A Lacanian analytic, by no means abnegating the place or importance of history, supplements Foucaultian historicism by allowing for absence, the non-meaning within representation, to irrupt upon alleged historical necessities.[11]

* * * *

In his initial reading of *Las Meninas*, Foucault observes that the spectator, like the painter-figure represented before the reversed canvas, appears in an incomplete liminality, in a threshold between total and effaced representation: "The painter is turning his eyes towards us only insofar as we happen to occupy the same position as his subject."[12] The subject of the painting, whom Foucault distinguishes as the sovereign figures, only appears in the mirror depicted at the left rear of the room. As the subject-figures who consolidate the occasion and purpose for the representation, the king and queen emerge in sharpened form, with the mirror reflecting nothing of the painter-figure, his canvas, the Infanta, or any other attendant personage. On the function of the mirror, Foucault writes that "[i]nstead of surrounding visible objects, this mirror cuts straight through the whole field of the representation, ignoring all it might apprehend within that field, and restores visibility to that which resides outside all view." The viewer's spectatorial representation only arises through the mirror, and for Foucault, the subject of the painting thus remains "doubly invisible." Not only does the mirror fail to reflect anything of the pictorial scene, but Velázquez renders the "original" position, the position in which the sovereign stands, as mimetically rather than immediately accessible to the spectator. Hence the image of the sovereign, given in reflective absence rather than in depicted presence, originates representative intelligibility for the spectator. The sovereigns "govern" the painting, despite their effectual absence, through the mere image of themselves, through a specular, relational gaze rather than through immanence. Foucault notes that in portraying the sovereigns through absence, Velázquez problematizes the relationship of subject to object, a relationship thought universal in accordance with classical-era paradigms of knowledge. The *subject* of the painting, which in a Cartesian register would endow the field of objects with sense and organization, is represented as a gazing *object* in the painting.[13]

Foucault determines the function of the constitutive gaze to be tripartite with respect to the subject positions in *Las Meninas*. First, he indicates, "there occurs an exact superimposition of the model's gaze as it is being painted." Here the sovereigns become "the model," reflectively represented as standing in the place of the spectator. The spectator's gaze "as he contemplates the painting" from the place of the sovereigns forms the second position. The third position comes in the figure of the painter, Velázquez himself, "as he compose[s] his picture" on the physical canvas. The three subject positions converge in a space "exterior to the picture: that is, an ideal point in relation to what is represented [...] that makes the representation possible." The three ideal points outside the picture correspond to three represented points in the picture: homologously, to the sovereigns in the mirror, to the visitor marginal to the painting, and to Velázquez in caricature. For Foucault, *Las Meninas* interlaces the relational gazes inside the picture with the relational gazes outside the painting to illustrate the central void underpinning its representative core. Despite the component subject positions coordinating respective gazes, only a vacuity remains in the spectator's position. The "very subject" who bestows sense upon the painting, as both the sovereign figures in whose place the spectator stands and the spectator standing in for the sovereign figures, "has been elided." The organization of the painting around a virtual nothingness allows "representation in its true form," an indeterminacy of origin, to emerge.[14]

Foucault cites the representational play of absence in *Las Meninas* as exemplary of the historical progression from representation and signs in the classical era to highly intricate, "organic" conceptual systems of knowledge in the "modern" era.[15] He first establishes the importance of representation for classical-era knowledge in his 1961 book *History of Madness*. He identifies "perception" as the representative mechanism through which scientific inquiry proceeded to tabulate madness, a mechanism visibly at work in *Las Meninas* as the gaze.[16] Throughout the eighteenth century, Foucault states, physicians responsible for diagnosing madness transitioned from treating madness in a chiefly spiritual capacity. Medical experts began to interpret madness as spiritual corruption through explicitly visible corporeal corruption. The widespread adoption of representation, carried out in the ostensible interest of assembling medical compendia, permitted physicians to detect madness through perceptible phenomena. Perception and empiricism, Foucault emphasizes, became the conceptual structures through which madness could be observed to speak through the body. Never the origin but always the scene of madness, the body gained a definitive place in the "order of causal proximity and succession," a place posterior to but always articulating the soul. Specifically, the body became the expressive medium that presented an image of the soul, a sign evidencing the soul's corruption.[17] Corporeal phenomena judged to signify madness became the signs that, according to the regime of re-presentation, spoke the truth of the contaminated origin, the soul.

In a section of *History of Madness* entitled "Theatrical Realisation," Foucault describes medical praxes physicians would employ to expose and to assuage madness with human reason. Physicians treating confined patients would indulge in the logic of the patient's "madness" in order to pursue it to extinction. According to Foucault, temporarily implementing the logic of madness "made the delirious object real, but at the same time exterior and if it made it perceptible to the senses of the sufferer, it forcefully delivered him from it." Such treatment displaced madness from its illusory "non-being" into a theatrical context, a context through which non-being could be rationalized by means of perception. The staging of madness showed that "the laws of being of delirium are nothing more than the appetites and desires of an illusion, the demands of non-being." The truth of non-being, surfaced through the "theatrical realisation" of non-being, consisted in the "confusion" the mad patient suffered in conflating image with presence. Foucault here emphasizes that theatrical performance, especially when successful in abating mad symptoms, signaled a triumph of empirical rationality against irrationality. As a result of its profound pertinence to classical-era scientific thought, perception would eventually propel systematicity to the forefront of post-classical thinking.[18]

In Aristotelian terms, the classical era marks for Foucault the period in which perception became a substantial form, a truth-telling apparatus substantivized by signs. Representation, qualified by signs gathered through perceptive means, served as the operative ground for scientific, medical, and aesthetic meaning: "nothing is given that is not given to representation."[19] As Foucault explains in *History of Madness*, the signs of madness, appositely interpreted, would indicate the truth about madness through representation.[20] Similarly, in his initial reading of *Las Meninas*, the specular image reflecting the sovereigns re-presents but never immanently shows the unifying context of the painting.[21] In balance, the spectatorial subject position, in which the sovereigns repose as hidden, serves as a visually absent node in a constellation of subject positions, none of which appear noumenally.[22] Foucault schematizes the move from classical to post-classical thinking by exploring the growing scientific unease with representation as a conceptual enterprise.[23] He characterizes the relationship between perception and percept as unendingly tenuous, arguing that classical-era structures of knowledge proffered no definitive termination to any chain of signification:

> No sign ever appears, no word is spoken, no proposition is ever directed at any content except by the action of a representation that stands back from itself, that duplicates and reflects itself *in another representation that is its equivalent*.[24]

Representation produced conceptual short-circuiting in the classical era, signifying but never showing, illustrating with absence but never demonstrating with presence. As with the gaze in *Las Meninas*, images, but never presence, originated meaning. The sign in its representational context emplaced visible phenomena in relation only to other signs, other representations, other names which themselves solely produced absence.[25]

* * * *

Shifting his analysis to post-classicism, Foucault argues that the function of the sign transforms in the nineteenth century, a transformation that would shape modern understanding of conceptual meaning. The sign, he explains, serves to reference phenomena already captured by "organic" systems of knowledge rather than to represent such phenomena. Put another way, the sign functions to recall knowledge from among pre-established, systematized truths:

> The general area of knowledge is no longer that of identities and differences, that of non-quantitative orders, that of a universal characterization ... but an area made up of organic structures, that is, of internal relations between elements whose totality performs a function.[26]

Post-classical thinking detains the vertiginous movement of endless representation by stabilizing the sign in conclusive relation to objects of systematic knowledge. By extension, systematicity subordinates perception to an exercise in self-referentiality, to repeating truths of determinate fact, cause, and effect captured in advance by knowledge systems. In this sense, classical-era *signification* yields to post-classical *anticipation*, as systematicity predestines as-yet unsystematized phenomena for "fixed forms of a succession which proceeds from analogy to analogy."[27] Historian of science Marvin Bolt echoes Foucault's characterization, asserting that what distinguishes modern science from its classical-era incarnation "natural history" is "an approach increasingly abstract, quantitative, experimental, and replicable, characterized by measurements, shared results, and *the expectation of novel discoveries*."[28] What was the "Order" of representation in the eighteenth century becomes "History" in the nineteenth century, and History, as Foucault argues, "*gives place* to analogical organic structures."[29]

In departure from the classical era, post-classical conceptual structures, by which objects of knowledge come to be posited, categorized, and thereby "known," serve as counterfeit "transcendentals" situated *a priori* "with the object." As Foucault clarifies, they pose as self-evident presence whose axiomatic functionality becomes shrouded through the systematicity that holds them as always "previously" applicable towards the interpretation of *any* phenomenal contingency. Post-classical conceptual structures presuppose systematicity itself as the ordering, historicizing machinery that transcends history. Conceptual systems, in other words, become in the nineteenth century and persist in the modern era as "a finally unified *corpus* of learning," wholly self-referential and representative only of prescribed knowledge structures. The ultimate dissociation of knowledge from representative abstraction guarantees for modern conceptual apparatuses a specious sense of cogency and stability still inconceivable in the classical era.[30]

Once modernity "eclipsed" the classical era, subordinating representation to referentiality, a figure Foucault terms "man" appeared in an "ambiguous position as an object of knowledge and as a subject who knows." Foucault differentiates modern "man," a dyadic subject–object of knowledge, from classical "man," by again turning to *Las Meninas*. In his initial reading, the painting stages the originary absence of representation through Velázquez's depiction of a subject who never appears. Each figure in the painting remains ancillary to the relational gazing effectuated by subject positions that represent through absence. Neither the spectator nor the sovereigns materialize, Foucault argues, so Velázquez effectively paints an empty, intermediary relationality between figures. Here, Foucault performs a second and concluding reading of *Las Meninas*, claiming that the painting permits an analysis of "modern man."[31] In his estimation, if each component gaze is taken in its atomized, partial relationship to the whole, each as a disconnected fragment, the painting illustrates the endless significatory drama of the classical era. In his second analysis, however, Foucault argues that if each atomized gaze reunites to comprise a gestalt figure in the spectator, then "man" is seen to gaze upon himself as an object of study. We observe "man" as an object to himself, he specifies, if we consider that, under modern conceptual systematicity,

> All the figures whose alternation, reciprocal exclusion, interweaving, and fluttering one imagined (the model, the painter, the king, the spectator) suddenly stopped their imperceptible dance, immobilized into one substantial figure, and demanded that the entire space of the representation should at last be related to one corporeal gaze.[32]

A logic of indissoluble unity, through which Foucault maps Velázquez's use of the gaze, allows systematic conceptuality to suppress representative uncertainty in favor of self-assuring structures of knowledge. Making a show of mastery, conceptual systems claim dominion over presence [*l'actuel*] by situating the origin of phenomena they seek to characterize as interior to their working parts and by then authorizing a search for that origin. The human becomes the intellectual vehicle of this search, as "necessarily the principle and means of all production." As principle, the human serves as *primum movens*, the force transcending the system he or she puts into motion. As means, the human serves to carry out the search for the truth of and within the system. The paradoxical role of "man," acting in modernity in both subject and object capacities, leads Foucault to term the human an "empirico-transcendental doublet." This "doublet" assumes an ambivalent relationship to knowledge, performing at once an *externalized* framing function that arbitrates the contents of knowledge and a systematically *internalized* function that collates all elements of knowledge. As Foucault puts it, the modern human becomes the examining subject and examined object of systematic knowledge, "a being such that knowledge will be attained *in* him of what renders all knowledge *possible*." Oxymoronically, then, the human serves as the "figure in which all the empirical contents of knowledge necessarily release, of themselves, the conditions that have made them possible."[33]

* * * *

Foucault draws his second reading of *Las Meninas* to a close by theorizing two functions, infinite finitude and origin, as key features of modern systematicity. He contends that infinite finitude and origin allow the human, aporetically, to maintain simultaneous empirical and transcendental access to conceptual knowledge. Classical subject–object dualism, singularized in the figure of the modern human, ensures in post-classicism that neither subject nor object roles will terminate in a lasting formulation of the human.[34] As we will see, Foucault's analysis of the immanent and unceasing subjective incompletion proffered by systematic conceptuality places him in significant, albeit limited alliance with Lacan. The guarantee of boundlessly partial identity Foucault ascribes to systematicity echoes Lacan's assertions concerning representation in art, language, and the subject. What Lacan calls this "relevant point of intersection," however, quickly becomes a point of departure marking two varying assessments of the role of historical eventuality for representation and the subject.[35]

Foucault observes the revisionary potential conditioning systematicity to lie within the absence undergirding representational media. Just as the relational gazing in *Las Meninas* produces meaning and context through absence rather than presence, for Foucault, systematicity depends upon an infinite finitude that perennially rends conceptual systems open. Each conceptual totality, such those he locates in labor, value, and language, asserts a refusal to close precisely because conceptual systems "are thoroughly imbued with finitude." "Heralded in positivity," Foucault continues, "man's finitude is outlined in the paradoxical form of the endless," a form that animates the power relations informing knowledge systems in a manner enabling their continued application."[36] Conferring limitless finitude upon particularized *Geschlecht* genres such as gender and race, modern conceptual structures fashion an origin for humankind out of categorial knowledge. A subject's enclosure within systems of knowledge grants him or her a representative lexicon through which to express predetermined parameters of subjectivity. As Foucault explains, to express subjectivity is to express conceptual systems that guard their origin from fluctuation in representation. The subject, he states,

> Rather than a cut [of signification], made at some given moment in duration [...] is the opening from which time in general can be reconstituted, duration can flow, and things, at the appropriate moment, can make their appearance.³⁷

As opening rather than closing, the subject always faces his or her origin as a retreat of origin. In this sense, the subject experiences both empowerment and disempowerment in every instance of representation. Espousing political, sexual, or racial identity, a subject mobilizes systematic knowledge in a move that originates solely the partial completion of any conceptual totality he or she invokes to frame subjectivity. Foucault further characterizes the "retreat" of the origin as "more fundamental than all experience, since it is in it that experience shines and manifests its positivity." Arguing that the retreat allows for historically contingent experience of phenomena, he locates the origin's manifestation decisively through its withdrawal. Yet Foucault here postulates a simultaneous, inverse operation to origin, complicating the conceptual horizon opened up by infinite finitude. He states that as origin withdraws, it also masquerades as the opposite of withdrawal, as definitive presence. Phenomenal origin remains inarticulate, Foucault argues, because it is never "contemporary" with its contemporaneity. In other words, an origin "is at the same time withdrawn and given as an imminence: in short, it is always concerned with showing how the Order, the Distant, is also the Near and the Same." Conceptual systems associate origin with an ahistorical immediacy by masking the historical conditions that instate them.³⁸

Modern systematic "Histories" hide the origin of humankind through dissimulative tendencies that, as Foucault claims, remain historically traceable in the passage from pre-classical to classical thinking.³⁹ In both readings of *Las Meninas*, Foucault stresses interpreting the painting as a mirror through which Velázquez exemplifies the instantaneous withdrawal and advent of origin in representative functionality. He charts each relational gaze, whether between the mirrored sovereign figures and the spectator or between the painter-figure and his putative subject, as merely reflective of presence. Alongside Lacan, Foucault cites the subject of *Las Meninas* as illustrative of the condition of subjectivity in general, a condition that saturates the subject with conceptual meaning while continually revoking its promise of presence. In contrast to Lacan, to whom we now turn, Foucault asserts that subjectivity, origin, and the final absence undergirding them result from discursive practices generated through distinctly historical developments.

Foucault's insistence upon quantifiable epochal characteristics, such as those he posits to differentiate pre-classical from classical thinking, obfuscates what Lacan sees as the *conditio proprio* for the epochal itself: the incessant displacement of representational meaning in the subject.

III

Lacan commences his analysis of *Las Meninas* in a manner parallel to Foucault, centering upon two forms, the reversed canvas and the Infanta, that for him accentuate representative functionality in the pictorial narrative.[40] Promptly, however, Lacan differentiates his methodological approach, contending that reading *Las Meninas* as a mirror confines critical engagement with the absence sustaining representation to the narrative dimension alone.[41] Transposing the analytic tenor from mirror to window, he argues the painting serves as a biform object of both literal and metaphorical potential. From a literal aspect, *Las Meninas* invites interpretation of its representative content, availing the spectator, as Foucault notes at length, of a conceptual object that portrays subject constitution through absent relational gazing. From a metaphorical aspect, the painting serves as a visual medium whose very translucence frustrates the spectator's hermeneutical labor.[42]

As window rather than mirror, *Las Meninas* functions as an object that at once permits spectatorial perspective while standing in the way of that perspective.[43] Lacan's transition from mirror to window bespeaks not only a crucial interpretive divergence from Foucault, but a divergence of the avenues through which their respective disciplines evaluate the subject in connection to representation and power. Whereas Foucault envisions the representative absence configuring conceptual structures as a product of evolving historical circumstance, Lacan argues *Las Meninas* precipitates interpretive failure in microcosmic illustration of representative functionality as such. While Lacan agrees with Foucault that "infinite" representative failure generates historical coherency, he argues that such failure intrudes concomitant to every phenomenally contingent instance of history in particular excess to the content of that history.[44] Representative failure, in other words, occurs not as a product of an historically inaugurated "infinite finitude" conditioning systematic conceptuality.[45] Rather, representation is itself the horizontal absence constitutive of historicity, the inhibiting, interstitial deficiency linking historical moment to historical moment.

* * * *

Reading the painting as a window rather than as a mirror allows Lacan to posit discontinuity over unity as the modality through which time and space converge in *Las Meninas*. Whereas a mirror reflects its content instantaneously, a window can splice "different times and places into a new present, a new place," thereby staging the spatiotemporal pastiche of representation rather than the linear, chronological consistency of historical narrative.[46] Beginning with the representation of space in *Las Meninas*, Lacan turns his attention to the reversed canvas that occupies the left-hand side of the painting. He highlights the canvas to contextualize *Las Meninas* as an object that hinders perception from instituting a categorical claim over the painting's narrative content. As object, the painting "is not only a representation, not only something one looks through or into but also something one must look at." Lacan characterizes his claim, according to Thomas Brockelman's analysis, by identifying the "key 'space'" of *Las Meninas* as the "foreground area *between* the depicted and the actual canvases," between the reversed canvas and "the actual 'picture plane'." Both the painter-figure standing before the canvas and the Infanta poised at the picture's center gaze into this "space" which, as Brockelman's scare quotes testify, more accurately comprises a spatial lapse. By producing a rift in the *visual* field, Lacan argues, Velázquez produces a *narrative* rift, disrupting spectatorial certainty and encouraging the viewer "to see that his painting [...] *is an object*: it is *not* the same as the space we look 'into' but stands in front of that."[47] As Lacan suggests, at the instant *Las Meninas* problematizes perception it demands the spectator to perceive its narrative, and in perceiving, finally to misperceive its representative absence as presence.[48] The painting poses misrecognition [*méconnaissance*] as the prerequisite to which spectatorial engagement becomes possible, a tendency that, as Lacan argues, exposes the spectator to the absence grounding representation.[49]

That the Infanta's gaze extends to the intermediary spatial lapse beyond the reversed canvas indicates that the painting *Las Meninas* remains an object beyond her perception. In a much-quoted passage from his analysis, Lacan imagines the painting, as object, speaking to the Infanta, declaring: "you do not see me from where I am looking at you."[50] Below I cite Lacan's statement at length:

> "You do not see me from where I am looking at you": since it is a formula minted in my style that is in question, I will allow myself to point out to you that in my style I did not say: "you do not see me, *there*, from where I am looking at you" (*tu ne me vois pas, là, d'ou je te regarde*) [...] *There is no "there"* that Velasquez [sic], if I make him speak, invokes, in this "you do not see me from where I am looking at you". In this gaping place, in this unmarked interval, there is precisely this "there," where there is produced the fall of what is in suspense under the name of o-object.[51]

Here Lacan enters into brief but direct dialogue with Heideggerian ontology, and in particular the notion of "being-there" [*Da-sein*] in which a "there" marks an existentially spatial, temporal, and social context. The place from "where" Lacan imagines the painting speaking, the spatial "where" of representation itself, consists not in a being-there but in a representative void. More precisely, *Las Meninas* positions its figures and their respective gazes into a configuration brought about by a relationality of absence. In this way, the painting renders perceptible its own "surface," indicating to the spectator its status as a partial object, what Lacan terms above the "o-object" and elsewhere the *objet a*. An object of only partial representative extension, the imperceptible, immaterial "where" into which the painter-figure and the Infanta gaze represents the visual relation the spectator must presuppose in imagining narrative coherency for the painting. The partial object protrudes, indiscernible but for its effect, as residual evidence of the accord struck between spectator and painting. Enacting partiality, Lacan explains, the spatially impalpable foreground marks *Las Meninas* as "representative of representation," superfluous to but constituent of its narrative drama.[52]

Lacan further elucidates his notion of the partial object by analyzing the representation of time in *Las Meninas*. Portraying a reversed canvas, he argues, permits Velázquez to reproduce the temporal discontinuity generative of and generated by representation.[53] Beholding the reversed canvas, the spectator perceives the surface on which the painter-figure depicts his subject, a subject to which the painter's gaze ostensibly ranges. If one considers the painter's gaze to extend to a spatially insubstantial "where," however, then the reversed canvas becomes a signifier rather than a surface, an empty symbol whose content is compromised through the very act of seeing. The reversed canvas exemplifies the inaccessibility representation imposes in relativizing the content it would bear: "the painter could have painted anything at all there; or, more radically, there need be no relationship between *Las Meninas* and the picture in the picture."[54] The unknowable content on the reversed canvas, in other words, obtrudes as a temporally *a posteriori* excess.

* * * *

Over the past twenty years, many critical theorists concerned with the role of representation in art, conceptual systems, and the subject have acknowledged the fundamental importance of Foucault's work. While intellectually indebted to Foucaultian theories about the subject, certain thinkers have critiqued Foucault's unremitting reliance upon history to outline the emergence of the subject in historical relations of power. As they see it, Foucault problematically uses history in description of representation, origin, and the subject, developing logically circular, self-contained frameworks themselves resembling the systematicity he critiques. Simply, they argue, Foucault employs an historical analytic to scrutinize oppressive, exclusionary accounts of history in an effort to establish "another" history, an alternate history cognizant of the power relations constituting it.[55] Specifically, the work of Joan Copjec and Slavoj Žižek illustrates how a stoic appreciation for the content of Foucault's assertions about subject representation can also contest the form through which he executes his analyses. Briefly reading these two theorists, both of whom broach Lacanian accounts of the subject, will provide grounding for an objection to Foucault's historicist epistemology.

In the introduction to her book *Read My Desire*, Joan Copjec defines historicism as "the reduction of society to its indwelling network of relations of power and knowledge." The problem of reducing a historically derived conceptual apparatus to its immanent relations of power is that doing so "limit[s] that regime to the relations that obtain within it." Working from within history, she argues, Foucault cannot but repeat conceptual system-building in the imposition of alternate histories, a move he would consider specifically causative of the types of regimes, such as the biopolitical, that he variously criticizes. In order to balance the context of Copjec's project, we must note she does not argue that in opposition to an historicist analytic one must accept the possibility of transcending the conceptual systems within which power operates. She instead understands a Lacanian analytic to surface the gaps and negation *within* historical accounts of the subject, gaps which themselves condition those historical formulations.[56]

In another critical exchange over the efficacy of historicist critique, Judith Butler criticizes the Lacanian formulation of the subject as "quasi-transcendental" in part of a larger published correspondence with Slavoj Žižek and Ernesto Laclau. She states that Lacan permits an analysis of the subject's constitution through misrecognition [*méconnaissance*], through the naturalization of conceptual structures which precede the subject. Yet, she continues, Lacan unwittingly presumes the universality of Freudian concepts, such as the Oedipus complex, and with it, heteronormative familial structures, as the transhistorical *a priori* upon which then to perform an analysis of the subject.[57] Here Žižek identifies a caveat to Butler's interpretation of Lacan, one stemming specifically from her espousal of a Foucaultian, historicist analytic. He finds Butler's reading of *méconnaissance* to be sound, but criticizes her "conflation" of "the endless political struggle of/for inclusions/exclusions *within* a given field" with a more "fundamental exclusion which sustains this very field."[58] Žižek elaborates that Lacan theorizes a productive antagonism to subjectivity, a "bar" to the total self-completion of the subject's identity, not in order to locate representation *outside* the subject as some sort of transcendental condition for subjective meaning. Instead, he argues, Lacan uses the notion of the "barred subject" to locate representative incompletion from *within* the historically contingent field of experience, as the self-negating, self-contradicting ground whose content founders upon the impossibility of its own universality.[59] On this contingent, conditional failure of representation, Žižek writes:

> In order for this very struggle to take place, however, its *terrain* must constitute itself by means of a more fundamental exclusion ("primordial repression") that is not simply historical-contingent, a stake in the present constellation of the hegemonic struggle, since it *sustains the very terrain of historicity*.[60]

To place Butler and Žižek's disagreement in Foucaultian terms, we must consider what Foucault and Lacan, respectively, understand to be most primordial in subject constitution. Foucault would claim the subject is constituted entirely by and in discursive practices that mandate the subject to route, for example, his or her expression of desire through sexuality, a highly intricate set of conceptual-*cum*-material practices. Such practices, both Butler and Žižek agree, appear *natural* but are in fact *naturalized*, both preceding and precedent to the subject as the condition upon which he or she might enter conceptual, and thus historical, intelligibility. Lacan, conversely, finds the subject as constituted through discursivity, through the act of symbolizing: not through *impossible* identities, but through the *impossibility* of identity. What remains at stake for Lacan regarding sexuality, for instance, is not that any and every historical formulation of sexuality will never fully accommodate the ever-expanding sexual pluralities of a given subject. Rather, as Žižek maintains, that the fundamental condition upon which any formulation of sexuality can be posed *will inevitably fail* remains the condition for postulating subsequent formulations. For Lacan, it is not that an historical field of sexual intelligibility fails to accommodate a subject's sexuality, but that historicity itself relies upon a structural, constitutive negation, a "particular" exception to every "universal" rule.[61]

* * * *

What perhaps constitutes Foucault's difficulty, and consequently the limits of his historicism, is the absence of a cogent distinction between representation's inhering self-referentiality and the potential works of art might have in performing that self-referentiality in a mode that would further disclose representation's central, eidetic void. In this respect, Foucault's overt historicism may, as methodology, limit his engagement with what he calls, when writing of literature, the "being" of words: that is, the final vacuity undergirding language's self-relation.[62] A Lacanian analysis avails us of what a Foucaultian analysis cannot here approach, that the "being" of words, in its endless play of self-relational emptiness, serves as the productive impediment, the generative antagonism, the faulty signified behind the insisting signifier, that conditions the possibility of language in the first place. Contextualized in Foucault's schematic of the nineteenth century, the self-referentiality comprising systematicity describes the condition of language as such for Lacan. In other words, for Lacan, language can only *ever* speak with itself in revelation of silence over sound, of absence over presence, of silence over substance. While certainly Foucault can see, and indeed compellingly scrutinizes the "being" of words, our mistaking the "being" of words for substantial presence, his commitment to its elucidation as a distinctly historical product pledges him to abjuring the following Lacanian observation: that the self-referentiality of signifiers allows words to circulate as meaningful.

In each historical invocation of language, as Foucault notes, language has "nothing to say but itself." Systematicity repeats itself as the structure allowing signifiers to voice subjectivity, signifiers at last only voicing the system in its insubstantiality. Similarly, as Foucault notes in his readings of *Las Meninas*, the relational gazes conditioning subject positions, whether fragmented or conjoined in description of "man," beget "nothing" but absent, intermediary echoes. Foucault would determine the infinite finitude suffusing conceptual systematicity as resulting from, and in turn informing historically derived exercises of power.[63] Lacan, on the other hand, would contextualize infinite finitude as the productive obstacle generating the foundation upon which representation, and thus representation of the subject through power, can take place.[64] In close proximity to Foucault, Lacan would confirm that systematicity permits an infinite search in which absence always emerges over presence. In close proximity to Lacan, Foucault would stress that representation, despite its relational emptiness, becomes the agential possibility through which the subject can navigate and criticize conceptual systems posing as natural. Their theoretical proximity here becomes distance, however, as Lacan would clarify that the conceptual systems in which one must affront the sheer impossibility of either mapping the "I" within any linguistic network, or mapping the spectatorial position within any visual network, primordially and not as an exclusive product of any historical chain of events, grounds the promise of ontological completion through perpetual incompletion.

As Foucault explains, the conceptual systems promulgating their own stability parade as *hic et nunc* transcendent preconditions to the content then found to exceed their parameters. Yet he misses that the infinity grounding finitude allows for a subject not only to posit the possibility of subjectivity, but as Lacan indicates, for the subject to presuppose transcendence as an impossible possibility, one that will never be realized. Under the latter framework, Lacan proffers a mode of agency resistant to oppressive conceptual regimes that operates *in concert with* and *through* representation rather than *against* the systematic forms at any particular historical juncture under examination. Indeed, if the historicism propelling Foucault's critique of history, one fastidiously dedicated to immanent, historically based events, were exercised unto its logical end, perhaps Foucault might have taken the Lacanian point that "the possibility for de-stabilization ... has stood *within* the constitution of the modern subject."⁶⁵ To pursue a Foucaultian metaphor from *Discipline and Punish*, "the soul is the prison of the body," but as Lacan allows us to see, the body's inability to confine the soul neatly within its bounds begets the possibility of conceiving both in the subject.

IV

Dasein, in Derrida's reading, names a principal relation-to-self which is not a relation to an ego (to an "I"), but rather to "a neutrality before ontic being, as in *In-der-Welt-Sein*" [being-in-the-world]. *Dasein* designates the neutral register opened up unto a horizontality that consists in a "preparatory" disposition towards the ontic meaning that would individuate "being-there" as "being-in-a-world," as being according to a particular set of signifying terms.⁶⁶ In his 2015 book *The Use of Bodies*, Giorgio Agamben maps this neuter mode of Being onto what he calls the "use-of-self," a mode in which the subject remains dynamically in relation to identity as identity's self-same capacity and realization.⁶⁷

Somewhat confoundingly, Derrida also describes the neuter register as a positivity, explaining that *Dasein* consists in an ongoing temperament toward ontic relationality that must, through temporality, embody numerous genres of being. Under such a reading, *Dasein* describes a non-teleological momentum rather than a congealed state of being, a recurrent process that remains horizontally alongside and particularly within relational meaning. Of this positivity, Derrida writes "[f]ar from constituting a positivity that the [...] neutrality of *Dasein* would annul [...] binarity itself would be responsible, or rather would belong to a determination that is itself responsible for this negativation."⁶⁸ The deconstructive potential of the differing, unravelling force of the neuter resides, in this very strict sense, in the positivity of oppositional structures, a positivity which, in its expression through *Dasein*'s genres of being, undoes itself through residual slippage. Hence for Derrida reading Heidegger, the neuter designates the ontological horizon of Being as it permits the positivizing of identity genres—as reducible to binary or multi-modal frameworks of meaning—and the destructive *qua* deconstructive force that retracts neutrality from potentiality, therein slotting *Dasein* into logics of meaning. As both potential and actualization, *Dasein* names the ongoing relationship a subject endures in connection with the genres of being that define the subject.

The "point of departure" from being-as-potential to being-as-genre bespeaks an originary "isolation," an alienation that illustrates to an individual their non-belonging in language. The problem of applying language to ipseity, to the purely ontological dimension of selfhood, here forms the same problem of "translating" self and other as symbolic premises. Here Derrida elucidates that "at a certain moment we will even come to see that the thinking of *Geschlecht* and the thinking of translation are essentially the same. The lexical swarm [*essaim*] brings together (or scatters [*essaime*]) the series 'dissociation,' 'distraction,' 'dissemination,' 'division,' 'dispersion.'" At a comparative, translational level—here between French and German— the above words carry an often negative sense, but "sometimes also a neutral or nonnegative sense." Thus the originary isolation also permits a "multiplication" of potential and yet-to-come signification, whether that signification arrives in the form of specific racial signifiers, or other genres conditioning the subject. As Derrida explains, "multiplicity [...] is not a simple formal plurality of determinations or determinities (*Bestimmtheiten*); it belongs to Being itself."[69]

The "originary, disseminal structure" of *Dasein* amidst discourses of identity categories is "dispersion," a term Derrida states is rather akin to his own use of the word "dissemination." Dispersion ought not to be thought to stand aloft and apart from spatial articulation, as it finds extension in language—although not in the Cartensian sense of *extensio*. Language, that is, carries within it the pathogenic, self-differentiating, dispersive force that undoes meaning and that conditions its formation and reformation across spatial contexts.[70] In other words, the neuter disposition of *Dasein* both positivizes and neutralizes its attendant genres of being, as those genres find decisive expression in language. Language is not separately a subtractive force and/or an additive force; rather, it besets upon the subject a vertiginous simultaneity stalled only through the election of certain significances over others. Thus, the function of dispersion is neither wholly positive nor negative but multilateral, insofar as *Dasein* is both a receptive preparedness for meaning, and what must proffer the subject an individuated "oneself," an alienating home in language in the form of "I."

One question upon which Derrida ends his essay reads as follows: "if one insisted on consigning difference within dual opposition, how does multiplication get arrested in difference?"[71] Turning now to Ellison's novel, we observe that biopolitics, control society, and medical discourse constitute a major force determining and enforcing racially particularized being. In a scene illustrative of biopolitical management, here perpetrated upon the narrator by hospital staff tending his wounds following a boiler explosion, an attendant holds up a large card and "thrusts it before [the unnamed narrator's] eyes."[72] Encased in a glass-like shell, a medical apparatus permitting the staff to observe him, the narrator reads the phrase "What is your name?" on the card. The narrator is called to identify with the most fundamental sign in the biopolitical regime of meaning, the name. The name is most fundamental, I argue, because it is supposedly the *most* individuated sign intended to mark the subject: firstly, as belonging to the order of speech, symbol, and meaning, what structural anthropologist André Leroi-Gourhan would call the "universal" order of the human, and secondly, as particularized within that order.[73] The narrator's response to beholding the card, and to his own subsequent inability to produce his name, bespeaks the racial conundrum in which he is embroiled throughout the novel, insofar as he cannot seem to identify with the nodal patterns of meaning characterizing "Black identity" itself. That is, he cannot so easily identify with the effects of the biopolitical injunction to meaning by wholly claiming Blackness, education, communist laborer, or even "hospital patient" as definitive of his own identity. The lattermost element is witnessed in the peculiarity of his condition, over which the medical staff bicker.[74]

Foucault cites the modern medical institution as one sector of the biopolitical episteme in which the "abnormality" of certain conditions signals not untreatable physiological aberrations but ideological crises of uncertainty over the stability of medical representations of aberration. In his 1974–5 lecture series *Abnormal* [*Les Anormaux*], Foucault characterizes "abnormality" by analyzing the figuration of the abnormal "criminal" as circumscribed by medical discourse, and specifically as detailed in psychiatric discourse. Foucault cites as "dangerous" the criminal who "is not exactly ill and who is not strictly speaking criminal." What marks the dangerous criminal as distinct from the normalized criminal is the radically *unmarked* style of his or her crime, the as-yet unclassifiable tendency that resists systematic categorization either within terms of madness or within a context of determinate criminality.[75] The abnormal crime, in other words, merely resembles crime, and as such produces no sign or empirical evidence of its meaning other than the fact of its own occurrence, a fact that in turn antagonizes the medico-juridical discourse that would manage it.

Yet at this juncture, Foucault clarifies that "danger" consists not in an aberrational property internal to crime, not in a palpable essence that would definitively demarcate conventional criminal behavior from unanticipated, unpredictable modes of dangerous crime. Rather, the "danger" within the otherwise quantifiable criminal population makes possible what Foucault calls the "theoretical foundation of an uninterrupted chain of medico-juridical institutions." The abnormal, materializing in psychiatric discourse through the figuration of the pervert, allows for medical and juridical meaning "to be stitched together." Here, Foucault identifies the counterpoint to the pervert in the figuration of the expert. The expert depends entirely upon the pervert, upon the significatory excess to psychiatric discourse, to legitimize his or her opinion as germane both to medicine and to law. In a sense, then, the expert conjures psychiatric discourse necessarily in the shadow of perversion, in radical proximity to the potentially contaminative, "perverting" force of the individual rendered as abnormal by psychiatric discourse.[76] On the subject of expert opinion, Foucault writes:

> The infantile language of expert opinion functions precisely to bring about the exchange of effects of power between judicial and medical institutions through the disqualification of the figure in whom these institutions are joined together.[77]

Medical and juridical discourses operate through the expert's disavowal of the pervert, through a sweeping gesture that at once renders peripheral and central the figuration whose indeterminate formulation in language allows for those discourses to continue compounding.[78] For this reason, Foucault argues that expert psychiatric opinion, insofar as it claims to access the truth of the human psyche, always repeats the same gesture. In short, expert psychiatric opinion conveys nothing of psychiatry, instead serving as an interstitial force whose object becomes the mere applicability and enforcement of law.

In the same way that structural anthropologist Leroi-Gourhan argues racism depends upon our first positing the figuration of the human as a primary ontological framework, so Foucault argues that neither medicine nor law but their caricature in expert opinion must be presupposed as the value conditioning legal decision-making. Expert opinion, in other words, *sensu stricto* remains neither medical nor juridical opinion. Rather, it emerges as the indistinction, as the variable negative force consisting of no juridical or medical property but that nevertheless permits legal decision, and thus nominal justice, to occur. As Foucault puts it, expert opinion "is consistent with neither law nor medicine," but that it nonetheless "has a major role in their institutional adaptation, *at their join*." Foucault understands expert opinion as an effectual point of contact between medicine and law, one "deployed" not "in a field of opposition, but in a field of gradation from the normal to the abnormal." Just as Socrates argues of sophistry in Plato's dialogues, expertise possesses no field or art [*techné*] of its own. Although expertise governs, it is not explicitly in the business of governing as one might assert of law: its *telos*, normalization, remains vacuous of any specific "craft knowledge" and incapable of any praxis other than self-replication.[79]

Foucault illustrates his theory of the abnormal by briefly examining the role of plague victims—an historical population most commonly deemed corporeally abnormal—in eighteenth-century European discourses of medicine and the metropolis. Instead of abandoning plague communities to survival in rural areas unregulated by the city, urban planners undertook what Foucault terms a "meticulous spatial partitioning" that allowed for the inclusion of plague victims within cities. Foucault contends that the move to include the plague community within city limits exemplifies the exertion of state power, one aiming not to alienate but specifically to integrate and to monitor populations considered "dangerous." For Foucault, power "extend[s] to the fine grain of individuality," operating not through exclusion but through "a close and analytical inclusion of elements." In order to assign the "dangerous" plague victim a place within spatial and temporal dimensions, power first and foremost functions to assign the plague victim a place within significatory dimensions, within a system of medical and legal meaning. Consequently, the circulation of power functions not only through *regimes* of legal, medicinal, and scientific power as materialized in physical practices, but also through *epistemes* of legal, medicinal, and scientific knowledge. The court and the judge normalize justice, and the hospital normalizes medicine, each through various imbricated networks of meaning that accumulate knowledge and provide it a context, namely the possibility of its dissemination and enforcement. In this sense, normalization is a positivism before it is a means to repress individuals.[80]

Certainly, Foucault might here note, exercises of power and discipline remain an important object of critique, as they often occur in the form of physical violence. Yet as the above analysis testifies, exercises of power follow upon the imposition of signifying constellations of which medical, legal, and political discourses become nodes. These highly organized, ideological centers of "truth" allow the subject to express meaning, and to be expressed meaningfully, according to the order of signs conditioning those constellations. The creation of sexual meaning, under Foucault's reading, permits an individual to become a sexualized subject and to voice that sexuality within an intelligible regime of meaning.[81] Here we might understand Foucault to reject the notion of power as a ubiquitous and de-personalized force imposed through the arbitrary rule of a sovereign or sovereign figure. What instead surfaces in his analysis is a power that repeats itself through all systematic discourse as highly personal and individualized. As a general course of ontology, biopolitics permits a subject to be a subject within a system of meaning, while demanding that the subject be *according* to the relations that obtain within that system. Biopolitical governance ensures its longevity, however, through the subject's ultimate inability to identify with the discourses and signifiers shaping the boundaries of his or her lived experience as a personified genre. As a result, biopolitical logic can continue to signify and re-signify the subject in a mode of caprice generated and sustained by significatory displacement, and in particular through disavowing language's metonymic and metaphorical constitution.

In the terms of medical discourse, Ellison's narrator cannot "properly" appear as an analyzable patient of medicine. Invisibility, as the metaphysical void around which discourses of medicine are built, irrupts in this instance as the forgetting of the name:

> A tremor shook me; it was as though he had suddenly given a name to, had organized the vagueness that drifted through my head, and I was overcome with swift shame. I realized that I no longer knew my own name.[82]

The doctor's gesture in holding up the card instates not self-recognition but an underlying vacuity to the narrator's identity, an emptiness for which the narrator serves as a placeholder within medical discourse. When the doctor holds up another card reading "Who are you?" the narrator thinks: "Who am I? I asked myself. But it was like trying to identify one particular cell that coursed through the torpid veins of my body." The narrator is able only to produce "himself," an immediacy of determinate non-meaning, a non-sign, as witnessed in the grammatical construction of the question "Who am I? I asked myself" wherein the subject-predicate "I," through questioning, speaks only to the emptiness of its object, "myself." Divested of memory and its images, he merely reflects upon the self as a linguistic function in the form of the emptied "I," and thus as a non-self: in other words, he sees himself as a pure, barren postulate of language.[83] The narrator's self-questioning depicts invisibility in its starkest form: not something that biopolitical meaning coerces the subject into, but the condition upon which subjectivity arises and founders. To pursue a brief metaphor, the sea makes a ship possible *qua* conceivable as a ship, ready to sail and thus purposive, but the sea also threatens, corrodes, and annihilates a ship, rendering it at one moment a ship and thus in separation from the sea, and at another moment virtually indistinct from the coursing water.

Laboring to rack his memory for familiar thoughts, the narrator declares, "I tried, thinking vainly of many names, but none seemed to fit, and yet it was as though I was somehow a part of them all, had become submerged within them and lost."[84] Here the narrator does not sift through the names he knows, acquiescing to assign value and meaning to some while rejecting others. Rather, he elucidates his subjectivity as the evacuated placeholder through which biopolitical power, here occurring as the name, passes in an entirely impersonal manner. More specifically, he reflects that the "I" becomes the movement that power, as meaning within a system of signs, attempts to hold in place, but that power ultimately cannot fasten to any one sign, even to the "I."

The medical staff continue attempting to solicit a name from the narrator, writing questions upon cards of a distinctly racializing logic, no doubt surmising that if the narrator cannot produce his own name, that surely he might answer such questions as "Who was Buckeye the Rabbit?" and "Boy, who was Brer Rabbit?" Here we note a different, more intensely contextualized biopolitical measure, a movement from the universal demand to identify—"What is your name?" viz. are you not a human, an agent of reason?—to the particularly racist—"Who was Buckeye the Rabbit?" viz. are you not a Black man?[85] The biopolitical measures here employed enact two movements, the humanizing and the racializing—reflected in the figures of the ontological and the ontic—in an effort to retrieve the narrator from what Foucault terms the indistinction of the abnormal and to emplace him in relation to biopolitically intelligible meaning.

As Foucault and Leroi-Gourhan's analyses show, ethnicity is made possible, and race as its corollary, through the abnormality–normality split. In the biopolitical regime of Ellison's novel, race is a metaphor that functions literally, just as every signifier is both fictive and real. More specifically, "Black" becomes a fiction in that its origin, its elucidation as a subject category through power, and the characteristics posited to furnish its formal parameters depend upon an interminable displacement of meaning that constitutes its fundament. It is this condition of significatory displacement, of what Paul de Man calls "un-decidability," that racial expertise, such as that Ellison's narrator experiences in the hospital, endeavors to disavow because it creates only a discourse of the unknown: of endless signification.[86] Again, however, under biopolitics race in general and Blackness in particular remain "real," as their metaphoricity operates concertedly to frame the Black body as subject to power. As metaphor, race masquerades as literal such that it becomes indistinguishable from the literal, therefore permitting expertise to substantivize it as reducible to particular racial "truths," as in the cultural *sign* of Brer Rabbit forming the putative *substance* of Blackness. But despite the claim of medico-juridical expertise, the question of race is never a question of reason, of rationality, but rather of systematicity and classification—of where particular racial significations have been situated within the biopolitical regime.

In the concluding passages to *Invisible Man*, Ellison's narrator poses the question of whether agency within biopolitical logic is possible. In a dream sequence following a fall into a New York City manhole, the narrator envisions the only mode of resistance that cannot be exclusively operationalized by biopolitical discourse: writing. Envisioning his castration at the hands of the various figures who, throughout the novel, seek to circumscribe *his* struggle as *their* struggle, the narrator perceives his genitals, dripping with blood, caught in the framing of a steel bridge:

> "I'm not afraid now," I said. "But if you'll look, you'll see … It's not invisible … "
> "See what?" they said.
> "That there hang not only my generation wasting upon the water—"
> […] "there's your universe, and that drip-drop upon the water you hear is all the history you've made, all you're going to make. Now laugh, you scientists. Let's hear you laugh!"[87]

Here as elsewhere, the ocularism of which Ellison's narrator speaks indicates a valence beyond seeing-as-apprehension, and indeed beyond invisibility as merely not being-seen. The narrator transposes the ocular from a literal to a metaphorical register insofar as those who do not see him cannot see beyond the varying biopolitical identities into which they would slot him. To live agentially, that is, in a manner signaling his particular embodiment within power, the narrator would write in a manner within but disruptive of the very boundaries that allow for his subjectivity to remain legible. In other words, he would choose the signifier in its radical inability to reduce, pinpoint, localize, or otherwise totalize his lived experience as the singular expression of power.

The writing of history, and especially of the personal histories of racial prejudice and oppression, may not permit a total reclamation or seizure of power over biopolitical meaning. What the writing of personal histories may permit, however, is a repudiation of the putative totality christened "History," a rejection of a master narrative claiming absolute truth over questions of race as applied to racialized, subjected individuals. Here the narrator becomes no more and no less invisible; he instead accepts invisibility as the condition for writing local histories *qua* genealogies insofar as writing those histories remains an ongoing and interminable project. Difference, or as he puts it, "division," remains the sole cause and effect of writing, and is the only way to communicate his singularity, as that singularity is only communicable as metaphor, as writing. That is, division, such as that between love and hate, or between denouncing and defending, becomes all the narrator can effectuate in writing, so division must be taken *in place of* singularity, which can never be communicated in itself.

In the final pages of the novel, the narrator admits that writing effaces his invisibility, as a sort of necessary positive act advanced against the void opened up by the non-presence of language: "So now having tried to put it down I have disarmed myself in the process."[88] Nevertheless, he deduces, the "disarmament has brought me to a decision," a decision to take up meaning in its self-alienating alterity, and to assert the "I" precisely because it communicates a non-essential coordinate to subjective experience. For this reason, the strength of Ellison's narrative lies in its refusal to hypostasize individuality, the "I," and invisibility in the same mode through which biopolitical discourse subjectivates the racialized subject: as a sign. Insofar as the circulation of meaning in the signifier effectuates continual dynamism over stasis, the signifier remains its own worst enemy in the most generative sense. In light of language's ultimate metaphysical failure, its failure to render present and actual [*l'actuel*] the figuration of race in general and Blackness in particular, Ellison reminds us that we ought not to abandon ourselves merely to the role of passive participants or observers of biopolitical subjectivation. As language users interested in the composition of dynamic genealogies of individuals rather than of static, totalistic

Histories of race, we need to prolong the circulation of meaning: to nourish the viral constitution and behavior of signification. As Ellison's *Invisible Man* testifies, the signifier's breakdown, reformation, and cyclicality become the operative possibility of heterogeneous meaning-production, one which would productively dislocate each subsequent figuration of race and history to come.

Notes

1. Jacques Derrida, "*Geschlecht* I: Sexual Difference, Ontological Difference," in *Psyche: Inventions of the Other*, vol. II, eds. Peggy Kamuf and Elizabeth Rottenburg (Stanford: Stanford University Press, 2008), 7–26.
2. Jacques Lacan, *The Object of Psychoanalysis*, trans. Cormac Gallagher, www.lacaninireland.com/web/wp-content/uploads/2010/06/13-The-Object-of-Psychoanalysis1.pdf, 210.
3. Thomas Brockelman, "The Other Side of the Canvas: Lacan Flips Foucault over Velázquez," *Continental Philosophy Review*, vol. 46 (2013), 2, 271.
4. Lacan, *The Object of Psychoanalysis*, 232.
5. Brockelman, "The Other Side of the Canvas," 272–3.
6. Lacan, *The Object of Psychoanalysis*, 210.
7. Brockelman, "The Other Side of the Canvas," 273.
8. Brockelman, "The Other Side of the Canvas," 283.
9. Lacan, *The Object of Psychoanalysis*, 232.
10. Brockelman, "The Other Side of the Canvas," 275.
11. In *History of Madness* (trans. Jonathan Murphy and Jean Khalfa, New York: Routledge, 2009) Foucault illustrates his awareness of the threat of non-meaning for conceptual understanding. He includes a brief notational aside in explanation of sixteenth-century religious views on spiritual aberration, arguing that historical "experience of the demonic" threatened to reveal "a tear in the fabric of the world" (597, n. 83). What Foucault cannot articulate here is that the threat of non-meaning conditions historicity itself, that conceptual understanding and its constituent power relations arise precisely in antagonistic reaction to "a tear" in representative functionality (597, n. 83).
12. Michel Foucault, *The Order of Things: An Archaeology of the Human Sciences* (New York: Vintage Books, 1994 [1966]), 4–5.
13. Foucault, *The Order of Things*, 5, 7–8.
14. Foucault, *The Order of Things*, 14–16.
15. Foucault, *The Order of Things*, 218.
16. Michel Foucault, *History of Madness*, trans. Jonathan Murphy and Jean Khalfa (New York: Routledge, 2009), 214.
17. Foucault, *History of Madness*, 214, 219.
18. Foucault, *History of Madness*, 332f.
19. Foucault, *The Order of Things*, 78.
20. Foucault, *History of Madness*, 219.

21 In chapter 6 of *The Order of Things*, "Exchanging," Foucault illustrates the prevalence of representation in the classical era through an analysis of value's changing relationship to coinage. In pre-classical systems of valuation, Foucault writes, in excess of the sovereign imprimatur, coins were valued for the precious metals innate to their constitution (202). In the eighteenth century, however, coins became a sign indicating value through absence rather than through the presence of precious metals (202). The axis of value tilted, permitting coins *to represent* rather than *to be* value: "*Value*, then, occupies exactly the same position in the analysis of wealth as structure does in natural history; like *structure*, it unites in one and the same operation the function that permits the attribution of one sign to another sign, of one representation to another, and the articulation of the elements that compose the totality of representations or the signs that decompose them" (202, italics in original). See 166–214.
22 Foucault, *The Order of Things*, 15.
23 Foucault, *The Order of Things*, 78.
24 Foucault, *The Order of Things*, 78; italics in original.
25 Foucalt, *The Order of Things*, 78–9.
26 Foucault, *The Order of Things*, 218.
27 Foucault, *The Order of Things*, 218.
28 Marvin Bolt, *Glass: The Eye of Science* (New York: Corning Museum of Glass, 2016), 2; italics in original.
29 Foucault, *The Order of Things*, 219; italics in original.
30 Foucault, *The Order of Things*, 244–5, 247, 250; italics in original.
31 Foucault, *The Order of Things*, 312.
32 Foucault, *The Order of Things*, 312.
33 Foucault, *The Order of Things*, 313, 318, 322; italics added.
34 Foucault, *The Order of Things*, 314.
35 Lacan, *The Object of Psychoanalysis*, 210.
36 Foucault, *The Order of Things*, 314.
37 Foucault, *The Order of Things*, 332.
38 Foucault, *The Order of Things*, 334–5, 339.
39 Foucault, *The Order of Things*, 339.
40 Lacan, *The Object of Psychoanalysis*, 232.
41 Brockelman, "The Other Side of the Canvas," 278.
42 Lacan, *The Object of Psychoanalysis*, 232.
43 Brockelman, "The Other Side of the Canvas," 280.
44 Slavoj Žižek, "Class Struggle or Postmodernism? Yes, Please!," in *Contingency, Hegemony, Universality: Contemporary Dialogues on the Left*, second edition (New York: Verso, 2011), 111.
45 Foucault, *The Order of Things*, 314.
46 Brockelman, "The Other Side of the Canvas," 283.
47 Brockelman, "The Other Side of the Canvas," 280; italics in original.
48 In contrast to his claims about psychoanalysis, the Lacanian approach produces the opposite of what Foucault describes as "theatrical realisation" in *History of Madness* (see above: n16). Foucault argues that in the eighteenth century, the proto-analytic physician joined in a "mad" patient's logic in order to assuage madness through the exercise of reason *qua* humanistic rationalism

(*History of Madness*, 332). Lacan's clinical approach involves precisely the contrary, bringing the subject to the profound *failure* of rationalism either to enclose entirely or to transcend the representative signs circumscribing existence.

49 Lacan, *The Object of Psychoanalysis*, 232; Lacan's interest here remains as much to emplace subjectivity and representation in relation to art as it remains to recapitulate general psychoanalytic insight into the subject's experience in a system of signs. As Brockelman explains, in the psychoanalytic session, the analyst aims to bring the analysand to the threshold of the fantasy objects structuring his or her reality in order to disclose the radical absence allowing for those fantasy objects (Brockelman, "The Other Side of the Canvas," 288).
50 Lacan, *The Object of Psychoanalysis*, 232.
51 Lacan, *The Object of Psychoanalysis*, 232; italics added.
52 Lacan, *The Object of Psychoanalysis*, 232–3.
53 Brockelman, "The Other Side of the Canvas," 287.
54 Brockelman, "The Other Side of the Canvas," 283; italics in original.
55 Brockelman, "The Other Side of the Canvas," 288–9.
56 Joan Copjec, *Read My Desire: Lacan Against the Historicists*, second edition (New York: Verso, 2015), 6f.
57 Žižek, "Class Struggle or Postmodernism? Yes, Please!," 109.
58 Žižek, "Class Struggle or Postmodernism? Yes, Please!," 108; italics in original.
59 Žižek, "Class Struggle or Postmodernism? Yes, Please!," 110.
60 Žižek, "Class Struggle or Postmodernism? Yes, Please!," 110f; italics in original.
61 Žižek, "Class Struggle or Postmodernism? Yes, Please!," 112–13.
62 Foucault, *The Order of Things*, 294–300.
63 Foucault, *The Order of Things*, 300, 312, 314, 318.
64 Brockelman, "The Other Side of the Canvas," 280.
65 Brockelman, "The Other Side of the Canvas," 289; italics in original.
66 Derrida, "*Geschlecht* I: Sexual Difference, Ontological Difference", 11.
67 Giorgio Agamben, "The Inappropriable" and "Epilogue: Toward a Theory of Destituent Potential," in *The Use of Bodies: Homo Sacer IV, 2*, trans. Adam Kotsko (Stanford: Stanford University Press, 2015), 80–94, 263–80.
68 Derrida, "*Geschlecht* I," 14–15.
69 Derrida, "*Geschlecht* I," 17–19.
70 Derrida, "*Geschlecht* I," 19, 20–1.
71 Derrida, "*Geschlecht* I," 26.
72 Ralph Ellison, *Invisible Man*, second edition (New York: Vintage, 1995), 239.
73 André Leroi-Gourhan, "Introduction to a Paleontology of Symbols," in *Gesture and Speech*, trans. Anna Berger (Cambridge: MIT Press, 1993), 269–80.
74 Ellison, *Invisible Man*, 236ff.
75 Michel Foucault, *Abnormal Lectures at the Collège de France 1974–1975*, trans. Graham Burchell, ed. Arnold I. Davidson (New York: Picador, 2003 [1999]), 34.
76 Foucault, *Abnormal Lectures*, 34, 36.

77 Foucault, *Abnormal Lectures*, 36.
78 Foucault, *Abnormal Lectures*, 26.
79 Foucault, *Abnormal Lectures*, 41–2; italics added.
80 Foucault, *Abnormal Lectures*, 46, 34, 48–9.
81 Foucault, *Abnormal Lectures*, 52.
82 Ellison, *Invisible Man*, 239.
83 Ellison, *Invisible Man*, 240.
84 Ellison, *Invisible Man*, 240–1.
85 Ellison, *Invisible Man*, 242.
86 Paul De Man, "Metaphor: Second Discourse," in *Allegories of Reading: Figural Language in Rousseau, Nietzsche, Rilke, and Proust* (New Haven: Yale University Press, 1979), 135–59.
87 Ellison, *Invisible Man*, 570; italics in original.
88 Ellison, *Invisible Man*, 580.

7

From Lectiocentrism to Gramophonology: Listening to Cinema and Writing Sound Criticism

David LaRocca

I

As William Carlos Williams reflected on the composition of *Paterson*, he wrote: "The noise of the Falls seemed to me to be a language which we were and are seeking and my search, as I looked about, became to struggle to interpret and use this language."[1] Williams, to my ear, addresses the translation of sounds from the world to the page, from the Falls in Paterson to its written, poetic expression in the poem, *Paterson*. He is pursuing, what I call here, a gramophonology: the discovery, use, and development of a *Geschlecht*, or more than one; Williams' "sound writing" exemplifies one variety of a translational hermeneutics, part of an attempt observable at the level of broad cultural and linguistic currents and also in individual experiments, such as a given poem or essay, to "move" something from one place to another—as the linguistic origins of *metaphor* attest (Gr. μεταφορά, *metapherein*, *meta* "over, across, beyond" + *pherein*, "carry, bear"; Lat. *metaphora*, "transference," "to transfer").[2] These labors involve a persistent test of transcription and translatability, and thus require an attendant openness to transcription errors and untranslatability; that is, to discerning what elements remain left out, left over, in surplus and deficit, falsely rendered or accidentally imported, or what creates lapses and lacunae.[3] Hence the "struggle to interpret and use this language." Indeed, it may be difficult to discern what in fact doesn't make the passage on any given occasion—what was left behind; as a result, one may be visited or overcome by the compulsion to recirculate such movements—say, in the spirit of the "repeat-after-reading" that Emily Apter describes as *lexilalia*, a kind of repetition disorder confronting the lexicographer (especially one attempting to translate the untranslatable).[4] Needless to say, *Geschlecht* itself, for all its abundance of denotations and connotations, remains vexingly beyond assured and satisfying equivalents. Even on occasion "decoded," it resists uniform or definitive delineation, precludes a complete list of synonyms: there are so many options on offer that they would seem to variously negate or subsume the others. *Geschlecht* is representative in this condition of unfixedness, because, as Ralph Waldo Emerson noted, more generally: "[...] all symbols are fluxional: all language is vehicular and transitive, and is good, as ferries and horses are, for conveyance [...]."[5] Hence the nervous condition that we call the *Geschlecht* complex, a network of intellectual and emotional agitations to prevailing standards of definition and expectations for judgment.

Among the polysemious possibilities, *Geschlecht* is taken to mean sex, race, type, coinage, kind, lineage, clan, tribe, and family, as well as generation, genus, genre, and gender.[6] Consider how the internal relationship between generation, genus, genre, and gender is especially propitious, for it suggests a way forward for thinking about the sound/image entity we have come to call in popular parlance "the movies."[7] Is this audiovisual creation one thing or two, or, instead, many; are we speaking of two genera under one name ("film"), and perhaps also several medial genres (photograph, motion picture, animation, computer-generated imagery [CGI], and a plethora of sound genres)? If we are, as I contend below, faced with a plurality of overlapping genres (genera, etc.), while holding vigil for what is not overlapping, we need at least to acknowledge (in a spirit of phenomenological disclosure) the state of affairs as such; perhaps only then shall we be poised to ask if there *are* ways of translating one genre to another, one medium to another, making these disparate existential domains cohere.

The screenwriter or playwright offers a script, which in turn must find its way from page to stage, from stage to screen; adapation-as-translation means finding images and sounds for written words. In a related gesture, when Williams "writes on" or "writes about" the Falls, he undertakes to translate one ontology to another: the poem is not loud, not wet, not subject to gravity, not made of H_2O, but it offers a genre in which to think and feel the fractal attributes of falling water. The film director Jim Jarmusch joins the artful activity of translation—from poem to page to screenplay to screen—in his *Paterson* (2016), which features the vocal recitation of poems attributed to the eponymous bus driver/poet (played by Adam

Driver), composed off screen by Ron Padgett. As Paterson speaks selected verses in voiceover, they are inscribed in real time on screen, appearing with just a slight delay (as if his voice was setting down text, word by word, by means of an invisible pen or some satisfying dictation app.) In *Paterson* the film, the circulation of images, sounds, and words continues, as inaugurated by *Paterson* the epic poem: the movement of water to words for Williams becomes words to water for Jarmusch (including the sound of the Falls). Such categorial and conceptual translations are ontological—the milieu of one substance passing through the poet to the matter of words; words, in turn, interpreted by the filmmaker as cinematic representation (including words written on screen). Together these forays (as fragments and refractions of one another) constitute what we are inclined to call a world, indeed, the world. As Stanley Cavell once attended to the ontology of the world viewed, so we agitate for renewed questions about the ontology of the world heard.[8] Not incidentally, it is in tracking the spirit of Cavell's solicitation to our sensibilities—by his generous invitation for us to address "matters that I hope you will be moved at some point to pursue further"—that such onward investigations are conducted.[9]

As demonstrated by earlier dispatches in this collection, we ask here after the ontology of genre—and its fecund proliferation as genres. Because sound is a medium, it is also, in a most basic, even etymological sense, a genre (or a series of interrelated and overlapping ones), e.g., the ambient sounds of nature (falling water, mist, rain), sounds that constitute what Kyle Stevens calls, glossing Cavell, "worldly silence"; and then there are also, of course, the sounds of speech, the acoustic voice that doesn't amount to coherent speech, melodic music, ambient noise, the voice in one's head, etc.[10] An idea or definition of *genre* has us thinking about kinds, styles, characteristic forms, and associated techniques. Old French, of course, used *gender* for the same, so we have been attuned to classification, prepared for taxonomizing. Where Williams translated the sounds of water into poetry, cinematic sounds—the sounds that movies make—offer another site of sonic translations. Because such sounds most often arrive in lockstep with moving images (that is, synchronized), they may have become familiar to the point of invisibility, even paradoxically, inaudibility. The *Geschlecht* of such sounds is deeply intriguing (how have we come to take for granted this remarkable marriage? This coupling of two genres?); yet a *further type* of translation calls my attention here: how we *write* cinematic sounds.

To be sure, there exists a robust and diverse set of scholarly engagements on the sounds *of* cinema, of sound *in* cinemas. Several precincts and practitioners come to mind—cognitive film theory (Lisa Zunshine), film studies (Rick Altman), sound studies (Trevor Pinch), the sound of written prose *and* the sound of text on screen (Garrett Stewart)—as does the indispensable, influential work of Michel Chion and Kaja Silverman, and perhaps most perspicuously and foundationally, Maurice Merleau-Ponty.

Given the scale of these important, field-defining contributions, and by contrast, the smaller scope of a chapter, I narrow the focus (or, shifting to sonic tropes, reduce the range of attunement) to a specific attribute of our thinking about the sounds of cinema: how it is that we think, if we do at all, about the *translation* of *hearing* cinema to *writing*. In short, if much has been said about sound's role in cinema (e.g., in relation to or in relationship with the [moving] image, etc.), do we have a coherent sense of what we undertake in writing "about" sound on film? Is this a translation whose success we can, or should, take for granted, or might we be more circumspect and consider that in writing (cinematic) sound into prose we are giving warrant to a rather remarkable transformation from one genre to another, from one medium to another, and thus from one ontology to another? As William Carlos Williams struggled to "interpret and use" the language of the "noise of the Falls," so also may we be attuned to a struggle—of interpretation and use—we did not know we have, or should be productively troubled by.

I do not aim to rehearse or reinvent anything already in circulation—not the still-generative pages of Merleau-Ponty's *Phenomenology of Perception*, or Chion's many volumes, including the essential *Audio-Vision* and *Words on Screen*—but rather to accept something like an unsolicited invitation heard in Oliver Sacks' "The Dog Beneath the Skin," where he presents an auspicious analogue: a case study for imagining a world without smell.[11] Changing genres yet again! But the shift from ear to nose is instructive, hence the invitation; we are thrown back upon ourselves to ask: what sort of a world do we have with, or by means of, one or more senses? What if a sense is intensified, muted, or lost altogether? And how does my perception and my experience of such sensuous input change as my *sensitivity*—indeed, my *sensibility* (in a lovely, meaningful double entendre)—transforms? (The real-world effects of such a loss or derangement are newly underscored by reports from deep into the global coronavirus pandemic in which the loss of smell, and its related somatic sense, taste, is among the most prevalent and sustained punishments of covid-19, for some, irrevocably altering experience of the world as they knew it.[12]) We are, by now, familiar with how Merleau-Ponty articulates the phenomenology of perception ("we must begin by reawakening the basic experience of the world"), of how Chion gives us a new appreciation for the role sound plays in our encounters with the sights of cinema (consider his "audio-logo-video" poetics as such a valuable theoretical innovation).[13] I am, or I think I am, doing something else, or at least, in league with them but imposing a different set of emphases, namely, asking as if from an ethnographic position, about the metaphilology of cinema studies—what terms the field uses, how it understands them individually and in tandem. I invoke the position of the philosophically inclined ethnographer because it may also be the case that a study of such philology involves—demands—an attunement to the ontology of such terms.

We seem certain and settled about the meaning of, say, a film genre (e.g., that it is a domain in which works of cinematic art arrange themselves, or are arranged, according to shared traits that are themselves, in turn, static and dynamic). The ontology of film sounds—of whatever type (speech—in diegetic space and in voiceover, additional/automated dialogue replacement [ADR], Foley work, computer-generated, music, room tone, the patterned noises of the projection apparatus, etc.)—prompts our thoughts of cinematic sounds as genres unto themselves; as a secondary effect, then, we have to contend with the art and practice of writing about them, undertaking the "transfer" of meaning from one domain of experience (e.g., mere cognitive registration at the level of sonic vibrations) to another (e.g., the work of the film theorist, historian, and critic who can speak competently about "sound design," the influence of music, the role of a soundtrack or score, and the interpretation of speech and dialogue). So much here feels deeply familiar and yet calling for further theorization; we watch movies all the time, and many of us write about them—and their sounds—without a second thought about the (successful) "carry over" from one genre to another, from one medium (sound) to another (writing). Repurposing Williams' sentiment at the outset, the sounds of cinema seem "to be a language which we were and are seeking," and the "search" has become a "struggle to interpret and use this language" as we, in turn, write about this "language" by means of another language.[14] These are matters, verily, in need of some translation.

II

In the context of the critical study of cinema, it may sound like a category mistake to ask "What is the gender of sound?" And yet, if we borrow from extensive reflections on *Geschlecht*, we may be able to translate the question, slightly but significantly, so it asks instead: "What is the *genre of sound*?" and "Do sounds form genres?"—Are these better, more vital questions? What might be usefully said in response to them? We have at our disposal this turn of phrase "hard of hearing." Have we given it some thought? Listen to the depiction shuffled a bit: it is hard to hear. So, is the phrase "hard of hearing" a euphemism? Why not say "hearing impaired," "going deaf," or "deaf"? Perhaps because there is something hard *about* hearing. It takes an effort to hear; sometimes we are told of a difference between hearing and listening (the former marking a capability, the latter a mode of cognitive attention). We could say the same for our eyes: that just because something is "right before our eyes," there is no assurance we will see it. For this, we have the apothegm "hiding in plain sight." When Gabriel Marcel assessed the attributes of film—their effect on human experience—he concluded "that to me who has always had a propensity to get tired of what I have the habit of seeing—what in reality, that is, I do not see anymore—this power peculiar to the cinema seems to be literally redeeming [*salvatrice*]."[15] Siegfried Kracauer ratified Marcel's observation so much so that he made the subtitle of his landmark *Theory of Film* "the redemption of physical reality."[16] A concentrated thought as much as a daydream can veil the eyes along with the common state of being lost in thought. And then we hear the person snapping her fingers in front of our face—"Hello. Are you in there?" The sound wakes us from oneirism.

How much the same, then, in our experience watching movies? For all the spectacle we are treated to—frame after frame, twenty-four or more frames per second—how hard it has been for us to *hear* what we see. Indeed, we have been trained by continuity, so-called "invisible" editing, to not hear. We exit the movie house speaking of scenes (*seens?*—even the pun works) and shots; we remark on framing and color grading, camera movement and blocking, costuming and editing, film stock and lighting, and so on. When we reference character dialogue, we seldom remark on *how* things said made their presence known to us (voiceover? voice arriving before a cut to the speaker?), but, as if we were reading a book or a screenplay, merely *what* was said. Even the imitation of a distinctive diction, a regional accent comes across as a fetish with a misplaced object. In all this and a dozen other ways, we are positioned—trained, practiced, comfortable—in, as it were, merely *watching* a movie. We went to "see a film"—and that is what we did.

For what it is worth, I would like to add a few notes here to a conversation about the sounds of cinema—the things we hear but do not speak of when we go to "see a movie." I am interested, in a broad stroke, with deafness to cinema, with the way a viewer may be, it would seem, naturally, habitually hard of hearing when it comes to the sounds that cinema makes (or are made in her company, what was during the errantly named "silent era" once called "accompaniment"—because "films were not projected in utter silence," as Karin Littau reminds us, and more provocatively and poetically, as Stanley Cavell tells us: "A silent movie has never been made."[17]). Why is this so?—Why this *is* so turns us back to our experience of the movies as a coupled phenomenon. What if hearing cinema were easier to notice, to speak about, indeed, easier to hear? As Walter Benjamin remarked how "the camera introduces us to unconscious optics as does psychoanalysis to unconscious impulses," perhaps we are positioned to investigate an "unconscious acoustics"—what sound summons in us, and how we might articulate that "language" in a language of our own (whatever language that might be).[18] Can that *translation* be achieved—even in part, partially, provisionally—and to what end or extent?

If it has been difficult—vexing, even—to "hear what we see," then what can be said of the project of "writing what we hear"? Writing *on* sound becomes the writing *of* sound. Etymology frames the issue: grámma (γράμμα, letter)—as if to write *a letter* (as a member of an alphabet, and also as a dispatch from an ongoing correspondence), and phōnḗ (φωνή, sound)—what is potentially audible for us, to us. The conjunction of writing and sound, in this context, proposes notions such as a "letter-sound" or a "sound-letter." Such versions and inversions make clearer how "inscription" passes between types of language, including the visible and the audible.

The project of gramophonology (γράμμα, letter; φωνή, sound or voice; λόγος, with various definitions, including speech and discourse) calls out to the logic and ontology of "lettering sound," or in more demotic variations, "sound writing" and "writing sound" (as more literally captured by the term phonograph: φωνή, sound; γραφή, writing)—that is, to sounds that stand in need of listening, and hence, of translation. Another variant definition for gramophonology: "discourse of sound writing," which amplifies the presence of λόγος. The chapter's subtitle, of course, puns "sound" to summon the logical sense of the word—thus inviting a doubleness that would deliver a "sound criticism of sound."[19] Note the adoption of a once-trademarked name spelled with a single m and an o, *gramophone*, rather than the more antique double-m with an a, *gramma*, familiar to projects such as Jacques Derrida's grammatology and Garrett Stewart's metagrammatology.[20] The allusion to the gramophone, cousin of the phonograph, directs us to archaic acoustic technologies and mechanics that, despite being superannuated, are evocative: they provide emblems for the scene of our encounters with sounds, whether they are audio, visual (especially in motion pictures), or textual (as in books, or text on screen); they remind us of the autonomous existence of sound-generating objects. Though one can imagine productive variant spellings, such as grammaphonology, there may be reason to hesitate, for example, by insinuating too much overlap between grammaphonology and grammatology. The present, or recommended, spelling sets out the terms for an independent, if related inquiry.

For all of Derrida's critiques of the West—especially as promulgated by Plato and later Rousseau—as phonocentric (that is, as privileging sound or speech over writing), the Western tradition, in time, has become *even more* lectiocentric—whether literally or figuratively as a culture offering "readings" and "lookings" (and, of course, including Derrida's own expansive contributions).[21] If the work of a gramophonology is kindred and complement to Derrida's grammatology, it remains productively out of alignment with it. Indeed, deconstruction, especially post-Derridean varieties, exhibits a striking tendency to "phonophobia," while gramophonology aims not only to hear more and different sounds (as it were, beyond the voice), but to find the terms and conditions for the translation of sounds, ones that are not merely permutations of those frameworks and lexicons familiar to readings and lookings.[22] To our surprise, a pronounced and celebrated critique of phonocentrism has not issued a robust and countermanding culture of sonic literacies (Lat. *literatus*, learned); instead, "writing sound," writing *about* sound remains a rarefied region of inquiry, and its exemplars rarer still.[23] In fact, it appears that lectiocentrism—with its abundant troping of readings and lookings, that is, of seeings, and thus, ocularcentrism, etc.—is compatible with, perhaps even reinforced by, phonocentrism, because, ironically, these readings and lookings are addressed to the "legible" human voice as heard on film (Lat. *legere*, to read). Chion refers to the prominence of speech in cinema as vococentrism—"a reminder that [cinema] almost always privileges the voice" above other kinds of sound.[24] Call this practice another incarnation of phonocentrism, one that perhaps inadvertently calls attention not just to types of sounds, but also to their *classes*: how many other kinds of sounds (besides the voice), do we not hear on screen? In the practice of film criticism, for instance, cinematic vocalizations (in speech, song, voiceover) garner primary attention, in part, because they present as interpretable objects (in dialogue, lyrics, metadescriptions of scenes), while other filmic sounds (diegetic and nondiegetic alike) may be diminished, deprioritized—left unheard—because we neither have the training to translate them nor the patience to try.

Garrett Stewart has observed about the present study that the "category-mashing visualization of screen sound in words is the flip side of the fascinating passing point in Chion's *Words on Screen* that the flashing past of a road sign, or billboard, or legible suicide note, or subtitle, you name it, breaks with the time of the image, as well as of off-screen sound, into the separate duration of extra-visual phonetic time."[25] Dedicated readers of Stewart's work will recognize, of course, how his invocation of Chion's project emerges seamlessly from Stewart's own, career-long obsession with subvocal literary enunciation.[26] Stewart has, for decades, articulated the ways written texts have voices (*our* voices or subvocalizations); thus, as I have turned to a thinking over of cinema's sonic realities—as unnoticed, unacknowledged, unheard, unincorporated, untranslated—Stewart has explored how "the process of subvocal text production" offers "a uniquely perceived instance of mutual supplementation of gramme and phone."[27] Indeed, it was only a few pages earlier in *Reading Voices* that Stewart had charted the structure of these relationships in his prescient development of a metagrammatology.[28] Thus, our cinematic gramophonology draws up a medial relation to the arrangements of the phonotext, both enterprises set upon "hearing things" (in league with Timothy Gould, and after Cavell[29]); the difference, of course, being that cinematic sound announces itself in *proximity* to the frame-by-frame or pixel-array-by-pixel-array and thereby often passes without comment, while written texts reinforce their silence by virtue of the literalness that marks them as self-same, unvoiced materiality (and yet an adjacent voice, our own, lurks). In the latter case, subsonic mental enunciation would require us to become, in Geoffrey Hartman's apt appellation, "earsighted"—and thereby poised to adopt Stewart's "method of 'phonemic' analysis."[30] Despite the aspiration, including these efforts to engage the mind's ear, talkies and texts remain vexed in their relationship to viewers/readers, which is to say, *listeners* who may not be aware of the contribution of sound to cinematic experience on the one hand nor to the generation of literary meaning (through metacognitive subvocalization) on the other hand.

If we currently occupy a time that speaks (often with casual confidence) about the end of theory, moving beyond theory, living post-theory, and finds various "elegies" for theory, it may be useful to recall how, not long ago, theory was a vital, variegated, liberating activity. Consider Lucy Ives' gloss on things a half-century ago:

> Critical cross-research is of course also relevant to Roland Barthes' intermedial readings—which propose a transdisciplinary rhetoric permitting images and other apparently non-linguistic items and processes to be systematically interpreted as text—along with the work of many other poststructuralist thinkers, who rejected philological approaches along with other forms of disciplinary silo-ing in favor of methodologies claiming forms of critical authority applicable beyond the halls of academe.[31]

In one respect, Ives' observation helps us appreciate one of the salutary benefits of the approach Barthes et al. made possible for cinema—namely, that moving pictures (and the sounds they carried as part of the broad bandwidth of popular culture) were legitimate "texts" worthy of critical reading, and theorizing. And yet, as cinema became a bona fide member of academic discourse—just another field among many others, and at that, across dispersed, diverse forms of media—it is easy to spot how the scopophilic, scopocentric attributes of cinema took precedence above other possible attributes (principally its most overt accomplice, sound); the abiding lectiocentrism of deconstructive assessment and theory-readings reinforced this asymmetry (both at the level of form and content). The irony, of course, is that the means of cinema's liberation to—that is, inclusion in—the mainstream of academic study (by way of popular culture) was made possible by an intellectual movement (emblematically figured by Derrida's *Of Grammatology*) that was in the business of saying that philosophy (or simply "modes of reading") should favor *writing*, while suppressing the importance of speech (that is, an activity defined by, embodied by sound).

No doubt, as we watch movies we are affected by its sounds—the *melos* (μέλος, song, tune) of melodrama drives us to tears, the disembodied footsteps from the basement terrorize, the particular voice of an actor feels familiar, like that of a friend—yet we do not notice, do not remark on these elemental attributes so much as interoceptively feel them, unconsciously incorporate their somatic effects into our thinking about what we *saw*. As such, these sounds—despite their prominent impact and concept-determining effect—remain unheard *as sounds*. What if, instead, the sounds of cinema were consciously part of what we marvel at when we marvel at movies? How would we theorize that hearing—speak of it in language, write about it in words? And what would that sonic attunement do, in turn, as it were reflexively, to our seeing? How would we bring these two worlds already so intimately, indistinguishably paired before us, on the screen, together in our own minds—and then, crucially, in or through some subsequent act of translation, onto the page, what we commonly call film criticism (or more broadly, "writing on film")? Ultimately, we may wish to avoid a contest between image and sound, or reversing the prevailing hierarchy, so that sound criticism would become a species of embodied cognition. Gramophonology may serve as part of such an endeavor, as a bid to be a little less hard of hearing.

III

We are launched, then, in an exploration of the metacinematic qualities of sound as cinematic genre and how theorizing its medium specificity (apart from but in association with moving images) yields new terms for how we write about what we hear. Such a sequence calls us to ask how we think about how films think (say, epistemological terms) and how we know what kind of things we are thinking about (for example, as ontologically distinguishable phenomena). These forays, then, are not playful exercises, with theorists chasing after puzzles created by (unthoughtful) thought experiments; rather, more direly, the work is part of a series of responses to the ongoing crisis—and thus questioning—of the documentary index.[32] As the ontology of sound and image have continued to evolve, we have become less sure what is real and what is simulacrum; and the doubt has given rise to a pernicious skepticism, one that will not be overcome by happenstance, or even, in many cases by our finest computational devices. Indeed, the very notion of the "sound as index" is in question, first, by mere physiology: as we remember that color blindness and focal distortions affect the nature of what we see (e.g., the optical blind spot is common to all humanity), the reception of sound is more than a matter of volume (decibels), because the very *shape of the ear* affects the *way* we hear and thus the *what* of what we hear.[33] Coupled with this bespoke, personalized mode of sound reception, the content of sound continues to be transformed by technologies that augment it at the level of the media that encodes it—thereby undermining the virtue and value of, for example, on-site recording (as animation, deepfakes, CGI, GIFs, and general adversarial networks [GANs] have racked the indexical nature of the visual image).[34] Still, as a holdover, as a muted index of sound, we might consider present-day sound environments beyond cinema as offering something that the time-image (now vanquished by the tricks of computational media) cannot: we visit a historic site, say the shoreline once the field of a famous battle: the war is over but the waves still crash, and will continue to do so, ceaselessly. Perhaps the sacredness of our memorial sites, at least the ones that are linked to their locations, draw their power mainly from the sonic atmosphere of the place itself. At this point, admittedly, such "sacredness" is likely more a matter of conceptual invention than anything like the consequence of indexical effects upon the eye and ear.

The marriage of sound and image—as we experience it in movies—continually announces such "conceptual inventions"; in the short term, call them feelings and ideas, and in time, memories; all of these mental effects are decidedly subjective. How to take that personal, private, impression and make it sharable, intelligible to others? Moving pictures are coupled with sounds (Chion speaks of them forming an "arranged marriage"[35]), and because we continually come into contact with their conjugation (if not yet coming to terms with them as independent phenomena), we are positioned to reflect on how such form/content relationships embody and reflect human values (viz., those that make up the work of ethics and aesthetics). Concerns with the ethics of film—by way of the aesthetics of its images and sounds—lie as a potent guiding force behind any such reflections. As Cornel West has said, we are time and again responding to specific cultural criteria that will give shape to our present and future: "Oh my god, the spiritual vacuity of the culture. The obsession with spectacle and image and things and commodities and status and money."[36] Contemporary life is figured anew each day and increasingly as a contest between substance and simulacra, between abiding concerns and fleeting ephemera. We are not "just theorizing," but trying to find our way a little bit, in the midst of daunting, despair-inducing conditions—as we have found them, inherited them, and may be creating them. If we have birthed this monster, we are then obliged to care for it, and contend with it.

The "mediating" of the relationship between sound and image can be profitably taken up as a double entendre—that we are working with a *medium* (i.e., in a medium, aware that something is being mediated or is itself a form of mediation); and negotiating between two figures or forms or, as the case may be, *genres* of cinema (image and sound). To discuss image and sound as *separable* means to think about their "fit" and "attraction" as well as their "intimacy" and "compatibility"—whether and how they go well together, as it were, join seamlessly. And yet, as with so many partnerships, marriages, it may be that one partner gets more attention than the other—that the imbalance in our thinking about the partnership says something peculiar about us (as "readers" of film, as "viewers" of it) and not just our physiology (where human eyes are positioned, how ears are shaped, etc.), but also our psychology, and even our philological habits. Our very language—so predominantly, so overtly lectiocentric and scopocentric—belies our often-unarticulated preferences, occludes who we favor in this marriage of mediating technologies.

In the cinematic examples invoked below, I explore the coupling of sound and image, and hopefully illustrate some of the uncanny ways in which sound and image are attracted to one another, and at times, repellant (perhaps becoming distorted to the point of monstrosity). The film instances, taken straightforwardly, can highlight sound's contribution to the meaning of the partnered image (a sequence we may come to think about as offering us the "sound" of the monstrous—as it were ahead of its image, a conjuring that may make the image itself redundant, an appurtenance). Yet, these filmic examples can also to illustrate—and make evident sonically—that what we so often call "the image" or the "motion picture" is, in fact, imbued with the powers afforded by an acoustic supplement that is anything but.

IV

Where once cinema was a marvel of time sequences—think of Eadweard Muybridge's score-settling innovations with twenty-four cameras firing off their shutters, tripped by horse legs—scholars have noticed how motion photography (zoopraxography, as Muybridge called it) was taken over by the logic of narrative. As a result, the display of cinematic *imagery* was an issue of space rather than time. Gilles Deleuze spent two volumes of *Cinema* making this point; Timothy Corrigan notes more laconically that "classical narrative cinema begins to privilege spatial movement."[37] When thinking of the Lumière brothers' *Arrival of a Train at La Ciotat*, Karin Littau says: "The modern perception of the world as ephemeral, fugitive, and contingent is protocinematic insofar as it involves the same two elements whose 'juncture' defines the cinema: 'movement and vision'."[38] What about sound? The same author writes, as if in reply: "Modern life, as any New Yorker or Londoner knows only too well, causes nervousness, because the unrelenting influx of visual stimuli perpetually threatens to overwhelm and overload us."[39] (New York and London, of course, are hardly as quiet as a monastery so there is no need to mention the multiform cacophony.) Yet, the contemporary critic fairs no better than one writing in 1912: Friedrich Freska notes that "rarely has a time suffered so much from eye-hunger [*Augenhunger*] as ours. [... W]orking people [...] are assaulted by a welter of images from all sides. [... To] satisfy this hunger, there is nothing so fitting as the cinématograph."[40] Let us add eye-hunger to our ocular-obsessed list of terms—along with voyeurism, ocularcentrism, the gaze, cinephilia, scopophilia, *schaulust*,[41] and the everyday words that encode visual sensation (spect-acle, spect-actor, per-spective, and the like) along with the default modes of addressing the medium ("watching a movie," "seeing a film," etc.). And yet a simple observation reorients us to the world of cinema even before the advent of sync-sound, namely, that, as noted, "films were not projected in utter silence. Apart from the accompaniment of piano music, there would often have been a showman commenting on the films displayed."[42] "Audience" and "audio" are among the very few commonplace words in wide circulation that intimate "hearing" (*audiens*, hearing; *audire*, to hear) and have been an integral part of the cinematic operation since its inception; despite the etymology, movie audiences are primarily treated as viewers, and it would appear, regard themselves accordingly.

By virtue of the physiology of the human ocular apparatus (with lens, pupil, cornea, rods, and cones, etc. to the retinal ganglion cell axons of the optic nerve that connect to the brainstem), persistence of vision allows for "continuity of space," and motion (in that space), thereby tricking the eye into a sense of presence—variously named realism, neorealism, indeed, "continuity" editing, etc.—by visual means. But sound and sounds, noises and acoustic elements, were early on a signature means by which to model and achieve such continuities; Chion is terrific on observing the tenacity with which sound binds images together—via perceived linkages, connections, and such.[43] By the late 1920s, sound would "arrive" (as the train in Lumières' film) with boldness, and reinforce editorial innovations by the likes of Edwin S. Porter and his inside/outside shots from the *Life of an American Fireman* (1903). As viewers, we were already familiar with cinema's hold on space—its ability to establish the frame of a given *mise-en-scène*.

When sound arrived, as we see it—and hear it, for example, in the mythopoesis provided by *Singin' in the Rain* (1952, dir. Stanley Donen and Gene Kelly), it is there to support the achievement of space, of scenes, of characters, of stories. The possession of voice—who has one, who can arrogate it, who is dispossessed of it—is a central theme of the narrative, and in this movie about "singin'," vitally, the voice provides the justification for the reality of the character: call her Lina, call her Kathy. It is thus the *location* of the voice that is the scandal, and thus what constitutes the narrative in its scenic varieties (sound stages, studio lots, song-and-dance set pieces, dream sequences, avant-garde experiments, and the like); MGM itself would later deploy the trick to impressive effect by giving its iconic roaring Leo the Lion the voice of a ... tiger.[44] In this ciné-example from the set and *mise-en-scène* of *Singin' in the Rain*, voice—the sound of voice—is about itself only insofar as it establishes and maintains the credibility of the characters (alive and dancin' within the diegesis); after Linda Williams, one wants to appreciate *Singin' in the Rain*'s acknowledgment of the "frenzy of the audible."[45] Perhaps not surprisingly, in a film that announces "singin'" and conjures a metacinematic celebration of sound's emergence in Hollywood, sound—here especially, the human voice, the singing voice—is commodified, a matter of contracts, property rights, and thus an issue of cinema space, the territory of the screen (that is, the location where we see what we hear). Corrigan again:

> The emergence of a classical cinematic subject within these practices has commonly been formulated according to a theatrics of vision that relates identity to the conquest and possession of property [...]. Both the psychoanalytic and the semiotic traditions informing these inquiries have usually developed the visual terms of these positions as "emplacements" by which the subject follows and is defined by movement within a theatrics of sight.[46]

While time's role in cinema remains debated (accounting for at least *half* of its reality according to Deleuze), time is, *at least* half of music, if not more. We may speak colloquially of music "filling a space," and describe the "acoustic qualities" of a theater, but music's primary preoccupation—as any conductor offers an embodied expression of—is time, timing, tempo, meter, measure, pace, and rhythm. In this way, when the "sound of music" meets the image, time is re-enchanted on screen; the moving image, perhaps beyond conscious recognition, is temporalized, returned to the earthly constraints of chronology. Peter Wollen writes commandingly of the several discourses already implicated in our discussion, when he summarizes the philological and philosophical stakes of sound in *Singin' in the Rain*:

> Thus the core issue in the film is that of the relationship between sound and image. Things can only end happily when, so to speak, a properly "married print" is produced, in which voice and image are naturally joined together. The underlying theme is that of nature as truth and unity, versus artifice as falsehood and separation. Kathy's voice becomes a kind of ornament which can be subtracted from her and added to Lina in defiance of its natural origins. This privileging of the bond between essence, body, and voice, as the *logos* on which truth must be founded, is precisely that which was later to be attached by the philosopher Jacques Derrida as the illusory basis of all Western metaphysics, from the time of the Greeks on. He associates this theory of the *logos*, normalized philosophically to the point where it is scarcely noticed, with the persistent philosophical denigration of writing as a form of artifice, obeying the logic of a supplement or additional ornament, rather than an integral reality. Read this way, *Singin' in the Rain* could be characterized as the purest example of the translation of such a metaphysics from the realm of language to that of cinema. Dubbing, here, represents the cinematic form of writing, through which sound is separated from its origin and becomes a potentially free-floating, and thus radically unreliable, semantic element.[47]

Wollen's masterful reading of and listening to *Singin' in the Rain* coalesces several strains of thinking and multiple categorial operations, especially, as he recognizes the hyper-metacinematic ways in which the Kelly and Donen film achieves exemplification as a site of translational hermeneutics. In scene after scene, the writers and directors—as well as performers and cinema technicians—explore the media forms they are using to represent those same media forms. As Wollen concludes: "the inevitable culmination of *Singin' in the Rain* has then to be an unveiling, which rolls back the grammatological curtain and reveals what must be, metaphorically, the naked truth: the *logos* made spectacle."[48] Not missing a chance to heighten the metacinematic richness of the film, Wollen adds that "it remains an endearing irony that, in reality, if I can so use the phrase, Debbie Reynolds' singing voice in the film was in fact dubbed by Jean Hagan, so that what we see and hear is the unveiling of a mystery which subverts its own appearance of authenticity."[49] As should be evident, Wollen is an unusually attuned analyst of the sound/image index, not least when he remarks: "It seems that, after all, the ear is more easily ensnared than the eye. Although, to tell the truth, to deceive the ear, deception of the eye is necessary too."[50]

In their now-canonical introduction to cinema, *Film Art*, David Bordwell and Kristin Thompson write: "sound is often treated as a lesser partner to the images, but we need to recognize that it can actively shape how to understand them."[51] This is a true statement, if also lackluster in its endorsement for the credibility of sound as a force—indeed, as a form of its own; Chion, by contrast, and across several books, testifies to the extraordinary (if regularly "overlooked") power of sound to transform the reception of images. Moreover, Bordwell and Thompson retain prevailing habits of regarding sound as a "partner to […] images," that is, as an additive that "shape[s]" how we understand images. But, putting some pressure on the apparent separability of these partners, let us ask in reply: how do we understand sound on its own terms? What helps sound become intelligible as an independent mode, or genre? And indeed, when we hear many different types of sounds (again, voice, music, sound effects, ambient noise, etc.), are these not one genre but many genres? Following Wollen, though, this sequence of questions becomes: how can (or should) images be taken as aids to the interpretation of the sounds they are partnered with? Can movie sound discover and delineate an intelligible independent existence apart from motion pictures? If marriage is the dominant trope of sound and image (despite being figured more intimately in the compound *audiovisual*), we are led to believe that they are separate and separable, where sound is vying for status ("a lesser partner"), and perhaps, at last, not translatable one "into" the other, so much as generative—the movie itself presenting as progeny.

Like Chion, I am hoping to make a more emphatic case than Bordwell and Thompson, among others, for the centrality of the image/sound pairing, coupling, and when needs be, separation, to help consider under different terms the habits of describing sound's "contribution" to the object or experience we refer to as "the movie." (As a quick, ready-to-hand, example: in a concert film, the music may regularly be a greater achievement than the *image* of the music as it is being played. The projector can be shuttered and yet the sound recording prevails in its distinctive, untrammeled glory; "concert recordings," with sounds that originally derived from on-location capture in synchronization with film, may be dignified as a genre unto themselves. Indeed, the quality of the images—perhaps at times out of focus, grainy, under-lit, overexposed, etc., is hardly an issue if the sound capture is clean and well-modulated.) Bordwell and Thompson seem to take seriously the diminishment of sound's affective presence as an achievement of the movies—as if a greater (or even much of any) conscientiousness of sound would break a spell, as if our lack of attunement to sound were an advantage for our capacity to be drawn into the cinematic diegesis.

> [... U]nless we're musicians or sound engineers, we've learned to ignore most sounds in our environment. Our primary information about the color, texture, and layout of our surroundings comes from sight, and so in ordinary life, sound is often simply a background for our visual attention. Similarly, we speak of *watching* a film and of being movie *viewers* or *spectators*—all terms implying that the sound track is a secondary factor. We're strongly inclined to think of sound as simply an accompaniment to the real basis of cinema, the moving images. This inclination lets sound designers create a world without our noticing.[52]

Even so, Bordwell and Thompson admit that "filmgoers have started to notice" sound on film, and consequently, "many modern films lead us by the ear. Not since the first talkies of the late 1920s have filmgoers been so aware of what they hear."[53] These claims are, clearly, contradictory (viz., "without our noticing" and "so aware of what they hear"), and yet, both may be true as readings of the history of our relationship with the media we call the movies.

It is telling that Deleuze's *Cinema* is printed in two volumes, that is, as separate entities—*Movement-Image* and *Time-Image*—because space and time do not seem to be separable, perhaps especially as we encounter their coupling in cinema. Moreover, like so many other books that form the nexus of cinema studies, the "image" takes precedence (Guy Debord's *Society of the Spectacle*, Stanley Cavell's *The World Viewed*, P. Adams Sitney's *Eyes Upside Down* and *Visionary Film*, Brian Winston's *Technologies of Seeing*, Alan Williams' *Republic of Images*, Stan Brakhage's *Metaphors of Vision*, Devereaux and Hillman's *Fields of Vision*,[54] Everett's *The Seeing Century: Film, Vision, and Identity*,[55]

Miller's *Seeing Through Movies*,[56] and bringing us back to Apter's work on the "looking" and the "reading," Petrie and Boggs' *The Art of Watching Films*,[57] David Thomson's *How to Watch a Movie* and James Monaco's *How to Read a Film*). We find similar tendencies in works of philosophy and literary criticism: Peirce's "How to Make Our Ideas Clear," Paul de Man's *Blindness and Insight*, Richard Rorty's *Philosophy and the Mirror of Nature*. Despite the perspicuous, plentiful, prominent presence of ocular metaphors in cinema studies and philosophy, the incisive Martin Jay has found an exception, or a place apart from this trend: France; hence his massive study, *Downcast Eyes: The Denigration of Vision in Twentieth-Century French Thought*.[58] Not surprisingly, given a certain Gallic irony, the "denigration" in question manifests itself as, in fact, an *obsession* with vision—case in point the above-mentioned landmark volume by Debord; to say nothing of the contribution the French and Francophones have made to cinema itself—from the Lumières and Méliès to Renoir, Bresson, Godard, Resnais, Marker, Melville, Truffaut, Tati, Demy, Varda, Assayas, Carax, the Dardenne brothers, Denis, Desplechin, Hansen-Løve, and many more; and by complement, the French contribution to writing about cinema, from Bergson, Bazin, Epstein, Metz, Barthes, Deleuze, the *Nouvelle Vague* theorists, and the especially pertinent Chion. Still, in the wake of this brief but hopefully sufficient batch of evidence from the field (where vision is, in fact, more, or often the most, pronounced sensory faculty), we may return to Deleuze with the intrigue posed by a postulation he and the others don't make—namely for a *sound-image*. What would this most obvious of alliances amount to? In phenomenological terms, perhaps the very "essence" of cinema (should we any longer be able to speak of such things)? No doubt, in the community of these cited books, it stands out as a mere proposal, and thus a prospective entity or idea in need of theorizing. Perhaps what follows will yield a modest bid in that direction.

As we move on, it is worth keeping in mind the abundant work in sound studies as its own field or genre of inquiry (and at that, often apart from film theory or operating without attention to film sound). After much reading in this domain, a couple of brief observations to consider: first, contributions often oddly retain a self-consciousness that further encodes the ghettoization of sound; like the invocation of reified racial and gender categories, the insistence on their existence enacts a separation from a shared domain rather than an integration. In this way, speaking of sound appears to create the conditions *ipso facto* for speaking outside or beyond the image (hence, again the promise of the notion of a sound-image, in cinema an almost-always-already joined phenomenon). Second, the separation of sound and image seems to give credence, ironically, to the privileging and ongoing predominance of the visual (including degrees of phonophobia). Paradoxically, an emphasis on sound—its reality, its contribution—somehow replicates and reinforces certain pro-scopic tendencies that allow the film image to possess sound as its own subservient feature (as its lesser partner). Even Chion's core claim about sound as offering "added value," presumes that the image-on-its-own has plenty of value *without sound*, indeed, may survive well enough in its absence.[59] Thus, sound is presented to us as a supplement rather than a constitutive element (e.g., a chapter on "The Visionary Soundtracks of Stan Brakhage" even makes a point to pun the filmmaker's sonic accomplishments in scopic terms[60]). Another salient moment: the cultural studies approach of *The Oxford Handbook of Sound Studies* advertises itself by saying that "the book considers sounds and music as experienced in such diverse settings as shop floors, laboratories, clinics, design studios, homes, and clubs, across an impressively broad range of historical periods and national and cultural contexts."[61] Aside from a single chapter on sound's role in digital animation (focusing on Pixar's shorts[62]), the five-hundred-plus pages have other business than cinema. "Through a diverse set of case studies, articles illustrate how sounds—from the sounds of industrialization, to the sounds of automobiles, to sounds in underwater music and hip-hop, to the sounds of nanotechnology—give rise to new forms of listening practices." Even a volume ostensibly aiming to sustain or extend the subfield, *Film Sound*, another five-hundred-page collection, devotes only one-fifth of its efforts to theorizing sound. And among its most high-profile contributors, Béla Balázs, we read a line that defeats the endeavor: "In a sound film there is no need to explain the sounds."[63]

V

By the second paragraph of his book, *Pursuits of Happiness: The Hollywood Comedy of Remarriage*, Stanley Cavell offered a metacritical comment on his approach to the films he addresses: "I habitually call these accounts of films 'readings' of them."[64] The quotation marks around "readings" show that he is aware of the oddness of the appropriation from literary and philosophical analysis to cinema, indeed, that the translation of such a term needs to be acknowledged in some manner; let us call this the way a philosopher of a certain training, of a particular generation, in both cases, Cavell's, goes about his study of the thought of film. Then again, one might have asked at any time during the last century—the first full century in human history that could claim cinema as an art—how else would such interpretation get done other than by means of reading? That Cavell was sufficiently self-critical— or aware of the application of a literary trope to a cinematic context—to make this observation or admission (and no less by the second paragraph of the book) is itself a mark of his canny skills as a reader, as an interpreter of cultural artifacts. The scare quotes, in short, inscribe an observation that may have otherwise gone unnoticed.

Still, Cavell is, no doubt in part because of such an emphasis on "reading" film, placing himself in a tradition of lectiocentrism; his membership is especially evident because transitioning from literary and philosophical texts to cinematic ones gives him an opportunity to, as it were, double down on familiar and effective methods. If books can be read, why not films? If he was already attuned to the human voice in the texts of philosophy (especially his own), why not also in films, filled as they are with voices of an even more apparent sort? While Cavell's work admits of the paradox of "reading sound" (as later Garrett Stewart will attend to "reading voices"), his distinctive, inimitable brand of interpreting films remains vital to the present and future of cinema studies.[65] That said, the dominant trope (of reading a film) calls us to ask after a complement to such "readerly" habits, including a new or renewed attention to form.

As we continue to consider the shift from lectiocentrism to gramophonology, Cavell's sense of "reading" becomes an instructive way of retaining the former as an aid to the latter, including the notion, or definition, of a genre—or genres. Indeed, both his accounts of "reading" and "genre" are essential, "internal" to his ontology of cinema—"what I think film is."[66] In this way, Cavell was concerned with noticing, and defending, the relationship between words on the page and, as it were, words on the screen (or, with our emphasis, words *as we hear them* on screen): "to believe, that is, that the visual facts of a movie you care about may survive the same kind of attention you would give the verbal facts of a literary text you care about."[67] Despite Cavell's characteristic verbal nuance, there is some conceptual slippage—where "visual facts" are in fact a metonym for the kinds of things people *say*, which is to say, "words for a conversation" that comprise the genre of remarriage comedy at issue in his book. It is perplexing, I think, to describe "the words *spoken* in the film" as "*visual facts*," but that peculiarity makes Cavell's account at once central to the motive here to think through these descriptions again, anew, and also to question how it is that we give accounts of the sounds we hear "on screen" (or fail to), that is, from the screen we see and as it were, the screen we also listen to (but do not acknowledge); moreover, the amplification of movie sound does not emit from the screen itself—but from behind or around the projection or display. As the eye/brain presents a unified scene, so we have grown accustomed to experiencing the cinematic (or televisual) sound/image as a single, unified phenomenon, when, in fact these two are unconsciously combined. If, as Cavell says, "film is a visual medium," it is also, we must add, something else as well as that.

Cavell's interest in the citationality of film—its ability to be quoted, for example, as a description of a scene, or by means of reference to the words spoken in a passage of monologue, dialogue, or voiceover[68]; and his reference to film as a "text" that can avail itself to "readings" (many of them, over time)[69]—should be coupled with our remembrance of Cavell's beginnings as a musician and a composer. When our philosopher writes autobiographically, then, with attention to the arrogation of voice, to the *sound* philosophy makes, etc., he calls his book *A Pitch of Philosophy*. We are meant to hear what he says on a certain register; later, he subtitles *Cities of Words* "pedagogical letters on a register of the moral life," so we are encouraged to meet him on the right measure as we encounter philosophy as an "enterprise that measures the value of our lives."[70] These sonic tropes are worth dwelling on and drawing from, as we seem to happen upon not merely moments of personal history but something like the anthropology of philosophers and filmmakers as they learn to speak to one another. So it is that this musician turned philosopher wrote in his first book of essays that "in philosophy it is the sound which makes all the difference."[71] And, indeed, it has been the sound of Cavell's own voice—"a voice like no other in philosophy, today or ever," according to Arthur Danto—that has insisted that philosophy, a labor largely conducted in written prose, considers, if metaphorically but no less vitally, that such writing can possess (and more often lack) a sound. Contending with received practices in his discipline, Cavell spoke of his efforts in *Cities of Words*, for example, as an attempt to preserve, imitate, or replicate "something of the sound of the original classroom lectures" on which the book is based.[72] As Cavell admits, "I love the sound of interesting, which means interested, academic learning."[73] An entire critical book has been devoted to reflections on the trope of sound in Cavell's oeuvre—*Hearing Things: Voice and Method in the Writing of Stanley Cavell* by Timothy Gould.[74] That is, we are meant to hear a "voice" in the writing, indeed that Cavell's voice—as written—figures as a methodology, a way of doing philosophy. Voice in writing and audibility on film (especially the audibility of female characters) have become a familiar tandem in the literature on Cavell's work.[75]

Yet another crucial contribution from Cavell is his theorizing of genre-as-medium—an account first offered in *The World Viewed: Reflections on the Ontology of Film*: "For a cycle is a genre (prison movies, Civil War movies, horror movies, etc.); and a genre is a medium."[76] It would appear there are transitive properties at work here (cycle = genre = medium), and so a translation of attributes is underway. This movement is especially arresting (and potentially fruitful for thinking about the writing of sound on film, and the subsequent writing about sound in prose) when we consider the way in which Cavell couples medium and idiom. For instance, he says that "[Jackson] Pollock made dripping into a medium of painting."[77] And so the movement, let us call it the "style," of Pollack's application of paint is itself treated as a medium. If we have become accustomed to thinking of paint-as-medium, we now can address a particular method under the notion of style-as-medium. Cavell has more to say on this point: "A medium is something through which or by means of which something specific gets done or said in particular [peculiar? idiomatic?] ways. It provides, one might say, particular ways to get through to someone, to make sense; in art they are forms, like forms of speech."[78] It is uncanny that we have arrived back at speech—at the *sound* of a form, for here, again, we are pressed to consider the particular/peculiar/idiomatic ways in which movement and sound are *written*, filmically encoded, and thus made available for prose interpretation—that is, translation—through concentrated acts of listening.

Picking up on Cavell's blended approach to reading, genre, and medium (all of them conspicuously—and not incidentally—caught up in various discussions of sound, voice, and speech), I would like to ask how an attunement to the meaning of *Geschlecht* can help us with the problem of the image's enduring dominance over sound, or indeed, with the image's *absorption* of sound to the point of its inaudibility—as if sound were not its own thing, but merely an add-on, an extra with no distinctive ontology of its own. At such a cleave point, one cannot help but notice how etymology becomes embodied in practice, when, for example, a genre/gender imbalance announces itself: as if image/sound were unconsciously inherited as yet another problematically asymmetrical masculine/feminine disparity. And not as the slash would have us believe—50/50—but some problematically disproportionate ratio; a viewer oblivious to sound might (inadvertently?) rate its cinematic contribution at zero, and so we can only go up from there. Cavell's radical attention to "the woman's voice" (often, no doubt, in so-called "women's pictures"—a subset of which Cavell describes as "melodramas of the unknown woman") thus becomes not only an issue for our reading of these Golden Age stories—comedies and melodramas alike—but the uncanny ways that cinematic sound as such has been treated in a secondary fashion, as an invisible/inaudible accomplice, as an afterthought, or not thought of at all. What a curious content/form parallel to discover "the woman's voice" and as it were *cinema's* voice sharing a common fate; while film history has largely moved on from the crisis Cavell isolated in films from the 1930s and 1940s, *the sounds of cinema* have barely changed in their relative status to a still-dominant privileging of the visual—even though, in many cases, the volume is decidedly turned up for the theatrical presentation of cinematic sound in the twenty-first century. Because we have, since the late 1920s, lived in the age of "sound film," we can also notice how, long ago, the modifier dropped away: so obvious a fact *of* film, the announcement of "sound" in the phrase "sound film" was made cumbersome, redundant; sound was naturalized to the point where it was made an indistinguishable part of the image. Image *presumed* sound, and in time, it *subsumed* sound. Look where we are a century later: largely left without a distinction that is, nevertheless, persistently presented to our senses, from frame to frame, measure by measure.

VI

In a series of articles and books, Emily Apter has, along with Barbara Cassin, opened for us a vista onto the prospective and probable regions of what remains untranslatable—from one language to another, from one medium to another, from one genre to another. Yet, like many perspicacious views, we should want notes on other senses—not just a vista, then. For instance, in an article entitled "Untranslatable? The 'Reading' versus the 'Looking,'" Apter traces the peculiar—perhaps pernicious—application of interpretive habits associated with visual perception as they come to inform art history, e.g., where "the looking" at a given work of art becomes "the reading" of that work. She marks this terminological shift as a possible point of mistranslation (and beyond that untranslatability an impasse, code unknown), for in what sense are we *reading* this (nonlinguistic) work of art? As she describes the situation, a visual impression is (or must be) translated into a "word-based model," and thus, at once, falls "into the prison-house of language."[79] Apter's observation reminds us of the widespread habit of speaking of artworks as "texts" that are more (or less) available to us as "readers," and thus as critics and analysts presumed to be in a position to offer "readings" of them (as the earlier dispatches from Cavell already established). But what happens to an artwork—say, a painting—when it is "read" as opposed to seen; or to a film, when it is "read" instead of heard? Our metaphors have created false equivalencies and thus a false confidence—as well as what may be unfulfilled "translations." How much film criticism, for example, is merely *visual* criticism? And stepping back, how much of that "merely visual criticism" is hampered by the author's confidence in offering a "reading" of a film as if it were (the equivalent of) a written text?

Sustaining Apter's apt critique of the faulty translation of habits that would take us uncritically from the looking to the reading, let us borrow her methods here and amplify the field of our encounters with art—in particular, extending it to that form of art known as cinema. This is to say, by coupling our lexilalia with attention to cinegraphia, we have occasion to note how cinematic works of art are often not merely moving pictures but are also "wired for sound." Even if we wanted to, in the cases of "sound film" (say, especially in those works made since 1927), we cannot merely transpose "the looking" for "the reading," but must also include the listening. If we are "reading" films-as-texts (already a problem in need of an explanation and a translation), then we are—or should be—hearing them as well, finding ways to make that transition. Consequently, we are positioned to add to Apter's deliberation over lectiocentrism the critical project of gramophonology. When presented with a film "to read," we can reply in kind: "But what does it sound like? What sounds does it make? How do those sounds relate to the images or non-images presented to us? What am I seeing but not hearing?" And subsequently: "What can we say or write about what we have heard?" How is that further translation possible, if at all?

Part of any replies to such questions, again with reference to Apter's and Cassin's foundational, indispensable, field-defining work on untranslatability, involves a re-thinking of genre as it intersects with the medium specificity of cinema. Importantly, then, one can distinguish between an engagement with (1) the rich and sophisticated history of thinking about genre films (melodramas, Westerns, musicals, etc.), (2) the ways in which specific films can be argued for or against membership in a given genre, and the theorizing that makes this categorial apparatus function (as articulated by, among others, Altman, Buscombe, Grant, Grindon, Neale, Schatz, Tudor, and Williams), and instead orient us to what could be described as (3) the ontology of a medium's genre(s). In what follows, I appraise issues germane to this third field of inquiry, namely, the ontology of cinema—its unique combinations of images and sounds—and ask: are we served at all by thinking of these partners as genres unto themselves (joined together and yet distinguishable)? In brief, is sound a (separate or separable) genre of cinema? Is cinematic sound, in particular, a distinct semantic domain that (merely) resides in another medium; or does it constitute one of its own? Were it possible, would a division of image-as-genre and sound-as-genre activate or otherwise enable a more fitting and robust translation of achievements among film theorists and critics? Because films continue to arrive with image and sound synchronized, the separation must remain conceptual, and the philosophical effect rhetorical—unless, that is, one goes to the trouble to mechanically or digitally separate them. Yet, even the proposal (at whatever degree of actualization) can productively unsettle some of the disciplinary habits that leave us "overlooking" and "underhearing" our artistic quarries.

In these decidedly cinematic conditions, genre can feel more akin to milieu or (again reaching for a linguistic analogy invoked above) idiom—as if we find the potter working in the milieu or idiom of clay. Can we, in turn, speak of the filmmaker working in the genre of sound (or with genres of sounds)? If these questions feel misguided—as if they might threaten, bypass, misunderstand, indeed (in a Bloomian sense) "misread," an established notion of genre, or may admit an easily identifiable category mistake—perhaps these concerns can be not just allayed, but productively transformed, by thinking of genre in terms of its *Geschlecht*. Namely, that we are calling to mind the traits that define a medium—what makes it so constitutionally, criteriologically—and thus are afforded a sense of not just what (sound) is *on* or *in* film, or even separable *from* film, but how sound *is* film (or, in a technical sense, a species of its form). As an aid to reflection on this point, consider select moments when sound is made the subject of the *fabula*, as in *Cleo from 5 to 7* (1962, dir. Agnès Varda), *The Miracle Worker* (1962, dir. Arthur Penn), *Land of Silence and Darkness* (1971, dir. Werner Herzog), *Days of Heaven* (1978, dir. Terrence Malick), *Stalker* (1979, dir. Andrei Tarkovsky), *Toute une nuit* (*A Whole Night* or *All Night Long* or *All One Night*, 1982, dir. Chantal Akerman), *Come and See* (1985, dir. Elem Klimov), *Children of a Lesser God* (1986, dir. Randa Haines), *Three Colors: Blue* (1993, dir. Krzysztof Kieslowski), *There Will Be Blood* (2007, dir. P. T. Anderson), *Under the Skin* (2013, dir. Jonathan Glazer), *Timbuktu* (2014, dir. Abderrahmane Sissako), *A Quiet Place* (2018, dir. John Krasinski), *Sound of Metal* (2019, dir. Darius Marder), *Coda* (2021, dir. Siân Heder), and many works by Robert Altman and Kelly Reichardt[80]; or conjure the figure of the sound recordist (and active listener) in *Medium Cool* (1969, dir. Haskell Wexler), *The Conversation* (1974, dir. Francis Ford Coppola), *Blow Out* (1981, dir. Brian De Palma), *Lisbon Story* (1994, dir. Wim Wenders), and *Das Leben der Anderen* (*The Lives of Others*, 2006, dir. Florian Henckel von Donnersmarck)—to appreciate a certain picture of sound at work in cinema, as cinema.

These parables, in the first cases, of life shaped by sound or its absence, and in the second set, of "sound capture," turn us anew to the medium itself. Do such films, which operate according to the prevailing logic of cinema (as image-centric, as the art of the motion picture), nevertheless, shuffle our attention such that these works, among related examples, seem to be made in or of a different genre, that is, by means of a different register of the same medium? These instances would appear to be "sound films" in a more literal sense, that is, standing apart as it were from those image-sound synchronizations well-known since the late 1920s. Indeed, the plurality of approaches epitomized by these films defers an inclination to settle on sound-as-genre and opens up the question of multiplicities, as if cinematic sounds created not one but many sound genres, among them: the sounds of nature, diegetic speech, diegetic music, voiceover, ADR, nondiegetic music, Foley work, sound effects, "worldly silence,"[81] and more. When these disparate forms are gathered, layered, "mixed" (in the standard trope of professional cinematic sound design), we are presented with a *blended* set of genres: artfully gathered, they are transformed into distinctive, comprehensible, even unified sonic landscapes. In these cases, sound reveals itself as not just "more than" image, but more than (mere) sound.

VII

In Barbara Cassin's *Dictionary of Untranslatables: A Philosophical Lexicon* (*Vocabulaire européen des philosophies: le dictionnaire des intraduisibles*), we read from Marc Crépon's entry on *Geschlecht*. The German word can be glossed as meaning, among other things, both *gender* and *genre*.[82] Likewise, as Heidegger and later Derrida have noted at length, these twin manifestations bespeak origins and fecundity, thus *generation*, and therefore creation (as an ontological category); in turn, existence summons types/typage (as a mode for keeping track of generic traits, commonly, now habitually according to gender/genre categories). In a project that announces defeat as its modus operandi, Cassin and company draw our attention to the "untranslatable"—at first, perhaps, as a provocation in search of a reply, a contest for achieved translations; then, in a different mood, as marking a willingness to contemplate what cannot be carried over. Thus, as translators from one language to another, from one mode or medium to another, from one genre/gender to another gender/genre, we are actively set upon the project of "finding equivalents" (or admitting when they cannot be found).[83] Where Heidegger and Derrida, and later Cassin and Apter, attend to the equivalents of *Geschlecht*—in short, how best to define it (so as to "assign identity"), while wondering if that appeal to primacy, much less completeness, is even possible—the foregoing notes on (cinematic) sounds ask, in kind, if these phenomena can be defined on terms that befit a role in "motion picture" history—a photography-based history that, from the first, appears to have casually (and in time, purposefully) written sound out of its purview, indeed, silenced sound at the level of everyday discourse (and thus to the point where "viewers" are no longer conscious of sound's presence and impact on the meanings of moving images). As a term of art, "talkies" proved a salient, if brief, exception to the scopocentric glossary. Despite the promising anomaly, however, cinematic sounds remain mysterious, an almost ineffable part of the experience of movies. (For your consideration, the first line of Noël Carroll's summative critical masterwork: "Though the philosophy of the motion picture—or, as I prefer to say, the moving image—began early in the twentieth century ...."[84]).

Crépon's fourth valence of a multivocal definition for *Geschlecht* states: "in a more abstract register, *Geschlecht* refers to the genus, in the sense of logical category, in the widest sense. It thus refers to the different genera of natural history as well as all sorts of objects and abstractions."[85] As *Geschlecht* has other bona fide definition-formations—such as sex and race—the topic of film sound may seem out of place, itself miscategorized, once again alienated from the class or genus that would recognize it as familiar, as indigenous, as deserving of inclusion and legitimate membership. Perhaps it is precisely because sound presents itself as a logical category of the film medium, one caught up in the *generation* of cinema for over a century, that we find a possible explanation for its stunted, halted, diminished or otherwise alienated status in the public imagination and critical praxis of moviemakers, movie watchers, and perhaps most oddly (but tellingly) film theorists and film critics: the sounds of cinema have yet to be recognizably, intelligibly translated; the *Geschlecht* of this "other half" remains—despite acknowledged efforts—largely unaccounted for, uncategorized, untranslated. (Is it, in fact, untranslatable?) One may say, with qualification duly noted, that cinematic sound has not achieved conspicuous representation, even if it has sporadically garnered the fervent attention of theorists. Instead of being part of the popular imagination of moviegoers, sound remains an occasionally inaudible, largely muted, and thus generally unheralded phenomenon.

To explore the etiology of such a condition, what if we take the "advent" (i.e., generation) of sound as the "introduction" (invasion?) of something foreign into an established and coherent genus (viz., the photographic image made moving image).[86] Still photography is the surprising progenitor of motion photography (Muybridge's zoopraxograph, the Lumières' cinématograph, Edison's kinetograph). Was it obvious to Muybridge, the Lumières, Méliès, and Edison that sound was "missing"? To Edison, perhaps, yes, because he invented the phonograph in 1877. Yet, recalling the case shared by Oliver Sacks, would it have been as odd for photogenetors to imagine that smells—odors, fragrances—were also missing from cinema's origins? Hardly, and we remain untroubled by the lack of such attributes and potential sensory effects in our continual encounters with screened entertainments. The slow emergence of augmented (AR) / mixed reality (MR) / virtual reality (VR) technologies, including haptic interfaces, may signal a shift in the expectations of consumers seeking a movie environment that exceeds the moving image—that draws in other senses for viable input.

A turn toward a gramophonology is, then, indebted to the nature of medium and genre conjured by the invention of cinema and its sibling technologies. Consider how "motion pictures"—imbuing the logic of its own *Geschlecht*—formed a community of images in a certain relation to one another (e.g., as variously sequenced, chronological, assigned a frame rate, and given a playback direction, etc.). At this early stage, in the late nineteenth century, the master terms of Deleuze's influential two-volume pair seem precisely right, if *avant la lettre*: a time-image and a movement-image are unified; the still photograph has come to life—been in-spired (*anima*) and thus appears *animated*. What then of sound as a foreign intervention, an invader from another genus? Crépon again: "*Geschlecht* thus concentrates [...] the risks involved with any designation of community: that of being led back to an order of belonging deriving primarily from generation and ascendency (thus from sexuality as well)—that is, the risk of contamination of politics by genealogy."[87] The image and later the *moving* image were not created with sound (as something native to its generation); rather, sound was, even from the beginning, an additive, a separable and thus separate technology, and therefore arrived with a different ontology; a visitor from another realm, it not only needed to be identified and if desired, integrated, it also needed first to be acknowledged on its own terms; strangely, while incorporation occurred (indeed, to the point of complete digestion), identification seems to have never happened. Moreover, the "generation and ascendency" of the art of motion pictures appears, even in those inchoate first stirrings of the film medium, to assure sound's ancillary status, its perpetual and perpetuated foreignness, its dispossession. Despite the obvious, long-standing intimacies of the genres of image and sound, the latter remained an unknown or unknowledged presence—that is, unless pointed out (a finger directed to the ear, as if to say "listen"); hence the pedagogical usefulness of films that adopt sound as a subject, or that manage to make sound an issue at the level of form.

If these sketches of cinematic history succeed as veritable at the mere level of description (something like a media anthropology, kin or kindred to Thomas Elsaesser's media archaeology), what follows may be more speculative, namely, that by the time sound "arrived" to meet and merge with its mate, to become "married" to the image—again, as if emerging from another world (an arrival, let us say, that begins officially, or at least with fanfare, in the late 1920s)—it was too late for its power, novelty, or identity to unseat the overtness and primacy of the image, whether still *or* moving. Any attempts at a genuine, equitable "marriage of mediums"—sound and image—seemed to demand imbalance, as if humans were not sensorially equipped to recognize and institute parity; hence asymmetry, hence "ascendency" of the one over/upon the other; or the one "inside" the other (as film seems to "contain" sounds, whereas a soundtrack, by contrast, is not treated as "containing" images—only calling them to mind from memory). Perhaps it need not have turned out this way: the historically situated and soon enough abandoned sobriquet "talkie" gave *preference* to sound with no trace of the image (moving or otherwise); drawing from the genre multiplicity explored above, we should note that despite the many sounds on offer after 1927, the sound of human speech (in the form of "talking") prevailed among other contenders (such as song, sound effect, etc.). Retrospectively, perhaps "talking picture" would have suggested a better, if not fully achieved balance (and, admittedly, in this case, *motion* is left aside, unacknowledged). The syntagma "sound film," as noted, prioritizes sound, places it first, thus lends credence to an ontology of film that always already involves the implacement of audio genres. In the long century since sound merged with moving pictures, sound's absence or asynchronization are rarer events; indeed, in the last half-century, they shuffle a work's status, making it "experimental" or "avant garde"—hence, names given to designate deviation and a willing distance from established norms. Not incidentally, experimental and avant-garde films, or even the partial implementation of their methodologies in mainstream movies, have given us better chances for noticing sounds.

Helpful or not, truthful or not, the gathered tropes of genealogy, intimacy, community, containment, contamination, etc., hint at sound as pollutant—something defiling the independence and even "purity" of motion pictures.[88] We must assume, then, that if olfactory and haptic technologies could have *preceded* sound innovations, our conversation about film ontology would have to contend with a wider range of "invasive" genres, however much those points of contact were beneficial and otherwise enriching for the gathered potency of (this, to us, as of yet unknown) aroma-haptic-cinema. In this counterfactual film history, smell and touch were already long-ago integrated into the cinematic environment and sound only recently began making itself known as a *Geschlecht* that might be "added" to cinema; indeed, as noted, "added value" is how Chion regards sound's contribution to or relationship with moving images.[89] Is this reordering of arrivals and mergers unthinkable because (technologically) unlikely, or unthinkable because incoherent? Any reply will search for a sense of how these genres-as-mediums come together, how they interact, yet also how they maintain distinct identities while contributing to a collectively realized work of art. Consider, for example, how we are struggling to articulate cinema's emerging relationship to—or as—VR, AR, MR, and other immersive environments. Are these up-to-the-minute interventions not as destabilizing as the "introduction" of sound was a century ago? Add to these computational transformations the rise of deepfakes and GANs, and the audiovisual landscape yields yet more genres to account for—to identify individually and translate collectively.

If we retain the language of a "community" of traits—where sound or, better, *sounds*, at last, present themselves as a set of genres (perhaps classified under prevailing sonic *genera*)—then we remain poised to regard them as "contaminants," or harmfully parasitic, instead of positively symbiotic and beneficially co-constitutive. Moreover, because the relationship is evidently generative—a productive and reproductive comingling—the question of "coupling" and the number of "partners" (or genres/genders) in play lends credence to the notion that sound and image—or the sound-image—is only nominally binary. No doubt the language in use here—the terms "chosen," or more likely passively inherited, and thereafter the definitions accepted or supplied to them—needs to come up against the phenomenological impulse so emphatically called for by Merleau-Ponty: "To return to things themselves is to return to that world which precedes knowledge, of which knowledge always *speaks*, and in relation to which every scientific schematization is an abstract and derivative sign-language, as is geography in relation to the countryside in which we have learnt beforehand what a forest, a prairie or a river is."[90] Our tropes for thinking sound suggest that we have faltered in our attempts to translate genres, to make them full partners to one another. Such a foray into the untranslatability of sound's *Geschlecht* may be part of our trouble because it would seem to heighten the terminological polysemy at issue (and along the way stoke an unexpected, although not unwelcome, ethical and political tumult). With Merleau-Ponty's admonishment at the ready, our perennial generic impasse comes into view rather clearly and compellingly as an interaction between the pre-linguistic sensation of cinema's varied attributes and our belated linguistic adventure in categorizing, typing, troping, etc., the phenomena we are said to, or say we, experience. There is something powerful about letting that dogged resistance to formulation rest under our attention, as if we could find solace in the lack of transmission, the failure to move from one region of phenomenal expression to another. Rather than advocating for sound's crendentializing—and competition with the image—we let it remain in its liminal state, perceptible, yes, but also beyond conceptualization. We are again *in utero*, head up against our mother's beating heart.

VIII

Amy Villarejo has given us language to think of a genre as "a category of [technological] production" and as something with static and dynamic attributes that must be perceived by audiences—according to practices of reception—in order to be interpreted (in her words, "as a description of practices of reception according to generic conventions and expectations").[91] Meanwhile, visuality as figured by films often feels defined by its own category of medial production—its own (ontological) genre (viz., what, materially, the visual representation is encoded upon, e.g., whether "on" film, tape, digital media, or through various computational programs and codes). The material culture (even if digital) suggests that visual media is caught up in practices of treating the representation a certain way—practices matured in logocentric and ocularcentric environments. Gramophonology counters these habits, appears as a gesture of recalibration. Even the many innovative theorems and critical observations of postmodernity—from the "male gaze" (and its cinema of "looks") to the "scopic regime" along with various portraits of simulacra, the hyper-real, and the like—have repeatedly privileged the *visual* aspects of cinema. With these cues from Villarejo (and Laura Mulvey as a presumed interlocutor), let us ask whether, or to what extent, we have systematically engaged what it would mean to contest the "objectification and fetishization" of the *sounds* of figures on screen.[92] The postulation is rhetorical, exposing yet another apparent category error, because what controversy—of, say, asymmetrical power—has been raised by the presence of sound on (near, behind, in, or beside) the screen? Where is the charged reaction to that unwritten work "Sonic Pleasure and Narrative Cinema"?

When writing about Laura Mulvey's seminal "Visual Pleasure and Narrative Cinema," Villarejo observes that "Mulvey effectively demonstrated how the vision (aesthetic, ideological) of classical Hollywood cinema is complicit with a menacing patriarchal vision that consigns women to the status of passive objects."[93] Notice the two instances of "vision," even while we wonder: but what about the *sounds* of classical Hollywood cinema? Mulvey's go-to for "fetishistic scopophilia" (Sternberg) and "the investigative side of voyeurism" (Hitchcock) used sounds, in significant measure, to achieve their cinematic effects.[94] Not that sound should *want* to take credit for any such "menacing," but it nevertheless bears out that it should be part of our critical reception of such celebrated and influential films.

In the context of Villarejo's account, such remarks fall under the domain of reception studies, because they are undertaken by film-philosophers and cinema critics rather than filmmakers. Yet how have these audiences-for-film engaged—"received"—the sonic register(s) of their appointed medium, film? If, by and large, these audiences have left sound relatively (or comparatively) un- or undertheorized, how might we take the present occasion (and those like it, which is to say, any occasion in which film presents us with sound—and perhaps even those moments when it goes silent) as an opportunity to fill in a crucial (almost painfully self-evident) lacuna? What then should be the project after making such initial observations? I have been trying to find terms for it, describing it variously as involving a thinking of "sound as medium," "medium as genre," and perhaps now, gathering lines laid above into a culminative coupling of those theoretical descriptions, "sounds as genres (*of the* medium)"—for sound is, as noted, (1) a category of (technological) production and (2) possesses static and dynamic attributes that must be perceived by audiences (according to practices of reception) in order to be interpreted.

Sound would appear, at first blush and even after further study, to qualify for both attributes of "genre" just adduced (viz., 1 and 2; as, no doubt, we can add and readily admit, does the image). Yet, customs of cinema studies speak of "film type" almost exclusively in terms of the visual content of films—e.g., which types and archetypes emerge from a series or cycle of films (e.g., the Western, yes, but also, the Cowboy [as a feature of a Western]; or the Western as parable of American political ideology, or as a coded critique of contemporary culture).[95] The appeal to "types" (and traits) puts us squarely within our catalogue of curiosities collected under the master term *Geschlecht*. In looking to screened content, we ask not so much *what* is a Western, but *when*? *There Will Be Blood* (2007, dir. P. T. Anderson) and *Days of Heaven* (1978, dir. Terrence Malick) look like they belong to the genre, but so do *Legends of the Fall* (1994, dir. Edward Zwick), *The Big Lebowski* (1998, dir. Joel and Ethan Coen), *The Last Samurai* (2003, dir. Edward Zwick), *The Assassination of Jesse James by the Coward Robert Ford* (2007, dir. Andrew Dominik), *3:10 to Yuma* (2007, dir. James Mangold), *Inglourious Basterds* (2009, dir. Quentin Tarantino), *The Revenant* (2016, dir. Alejandro González Iñárritu), and *Once Upon a Time ... in Hollywood* (2019, dir. Tarantino). Frames of reference are crucial for such accounting (John Ford's *Stagecoach* [1939] or *The Searchers* [1956]?), as we are speaking to the way film instances communicate with the specifics of precedents: moods, thematics, characters, stars, plotting, and moral landscape. Indeed, the profoundly masculine catalogue here itself comes in for reconsideration and reconception on account of films by Kelly Reichardt.[96] Ryan Gilbey calls *Meek's Cutoff* (2010, dir. Reichardt), "a western that prioritizes the female perspective." Reichardt says that in the Westerns she knows, "women are usually the objects. But I always wondered what, say, John Wayne in *The Searchers* must have looked like to the woman cooking his stew."[97] Not only does Reichardt offer novel perspectives on the Western—what it was and might yet be (see also, more recently, *First Cow* [2019])—her films also remind us how "moods, thematics, characters, stars, plotting, and moral landscape" are affected by the sounds of the genre.

Moving further in the direction of the genres of sounds, or sounds-as-genres—in particular, we chart a two-step: first, after Apter, Cassin, and company, approaching sound as *medium* (or a set of them) by way of its *Geschlecht* (that is, its particular residency in the material of film); and second, we encounter genre-as-medium (Cavell) or medium-as-genre (Villarejo), that is, where film's expressivity of, and participation in, an identifiable ("particular" in Cavell's parlance) set of traits conjures associations to other film worlds and our own. If this logic holds, we arrive at the present, hybridized postulation, namely sound-as-genre, or, again, perhaps better in plural—sounds-as-genres. By way of sound's categories of (1) technological production and (2) the static/dynamic attributes that make sound recognizable from one moment to the next, *sounds-as-genres* presents itself as a series of layered and mixed acoustic environments—ones that however much they lend distinctive contributions to sensory experience are often indistinguishably embedded in the medium dominated by the image.

We can situate these genres of sounds by thinking of the specific (again, "particular") ways in which sounds distinctively reveal themselves in, or in the company of, moving pictures, namely, through Foley work, sound effects, spoken dialogue, voiceover, score, diegetic music, nongietic music, noise, natural sounds, etc. Each has or offers its own world of characteristics and references, thus each appears to exist as a genre unto itself. Additionally, as these genres coalesce as the sounds *of* cinema—that is, what we hear when we "watch" a movie—these genres point to sounds-as-such, what we may call the media of sound, or a constellation of sonic *genera*. In their heterogeneity, sounds arrive with already impactful ontologies (ones, for instance, that signal an awareness of our own embodiment, that is, as the kinds of creatures who can experience the effects of sounds), yet the critical expression or articulation of such ontological traits has long been overshadowed (another visually troubling verb?), or rather undersung, by our attention, our preoccupation, with moving pictures. Indeed, how often do elements of visual content (scene, star, dialogue, diegetic event) claim the somatic and sensory effects of sound as their own?

IX

Let us turn to another exercise in "reading" that is meant to include "listening"—translating sound as we find it in/on/as film, or finding ourselves befuddled by its untranslatable presence in/on/as cinema. Turning to Hollis Frampton's *Hapax Legomena* (as Frampton glossed the syntagma, "things said once," a definition that presents as a comic inversion of Apter's lexilalia—namely, the compulsive repetition of things said), we find a work entitled *Critical Mass* (1971, 25 min. 11 sec., black and white, mono).[98] When "screened," *Critical Mass* provides a potent figuration of sound's presence, and in particular, evidence for thinking of *sounds-as-genres*.[99] In *Alone. Life Wastes Andy Hardy* (Martin Arnold's film that will be addressed below), we watch a boy turn away from his mother and father and toward a girl; the film ends with the boy and girl's anxious initial point of contact—one that doubles lustful union (a kiss) with repellant animalistic signals of imminent danger (a hiss). In *Critical Mass*, by contrast, we are on the other side of a relationship, as it collapses, comes apart. She says: "That's what you are—a fucking little boy. What you need is a mommy, that's what you need.... I look like your mother, huh? I sound like your mother, too, right?" He says: "You *act* like somebody's mother."[100]

One of our most astute readers of sound in/on/as film, Rick Altman, wrote a brilliant expose-cum-manifesto, "Four and a Half Film Fallacies," where he begins by saying:

> Logically, every theory of cinema should address the problem of film sound. Practically speaking, such has hardly been the case. On the contrary, a surprising number of theoreticians blithely draw conclusions about the nature of cinema simply by extrapolating from the apparent properties of the moving image. If this were just a question of oversight, the problem would be rapidly corrected. In fact, theoreticians who overlook sound usually do so quite self-consciously, proposing what they consider strong arguments in favor of an image-based notion of cinema.[101]

My remarks are obviously indebted to the spirit and the letter of Altman's astute observation, including his critique of prevailing mores. Speaking of awareness, though, and whether or not Altman is himself "self-conscious" on this point, we could pause to notice the dominance of ocular metaphors in the coursings of our language, such that Altman addresses those who would "overlook" sound. Thus, as a matter of "oversight," let us consider how to compensate for these excesses, for instance, how to *overhear* cinema.

Situating research in this chapter (as it aims to translate certain tuitions from Apter, Cassin, Cavell, Villarejo, and others), and in the context of Altman's corrective to film studies, I would describe the project as, in part, combatting the ontological fallacy. Altman traces the error to at least Rudolf

Arnheim and Béla Balázs, who "make the formal case that the image without sound still constitutes cinema, while sound without an image is no longer cinema." The history of cinema is rife with examples that illustrate how "sound-oriented proclivities regularly confront image-based tendencies," and thus, how the ontological argument is "falsely ontological." Still, "so strong is the apparent appeal of [the] ontological claim [made by Arnheim et al.] that it regularly reappears in the writings of current theoreticians." And what is more, so often, "not from the enemies of sound, but from its greatest defenders"; Altman cites Theodor Adorno and Hans Eisler as exemplars of the latter.[102]

As for my contribution to the conversation, and though I am decidedly in league with Altman on the matter of sound's odd repression and distortion in cinema studies, I should hazard that I am in fact responding to the ontological fallacy *with more ontology*. I am trying to articulate sound's identity as an ontological presence (in or as its medium, genre, and *Geschlecht*): whether it is coextensive with the image, separable from it, or something of both (depending on the film and the conditions of its reception), requires further study. Metacinematic movies, of course, launched the inquiry long ago: we can hear the dismissive "It's just a fad" shouted anxiously from the screening room of the first sync-sound film presented in *Singin' in the Rain*, and then laugh at the hasty declaration, because we know how wrong the dismissal turned out to be—historically *and ontologically*. If the development of *sound's identity as cinema* has been oddly forestalled by detractors of sound and fans alike, then, even thirty years after Altman's intervention, and despite the welcome expansion and enrichment of sound studies (though, again, so often beyond the study of cinema's sounds), we are continuing to reckon with the sound-image partnership—the nature of the coupling, the peculiarities of these paired ontologies; and as this query attests, also, the differences, the resistance to integration, the otherness—and hence estrangement. As it happens, a case for ontological harmony may yet be illustrated when things fall apart, when the "couple" has a falling out, when the partnership is fraught, nerves frayed, sympathies forgotten. That is, when they do not communicate—remain unheard, speak past one another.

In *Critical Mass*, Frampton, like Arnold, employs looping as a technique. Yet *Critical Mass* helps us perceive an attribute of Arnold's *Alone.*, namely, that for all of Arnold's manipulation of playback speed and direction, and his extensive use of looping, sound always remains intimately aligned, coupled with the image—indeed, by means of Arnold's technique, sound seems even more inherent than our customary viewing of standard moving pictures encourages us to perceive. In short, despite the radical interference of Arnold-as-artist, as cinematic psychoanalyst-cum-ciné-magician, he keeps the sound/image marriage intact. Not so in Frampton's *Critical Mass*. Plainly, openly in *Critical Mass*, form and content are in dialogue in a destabilizing way, one that reveals, in time, that a troubled relationship between lovers (here a woman and a man, Barbara DiBenedetto and Frank Albetta, two romantically involved university students in 1971[103]), is mirrored by a troubled relationship between sound and image. It seems neither pair can stay together.

Critical Mass was Frampton's first film with sync sound, or especially suitable in this case, lip sync—another cinematic term of art that bears on the relationship between media (as it does people), and the respective potentiality for comprehension, mutual or otherwise; "lip sync" also draws our attention to the mouth as locus, thus, to the sound of speech as it aligns with, or detaches from, labial movements in partnership with teeth and tongue. *Critical Mass* is dominated by the sound of human voices. Frampton recalls: "Larry Gottheim crewed on the job as sound recordist: at the time I didn't know a Nagra from my elbow."[104] The film historian, Scott MacDonald takes us further into the context of the film's creation—and the way the piece functions as a social *and* cinematic critique: the "film provides an implicit" (that is, at the level of the film's ontology) "conceptual riff on the commercial cinema's dependence on sync sound, particularly in films focusing on romantic relationships."[105] At the time *Critical Mass* was filmed (March 1971) and edited (later that year), Frampton himself was in the process of separating from his wife, Marcia Steinbrecher; they divorced a few years later, in 1974; in 1971, Frampton began seeing photographer Marion Faller, whom he later married. MacDonald continues along lines that blend personal, social, and cinematic commentary:

> In commercial films, sync sound has always been most important for spoken dialogue, and traditionally this required a double system: that is, sound and image were worked on separately and "married" during the final stage of production (in celluloid cinema a "married print" cannot be edited—since the sound that accompanies a particular image is located several frames away from the gate of the projector). Frampton seems to have understood the pun implicit in "marrying" image and sound: so many Hollywood films made during the 1930s to 1950s, when Frampton was growing up, end in marriage or assume that marriage is the culmination of whatever romantic action and dialogue fuels the narrative. As a filmmaker committed to working independently ("independent," specifically, from the film industry), Frampton used his first sync-sound film as a way of critiquing the assumption that marrying is the endgame of both narrative romance and film production.[106]

As the quarrelling students rehearse a relationship argument through clichés—clichés because true—and those clichés are themselves repeated, replicated within the confines of the argument-slash-dialogue that Frampton has created through editing, we are made to wonder about the clichés surrounding the relationship between image and sound. Not to be missed, MacDonald has come to describe Frampton's *Critical Mass* as offering us a cinema of "de-marriage"—that is, a de-coupling that stands at odds with Cavell's canonical notion of "remarriage."[107] (And in a moment of apropos duplication, MacDonald himself describes his professional relationship with Cavell's writing as "troubled.") Image and sound, Frank and Barbara: together for so long and yet so unknown to one another, the same arguments rehearsed again and again and again. Despite the steady repetition and ardent emphasis of these sounds, or perhaps because of them, we may not have ears for them. Aural reception becomes a matter of linguistic sense as well as physiology.

X

Shifting to another location of experimental and avant-garde cinema, I will pick up from something I developed in a chapter for *Metacinema*, and here offer a further study, or more accurately, an extension of that research: dwelling at more length, diving more deeply into the secondary literature on the practice of reading as translational, and as the manipulation of formal entities (often just called media or art) that may induce confusions and false leads, and as the case may be, false or misleading conclusions.[108] In this way, the analysis begun elsewhere is now drawn into proximity with specific issues of intelligibility as they align with questions of the untranslatable. Here, again, the looking and listening are at issue, especially as those embodied activities approach and assess works of art that present moving images and make sounds. To what extent do we see and hear projections from our mental landscapes, and to what extent are we capable of receiving them from the media on offer? This interstitial space—truly, the conditions for the possibility of criticism as such—announces its fraught position: crossing this divide in both directions (in one, as witness; in the other, as reader) proclaims the stakes of film criticism as translational practice.

As experimental filmmaker and trained psychoanalyst, Martin Arnold, himself said: "I am not a film theorist and I did not try to filmically translate any theory of gender politics. [... T]heories that film artists themselves attribute to their work are to be taken with a grain of salt."[109] Arnold is referring to his remarkable, memorable trilogy of black-and-white films exploring (and exploiting) experimental cinematic techniques commonly referred to by the name *The Cineseizure*: *Pièce touchée* (1989, 16 mins.), *Passage à l'acte* (1993, 12 mins.) and the aforementioned *Alone. Life Wastes Andy Hardy* (1998), a fifteen-minute film whose ostensible content is coextensive with a 1940 movie entitled *Andy Hardy Meets Debutante* (dir. George B. Seitz) starring a young Judy Garland and Mickey Rooney, and a

1939 Busby Berkeley movie, *Babe in Arms*.[110] Thus, while it is true that we critics can on the one hand advocate apart from, or by dismissing, authorial intention, we may, on the other hand, be seduced by authorial hints subsequently deployed to ratify theory; indeed, the media itself may resist our efforts or register its own effects. One may want to claim, for example, that *Alone.* reveals or discloses subtextual psycho-sexual elements, and yet, with heightened attention to Arnold's methods, the effort by some critics to achieve a translation from the hidden to the revealed is, in fact, undermined. Invoking a certain Wittgensteinian spirit and sentiment, "No such thing was in question here."[111] In short, the Andy Hardy and Busby Berkeley movies do not "contain" the many latent meanings ascribed to these works, rather we do—as viewers, critics, and crucially here, as listeners.

The engagement with the secondary literature on Arnold's work to follow is meant to create a context for thinking about interpretable objects, especially audiovisual ones that arrive in unfamiliar ways. With decades worth of "training" in watching narrative film, we may be caught off guard by experimental and avant-garde works; new ways of watching and listening may need to be developed before theories are "applied" or meanings "discovered"—or in Michael Zryd's Freud-laced phrasing, "refound."[112] Imagine we screened Arnold's work to the original audiences for the Andy Hardy and Busby Berkeley movies circa 1940. For one thing, they would lack our varied theoretical apparatuses (poststructuralist, genderqueer, critical race, feminist, film theory, media studies, etc.). Indeed, to an audience from this earlier era—even one familiar with the movies and criticism of them—Arnold's suite of films may read simply as works suffering a number of mechanical errors all at once (a major glitch in playback, a technical problem with sound, etc.). This bit of imagined time travel jolts us to reconsider the importance of spatio-temporal location for reception, including the available "theories" and frames of reference on offer or in wide circulation. Although Sigmund Freud died the year the Berkeley movie was released, should we expect popular audiences for *Babe in Arms* to have a familiarity with Freud's work, or Freudianism, or psychoanalysis, such that *Alone.* would appear intuitively revelatory of otherwise hidden psychoanalytic or psychosexual content? For instance, in approaching a film of novel production and projection (such as *Alone.*), are we equipped to say with confidence how much of a work contains its meaning and how much of that meaning is contained in us? There are different presiding tropes on offer: a model of discovery in which we uncover and unconceal (in the spirit of *aletheia*, ἀλήθεια); and another model, say (in a canny cinematic pun), of projection—by which we the audience ascribe qualities to a work. These are two modes, and it would seem interpretation often involves some overlap of them. Yet there are times when one model or the other is applied to a work for which it is ill-suited. Readings of Arnold's *Alone.*—and the family of films known as *The Cineseizure*—appear to be such an arresting case.

In the chapter from *Metacinema*, I aimed to articulate how Arnold's work—in *The Cineseizure* generally and *Alone.* specifically—amounted to metaformal innovations; in that context, I argued that—contrary to much prevailing film criticism on the trinity of films in *The Cineseizure*—psychoanalytic content was not hidden or "latent" in the original footage, but an epiphenomenon of audience reception prompted by formal invention by way of metaphorical intervention ("inscriptions" in Arnold's parlance) into the found materials, thus making the audience and/or Arnold the proper source of such meanings. Now, as part of the present effort to closely examine what it means to listen to films as a mode of "reading" them—as part of the shift from lectiocentrism to gramophonology—we are moved to explore some salient moments in the two decades of interpretation Arnold's 1998 experimental film has received. Watching and listening to *Alone.* in company with these interpreters, I suggest, highlights metaphilosophical concerns that lie at the core of the *Geschlecht* complex, namely, how critics interpret formal attributes as opposed to cognitive *responses* to those aggregated traits (simply known as "the work" or "the film" called *Alone.*). We are pressured to ask: when does a rather empirical etiology and description of a film slip into a report on one's feelings about the film? The slippage, itself, of course, can amount to an intriguing moment of translation—of moving from one realm to another, but then, we have left the work and entered the arena of autobiography and psychological testimony.

To this end, let us sustain Arnold's admonition that we be on guard for artists who theorize—even those, such as himself, well-trained in the type of theory at issue, namely, Freudian psychoanalysis—while attending to some of the abundant critical, so often strikingly positive, reception of his work—a reception that is not only in awe of Arnold, but regularly in general agreement (perhaps another indication that something has gone awry methodologically). Rather than claim, then, that *Alone.* issues a gender politics or psychoanalysis of culture, or film history; that it has at last delivered meaning from the eighty-year-old films hiding, somehow, in plain sight (and unplugged ear)—no such translation was on offer—we should be more circumspect, considering instead how the reception of work informs the theoretical valences and commitments we otherwise might wish to credit to the work. In this case, "the work" is not just one thing, but two: (1) found footage from Hollywood (*Andy Hardy Meets Debutante* and *Babe in Arms*, as well as the other source films[113]) and (2) a registration of mechanical, photo-optical playback effects created by Arnold himself. What the footage contains is one thing, what it shows—in *Alone.*—is quite another. And we may be obliged to add a third category when accounting for the meaning of Arnold's metaformal interventions in the critical literature—meaning that is, as it were, neither "in" the found footage, nor even "in" Arnold's crafted metaworks.

In place of a list of films or a constellation of titles that evoke a genre, we have at hand a single filmic example—or unified artistic method—that may help us address existing habits of theorizing and their attendant imbalances; a film, or set of films, that cultivates, indeed, demands, an attunement to its sounds. From a technical view, Arnold used an optical printer to achieve the loops, stutters, slow-motion, and other photo-and-sonic effects that define this work "sampled" from existing movies; such a brief, technical description of his approach will be the easiest, most straightforward claim to make about this remarkably fecund film.

The belief that Arnold conjured a psychoanalytic subtext—hiding in plain sight—has drawn deserved critical attention, and more especially critical praise. That is, critics, by and large, seem awestruck and entranced by what appears to be Arnold's capacity to uncover and illuminate veiled attributes from the otherwise everyday movements of familiar cinematic figures. *The Cineseizure* is a "trilogy of compulsive repetition," as Dirk Schaefer remarks,[114] and at more length, Michael Zryd decodes the stirring discoveries on offer in Arnold's experimental triad:

> Arnold's signature style applies the technique of forward-and-back looping—images repeated in a kind of two steps forward, one step back pattern—to banal interstitial sequences from classical Hollywood films, propelling the characters through a scene in stuttering slow motion. The repeated gestures are indeed made compulsive; frozen and replayed, they seem to capture moments of unconscious desire and repression unwittingly trapped between the 24 frames per second which ground cinematic movement. Arnold, trained in psychoanalysis in Vienna, carries Freud's investigation of the "Psychopathology of Everyday Life" into the placid surface behavior of the classical film text, shattering those carefully contained fantasies by elevating them to staged psychic tableaux. Moreover, Arnold's virtuosic image and sound editing creates a hypnotically rich rhythmic visual and sonic field which lends both grace and savagery to the films' analytical work. The physical vitality re-found in the image, accompanied by equally complex variations on the soundtrack, make his films work as dance and music as much as ironic inquiry.[115]

That Zryd's nuanced reading of *Alone.* involves such balanced attention to image and sound suggests we have found a film text that, indeed, lays bare the potential for repressions to be released—at once seen and heard. Here is a film—a work of art made from so-called "found footage" that in characteristically Freudian terms "re-finds" what it contains. ("The finding of an object is in fact a refinding of it," we are told by Freud in *Three Essays on the Theory of Sexuality*.[116]) Although upon first (and second and third) viewings (that is, our own repetitions mimicking those in the film), the visual effect of looping may remain the dominant element—what shocks, but also what hypnotizes, it is, arguably, the sound that makes the visuals terrifying, that provides the counterpoint to baby-faced Andy (Mickey Rooney) and debutante Betsy Booth (Judy Garland) with their writhing teenage bodies— ones expressive of an interpolated and embodied agonism with parental authority, existential desire, and social mores that confound and constrain at every turn. As in many horror films, it is sound that gives us the cue to listen for—and thus experience—the critical, antic commentary achieved through Arnold's artful manipulation of the original film, a work that masks its genius by masquerading under the guise of populist, conventional, and thus acceptable dreams.

Arnold has nicely narrated essential features of his process and his sources: "I work with feature film scenes, with popular cinema, so for my work the image itself is also very important, because the imagery doesn't only show certain places, actors and actions; it also shows the dreams, hopes, and taboos of the epoch and society that created it."[117] Yet, we should keep in mind what Arnold means by—or what we should understand as— "show" or "shows." The scenes from popular feature films do, with the help of some capable cultural criticism, exhibit the "dreams, hopes, and taboos" of a given time and place. But this is not the showing that Arnold is up to in his work; rather, his point in his written remarks is that he recognizes how, like many mainstream cultural artifacts, popular films possess (or encode) elements—such as dimensions of the politics of gender and sexuality—that are apparent at the time of release and continue to evolve as meaningful representations as time goes on.

Yet, it is precisely the context-dependent nature of reception that makes *Alone.* (and *The Cineseizure*, more generally) such a potent field for reflecting on what a work "contains" and what is contained within us. What we (can) see and hear is shaped, with striking prominence and yet rarely acknowledged, by the available conceptual apparatuses of culture and criticism. Arnold adds a pertinent gloss on the motivation of his experiments: "Probably I also sensed that it is especially interesting to observe those things which we (falsely) think we have seen a million times."[118] As an example, he says: "The husband coming home and the wife waiting for him are familiar images to everyone, especially because that scenario is used in all genres of conventional cinema."[119] Indeed, merely "the entering and leaving of rooms is itself a central impulse in conventional narrative cinema of the fifties."[120] Here Arnold is being the good media critic we need, for one thing, noticing genre conventions, narrative themes, scenic structures even (viz., man returning/woman waiting; entering and leaving rooms) that can transform systematic readings of individual films and the genre(s) they contribute to and constitute. However, where we just spoke of the way film representations "show" us things, here Arnold speaks of "observing" them—and it should be noted that this observation is not made possible by some new technological change (e.g., selection of images, optical printing, repetition of frames, forward/backward/forward movement, playback rate, etc.) but something more like having (new) eyes and ears for (old) things. The change is in us. There is slippage, then, when we hear a critic say of his film work: "Arnold uses his optical printer to lay bare the gender-political implications of the husband's arrival [...]"; or, "Again, Arnold lays bare the politics of a conventional media moment."[121] Arnold's films may return us to the original/source films and give us a chance to see them anew (e.g., *Andy Hardy Meets Debutante* and *Babe in Arms*), but this revelation is not what we have experienced in experiencing *Arnold's* films.

Conceptual slippage—two steps forward, one step back—may be a fitting analogue for (any) criticism of Arnold's filmic trio here under discussion, where writing about his work takes on the qualities of the films themselves. We repeat ourselves, we advance, and then retreat. We take promising paths and then errant ones, missteps. We are as often stymied by the films and the remarks made about them—left "stuttering" and "limping"—as we are fortified.[122] Not a bad effect for art to have, in fact. But it would be handy to have a more solid hold on what Arnold's films bring about and what the source footage achieves on its own.

In *24× a Second*, Laura Mulvey writes that Arnold "re-edits fragments of old Hollywood movies and, in the process, transforms the movement of celluloid figures into empty gestures with no beginning, end, or purpose."[123] "Re-editing" seems incomplete, for we are not just talking about tacking one shot to another, say, like a newsreel. "Transforms the movement" is much better—and "transforms" should be a master term for speaking of Arnold's practice as it is both accurate and a word he uses to describe the results of his labors (as seen just above). But again, "empty gestures" seems hugely at odds with the surplus of meaning most critics find in those same movements; "empty," yes, in the sense that they are not natural (e.g., played at a standard rate, a single, brief, and gentle squeeze of an arm becomes, in Arnold's machination, a pulsing, extended, and insistent hump), but not in the sense that those same gestures—played at regular speed and forward direction—are charged with and full of referential power (hence all of our nervous giggles). Looking to the "old Hollywood movies" themselves—their fate in Arnold's hands—Mulvey is spot on: "These experiments accentuate the vulnerability of old cinema and its iconic figures."[124] For Arnold's intervention into the found footage, the characters "lose their protective fictional worlds."[125] What a helpful depiction: Mickey Rooney, Fay Holden, Judy Garland, et al. no longer (safely?) exist within their home storyworlds, the fictional realm of young Andy Hardy. Arnold has, rather, usurped the power regularly given to screenwriter, actor, director, sound designer, and editor and installed himself as chief choreographer of the enterprise. As David Clark writes: "By repeating, scrubbing, and elongating individual frames he re-animates the motion and sound of individual scenes to create what seem like monstrous puppets spewing emphatic utterances."[126] In this way, as puppet master, Arnold is entirely in charge of the "manipulation of human gesture."[127]

In two chapters of *Ex-Cinema*—"Cinemnesis" and "Digesture"—Akira Mizuta Lippit directs his attention to the same trilogy of Arnold's found-footage films that occupied Mulvey's interest and holds our attention here. One finds in *Ex-Cinema* many promising directives, for example, as when Lippit concludes that Arnold's films "seem ecstatic, or seem to unleash a hypermnemic force that writes as it projects [...] because the outside has come to resemble [...] a form of radical interiority."[128] Here "writing" finds kinship with Arnold's use of "inscription" (above) and "projects" (as in projection) keeps us close to the cinematic "writing" of light on the screen. Even more crucially, though, and problematically, is the "come to resemble"—that moment when, in short, the spectator is *tricked* to believe that, say, the erotic or aggressive or melancholic forces *we feel* when watching Arnold's films are (somehow) "in" the interiority of the characters, in the diegesis of the film world. Let us call this effect, after Lippit, an "impossible grammatology of the unconscious," because it is not the characters' unconscious that we are mining—or the culture in which, for example, *Andy Hardy Meets Debutante* would be produced—but rather our own. No wonder Arnold's films are terrifying stuff—conjuring resonances of the sublime, that is, when exhilaration from insight is matched by a vertiginous sensation of danger.

Lippit felicitously captures Arnold's value-added practice of filmmaking when he says *Alone*. "*feels* against the order of the original feature films. It expresses a feeling that originates elsewhere, at once within and without the reworked passage of film. Arnold's cinema represents a mnemic technology not only because it writes but also because it reads and feels."[129] For some, "reworked" is a term of art in pottery, and it seems in this case successfully translated to filmmaking, as Arnold's "manipulation" of found footage "reworks" them into new pieces of art. (Drawing on Arnold's preferred analogue, hip-hop music, I have earlier described *The Cineseizure* as a series of "remixes."[130]) Yet, I am less sure about what to do with Lippit's anthropomorphism, namely, where Arnold's cinema "reads and feels." Lippit's own more helpful notion of "has come to resemble" just cited appears as a necessary self-corrective, for we are interested not in the interiority of the (manipulated, reworked, remixed) characters but in our own spectatorial/auditorial encounter with their reworked gestures—that is, how we read them, how we hear them, how they make us feel.

Lippit's neologism "digesture" gives us some language for interpreting what it is we think is happening with the figures of the former profilmic space (viz., the original footage) and what is happening in Arnold's altered cinematic landscape. Digesture, in Lippit's nomenclature, is a combination of digest and gesture, where "the apparatus possesses the body, takes it over, and erases the organic body and its gestures, inscribing onto the images of bodies a series of secondary gestures."[131] The digesture—or secondary gesture—is precisely what Arnold (as puppet master) brings to the found footage: "Arnold reanimates these bodies, establishing a form of movement [...]. One gesture inscribed over another, one gesture absorbed by another, digested. Bodies absorbed by the cinema, digested, regestured, and reinscribed over other bodies and gestures."[132] Arnold's technical/mechanical practice "reworks" through "dismantling" the prevailing, inherited order (e.g., twenty-four frames a second, forward movement only, the standard projection of the profilmic scene) and then writes-over/rewrites/inscribes/remixes an algorithm for projection.[133] For example, in speaking of *Passage à L'acte*, Arnold shares this code: "I start with frame x, go forward to frame $x+1$ and then from $x+1$ back again through x to $x-1$."[134] Lippit accounts for the results: "Arnold generates in his recycled bodies a repertoire of new gestures: nervous ticks [sic], extensive stutters, apparent seizures, involuntary jerks and spasms, exaggerated signals, overexposed affect, and minute movements like the quivering of fingers between two frames."[135] How aptly stated. With it we can appreciate how digesting the (inherited, "found") gesture in Arnold's capable hands culminates in "a repertoire of new gestures" that are familiar enough to us to have them "come to resemble" something else altogether from where they began. Thus, the father's single slap conjures stern patriarchy, whereas Arnold's repetition and slowing of the slap becomes the occasion—in *Alone.*—for a scene of the son's simmering resentment and nascent rebellion. Andy Hardy speaks: "Alright [followed by a loaded, lingering pause added by Arnold, along with two extra slaps], dad." Despite all of this tremendously perceptive reading of Arnold's re-gesturing of bodies, Lippit concludes, in keeping with Mulvey cited earlier, that "Nothing is left in Arnold's cinema except empty gestures [...]." Like I said, two steps forward, one step back.

When David Bering-Porter comes to write about Arnold's films, after Mulvey and Lippit and Zryd, he begins, in his first sentence, by saying Arnold "seems to open up the [original] films to reveal additional layers of meaning."[136] Bering-Porter encourages an interpretive assessment wherein *Alone.* and its companion pieces "uncover a hidden aspect or latent content of the film and reveal an uncanny, libidinal economy at work; a film beneath the surface of another film."[137] As cited above, and resituated here to underscore an alternative to Chion's valued-added approach, he claims: "one does get the impression that Arnold is not so much adding to or changing the existing film, but rather revealing something that existed all along—trapped, as [Michael] Zryd puts it, in between the 24 frames per second of the film itself."[138] And serving as a final indication of this line of approach: "Arnold brings to light a truth embedded in the relation between the characters on-screen [sic]: an underlying impulse or drive that works below their actions, made visible through cinematic devices."[139] Zryd's point, according to Bering-Porter? That Arnold "unveils new insights."[140] As a moment of pushback, then, what if we regarded Arnold's figures as *no longer* "characters on screen"—but (also?) representations that have been taken over by Arnold to become as it were "re-characterized" (as someone or something else)? We could classify this description and new status as an extradiegetic version or variant of the characters, while holding fast to the recommendation that we are no longer in the company of Andy Hardy.

In *Doubting Vision*, Malcolm Turvey identifies a "revelationist tradition" in cinema—with conspicuous although varied contributions from Jean Epstein, Dziga Vertov, Béla Balázs, and Sigfried Kracauer—which addresses how cinema is an aid to the (limited) human eye; where the camera is said, in a word, to "reveal" things we are liable to miss, or must necessarily remain unaware of, because of ocular biophysiology. Turvey writes that "the basic argument made by these four theorists and filmmakers is that certain cinema techniques—the close-up, slow motion, time-lapse photography, editing—can reveal features of reality that are invisible in the sense that it is impossible for the human eye to see them without assistance."[141] Indeed, Turvey goes further than saying that the camera (a synecdoche for subsequent recordings on celluloid that can be studied) affords the revelation of "something otherwise hidden from human perception" *and* of "the truth of nature as well," but, indeed, that the camera also uncovers "the true nature of *social* reality."[142] This last claim is both pertinent and problematic to the study of Arnold's films. The revelationists advocate for cinema-as-prosthesis, and we can all sign on for this assessment of cinema's technological past as well as its ongoing service to the present and future of (digital) motion pictures. But this forensic revelationism isn't our issue with Arnold's work. We are not trying *à la* Muybridge to study whether the horse's gallop, in fact, includes a moment of levitation (it does), but what after-effects we can analyze in the wake of Arnold's metamedial reconstitution of found footage. In this respect, Arnold's work is not meant to serve as evidence for what was "hidden" (until now) and was, in fact, "actually happening" in the "reality" of gender politics circa 1940 (or, with the entire Andy Hardy arc in mind—from 1937 to 1946, with a capstone feature film in 1958, *Andy Hardy Comes Home*). Rather, Arnold's films offer us—contra the revelationists—something more like a Rorschach test for what is actually happening for spectators—*whenever* they watch his films—in their own, present realities. We are not seeking illumination about what is "in" the film, but instead what is "in" us. The subject of our psychoanalytic study has been misplaced from the start: Arnold's films aren't on the couch, we are.

Bering-Porter seems right, though, to draw in Walter Benjamin's interests for a moment of comparison with Arnold's, saying: "Arnold's cinematic project shares with Benjamin an investment in isolating and analyzing moments of everyday life in order to bring something new to light."[143] Like Benjamin, with Freud's *Psychopathology of Everyday Life* in mind, there is reason to see cinema as being in the service of "defamiliariz[ing] the content of habitual experience"—a *Verfremdungseffekt* essential to Bertolt Brecht's epic theater. While alienation or defamiliarization is a potentiality of cinema, however, it is not its default mode, at least, say, in popular cinema; just the opposite. Indeed, it is the metaformalists of structural filmmaking, and the wider scope of ciné-experimentalists and avant-garde film practitioners, who have kept alive the viability of *ostranenie* as a method for bringing "something new to light" in the humdrum of ordinary life (on this front, consider experiments in "the home movie"—quintessential art of the everyday, the amateur, and the unprofessional[144]).

Despite his advantageous textual touchstones, however, Bering-Porter sees support for "the connection between Arnold and the revelationist tradition," thereby arriving at the misleading conclusion that "the aesthetic possibilities of visual media reveal what would otherwise escape human vision and attention: a continuum of unconscious social and physical relations that structure everyday experience."[145] Hence my earlier appeal to the Wittgensteinian reminder that "[n]o such thing was in question here." Although Cavell illuminated for us—in the context of his study of the remarriage genre (yet another repetition to take hold of)—that for Freud "the finding of an object is in fact the refinding of it,"[146] Arnold's work doesn't make this case for itself. Rather, we could say: in our encounter with Arnold's films, we are not so much finding (or refinding) an object but founding it—taking note of what Arnold has added, has created, not discovered (as words such as "revealed," "uncovered," "unveiled," "liberated," "brought to light," etc., lead us to believe). Bering-Porter sums up: "What is unsettling about Arnold's films is the way they [...] are suggestive of alien or unconscious motivations behind our gestures."[147] What is unsettling about Arnold's films, I would counter, is his success in making Bering-Porter's claim *feel* legitimate—rather than, as Arnold's art appears to be: a bit of legerdemain that has evacuated the space of character agency so that he can take over, and in turn, we might attribute weighty significance to otherwise "empty gestures." It is not that the "unconscious" is "revealed" to us by Arnold (who somehow "explore[s] the fractured world beneath the surface of the film"[148]) but that—if we look to the metaformalism of his practice—we are given a chance to study our own affective responses to uncanny movements and sounds on the surface of the manipulated medium. Thus, movement in the behavior of the film's sounds and images, in turn, affects *our* behavior—and, quite consequentially, the impressions and thoughts that form in the wake of such a personal experience, such an intimate encounter. Some of these effects travel under the name film criticism.

When Martin J. Zeilinger takes stock of a selection of representative film criticism of *Alone.*, he writes with confidence and clarity:

> With minor variations, all reviewers and critics interpret Arnold's sampling technique as aimed toward the exposition of underlying meanings contained in the original (the Andy Hardy films) through an analytical close reading (contained in Martin Arnold's *Alone*). This analysis is seen to expose a return of unconscious or repressed content from the Andy Hardy series and the shifting sociocultural, historical, and political climate of the period (1937–1958) during which it was produced.[149]

Well, at least Zeilinger leaves room for "minor variations," such as my own. "Virtually all commentary," Zeilinger continues, "on the film [*Alone.*] describes a constellation in which *Alone* is what the original Andy Hardy films become once they are lying on the analyst's couch, so to speak, instructed to recall, explore, and work through the true meaning of the action portrayed in the originals."[150] In addition to announcing what may be a troubling interpretive consensus, Zeilinger's anthropomorphism offers a figuration that may also give us pause, for we are not (are we?) prepared to say such things about "true meanings" that stand in need of being confessed by a film—as if the found footage needs to be tested and tortured to give up its secrets. In a phrasing complementary to Zeilinger's formulation, Zryd has described the source footage as containing "moments of unconscious desire and repression unwittingly trapped between the 24 frames per second."[151] No doubt Zeilinger and Zryd—and apparently "with minor variations, all reviewers and critics" of Arnold's work in *The Cineseizure* series, "virtually all commentary" on these films—push us to understand a new degree of intimacy, indeed, problematic isomorphism, between psychoanalysis and cinema. Better, we may think, to take up a different line of approach, one offered by Zeilinger himself, where we "shift attention from the past of the sampled content to the present of the sampling itself and thus from the repetition to the subject who repeats."[152] Yes, this last suggestion sounds much more promising and in keeping with the productive insights afforded by Arnold's metaformalist innovations.

The humor of finding theoretical repetitions of theme and of assessment is not lost on me. Of course, the "repetition compulsion" of reading Arnold in a quite specific—and rather homogeneous—manner can, at this point, allow my own interpretive anxiety to manifest itself as a symptom of divergence; the *Geschlecht* complex makes itself known in such nervous conditions. One can feel alone in reading *Alone.* (cultivating a "minor variation" at odds with a supposed—and celebrated—consensus). And yet, it is not an apparent wrong-headedness in the consensus that I am tracking, but something like an intriguing theoretical slippage (and repetition) to match the medial slippage (and repetition) in Arnold's films—a doubleness no doubt fit for metacinema as film and metaphilosophical film criticism. The effect of his "magic" (in the old fashioned cinematic sense—a variant of "trick photography" and the "cinema of attractions") has been taken as proof of what, in "A Cinephilic Avant-garde," Erika Balsom describes as Arnold's exploration of the "latent libidinal energies of the family as depicted by classical Hollywood cinema."[153] By this point, the interpretive patterns (can we now call them tics?) should be clear along with my concerned and concerted response to them, for in Arnold's films we are not witness to anything "latent" but rather imposed, and we are sure that that intervention is not made by "classical Hollywood cinema" ("and the shifting sociocultural, historical, and political climate of the period [1937–1958] during which it was produced"[154]) but instead "depicted"—or re-picted—by Arnold, the hip-hop artist of found footage. And yet, the trend persists, as when Balsom writes:

> Arnold accentuates this capability of the apparatus [where, in Benjamin's phrase, "consciousness gives ways to a space informed by the unconscious"] by according attention to minute, overlooked gestures, not endowing them with new significance so much as revealing that which lies dormant, prompting the repressions of the classical form to manifest themselves as external symptoms.[155]

Arnold's certainly lavishes "attention [on] minute, overlooked gestures"—overlooked because, as per the revelationists, we cannot possibly fathom them when cinema is played at twenty-four frames a second. But it is precisely that attention—what we know to be Arnold's elaborate, painstaking, time-consuming, and subsequently cinematically time-elongating labors of intervention—which, as so many film scholars have repeatedly attested, "transforms" the original work, that we should by now (a quarter century after *Alone.* [1998], and more than thirty years since the sequence began in 1989) at last declare in something of chorus that (*pace* Balsom, because I am inverting her statement): Arnold doesn't so much reveal that which lies dormant as endow found footage with new significance; we have been distracted by content when the action is in form.

Balsom invokes MacDonald's comment about how Arnold's work may be taken up as "'revenge on film history' for having forgotten the lessons of the pioneers," but it is precisely, as Balsom puts it, the "analytics of motion and magic" that remind us where or how to locate Arnold's contribution to that history. Balsom glosses Arnold's response to MacDonald's suggestion about "revenge" as evidence that he, Arnold, "is not attempting to circumvent the narrative tradition entirely, but to demonstrate that the 'attraction' (in Gunning's sense) is not opposed to narrative but lurks within it."[156] While it may be psychoanalytically satisfying to probe old Hollywood films for "lurking," "latent libidinal energies," we only need be reminded by Balsom of the "analytics of motion and magic"—of those talented ciné-pioneers—to call us back to Arnold's invention by intervention. Just as we wouldn't say that a record album played backwards (what is called "backmasking") announces the siren call of Satan or news that Paul McCartney has died,[157] so we wouldn't say that the trick of Arnold's unnatural or de-naturalized motion of gesturing bodies—and their sounds—shows us what we couldn't otherwise see or hear. These hidden things were never hidden because they were never there. Rather, the "message" (i.e., whatever interpretive strategy we want to apply) in such cases of metaformal interference/sampling/shuffling/scratching/remixing and the like is emergent, not inherent. Time spent with *The Cineseizure* doesn't reveal essences but instead epiphenomena.

One of the conceptual motifs of Arnold's work is the act of "inscription," which, as noted, happens at the mechanical level—manipulating the image, frame rate, playback direction, etc. Arnold says: "I think that in the sixties, avant-garde film was concerned with inscription into the medium, whereas in the eighties it was concerned with inscription into the tradition of representation."[158] Arnold is quick to add: "In any case, I don't see any contradiction between the two approaches." (And we should be just as quick to underline how Arnold's notion of "inscription" is a trope for cultural commentary, for remixing the existing, for replaying history after a new fashion.) That said, it may be that the "two approaches" aren't contradictory, and yet, they are different, and Arnold's work stands in need of being situated with respect to them, or perhaps in a separate tradition. While for some avant-garde filmmakers of the sixties and seventies, it is true they were literally inscribing film (Stan Brakhage's work comes to mind as representative, as do works by Naomi Uman, such as *Removed*, made the year after *Alone.*), Arnold engages film material but does not literally inscribe it; rather, as noted, he re-presents it to us through selective printing and projecting techniques; "inscribing" as metaphor, then, has mainly to do with image selection, duration, repetition, and direction of playback. Secondly, when we viewers/listeners/critics come to watch and hear Arnold's work, we need to be on guard for conflating the (potential) meaning of originals and new works of art, that is, the projection of, say, *Andy Hardy Meets Debutante* and the newly digested, digestured, re-gestured, or re-picted film known as *Alone.* That is to say, *Alone.* enters "the tradition of representation" at a different point in time (1998) than *Andy Hardy Meets Debutante* (1940), so it should be seen and heard with its (newer) time-stamp firmly in place. Watching and listening to *Alone.* in the early 2020s—in the midst of the #MeToo movement—will no doubt conjure yet another range of striking interpretive outcomes. For all these reasons, we do not want to say *avant la lettre* that *Andy Hardy Meets Debutante* contains meanings or comments on social-sexual-gender mores in ways that should be more accurately attributable to the effects of *Alone.* itself (as an independent work of art), which is, at the same time, not to claim something for Arnold's intentions for those effects. Arnold seems as surprised as we are that his films activate such feelings in the audience; we should join him in marveling.

Arnold's training in psychoanalysis, and therefore his reasonable proclivity to see its pertinence to film generally and his films in particular, should be taken seriously. (One hopes that one can take his remarks sincerely as well, and can presume he is not, like his films under discussion, playing a trick on otherwise unsuspecting and well-meaning critics laboring in good faith.) As Arnold himself reminds us: "I am not a film theorist and I did not try to filmically translate any theory of gender politics. [... T]heories that film artists themselves attribute to their work are to be taken with a grain of salt."[159] Still, a grain of salt taken up with abandon can register an effect—distract us, turn us around, etc. So, although Arnold doesn't intend to theorize with his films (thank goodness) and also admits that his role is that of artist not critic, we can proceed with caution to his own "analytical" assessments of his work and their function in "the tradition of representation," however cryptic those comments may occasionally be:

> The cinema of Hollywood is a cinema of exclusion, reduction, and denial, a cinema of repression. In consequence we should not only consider what is shown, but also that which is not shown. There is always something behind that which is being represented, which was not represented. And it is exactly that that is most interesting to consider.[160]

Such a psychoanalytically-minded comment seems just the sort of shiny bobble that would lead a well-meaning film theorist astray. Arnold's comfort speaking about such formidable forces such as "repression" and "revenge," and his bifurcation of shown/not shown, ahead/behind, represented/not represented, may lure one to suspect, for example, that the lessons and effects of *Alone.* were somehow lying in wait in *Andy Hardy Meets Debutante* since 1940, and we just needed Arnold's aid to see them. This is Arnold-as-revelationist—alas, not a productive direction to go in, however psychoanalytically satisfying it may be. Arnold is not only, or even mainly, a revelationist of mid-twentieth-century culture otherwise, or until now, obscured. Rather, what Arnold says about repression in the cinema of Hollywood (in the display quote above) can be true, and yet not true about *Alone.* The meaning of *Alone.* was not repressed, because *Alone.* did not exist to have its meanings repressed. Now that *Alone.* exists, it is availed to us to criticize—that is, to find meaning in it, to ascribe meaning to it, and some of those meanings, no doubt, will trade on "the tradition of representation," which, of course, includes *Andy Hardy Meets Debutante.* But these meanings were not "not shown," "not represented" all these years, lurking "behind" the 1940 film. With my suggested corrective in mind, read Arnold's repetition and revision:

> To put it in general terms: in the symptom, the repressed declares itself. Hollywood cinema is, as I said earlier, a cinema of exclusion, denial, and repression. I inscribe a symptom into it, which brings some of the aspects of repression to the surface, or, to say it in more modest words, which gives an idea of how, behind the intact world being represented, another not-at-all intact world is lurking. Maybe this is the revenge on film history you [Scott MacDonald] mentioned earlier.[161]

Yes, "in the symptom, the repressed declares itself." Yes, Arnold does "inscribe a symptom into" Hollywood cinema. But, no, this "inscription" does not bring "some of the aspects of repression to the surface." A film theoretic reading of *Andy Hardy Meets Debutante* may do that, but not *Alone. Alone.* is not a theory of *Andy Hardy Meets Debutante*; *Alone.* is not a psychoanalytic reading of *Andy Hardy Meets Debutante*. *Alone.* is an independent work of art that stands open for us (including Arnold) to offer a theory of, including a psychoanalytic reading of, one among other possibilities. In such film critical or psychoanalytical interpretations of *Alone.*, we may be able to identify and explore some of the "symptoms" Arnold alludes to—feeling as if they are "lurking," "latent," "behind the intact world"—but these symptoms are not revealed by the profilmic content of *Andy Hardy Meets Debutante*, but instead, by Arnold's medial "analysis" of metaform we have been invited to call *Alone.*

Concluding this revisitation to Arnold's late-twentieth-century film experiments, I wish to underscore how the work of love in *The Cineseisure* is made monstrous through the acoustic landscape and sonic textures of the film. The vibrating hum of the medium itself creates a Lynchean air of menace—even before we hear the clicks and hisses, the tics and slaps, and above all the words (what is said, what is sung), and what is held back, what is not allowed to make forward progress to audible, intelligible speech. My invocation of *Alone.* in the context of our collective effort to revisit and reengage *Geschlecht* is meant to articulate a set of questions and observations that build upon Schaefer and Zryd's close analysis: namely, to ask, in what sense can we offer a full and satisfying "reading" of this film solely from a "looking"? How much (more?) of the meaning—the terror, the desire, the romance, the savagery, the repetition, the repression, the compulsion, the humor, the horror, the hypnotism—derives also from a listening?

While *Alone.* remains visually peculiar, no doubt demanding double-takes and serial re-viewings, consider also how complicated—how unintelligible—the sonic atmosphere of the diegesis becomes. The movements of the figures in the film, it turns out, hinge on their possession by sound, or the distortion thereof; so as we hear the sound we figure it as well—become attuned to its

Geschlecht in the company of these moving images, and navigate our way to the genres of these sounds (not one but several: speech, breath, song, the friction of material textures, ambient noise, etc.). The tics and hisses of mouths; the clicks and taps of bodies; the unconscious admissions of breathing and sighing; the voice stuck in the throat—these elements are the sonic partners of the shuttering, stuttering, refractive moving images, shackled as they are by this looping "cineseizure."

The reading demands a looking and a listening. To see *Alone.*, we must hear it. Yet in what sense have we ever spoken of "a reading" as an act of aural judgment—instead of a (purely?) ocular one? The obviousness of listening's elemental partnership with seeing is as overt as sound's accidental, seemingly cumbersome and somehow secondary presence in the frame of our critical reception of motion pictures. Although the habilitation of sound has been underway for some time, we are asking what it might mean to write sound, to write about sound, in particular, to heed the potentially special task of translating between the *Geschlechts* and genres of moving image and audio. What happens, for example, when listening must undergo a translation into writing? This metaphilosophical and methodological question, no doubt, implicates the present research, as it finds me laboring after such a translation. Am I writing *on* sound? *About* sound? Is this writing a "reading" *of* sound, or a "listening" *to* it? In the wake of the detours and disquieting conclusions of selected moments in the secondary literature on Arnold's film, for example, what would it mean to achieve sound criticism?

Arnold's work has occasioned an opportunity to address our variable senses for sound in relation to motion pictures: sound "in" film, sound "on" film, sound "as" film, forgetful as we often are that film is (also) a medium "of" sound. Arnold said, in a final, fitting repetition, that "the cinema of Hollywood is a cinema of exclusion, reduction, and denial, a cinema of repression." It is a cinema, we could say, whose revelations are repressions in part owing to its pre-history in legerdemain: it aimed to make a show without showing how. The visual impact—through shot-style and editing—has provided over a century of tricks, but if there was any phenomenon that has remained largely "hidden," it has been sound, a loyal accomplice often inaudible even when within earshot.

XI

Like gender, genre has come in for a wholesale reckoning. Borders and boundaries, long assumed to inhere essentially, that is, ontologically, have been redefined linguistically—indeed, as something more like constructs of culture. In turn, the practices of making and thinking about art have been transformed. In an identitarian age—when sorting, sifting, fixing, mixing, and aligning are the order of the day (not to exclude and rank but to include, combine, and make flat), the disturbing of genre's conceptual priority presents itself as the latest category we are asked to render—or to recognize as—untranslatable. This isn't necessarily a cynical move, but merely one more effect of the long cultural moment we inhabit, one that has shifted to the clarifying, purifying, and policing of categories (including genres). Writing from within a global pandemic, we are serially faced with what will regress and what will evolve, what will remain and what will be eclipsed. While theoretical industry has been applied to restoring sound to the conversation about the image, to fathoming sounds as genres, to finding terms for "writing sound," we may have nevertheless reached the era of "post-genre," when such debates will no longer be recognizable, and thus, viable. As Wittgenstein worried long ago, yet in a similar frame of mind: "At present we are combating a trend. But this trend will die out, superseded by others, and then the way we are arguing against it will no longer be understood; people will not see why all this needed saying."[162]

The decentering of the subject has been made a hallmark of those favoring speculative realism and its varied incarnations among the object-oriented ontologists. Like Plato's (classical) realism, these experiments in speculative realism address millennia-old conundrums about the one and the many, the nature of kind, and the human role in adjudicating apparent differences. The world—of things—seems suddenly fine without us (without our "thoughts"), and yet we are beckoned to comment, and appear to do so habitually, compulsively. Aspects of the present investigation bear resemblance to certain strains of OOO, especially where the varieties of material life announce clues for our understanding beyond our merely personal impressions of things, that is, when objects—and their relations—are given a chance to make themselves known.[163] As Graham Harman writes: "OOO endorses the basic formalist principle of the self-contained object, while flatly rejecting the further assumption that two specifics *kinds* of entities—human and non-human object—must never be permitted to contaminate each other."[164] The translational hermeneutics I commended at the outset, and have been aiming to enact since, echoes at the least a suppression of the human-as-prior or as-priority-above-all-else while holding fast to the essentials of a humanism; in short, it invites a measure of humility in one's interpretive practice. As indicated by the foregoing comments, by me and others, anthropocentrism can be modulated and yet must remain a vital and necessary component of such deliberations. The emancipation of (non-human) objects does not forestall the fascinated interest of the humans who share their space.

Among our needs may be a new ruling trope—something that captures our commitments to art and object, method and concept. Perhaps Karen Barad's use of diffraction (i.e., wave interference) or "entanglements" is appealing, or George Dyson's movement of recovery "from analog to digital and back," that is, his sense of a shift away from the digital (which has dominated the last half-century) back to—or rather onward to—the analog (as a much more robust and reliable computational system than the digital).[165] Why have just two options—ones and zeroes—when a multiplicity lies in wait? Dyson notes that "a mathematical conjecture known as the continuum hypothesis, suggests that the powers of analog computation, transcending the bounds of algorithms, or step-by-step procedures, will supervene upon the digital and reassert control. Electrons, treated digitally, became bits; bits, treated statistically, have become electrons. The ghost of the vacuum tube has returned." And so, where will we find intrusions into this "continuum" when all the boundaries and binaries have gone? The troubling trope of the mind-as-computer may be giving way to the ancient practices of nondual metacognition, ones that seemlessly unify brain and body, mind and interoceptive awareness.

Hollis Frampton and Martin Arnold's experimental cinemas intimate that we should not seek for image and sound a peaceable, equitable marriage of intelligible entities (for the most part, they already inhabit that reality), but rather the specter of ongoing and productive generic contest. These two historically asymmetrical genres of media should remain antagonistic, for if they commonly achieve the satisfying illusion of reproducing the world, they can just as often render a series of encounters with the ineffable—traveling in this volume principally under the aegis of the untranslatable.[166] In these latter cases, genre crisis means genre opportunity. From the image, we should not expect pure visibility (one without distortions, blind spots, or an observing human subject), and from sound, the calibration of equilibrium, but something much more like silence—an ultimate and poignant figure of the untranslatable.

In contemplating and consolidating lessons on the human encounter with the sounds of cinema, an exceptional outcome appears to be an improved semblance of listening itself—an activity that may not exceed its operations within the listener. We can shut our eyes, but not close our ears: the sonic space (the silence) between sounds makes the world audible (provides shutters that ear canals lack), and yet cinematic images are an unreliable ally for hearing—drawing attention to sound at one moment and masking its incidence in another. Paradoxically, "silent film"—that officially sanctioned syntagma—could not give us purchase on silence (only the "talkie" could do that). And neither can audio-only, as with the radio, deliver us silence merely by being turned down or muted. Rather, cinema—the art of image *and* sound—has afforded occasional contact with the "worldly silence" we crave.[167] Moving pictures that avail worldly silence, then, may come to exemplify some precipitates of sound criticism: states of immersion, embodied concentration, and attunement to attempted exchanges between internal and external phenomena (including the radical act of accounting for sound in prose). As an audience for sound film, as listeners, we are the site of the as-yet untranslated.

The readings and lookings of lectiocentrism find their translations in writing, and a cognate exercise in the listenings of gramophonology invites yet further linguistic remarks (i.e., further readings); a distinctive, "unlettered" mode for the translation of sound *to* writing is not forthcoming. Like the image theorist, we cinematic listeners remain an intermediary, situated between sound film and sound writing. Arnold's work illustrates that instead of finding meaning *in* cinema, genres of sound and image mix within us—make themselves known (or remain unknown), find articulation in response, or pass without notice. In these respects, embodied consciousness is the scene of potential interpretation and thus prospective translation—but so is it also the condition for misinterpretation, mistranslation, impasse, and the impossibility of conversion. (Even when all sound levels are diminished, the rhythm of the breath remains—a whispered declaration of one's continued existence and the final boundary between consciousness and extinction.) Sounds may be heard but remain inconvertible; an experience of sound does not mean one can speak of it; hearing cinema may not yield a report of what was heard. As a further practice of sound criticism, gramophonology seeks viable instances of success and criteria for onward development.

Entranced by certain works of film art, we return briefly to the present with calm, momentarily countermanding a certain lostness in thought. Listening to the sounds of cinema—especially works that make genres of sound a cinematic issue—can result in a rare sense of presence. These films, or segments of films, beneficially join one's own incessant mental chatter; layers of sound can be discerned: spoken dialogue, sound effects, ambient noise, subvocal enunciation of subtitles, one's inner monologue of observations (both on the film and in the stream of thoughts that reinforce cinematic immersion, or that break its spell). Hollis Frampton's and Martin Arnold's experimental films do this, and so does, I argue elsewhere, the contemplative cinema of Kelly Reichardt.[168] In the latter case, a slow or transcendental method of making movies operates with the familiar standards of synchronized sound and image; in the former films, by contrast, we are faced with refractive, metacinematic forays into the non-synchronized. In the art and act of "serious noticing," as James Wood adroitly formulates it, we are given a chance to observe these differences, and to register their effects upon us—to practice a coming to awareness of the interface between consciousness and the world it encounters and in turn constitutes.[169] Such an activity involves a perpetual translational hermeneutics, one that is decidely enhanced by an openness to a wider range of experiences—alas, and at last, not just "the reading" and "the looking" but also the listening. Genres of consciousness thus come into contact with genres as modes of giving shape to the world.

Writing about one of those genres—music genres, and the prevailing discourse about them—Amanda Petrusich gives the impression that the inherited categories by which we have collected, organized, and experienced music may have reached their end. Petrusich writes that "genre feels increasingly irrelevant to the way we think about, create, and consume art."[170] Genre was a "practical tool for organizing," but now that "all music feels like a hybrid," the taxonomical benefits of its application appear antiquated.[171] Not surprisingly, an *au courant* discussion of genre would link up with sentiments about people as genres (as individuals and in the aggregate), or, as the case may be, living in the wake of them: "Now the idea of identity as a fixed and narrow concept, and of taste as inherently cloistered, feels bizarre, punitive, and regressive."[172] Reaching for an analogue in film studies, consider Lev Manovich's sage prophecy from the mid-1990s: "From the perspective of a future historian of visual culture, the differences between classical Hollywood films, European art films, and avant-garde films (apart from abstract ones) may appear less significant than this common feature: that they relied on lens-based recordings of reality."[173] We now collectively occupy the position of this "future historian of visual culture"—including the sonic culture of music and sound films—so we can appreciate how accurate Manovich's claim has turned out to be. The "super-genre" of cinema defined by its qualities as lens-based, live action has evolved precisely according to Manovich's logic; in the present moment, as the coronavirus pandemic unsettles patterns of film production, distribution, and exhibition like no other event in the last century, including world wars, we may be in need of another prophecy.

When Petrusich writes of music—"what we mean by 'pop' or 'jazz' or 'country' is not a static, immovable idea but a reflection of an audience's assumptions and wants at a certain point in time," especially as "our aesthetic expectations [...] are tangled up in discriminatory ideologies"[174]—I hear, first, Thomas Schatz's reliable account of film genres as comprising both "static and dynamic elements"[175] and something of my own efforts above, namely, to recall the extent to which the meaning of art is enmeshed with audience reception (including its training, temperament, and perhaps unarticulated but no less forceful desires). Although we can meditate on deeper attributes of cinema or music as well as on superficial features, genre shows itself to be radically unstable, despite signs of durability. We may recognize patterns across independent works—shared traits, etc.—but we are also compelled to notice moments of deviation. Perhaps this is why scholars and critics of film will engage the logic of "cycles" as a conceptual bid to sidestep the imbrications of genres.[176]

Yet another tack may be to see genre itself, in Petrusich's view, "as a reductive, old-fashioned, and inherently problematic idea," one "we should all be eager to see rendered moot."[177] #CancelGenre? There is an oddness to the agency here: are we empowered to move beyond genre or is there something "inherent" about genre that disqualifies it for our present and future purposes? Such an amphiboly feels appropriate to our investigation because the ambiguity of genre's role in our lives—is it something we use or are used by?—lies at precisely those moments of impasse that we, in this volume, have been contending with as untranslatable, or as resistant to translation.

Wordly silence is not the absence of sound but the precondition for hearing, and in turn, the further art of listening. For humans, a recognition of such a phenomenology of sound appears to ratify the prospects of what we have been calling a gramophonology: to move on from a lectiocentrism, sound must become of interest to us on its own terms, and as it functions ontologically in co-presence with moving pictures. The genres of sounds (or treating sounds as genres) becomes the *Geschlecht* of gramophonology, that is, the means by which any such hope of "writing sound" could be regarded as offering a semblance of translation. Yet, how can we inaugurate, extend, or sustain a gramophonology—a listening to cinema along with the attendant endeavor to write sound criticism—without the logic, ontology, and epistemology of genre? For her part, and despite displaying a bracing willingness to jettison the territories of intellectual investigation delineated by genre and genre theorizing, Petrusich appears sanguine about prospects: "I remain curious about the contours of a post-genre world—what that might open for the future, and what might be sacrificed."[178] However one relates to Petrusich's conclusion that genre is "inherently backward-looking"—if only because one cannot see traits and trends from within a moment as well as one can from a position beyond it—her observations about music yield affordances for "thinking genre" in a new spirit, indeed, where and when such categorical locations, borders, limits, constraints, etc. are at last effaced. Would such a world-without-genre be rendered less richly nuanced, defined, ordered, ranked—perhaps; but with that eschewal, would not also the passive inheritances of power be disowned or redistributed, thus availing more diverse inhabitations in wider zones of experience? Taxonomies by design seem to invite transgression, the cross-fertilization familiar to collaborative acts across type. Some artists and theorists may be more troubled by liberation from constraints than the imposition and defense of them: obstacles are, after all, instructive.[179] Yet, if Petrusich's approach and attitude is an indication of where we are and where we are heading (with her serving, in this respect, as our new sentinel), then we may not only need to rethink genre theory, but how the creation of art is possible in a post-genre circumstance.

The final quandary proffered on this occasion places us at an edge, perhaps also on edge, namely, whether there is reason to believe in and defend genre—for example, that its "static and dynamic" features provide aesthetic, concept-determining classifications, and perhaps also a moral service; or whether, as with the dissolution of musical categories, the role of genre in thinking about media of all types, especially including cinema, is not just outmoded but evacuated. On this second front, there is no boundary to transgress.

With Stanley Cavell, we saw how a modernist and perfectionist philosopher collapsed high and low culture, popular and avant-garde, cinema and prose, music and poetry, Hollywood films and philosophy, Anglo-analytic logical positivism and American transcendentalism, and so on.[180] Genres of philosophy proliferated. Cavell's radical couplings were electrifying (indeed, remain so), and the steady expansion of philosophy's purchase on the everyday proved intoxicating. In his wake, we could suddenly talk about *Mr. Deeds Goes to Town* (1936, dir. Frank Capra) in the same breath as Henry David Thoreau at Walden Pond and Immanuel Kant in Königsburg. And in time, we found our suitable equivalents—Charlie Kaufman, Terrence Malick, Werner Herzog, Rithy Panh, Kelly Reichardt, Martin Arnold, and so on.[181] (Cornel West, a student of Cavell's capacious, inclusive methodology, operates his subsequent and accomplished prophetic project in a similar, Cavellian vein—drawing in Socrates and Chekhov, Jesus and John Coltrane, Public Enemy and C. S. Peirce, Karl Marx and *The Matrix*, Antonio Gramsci and Fanny Lou Hamer.) Yet if the boundaries of the genre formerly known as "philosophy" were unsettled, multiplied, distributed—what's next? The end of judgment? The end of criticism? The end of art? Watching decadence dissolve culture into a vast, undifferentiated mass of entities? Dire questions, and yet they appear to track closely with the urgency of theorizing genre—once and ongoing. The recent sale at auction of Mike Winkelmann's *Everydays: The First 5,000 Days* (2021)—the third highest sale by a living artist—announced the transcendence of material art into the vapors of computation. Aside from the astromical sale price, and the scandal of the non-fungible token—soon to be normalized and commodified like many such intrepid technologies—there is the more worrying question of the aesthetic merit of the art. Not only a single work of art, verily, but five thousand of them. Not just the everyday, but every day. Hence, no discernment, no distinction, no category, no curation—no genre. In turn, no boundary, and thus, no translation.

Are we to treat genre as a conceptual overlay to our experience of music, of movies, of philosophy that has run its course? And if genre now seems antiquated, perhaps even perniciously so, what follows from the removal of these families and the (formerly?) necessary attention to traits of their members? A sea of undifferentiated and uncomparable content—and thus only contact with raw, unnamed sensation? Sheer music (as sounds)? Unmitigated audiovisual media (as visual stimuli)? The collapsing of the movie house and television, of cable and broadcast, of studio and independent, of documentary and deepfake, of home movie and online clip, of advertising and so on, add further illustrations of the "merging lanes" Petrusich describes: all for one and one for all. To what extent, though, is judgment—aesthetic and moral—dependent on genre, which is to say, the power to differentiate and discriminate (the latter term in its eighteenth-century tenor)? Hence, a worry that the prominent end of genre also, but more covertly, culminates with the end of criticism.

We inhabit an inflection point between an apathy about the usefulness of categories ("genre feels increasingly irrelevant to the way we think about, create, and consume art") and an insufficient defense of the evident vitality of genre-as-method across media types and disciplines. Partly this mood of ambivalence allows for false equivalents, where we might otherwise negotiate genuine common ground (moving, say, from the sclerotic insistence on metaphysically dubious racial differences to the more conceptually, morally, politically, and scientifically defensible realm of a single, unified humanity—a humanity understood as members of a single existential genre); race as genre, or in a related context gender as genre, then, may be instructive, if only to show that genre doesn't serve contemporary commitments and therefore can be relinquished without loss or regret. But misapplications and expropriations need not wreck the field of genre studies; indeed, they may make it all the more poised for exhibiting its relevance. Transcending category distinctions—or errors—lights the way, for instance, by eliding, on the one hand, the artificially or arbitrarily, that is, culturally imposed or, on the other hand, the naturally occurring but uninformative. In sum, what remains untranslated may remain so without harm; it can abide as a liminal space that continues to reward investigation, even as it nevertheless imposes a limit on our approach to vital, empirical issues. Thus, the politics of the limit, whatever that threshold may be, doesn't mean we must fail to think beyond it; recognition is a necessary step, although not a sufficient one, for the ultimate act of transcendence (what in this context may simply travel under the notion of successful or satisfying translation).

Our abiding question, then, is whether and what kinds of creations—artistic and otherwise—deserve our continued effort to assign genres to them, and therefore theorize and defend them generically. Maybe cinema is one. Maybe not. The present, covid-era shift from the cineplex to the living room movie release suggests that a criterion for authority and artistic accomplishment cannot be merely an in-person theatrical premier; the institutional theory of art cannot survive the pandemic unchanged. In an identitarian age, we are forced to contend with our commitments to nominalism and realism: what do we think is contained in a name? Do we find constraint and deprivation in a category, or the potency to manifest liberation? What happens when we try to move between names, between categories, between discourses—between genres—to fathom a constant and robust circulation? The puzzling power of genre thinking has always disclosed a profound coupling of uncanny clarity and protean flexibility. Perhaps our era of flux and reformation, of radical reconception of terms and traits, means it is not just too soon to jettison genre, but instead a fitting occasion to double down on its as yet untapped potential. Hopefully, present efforts lend exhibition to the viability of such suggestions. Do we seek the retention and proliferation of genres, or the collapse and dissolution of genre altogether? Our reply to this tandem solicitation will establish the conditions for any next steps—including most especially where our concepts and commitments make contact.

Notes

1. William Carlos Williams, "A Statement by William Carlos Williams about the poem Paterson," in *Paterson*, revised edition prepared by Christopher MacGowan (New York: New Directions, 1992), xiv.
2. For more on metaphor, see my *Emerson's English Traits and the Natural History of Metaphor* (New York: Bloomsbury, 2013).
3. See also LaRocca, "Translating Carlyle: Ruminating on the Models of Metafiction at the Emergence of an Emersonian Vernacular," *Religions*, eds. Kenneth S. Sacks and Daniel Koch, vol. 8, no. 8 (2017).
4. Emily Apter, "Lexilalia: On Translating a Dictionary of Untranslatable Philosophical Terms," *Paragraph*, vol. 48, no. 5 (2015), 164.
5. Ralph Waldo Emerson, "The Poet," in *Essays: Second Series*, *The Complete Works of Ralph Waldo Emerson*, vol. III (Boston: Houghton, Mifflin and Company, 1903–4), 34.
6. David Farrell Krell, *Phantoms of the Other: Four Generations of Derrida's Geschlecht* (Albany: State University of New York Press, 2015), ix.
7. See index entries on genes, genesis, genius, genotype, and genus in my *Emerson's English Traits and the Natural History of Metaphor*.
8. See Kyle Stevens, "The World Heard," in *The Thought of Stanley Cavell and Cinema: Turning Anew to the Ontology of Film a Half-Century after* The World Viewed, ed. David LaRocca (New York: Bloomsbury, 2020); see also my "Contemplating the Sounds of Contemplative Cinema: Stanley Cavell and Kelly Reichardt," in *Movies with Stanley Cavell in Mind*, ed. David LaRocca (New York: Bloomsbury, 2021), 274–318.
9. Stanley Cavell, "*It Happened One Night*," in *Cities of Words: Pedagogical Letters on a Register of the Moral Life* (Cambridge: The Belknap Press of Harvard University Press, 2004), 156.
10. Kyle Stevens, "The World Heard," in *The Thought of Stanley Cavell and Cinema*, 81.
11. Oliver Sacks, *The Man Who Mistook His Wife for a Hat and Other Clinical Tales* (New York: Gerald Duckworth, 1985), 156–60.
12. Tejal Rao, "Will Fish Sauce and Charred Oranges Return the World Covid Took from Me?" *The New York Times*, March 2, 2021, nytimes.com.
13. Maurice Merleau-Ponty, *Phenomenonology of Perception*, trans. Colin Smith (Delhi: Motilal Banarsidass, 1996), viii. Michel Chion, *Audio-Vision: Sound on Screen*, second edition, ed. and trans. Claudia Gorbman (New York: Columbia University Press, 2013), 147–71.

14 William Carlos Williams, "A Statement by William Carlos Williams about the poem Paterson," in *Paterson*, xiv.
15 Gabriel Marcel, "Possibilités et limites de l'art cinématographique," *Revue international de filmologie*, vol. 5, nos. 18–19 (July–December 1954), 164.
16 Siegfried Kracauer, *Theory of Film: The Redemption of Physical Reality* (Princeton: Princeton University Press, 1997; orig. pub. Oxford University Press, 1960), 304.
17 Karin Littau, "Silent Films and Screaming Audiences" [on *Arrival of a Train at La Ciotat*], in *Film Analysis: A Norton Reader*, second edition, eds. Jeffrey Geiger and R. L. Rutsky (New York: Norton, 2013), 31. Stanley Cavell, *The World Viewed: Reflections on the Ontology of Film*, Enlarged Edition (Cambridge: Harvard University Press, 1979 [1971]), 149. See also André Gaudreault, "Showing and Telling: Image and Word in Early Cinema," trans. John Howe, in *Early Cinema: Space, Frame, Narrative*, ed. Thomas Elsaesser (London: BFI, 1990), 274–81; and Mathew Abbott, "On Film in Reality: Cavellian Reflections on Skepticism, Belief, and Documentary," in *The Thought of Stanley Cavell and Cinema*, 228–44.
18 Walter Benjamin, "The Work of Art in the Age of Mechanical Reproduction," in *Illuminations*, trans. Harry Zohn, ed. Hannah Arendt (New York: Schocken Books, 1968), 237.
19 A similar doubleness for the senses of "sound" is apparent in *Sound Theory, Sound Practice*, ed. Rick Altman (New York: Routledge and the American Film Institute, 1992).
20 Garrett Stewart, *Reading Voices: Literature and the Phonotext* (Berkeley: University of California Press, 1990), 117–25.
21 In addition to Derrida's abundant work on the subject of phonocentrism, e.g., conspicuously in *Of Grammatology*, trans. Gayatri Chakravorty Spivak (Baltimore: Johns Hopkins University Press, 1974/2016), see also, Jürgen Habermas, "Beyond a Temporalized Philosophy of Origins: Jacques Derrida's Critique of Phonocentrism," in *The Philosophical Discourse of Modernity: Twelve Lectures*, trans. Frederick G. Lawrence (Cambridge: MIT Press, 1987), Lecture VII, 161–84. For notes on lectiocentrism, see Emily Apter, "Untranslatable: The 'Reading' versus the 'Looking,'" *Journal of Visual Culture*, vol. 6, no. 1 (2007).
22 Chion, *Audio-Vision*, 5.
23 Ben Kirbach, "Reading for the Apparatus: An Interview with Garrett Stewart," September 17, 2019, https://english.uiowa.edu/resources/news.
24 As indicative of promising and positively impactful forays, see Rick Altman, *Silent Film Sound* (New York: Columbia University Press, 2004), and James Buhler, *Theories of the Soundtrack* (Oxford: Oxford University Press, 2019).
25 Lucy Ives, "After the Afterlives of Theory," Lucy Ives, *The Baffler*, no. 39, May 2018, https://thebaffler.com/salvos/after-the-afterlife-of-theory-ives.
26 Correspondence: Garrett Stewart and David LaRocca, July 2, 2021. See also Michel Chion, *The Voice in Cinema* (*La voix au cinéma*, 1982; English trans. 1999 by Claudia Gorbman, Columbia University Press), and his taxonomical inventory in *Words on Screen* (*L'écrit au cinéma*, 2013; English trans. 2017 by Claudia Gorbman, Columbia University Press). See also Garrett Stewart, "'Assertions in Technique': Tracking the Medial 'Thread'

in Cavell's Filmic Ontology," in *The Thought of Stanley Cavell and Cinema*, 23–40, and 289 n100; and his "A Metacinematic Spectrum: Technique through Text to Context," in *Metacinema: The Form and Content of Filmic Reference and Reflexivity*, ed. David LaRocca (Oxford: Oxford University Press, 2021), 63–83.

27 The book that formally launched Stewart's contribution to and shaping of the topic is *Reading Voices: Literature and the Phonotext* (Berkeley: University of California Press, 1990), "with a title intended as clause, not phrase," and "written back in 1990 as a riposte to a deconstruction less subtle than Derrida about inscription versus enunciation." More recently, *The Deed of Reading: Literature * Writing * Language * Philosophy* (Ithaca: Cornell University Press, 2015) has presented itself as a further dispatch in which he grapples conspicuously with phonetic reading (linked, in fact, to Cavell there in a treatment of Edgar Allan Poe entitled "Imp-aired Words"). Most recently, see his *Book, Text, Medium: Cross-Sectional Reading for a Digital Age* (Cambridge: Cambridge University Press, 2020).

28 Stewart, *Reading Voices*, 134.

29 Stewart, *Reading Voices*, 117–25.

30 See Timothy Gould, *Hearing Things: Voice and Method in the Work of Stanley Cavell* (Chicago: The University of Chicago Press, 1998).

31 Geoffrey H. Hartman's comments are drawn from an endorsement of Stewart's *Reading Voices*.

32 See my "Memory Translation: Rithy Panh's Provocations to the Primacy and Virtues of the Documentary Sound/Image Index," in *Everything Has a Soul: The Cinema of Rithy Panh*, eds. Leslie Barnes and Joseph Mai (New Brunswick: Rutgers University Press, 2021), 188–201; "Object Lessons: What Cyanotypes Teach Us About Digital Media," in *Photography's Materialities: Transatlantic Photographic Practices over the Long Nineteenth Century*, eds. Geoff Bender and Rasmus S. Simonsen (Leuven: Leuven University Press, 2021), 209–35; "Virtual Round Table: An Experiment," *Cinema: The Journal of Philosophy and the Moving Image*, vol. 12, Images of the Real: Philosophy and Documentary Film (2021), 175–215; and "Shooting for the Truth: Amateur Documentary Filmmaking, Affective Optics, and the Ethical Impulse," *Post Script: Essays in Film and the Humanities*, vol. 26, nos. 2 and 3 (Winter/Spring/Summer 2017), 46–60.

33 Veronique Greenwood, "How the Shape of Your Ears Affects What You Hear," *The New York Times*, March 6, 2018.

34 See, for example, the researches of *Radiolab*, "Breaking News," July 27, 2017, http://www.radiolab.org/story/breaking-news/.

35 Chion, *Audio-Vision*, 177–8.

36 Cornel West, *The Brian Lehrer Show*, WNYC Studios, April 4, 2018, 08:56.

37 Timothy Corrigan, *The Essay Film: From Montaigne, after Marker* (New York: Oxford University Press, 2011), 135.

38 Karin Littau, "Silent Films and Screaming Audiences," *Film Analysis*, 22.

39 Littau, "Silent Films and Screaming Audiences," 23.

40 Littau, "Silent Films and Screaming Audiences," 29.

41 As Littau notes: "*Schaulust* is the German term for rubbernecking, which has been widely, and rather misleadingly, translated from Freud and Walter Benjamin as scopophilia (pleasure of looking) rather than what it means literally and connotes very physically: the lust of the eyes." Littau, "Silent Films and

Screaming Audiences," 34; cf. also Karin Littau, "Eye-Hunger: Physical Pleasure and Non-Narrative Cinema," in *Crash Cultures: Modernity, Mediation, and the Material*, eds. Jane Arthurs and Iain Grant (Bristol: Intellect, 2002), 35–51.
42 Littau, "Silent Films and Screaming Audiences," 31.
43 Chion's insights along these lines begin on page 1 of *Audio-Vision*.
44 See Mark Mangini, "The MGM Lion," April 15, 2020, markmangini.com.
45 See Linda Williams, *Hard Core: Power, Pleasure, and the "Frenzy of the Visible"* (Berkeley: University of California Press, 1989).
46 Corrigan, *The Essay Film*, 135. "Read within classical narratives, the action of a central character mediates time through space, so that the time of those actions ultimately becomes meaningful and legible in the progressive or continuous conquest or stabilization of the spatial field that absorbs temporality. Lost within space, the time of classical cinema as continuous duration of 'endurance' is thus, in one sense, not too far from Benjamin's notion of a 'homogenous, empty time' ([in] 'On the Concept of History,' 396)."
47 Peter Wollen, *Singin' in the Rain* (London: BFI and Palgrave Macmillan, 1992), 55–6.
48 Wollen, *Singin' in the Rain*, 56.
49 Wollen, *Singin' in the Rain*, 56.
50 Wollen, *Singin' in the Rain*, 56.
51 David Bordwell and Kristin Thompson, *Film Art: An Introduction*, tenth edition (New York: McGraw Hill, 2013), 268.
52 Bordwell and Thompson, *Film Art*, 267.
53 Bordwell and Thompson, *Film Art*, 267. For more on filmmakers who make sound a more distinguished part of their filmmaking practice, that is, inviting us to notice sounds as well as images—and therefore, as more than mere "accompaniments," see my "Contemplating the Sounds of Contemplative Cinema," *Movies with Stanley Cavell in Mind*, 274–318.
54 Leslie Devereaux and Roger Hillman, eds., *Fields of Vision: Essays in Film, Visual Anthropology, and Photography* (Berkeley: University of California Press, 1995).
55 Wendy Everett, ed., *The Seeing Century: Film, Vision, and Identity* (Amsterdam: Rodopi, 1994).
56 Mark Crispin Miller, ed., *Seeing Through Movies* (New York: Pantheon Books, 1990).
57 Dennis Petrie and Joseph Boggs, *The Art of Watching Films*, eighth edition (New York: McGraw Hill, 2012).
58 Cf., e.g., 14–15 for a list of Jay's chosen figures—after Descartes, then Bergson, Bataille, Breton, Sartre, Merleau-Ponty, Lévinas, Foucault, Althusser, Debord, Lacan, Irigaray, Barthes, Metz, Derrida, and Lyotard.
59 Chion, *Audio-Vision*, e.g., 4–9, 12–13, 19–21, 182, 211.
60 See Eric Smigel, "Sights and Sounds of the Moving Mind: The Visionary Soundtracks of Stan Brakhage," in *The Music and Sound of Experimental Film*, eds. Holly Rogers and Jeremy Barham (Oxford: Oxford University Press, 2017), ch. 5.
61 See press description for *The Oxford Handbook of Sound Studies*, eds. Trevor Pinch and Karin Bijsterveld (New York: Oxford University Press, 2011).
62 William Whittington, "The Sonic Playpen: Sound Design and Technology in Pixar's Animated Shorts," in *The Oxford Handbook of Sound Studies*, ch. 15.

63 Béla Balázs, "Theory of the Film: Sound," in *Film Sound: Theory and Practice*, eds. Elisabeth Weis and John Belton (New York: Columbia University Press, 1985), 117.
64 Stanley Cavell, "Introduction: Words for a Conversation," in *Pursuits of Happiness: The Hollywood Comedy of Remarriage* (Cambridge: Harvard University Press, 1981), 2.
65 See for example Catherine Wheatley, *Stanley Cavell and Film: Scepticism and Self-Reliance at the Cinema* (New York: Bloomsbury, 2019); Rex Butler, *Stanley Cavell and the Arts: Philosophy and Popular Culture* (New York: Bloomsbury, 2020); *The Thought of Stanley Cavell and Cinema: Turning Anew to the Ontology of Film a Half-Century after* The World Viewed, ed. David LaRocca (New York: Bloomsbury, 2020); *Inheriting Stanley Cavell: Memories, Dreams, Reflections*, ed. David LaRocca (New York: Bloomsbury, 2020); and *Movies with Stanley Cavell in Mind*, ed. David LaRocca (New York: Bloomsbury, 2021).
66 Cavell, *Pursuits of Happiness*, 2.
67 Cavell, *Pursuits of Happiness*, 11.
68 Cavell, *Pursuits of Happiness*, 11.
69 Cavell, *Pursuits of Happiness*, 35.
70 Cavell, "In the Place of the Classroom," in *Cities of Words*, 7.
71 Cavell, *Must We Mean What We Say? A Book of Essays* (Cambridge: Cambridge University Press, 2002 [1969]), 36.
72 Cavell, Preface, *Cities of Words*, ix.
73 Cavell, Preface, *Cities of Words*, x.
74 See my review of Gould's book in *The Review of Metaphysics*, vol. LIII, no. 4 (June 2000), 931–3.
75 See Andreas Teuber, "Cavell's Ear for Things," in *Inheriting Stanley Cavell*, 199–206; and Catherine Wheatley, "Passionate Utterances: Cavell, Film, and the Female Voice" (175–9) and my "Contemplating the Sounds of Contemplative Cinema" (274–318), both in *Movies with Stanley Cavell in Mind*.
76 Cavell, *The World Viewed*, 36. See also Stephen Mulhall, "What a Genre of Film Might Be: Medium, Myth, and Morality," in *The Thought of Stanley Cavell and Cinema*, 88–104.
77 Cavell, *The World Viewed*, 31–2.
78 Cavell, *The World Viewed*, 32.
79 Emily Apter, "Untranslatable: The 'Reading' versus the 'Looking,'" *Journal of Visual Culture*, 149.
80 See Charles Warren, "Cavell, Altman, Cassavetes: The Melodrama of the Unknown Woman in *A Woman Under the Influence* and *Nashville*" (191–8) and my "Contemplating the Sounds of Contemplative Cinema" (274–318), both in *Movies with Stanley Cavell in Mind*.
81 Kyle Stevens, 81.
82 Marc Crépon, "*Geschlecht*," in *Dictionary of Untranslatables: A Philosophical Lexicon*, ed. Barbara Cassin; trans. eds. Emily Apter, Jacques Lezra, and Michael Wood (Princeton: Princeton University Press, 2014), 394–6.
83 Crépon, "*Geschlecht*," 394.
84 Noël Carroll, *The Philosophy of Motion Pictures* (Oxford: Blackwell, 2008), 1.
85 Crépon, "*Geschlecht*" 395. See also n. 7 above.

86 For more on the interaction between photography and motion pictures, see Stanley Cavell, "What Photography Calls Thinking: Theoretical Considerations on the Power of the Photographic Basis of Cinema," in *The Philosophy of Documentary Film: Image, Sound, Fiction, Truth*, ed. David LaRocca (Lanham: Lexington Books of Rowman & Littlefield, 2017), 57–74.
87 Crépon, "*Geschlecht*," 396.
88 For a study of purity metaphors, see also my *Emerson's English Traits and the Natural History of Metaphor*.
89 Chion, *Audio-Vision*, e.g., 4–9, 12–13, 19–21, 182, 211.
90 Merleau-Ponty, Preface, *Phenomenology of Perception* ix; italics in original.
91 Amy Villarejo, *Film Studies: An Introduction*, second edition (New York: Routledge, 2013), 139.
92 Villarejo, *Film Studies*, 140–1.
93 Villarejo, *Film Studies*, 140.
94 Laura Mulvey, "Visual Pleasure and Narrative Cinema," in *Visual and Other Pleasures*, second edition (New York: Palgrave Macmillan, 1989), 22–4.
95 See Robert B. Pippin, *Hollywood Westerns and American Myth: The Importance of Howard Hawks and John Ford for Political Philosophy* (New Haven: Yale University Press, 2012).
96 See my "Contemplating the Sounds of Contemplative Cinema," in *Movies with Stanley Cavell in Mind*, 274–318.
97 Ryan Gilbey, "How I Trekked Across Oregon for *Meek's Cutoff* Then Returned to Teaching," *The Guardian*, April 8, 2011, https://www.theguardian.com/film/2011/apr/09/kelly-reichardt-meeks-cutoff
98 "Filmed on two one-hundred-foot rolls of black-and-white 16mm stock during February of 1971, on the same SUNY Binghamton campus where Ernie Gehr had photographed his stroboscopic still life *Serene Velocity* the year before." Chuck Stephens, "Exploded View: Hollis Frampton's *Critical Mass*," *CinemaScope*, http://cinema-scope.com/columns/exploded-view-hollis-framptons-critical-mass-by-chuck-stephens/.
99 One of the group of Frampton's films known collectively as *Hapax Legomena*—a Greek phrase which the filmmaker parsed alternately as "unique words" (i.e., words unique in an author's corpus), and as "things said once" (Stephens, "Exploded View: Hollis Frampton's *Critical Mass*," *CinemaScope*). As an example of the first: the word "lemon" appears once in Joyce's *Ulysses*.
100 *Critical Mass*, 00:10:00.
101 Rick Altman, "Four and a Half Film Fallacies," in *The Philosophy of Documentary Film: Image, Sound, Fiction, Truth*, ed. David LaRocca (Lanham: Lexington Books of Rowman & Littlefield, 2017), 363. Cf. also Altman's companion piece, "Sound Space," in *Sound Theory/Sound Practice*, ed. Rick Altman (New York: Routledge, 1992), 46–64.
102 Altman, "Four and a Half Film Fallacies," *The Philosophy of Documentary Film*, 365ff.
103 See Scott MacDonald, *Binghamton Babylon: Voices from the Cinema Department, 1967–77* (Albany: State University of New York Press, 2015), 92–6, 214–15.
104 MacDonald, *Binghamton Babylon*, 93.
105 MacDonald, *Binghamton Babylon*, 215.

106 MacDonald, *Binghamton Babylon*, 215.
107 Scott MacDonald, "My Troubled Relationship with Stanley Cavell: In Pursuit of a Truly Cinematic Conversation," in *The Thought of Stanley Cavell and Cinema*, 107–20. For "de-marriage," see 166.
108 See my "*Alone.*, Again: On Martin Arnold's Metaformal Invention by Intervention," in *Metacinema: The Form and Content of Filmic Reference and Reflexivity*, ed. David LaRocca (Oxford: Oxford University Press, 2021), 291–317.
109 Scott MacDonald, *A Critical Cinema 3: Interviews with Independent Filmmakers* (Berkeley: University of California Press, 1998), 350, 354. MacDonald's *Critical Cinema* interview with Martin Arnold (347–62) is a version of an earlier engagement: "Sp ... Sp ... Spaces of Inscription: An Interview with Martin Arnold," *Film Quarterly*, vol. 48, no. 1 (Autumn 1994), 2–11.
110 See details at The Film-Makers' Coop: http://film-makerscoop.com/filmmakers/martin-arnold. For selected texts on Arnold's work from 1992 to 2018, see https://www.martinarnold.info/texts/. For more on Andy Hardy films, although predating (and arguably anticipating) Arnold's *Alone.*, see Robert B. Ray, *The Avant-Garde Finds Andy Hardy* (Cambridge: Harvard University Press, 1995) and "How to Start an Avant-Garde," in *How a Film Theory Got Lost and Other Mysteries in Cultural Studies* (Bloomington: Indiana University Press, 2001), ch. 5.
111 Ludwig Wittgenstein, *Philosophical Investigations*, trans. G. E. M. Anscombe (Englewood Cliffs: Prentice Hall, 1953), §1.
112 Michael Zryd, "Alone: Life Wastes Andy Hardy," *Cinémathèque Annotations on Film*, *Senses of Cinema*, no. 32, July 2004, sensesofcinema.com.
113 An eighteen-second shot from *The Human Jungle* (1954, dir. Joseph M. Newman) is used in *Pièce touchée*; shots from *To Kill a Mockingbird* (1962, dir. Robert Mulligan) are deployed in *Passage à l'acte*.
114 Dirk Schaeffer, "Alone: Life Wastes Andy Hardy," Program notes, *Views from the Avant-Garde*, curated by Mark McElhatten and Gavin Smith, New York Film Festival, October 10–11, 1998.
115 Zryd, "Alone," *Senses of Cinema*.
116 Sigmund Freud, *Three Essays on the Theory of Sexuality* (Vienna: Franz Deuticke, 1905), 222.
117 MacDonald, *A Critical Cinema 3*, 349.
118 MacDonald, *A Critical Cinema 3*, 350.
119 MacDonald, *A Critical Cinema 3*, 350.
120 MacDonald, *A Critical Cinema 3*, 350.
121 MacDonald, *A Critical Cinema 3*, 348.
122 MacDonald, *A Critical Cinema 3*, "limping," 348; "stuttering," 361–2.
123 Laura Mulvey, *Death 24× a Second: Stillness and the Moving Image* (London: Reaktion Books, 2006), 171.
124 Mulvey, *Death 24× a Second*, 172.
125 Mulvey, *Death 24× a Second*, 172.
126 See the section "Time Frames and Frames of Mind," in David Clark, "The Discrete Charm of the Digital Image: Animation and New Media," in *The Sharpest Point: Animation at the End of Cinema*, eds. Chris Gehman and

127 Mulvey, *Death 24× a Second*, 172.
128 See Akira Mizuta Lippit, *Ex-Cinema: From a Theory of Experimental Film and Video* (Berkeley: University of California Press, 2012), ch. 3.
129 Lippet, *Ex-Cinema*, ch 3; italics in original.
130 See my "*Alone., Again*," *Metacinema*, 291–317.
131 Lippit, "Digesture," ch. 7.
132 Lippit, "Digesture," ch 7.
133 Lippit, "Digesture," ch 7.
134 MacDonald, *A Critical Cinema 3*, 361.
135 Lippit, "Digesture," ch. 7.
136 David Bering-Porter, "The Automaton in All of Us: GIFs, Cinemagraphs, and the Films of Martin Arnold," *The Moving Image Review and Art Journal (MIRAJ)*, vol. 3, no. 2 (December 2014), 179.
137 Bering-Porter, "The Automaton in All of Us," 180.
138 Bering-Porter, "The Automaton in All of Us," 180.
139 Bering-Porter, "The Automaton in All of Us," 180.
140 Bering-Porter, "The Automaton in All of Us," 180; see also Zryd, "*Alone: Life Wastes Andy Hardy*," *Senses of Cinema*.
141 Malcolm Turvey, *Doubting Vision: Film and the Revelationist Tradition* (Oxford: Oxford University Press, 2008), 5.
142 Bering-Porter, "The Automaton in All of Us," 180; Turvey, *Doubting Vision*, 32; italics in original.
143 Bering-Porter, "The Automaton in All of Us," 181.
144 See my "On the Aesthetics of Amateur Filmmaking in Narrative Cinema: Negotiating Home Movies after *Adam's Rib*," in *The Thought of Stanley Cavell and Cinema*, 245–90.
145 Bering-Porter, "The Automaton in All of Us," 181.
146 See earlier, Cavell, *Pursuits of Happiness*, 149 and later, Cavell, *Cities of Words*, 299.
147 Bering-Porter, "The Automaton in All of Us," 182.
148 Bering-Porter, "The Automaton in All of Us," 182.
149 Martin J. Zeilinger, "Sampling as Analysis, Sampling as Symptom: Found Footage and Repetition in Martin Arnold's *Alone. Life Wastes Andy Hardy*," in *Sampling Media*, eds. David Laderman and Laurel Westrup (New York: Oxford University Press, 2014), 162.
150 Zeilinger, "Sampling as Analysis, Sampling as Symptom," 162; see also 164.
151 Zryd, "*Alone: Life Wastes Andy Hardy*," *Senses of Cinema*.
152 Zeilinger, "Sampling as Analysis, Sampling as Symptom," 163.
153 See Tom Gunning, "Before Documentary: Early Nonfiction Films and the 'View' Aesthetic," in *The Philosophy of Documentary Film: Image, Sound, Fiction, Truth*, ed. David LaRocca (Lanham: Lexington Books of Rowman & Littlefield, 2017), 159–74; see also Erika Balsom, "A Cinephilic Avant-garde: The Films of Peter Tscherkassky, Martin Arnold, and Gustav Deutsch," in *New Austrian Film*, eds. Robert von Dassanowsky and Oliver C. Speck (New York: Berghahn Books, 2011), 269.

Steve Reinke (Ottawa: YYZ Books/Ottawa International Animation Festival and the Images Festival, 2005). Also available at http://chemicalpictures.net/writing/the-discrete-charm-of-the-digital-image/.

154 Zeilinger, "Sampling as Analysis, Sampling as Symptom," 162.
155 Balsom, "A Cinephilic Avant-garde," 269.
156 Balsom, "A Cinephilic Avant-garde," 269.
157 See Bill Billiter, "Satanic Messages Played Back for Assembly Panel," *Los Angeles Times*, B3 (latimes.com) and Davis Erik, "What exactly lurks within the backward grooves of 'Stairway to Heaven'?," *Salon*, June 24, 2017, salon.com.
158 MacDonald, *A Critical Cinema 3*, 354.
159 MacDonald, *A Critical Cinema 3*, 350, 354.
160 MacDonald, *A Critical Cinema 3*, 354.
161 MacDonald, *A Critical Cinema 3*, 362.
162 Ludwig Wittgenstein, *Culture and Value*, trans. Peter Winch, ed. G. H. von Wright (Chicago: The University of Chicago Press, 1980), 43.
163 See my "Object Lessons," *Photography's Materialities*, 209–35.
164 Graham Harman, *Art and Objects* (Cambridge: Polity, 2020), x; italics in original.
165 See Karen Barad, *Meeting the Universe Halfway: Quantum Physics and the Entanglement of Matter and Meaning* (Durham: Duke University Press, 2007), and George Dyson, "From Analog to Digital and Back," *OneZero*, August 18, 2020 (www.onezero.medium.com) and *Analogia: The Emergence of Technology Beyond Programmable Control* (New York: Farrar, Straus, and Giroux, 2020).
166 For a related study, one that addresses translation as a mode of international influence and transnational communication, see *A Power to Translate the World: New Essays on Emerson and International Culture*, eds. David LaRocca and Ricardo Miguel-Alfonso (Hanover: Dartmouth College Press, 2015), part of the Dartmouth Series in American Studies "Re-Mapping the Transnational" from series editor Donald E. Pease.
167 Stevens, "The World Heard," *The Thought of Stanley Cavell and Cinema*, 81.
168 See my "Contemplating the Sounds of Contemplative Cinema," *Movies with Stanley Cavell in Mind*, 274–318.
169 See James Wood, *Serious Noticing: Selected Essays* (New York: Farrar, Straus and Giroux, 2019).
170 Amanda Petrusich, "Merging Lanes," *The New Yorker*, March 15, 2021, 68.
171 Petrusich, "Merging Lanes," 68.
172 Petrusich, "Merging Lanes," 68.
173 Lev Manovich, "What is Digital Cinema?" (1995), in *Critical Visions in Film Theory*, eds. Timothy Corrigan, Patricia White, and Meta Mazaj (New York: Bedford/St. Martin's, 2011), 1060.
174 Petrusich, "Merging Lanes," 70.
175 Thomas Schatz, *Hollywood Genres: Formulas, Filmmaking, and the Studio System* (New York: McGraw-Hill, 1981), 16.
176 See my "'One of the Most Phenomenal Debut Films in the History of Movies': *The Sugarland Express* as Expression of Spielberg's 'Movie Sense' and as Contribution to a Genre Cycle," in *A Critical Companion to Steven Spielberg*, eds. Adam Barkman and Antonio Sanna (Lanham: Lexington Books, 2019), 39–50.
177 Petrusich, "Merging Lanes," 72.

178 Petrusich, "Merging Lanes," 72.
179 See my "The Limits of Instruction: Pedagogical Remarks on Lars von Trier's *The Five Obstructions*," *Film and Philosophy*, vol. 13 (2009), 35–50.
180 See Cavell's *Cities of Words* and also *Emerson's Transcendental Etudes*, ed. David Justin Hodge (Stanford: Stanford University Press, 2003).
181 See, for example, my *The Philosophy of Charlie Kaufman*, ed. David LaRocca (Lexington: University Press of Kentucky, 2011; updated edition, 2019); "Thinking of Film: What is Cavellian about Malick's Movies?" in *A Critical Companion to Terrence Malick*, ed. Joshua Sikora (Lanham: Lexington Books, 2020), 3–19; "'I Am What My Films Are': Listening to Herzog's Ecstatic, Essayistic Pronouncements," in *The Philosophy of Werner Herzog*, eds. M. Blake Wilson and Christopher Turner (Lanham: Lexington Books, 2020), 1–20; "Memory Translation," *Everything Has a Soul*, 188–201; "Contemplating the Sounds of Contemplative Cinema," in *Movies with Stanley Cavell in Mind*, 274–318; and "*Alone.*, Again," *Metacinema*, 291–317.

Appendix III
Genre Unlimited/Genre Ungenred

Apter | Barthes | Cavell | Chartier | Crimmins | Croce |
Derrida | Jauss | Wells

If the german word *Geschlecht* can be translated to mean "genre"—a word that itself lives precariously between English and French—what, in fact, is the genre of *Geschlecht*? Can we speak to its history, kinship, and traits? What delimits the genre of *Geschlecht*—or because of the word's inherent, endogenous polysemy, should we instead regard its multivocity as issuing a set or series of genres? As one or more genres, does *Geschlecht* have a singular form or network of them; does it persist in a medium or travel across many media? Then there is the reader—or translator—of *Geschlecht* to consider. In this third appendix, like the earlier experimental collages, we welcome readers to a florilegium of excerpts and extracts that do work of their own, but also seem to work upon one another: there is, to be sure, collegial communion and conversation—but also transgressive crossings, infringements, overlaps, and repetitions. Although the writers use the "same" word—genre—their findings for its definition differ. Meanwhile, what do we readers, working from the univocity of these texts (appearing or translated into) in English, do with such a purposeful sequencing? Such selections and orderings do not happen by accident, yet our editorial deliberateness doesn't mean there aren't delightful moments of play and uncanny interactions, and thereby, intimacies to be enjoyed, insights to be gleaned.

When speaking of media objects—film, television, novel, criticism, music, painting, and so on—we seem to know, at a glance, where our bid for genre containment would be. This is a Western. This is a metadocumentary. Here is a work of autofiction. And how about this bit of New Criticism. Over there a Baroque chamber piece. And here a modernist portrait. Yet, can one genre turn into another? (For example, how has film become television but also remained distinctly television—while, surreptitiously, television has also become film?) Do answers depend on content or form, or something of both? What about the context of judgment or the framing of reception?

Along another tack, what happens, say, if a genre is taken to be without limits, as, for example, the novel—the only and "as yet uncompleted genre," as Bakhtin put it.[1] Can genres *become* unlimited, exist without limitation, hovering endlessly in transposition from one catalogue of artistic convention to another, or, again, somehow forever placed in between (occupying the *trans* permanently)? For all our efforts to define one genre from another, would such genres—in aggressive expansion and unself-conscious overlap—defy us to become "ungenred," at last stripped of their very genreness?

We editors have retained the timecodes of these various portions to mark out something of the evolution of genre thinking, yet in our contemporary moment—and in the future that soon awaits—there appear increasing indications that genre is, in fact, an antiquated notion (like what else?—liberal democracy? privacy? the natural? the self?). And so as human identity has become untethered from the binary (one genre of gender set against and distinguishable from another, "opposing" genre of gender), so genres of art may eclipse any reliance on inherited definitions of type, trait, kinship, and kind. The unclassifiable becomes the norm—a sea of ungenred entities.

For our particular metacuratorial experiment in what follows—gathering and compositing notes on genre in order to reflect on the genre such remarks might contribute to, or obliterate—we have interjected a further feature to this final appendix, namely, a glimpse of Stanley Cavell's contribution to the conversation conducted over the course of decades. Here, in this longitudinal study, you will find a first dispatch from the early 1970s—a full chapter from *The World Viewed*. Then we select from an article published a decade later, in which Cavell takes stock of his terminology and how it holds up in the context of additional media forms, types, and modes of experience. Lastly, in the new millennium, Cavell offers a striking referendum on his findings from the seventies: it turns out, much has changed. In this chronology of Cavellian notes on genre, we encounter a specific strain of thought worth attending to. And given the temporal sequencing, we are, no doubt, pressed into service to offer our own contributions, in this volume and elsewhere.

OSCAR JANSSON AND DAVID LAROCCA

* * *

The development of a theory not infrequently has an unrecognized or essentially unreflected dependency on the kind and the limitations of the object through which the theory is to be exemplified or to which it is to be applied. This is especially the case with the theory of literary genres.

> Hans Robert Jauss, "Theory of Genres and Medieval Literature," *Modern Genre Theory*, trans. Timothy Bahti, ed. David Duff (London and New York: Routledge, 2014), 128.

Theorists who appeal to scientific, mathematical, or logical schematics to naturalize their argument operate with the formal bias. Theorists who appeal to cultural, functional, or historical mechanisms operate with the genre bias. Although contemporary genre theorists have tended to shift away from understanding genre as a taxonomical system towards understanding genre as the cultural conditions that enable textual production, vestiges of both biases persist.

> Jonathan Crimmins, "Gender, Genre, and the Near Future in Derrida's 'The Law of Genre,'" *diacritics*, vol. 39, no. 1 (2009), 46.

What is the relation, for us, between rhetorical genres (or kinds, or modes) and literary genres? How do these two genres of genres combine or overlay one another?

> Susan Wells, "Genres as Species and Spaces: Literary and Rhetorical Genre in *The Anatomy of Melancholy*," *Philosophy and Rhetoric*, vol. 47, no. 2 (2014), 114.

As soon as the word "genre" is sounded, as soon as it is heard, as soon as one attempts to conceive it, a limit is drawn. And when a limit is established, norms and interdictions are not far behind: "Do," "Do not" says "genre," the word "genre," the figure, the voice, or the law of genre. And this can be said of genre in all genres, be it a question of a generic or a general determination of what one calls "nature" or *physis* (for example, a biological *genre* in the sense of *gender*, or the human *genre*, a genre of all that is in general), or be it a question of a typology designated as nonnatural and depending on laws or orders which were once held to be opposed to *physis* according to those values associated with *technè*, *thesis*, *nomos* (for example, an artistic, poetic, or literary genre).

> Jacques Derrida, "The Law of Genre," trans. Avital Ronell, *Critical Inquiry*, vol. 7, no. 1 (Autumn 1980), 56.

Hence follow a series of consequences. The first one is to widen the notion of genre beyond the textual real and to consider that public ceremonials, religious rituals, and everyday practices constitute different "genres," the "social energy" of which is encoded and refashioned by their representation or appropriation. The second is that the genres remain a pertinent way for delineating specific aesthetic experiences (theatrical practice, for example, implies a manner for separating artistic practices from social practices that is not the same in other literary genres) and for characterizing even within the same realm of experiences different types of exchanges between social anxieties and literary writing.

> Roger Chartier, "Genre between Literature and History," *Modern Language Quarterly*, vol. 67, no. 1 (March 2006), 131.

Genres are not to be mixed. I will not mix genres.

> Jacques Derrida, "The Law of Genre" (1980), 55.

Imagine someone (a kind of Monsieur Teste in reverse) who abolishes within himself all barriers, all classes, all exclusions, not by syncretism but by simple discard of that old specter: *logical contradiction*; who mixes every language, even those said to be incompatible; who silently accepts every charge of illogicality, of incongruity; who remains passive in the face of Socratic irony (leading the interlocutor to the supreme disgrace: *self-contradiction*) and legal terrorism (how much penal evidence is based on a psychology of consistency!). Such a man would be the mockery of our society: court, school, asylum, polite conversation would cast him out: who endures contradiction without shame?

> Roland Barthes, *The Pleasure of the Text*, trans. Richard Miller (New York: Hill and Wang, 1975), 3.

Following a classical precedent, one has deemed natural structures or typical forms whose history is hardly natural but, rather, quite to the contrary, complex and heterogeneous. [...] Genette insists at length on this naturalization of genres: "The history of genre-theory is strewn with these fascinating outlines that inform and deform reality, a reality often heterogenous to the literary field, and that claim to discover a natural 'system' wherein they construct a factitious symmetry heavily reinforced by fake windows."

> Jacques Derrida, "The Law of Genre" (1980), 60.

Genre theory is infiltrated with metaphors of natural selection, a powerful framework for understanding how species emerge, change, and die. These evolutionary schemes and tropes are sometimes quite explicit. In a typical essay, Michael Shepherd and Carolyn Watters observe that cybergenres demonstrate that "the new functionality afforded by the new medium drives the evolution ... of replicated genres ... through variations on those genres until novel genres emerge that are significantly different from the original genres" (1998, 98). Scholars discussing hybrid genres come close to imagining that two genres can get together and make genre babies.

Susan Wells, "Genres as Species and Spaces" (2014), 114–15.

I repeat: genres are not to be mixed. I will not mix them.

Jacques Derrida, "The Law of Genre" (1980), 55.

* * * *

Around this point our attention turns from the physical medium of cinema in general to the specific forms or genres the medium has taken in the course of its history.

Both Panofsky and Bazin begin at the beginning, noting and approving that early movies adapt popular or folk arts and themes and performers and characters: farce, melodrama, circus, music hall, romance, etc. And both are gratifyingly contemptuous of intellectuals who could not come to terms with those facts of life. (Such intellectuals are the alter egos of the film promoters they so heartily despise. Roxy once advertised a movie as "Art, in every sense of the word"; his better half declaims, "This is not art, in any sense of the word.") Our question is, why did such forms and themes and characters lend themselves to film? Bazin, in what I have read of him, is silent on the subject, except to express gratitude to film for revivifying these ancient forms, and to justify in general the legitimacy of adaptation from one art to another. Arnold Hauser, if I understand him, suggests wrong answers, in a passage that includes the remark "Only a young art can be popular,"[2] a remark that not only is in itself baffling (did Verdi and Dickens and Chaplin and Frank Loesser work in young arts?) but suggests that it was only natural for the movies to pick up the forms they did. It *was* natural—anyway it happened fast enough—but not because movies were destined to popularity (they were at first no more popular than other forms of entertainment). In any case, popular arts are likely to pick up the forms and themes of high art for their material—popular theater naturally *burlesques*. And it means next to nothing to say that movies are young, because we do not know what the normal life span of an art is supposed to be, nor what would count as a unit of measure. Panofsky raises the question of the appropriateness of these original forms, but his answer is misleading.

> The legitimate paths of evolution [for the film] were opened, not by running away from the folk art character of the primitive film but by developing it

within the limits of its own possibilities. Those primordial archetypes of film productions on the folk art level—success or retribution, sentiment, sensation, pornography, and crude humor—could blossom forth into genuine history, tragedy and romance, crime and adventure, and comedy, as soon as it was realized that they could be transfigured—not by an artificial injection of literary values but by the exploitation of the unique and specific possibilities of the new medium.[3]

The instinct here is sound, but the region is full of traps. What are "the unique and specific possibilities of the new medium"? Panofsky defines them as dynamization of space and spatialization of time—that is, in a movie things move, and you can be moved instantaneously from anywhere to anywhere, and you can witness successively events happening at the same time. He speaks of these properties as "self-evident to the point of triviality" and, because of that, "easily forgotten or neglected." One hardly disputes this, or its importance. But we still do not understand what makes these properties "the possibilities of the medium." I am not now asking how one would know that these are *the* unique and specific possibilities (though I will soon get back to that); I am asking what it means to call them possibilities at all.

Why, for example, didn't the medium begin and remain in the condition of home movies, one shot just physically tacked on to another, cut and edited simply according to subject? (Newsreels essentially did, and they are nevertheless valuable, enough so to have justified the invention of moving pictures.) The answer seems obvious: narrative movies emerged because someone "saw the possibilities" of the medium—cutting and editing and taking shots at different distances from the subject. But again, these are mere actualities of film mechanics: every home movie and newsreel contains them. We could say: To make them "possibilities of the medium" is to realize what will give them *significance*—for example, the narrative and physical rhythms of melodrama, farce, American comedy of the 1930s. It is not as if filmmakers saw these possibilities and then looked for something to apply them to. It is truer to say that someone with the wish to make a movie saw that certain established forms would give point to certain properties of film.

This perhaps sounds like quibbling, but what it means is that the aesthetic possibilities of a medium are not givens. You can no more tell what will give significance to the unique and specific aesthetic possibilities of projecting photographic images by thinking about them or seeing some than you can tell what will give significance to the possibilities of paint by thinking about paint or by looking some over. You have to think about painting, and paintings; you have to think about motion pictures. What does this "thinking about them" consist in? Whatever the useful criticism of an art consists in. (Painters before Jackson Pollock had dripped paint, even deliberately. Pollock made dripping into a medium of painting.) I feel like saying: The first successful movies—i.e., the first moving pictures accepted as motion pictures—were not applications of a medium that was defined by given possibilities, but the *creation of a medium* by their giving significance to specific possibilities. Only the art itself can discover its possibilities, and the discovery of a new possibility is the discovery of a new medium. A medium is something through which or by means of which something specific gets done or said in particular ways. It provides, one might say, particular ways to get through to someone, to make sense; in art, they are forms, like forms of speech. To discover ways of making sense is always a matter of the relation of an artist to his art, each discovering the other.

Panofsky uncharacteristically skips a step when he describes the early silent films as an "unknown language ... forced upon a public not yet capable of reading it."[4] His notion is (with good reason, writing when he did) of a few industrialists forcing their productions upon an addicted multitude. But from the beginning the language was not "unknown"; it was known to its creators, those who found themselves speaking it; and in the beginning there was no "public" in question; there were just some curious people. There soon was a public, but that just proves how easy the thing was to know. If we are to say that there was an "unknown" something, it was less like a language than like a fact—in particular, the fact that something is intelligible. So while it may be true, as Panofsky says, that "for a Saxon peasant of around 800 it was not easy to understand the meaning of a picture showing a man as he pours water over the head of another man," this has nothing special to do with the problems of a moviegoer. The meaning of that act of pouring in certain communities is still not easy to understand; it was and is impossible to understand for anyone to whom the practice of baptism is unknown. Why did Panofsky suppose that comparable understanding is essential, or uniquely important, to the reading of movies? Apparently he needed an explanation for the persistence in movies of "fixed iconography"—"the well-remembered types of the Vamp and the Straight Girl ... the Family Man, and the Villain," characters whose conduct was "predetermined accordingly"—an explanation for the persistence of an obviously primitive or folkloristic element in a rapidly developing medium. For he goes on, otherwise inexplicably, to say that "devices like these became gradually less necessary as the public grew accustomed to interpret the action by itself and were virtually abolished by the invention of the talking film." In fact such devices persist as long as there are still Westerns and gangster films and comedies and musicals and romances. *Which* specific iconography the Villain is given will alter with the times, but that his iconography remains specific (i.e., operates according to a "fixed attitude and attribute" principle[5]) seems undeniable: if Jack Palance in *Shane* is not a Villain, no honest home was ever in danger. Films have changed, but that is not because we don't need such explanations any longer; it is because we can't *accept* them.

These facts are accounted for by the actualities of the film medium itself: types are exactly what carry the forms movies have relied upon. These media created new types, or combinations and ironic reversals of types; but there they were, and stayed. Does this mean that movies can never create individuals, only types? What it means is that this is the movies' way of creating individuals: they create *individualities*. For what makes someone a type is not his similarity with other members of that type but his striking separateness from other people.

Until recently, types of black human beings were not created in film: black people were stereotypes—mammies, shiftless servants, loyal retainers, entertainers. We were not given, and were not in a position to be given, individualities that projected particular *ways* of inhabiting a social role; we recognized only the role. Occasionally the humanity behind the role would manifest itself; and the result was a revelation not of a human individuality, but of an entire realm of humanity becoming visible. When in *Gone With the Wind* Vivien Leigh, having counted on Butterfly McQueen's professed knowledge of midwifery, and finding her as ignorant as herself, slaps her in rage and terror, the moment can stun us with a question: What was the white girl assuming about blackness when she believed the casual claim of a black girl, younger and duller and more ignorant than herself, to know all about the mysteries of childbirth? The assumption, although apparently complimentary, is dehumanizing—with such creatures knowledge of the body comes from nowhere, and in general they are to be trusted absolutely or not at all, like lions in a cage, with whom you either do or do not know how to deal. After the slap, we are left with two young girls equally frightened in a humanly desperate situation, one limited by a distraction which expects and forgets that it is to be bullied, the other by an energetic resourcefulness which knows only how to bully. At the end of Michael Curtiz's *Breaking Point*, as the wounded John Garfield is carried from his boat to the dock, awaited by his wife and children and, just outside the circle, by the other woman in his life (Patricia Neal), the camera pulls away, holding on the still waiting child of his black partner, who only the unconscious Garfield knows has been killed. The poignance of the silent and unnoticed black child overwhelms the yarn we had been shown. Is he supposed to symbolize the fact of general human isolation and abandonment? Or the fact that every action has consequences for innocent bystanders? Or that children are the real sufferers from the entangled efforts of adults to straighten out their lives? The effect here is to rebuke Garfield for attaching so much importance to the loss of his arm, and generally to blot out attention to individual suffering by invoking a massive social evil about which this film has nothing to say.

The general difference between a film type and a stage type is that the individuality captured on film naturally takes precedence over the social role in which that individuality gets expressed. Because on film social role appears arbitrary or incidental, movies have an inherent tendency toward the democratic, or anyway the idea of human equality. (But because of film's equally natural attraction to crowds, it has opposite tendencies toward the fascistic or populistic.) This depends upon recognizing film types as inhabited by figures we have met or may well meet in other circumstances. The recognized recurrence of film performers will become a central idea as we proceed. At the moment I am emphasizing only that in the case of black performers there was until recently no other place for them to recur in, except just the role within which we have already met them. For example, we would not have expected to see them as parents or siblings. I cannot at the moment remember a black person in a film making an ordinary purchase—say of a newspaper, or a ticket to a movie or for a train, let alone writing a check. (*Pinky* and *A Raisin in the Sun* prove the rule: in the former, the making of a purchase is a climactic scene in the film; in the latter, it provides the whole subject and structure.)

One recalls the lists of stars of every magnitude who have provided the movie camera with human subjects—individuals capable of filling its need for individualities, whose individualities in turn, whose inflections of demeanor and disposition were given full play in its projection. They provided, and still provide, staples for impersonators: one gesture or syllable of mood, two strides, or a passing mannerism was enough to single them out from all other creatures. They realized the myth of singularity—that we can still be found, behind our disguises of bravado and cowardice, by someone, perhaps a god, capable of defeating our self-defeats. This was always more important than their distinction by beauty. Their singularity made them more like us—anyway, made their difference from us less a matter of metaphysics, to which we must accede, than a matter of responsibility, to which we must bend. But then that made them even more glamorous. That they should be able to stand upon their singularity! If one did that, one might be found, and called out, too soon, or at an inconvenient moment.

What was wrong with type-casting in films was not that it displaced some other, better principle of casting, but that factors irrelevant to filmmaking often influenced the particular figures chosen. Similarly, the familiar historical fact that there are movie cycles, taken by certain movie theorists as in itself a mark of unscrupulous commercialism, is a possibility internal to the medium; one could even say, it is the best emblem of the fact that a medium had been created. For a cycle is a genre (prison movies, Civil War movies, horror movies, etc.); and a genre is a medium.

As Hollywood developed, the original types ramified into individualities as various and subtle, as far-reaching in their capacities to inflect mood and release fantasy, as any set of characters who inhabited the great theaters of our world. We do not know them by such names as Pulcinella, Crispin, Harlequin, Pantaloon, the Doctor, the Captain, Columbine; we call them the Public Enemy, the Priest, James Cagney, Pat O'Brien, the Confederate Spy, the Army Scout, Randolph Scott, Gary Cooper, Gable, Paul Muni, the Reporter, the Sergeant, the Sheriff, the Deputy, the D.A., the Quack, the

Shyster, the Other Woman, the Fallen Woman, the Moll, the Dance Hall Hostess. Hollywood was the theater in which they appeared, because the films of Hollywood constituted a world, with recurrent faces more familiar to me than the faces of the neighbors of all the places I have lived.

The great movie comedians—Chaplin, Keaton, W. C. Fields—form a set of types that could not have been adapted from any other medium. Its creation depended upon two conditions of the film medium mentioned earlier. These conditions seem to be necessities, not merely possibilities, so I will say that two necessities of the medium were discovered or expanded in the creation of these types. First, movie performers cannot project, but are projected. Second, photographs are of the world, in which human beings are not ontologically favored over the rest of nature, in which objects are not props but natural allies (or enemies) of the human character. The first necessity—projected visibility—permits the sublime comprehensibility of Chaplin's natural choreography; the second—ontological equality—permits his Proustian or Jamesian relationships with Murphy beds and flights of stairs and with vases on runners on tables on rollers: the heroism of momentary survival, Nietzsche's man as a tightrope across an abyss. These necessities permit not merely the locales of Keaton's extrications, but the philosophical mood of his countenance and the Olympic resourcefulness of his body; permit him to be perhaps the only constantly beautiful and continuously hilarious man ever seen, as though the ugliness in laughter should be redeemed. They permit Fields to mutter and suffer and curse obsessively, but heard and seen only by us; because his attributes are those of the gentleman (confident swagger and elegant manners, gloves, cane, outer heartiness), he can manifest continuously, with the remorselessness of nature, the psychic brutalities of bourgeois civilization.

Stanley Cavell, "Types; Cycles as Genres," *The World Viewed: Reflections on the Ontology of Film*, Enlarged Edition (Cambridge: Harvard University Press, 1979 [1971]), 29–37.

* * * *

Lectiocentrism is an old problem in the historiography of art history, but increasingly, it is being framed as an issue for translation studies. The investigation of zones of translatability across languages has long been extended to the analysis of visual data and non-verbal art, but there have been relatively few self-conscious attempts to challenge the word-based model of "the reading," by, as it were, translating "the reading" into "the looking." Such a task is complicated by the obvious fact that "lookings"—once they become verbally articulated—fall into the prison-house of language.

"The reading" attained its status as master-model during the heyday of deconstruction and poststructuralism through the work of Jacques Derrida,

Harold Bloom, Shoshana Felman, J. Hillis Miller, Barbara Johnson, and Paul de Man, each of whom practiced a distinct mode of rhetorical interpretation infused with Nietzschean irony. Their readings may have paused at the conceptually amorphous boundaries between lexeme and grapheme, sign and glyph, verbal and visual sign, but in the end they privileged *literary* exegesis. De Manian technics revealed the infinite translatability of signs in questioning the limits between natural language and code in ways that anticipated the intermedial transfer of digital information. In his late writings, moreover, de Man was preoccupied with the materiality of inscription. Ultimately, however, de Man's readings reinforced a generic fidelity to texts in their dedication to the investigation of "linguicity" and the aporia structuring verbal expressionism.

> Emily Apter, "Untranslatable? The 'Reading' versus the 'Looking,'" *Journal of Visual Culture*, vol. 6, no. 1 (2007), 149.

The question of the literary genre is not a formal one: it covers the motif of the law in general, of generation in the natural and symbolic senses, of birth in the natural and symbolic senses, of the generation difference, sexual difference between the feminine and masculine genre/gender, of the hymen between the two, of a relationless relation between the two, of an identity and difference between the feminine and masculine.

> Jacques Derrida, "The Law of Genre" (1980), 74.

Spivak seconds Luce Irigaray in positing gender difference as irreducible, a natural condition of an anatomical form.[6] Conversely, Judith Butler, reacting against the compulsory heterosexuality that results from giving first priority to gender and second priority to sexuality as its expression, argues that identification precedes identity, that the performance of historically situated gender roles precedes a (forever displaced) gender identity. These two positions represent the dual problematic that gender shares with genre—a problematic that "covers the motif of the law in general, of generation in the natural and symbolic senses, of birth in the natural and symbolic senses"— namely the reciprocal dependence of the formal bias and the genre bias in the entangled fields of genre and gender.

> Jonathan Crimmins, "Gender, Genre, and the Near Future in Derrida's 'The Law of Genre'" (2009), 46–7.

What about a neutral genre/gender? Or one whose neutrality would not be negative (neither ... nor), nor dialectical, but affirmative, and doubly affirmative (or ... or)?

> Jacques Derrida, "The Law of Genre" (1980), 74.

In fact, the idea of a hybrid genre is striking evidence of the strength of species models of genre: a hybrid text is seen as a descendent of two "parent" genres: the prose poem, the horror comedy. The genre hybrid, like the horticultural hybrid, is expected to be showy and vigorous. Although the term "genre hybrid" is associated with innovation and experimentation, it quite conservatively assumes that genres are essentially tools for classification.

Susan Wells, "Genres as Species and Spaces" (2014), 131.

Thus, as soon as genre announces itself, one must respect a norm, one must not cross a line of demarcation, one must not risk impurity, anomaly, or monstrosity.

Jacques Derrida, "The Law of Genre" (1980), 57.

* * * *

To say that the primary object of aesthetic interest in television is not the individual piece but the format is to say that the format is its primary individual of aesthetic interest. This ontological recharacterization is meant to bring out that the relation between format and instance should be of essential aesthetic concern. There are two classical concepts in talking about movies that fit the requirements of the thing I am calling a format, as it were, an artistic *kind*: the concepts of the serial and of the genre. The units of a serial are familiarly called its episodes; I will call the units of a genre its members. A thesis it seems to be worth exploring is that television, for some reason, works aesthetically according to a serial-episode principle rather than according to a genre-member principle. What are these principles?

In traditional terms, they would not be apt to invoke what I mean by different principles of composition. What is traditionally called a genre film is a movie whose membership in a group of films is no more problematic than the exemplification of a serial in one of its episodes. You can, for example, roughly *see* that a movie is a Western, or gangster film, or horror film, or prison film, or "woman's film," or a screwball comedy. Call this way of thinking about genre, genre-as-cycle. In contrast, in *Pursuits of Happiness*, the way I found I wanted to speak of genre in defining what I call the Hollywood comedy of remarriage, I will call genre-as-medium.

Because I feel rather backed into the necessity of considering the notion of a genre, I feel especially in need of the reader's forbearance over the next half dozen or so paragraphs. It seems that the notion of a genre has lately been receiving renewed attention from literary theorists, but the recent pieces of writing I have started to look at on the subject (so far, I realize, too unsystematically) all begin with a sense of dissatisfaction with other writing on the subject, either with uses to which it has been put, or both. I am not interested here in joining an argument but rather in sketching the paths of two (related) ideas of a genre; it is an interest in coming to terms with what seem to me to be certain natural confusions in approaching the notion of a genre, and I went no further with it than the concrete motivations in reading individual works seemed to me to demand. With that in mind, in the present essay I am beginning, on the contrary, with certain intuitions concerning what the general aesthetic powers of video turn upon, and I am hoping to get far enough in abstracting these powers from the similar, hence different, powers of film, to get in a position to test these intuitions in concrete cases. (I may, however, just mention that two of the books I have been most helped by are Northrop Frye's *A Natural Perspetive* and Tzvetan Todorov's *The Fantastic*.[7])

Before going on to give my understanding of the contrasting notions of a genre, I should perhaps anticipate two objections to my terminology. First, if there is an established, conventional use of the word "genre," and if this fits what I am calling genre-as-cycle, why not keep the simple word and use some other simple word to name the further kind of kind I am thinking of, the kind I am calling genre-as-medium—why not just call the further kind a set or a group or a pride? Second, since film itself is thought of as a medium (for example, of art), why insist on using the same word to characterize a gathering of works *within* that medium? As to this second objection, this double range of the concept of a medium is deployed familiarly in the visual arts, in which painting is said to be a medium (of art, in contrast, say, to sculpture or to music—hardly, one would think, the same contrast), and in which gouache is also a medium (of painting, in contrast to water color or oil or tempera). I wish to preserve, and make more explicit—or curious—this double range in order to keep open to investigation the relation between work and medium that I call the revelation, or acknowledgment, of the one in the other. In my experience, to keep this open means, above all, resisting (by understanding) the temptation to think of a medium simply as a familiar material (for instance, sound, color, words), as if this were an unprejudicial observation rather than one of a number of ways of taking the material of a medium, and recognizing instead that only the art can define its media, only painting and composing and movie making can reveal what is required, or possible (what means, what exploits of material), for something to be a painting, a piece of music, a movie. As to the first objection—my use of "genre" in naming both of what I claim are different principles or procedures of composition—my purpose is to release something true in both uses of the word (in both, there is process of generating in question), and to leave open to investigation what the relation between these processes may be. The difference may be consequential. I think, for example, that it is easier to understand movies as some familiar kind of commodity or as entertainments if you take them as participating not in a genre-as-medium but in genres-as-cycles, or if you focus on those movies that *do* participate, without remainder, in genres so conceived. Movies thought of as members of genres-as-cycles is the name of the way of taking them that I earlier characterized as evanescent. The simplest examples of such cycles used to be signaled by titles such as *The Son of X, The Curse of X, X Meets Dracula*, and so on. Our sophistication today requires that we call such sequels *XII, XIII*, and so on, like Super Bowls. It is part of Hollywood's deviousness that certain sequels may be better than their originals, as perhaps *The Bride of Frankenstein* is, or Fritz Lang's *The Return of Frank James*.

Still another word about terminology, before going on to consider the thesis that television works according to a serial-episode rather than a genre-member principle. In picking up the old movie term "serial" to mark the contrast in question, I am assuming that what used to be called serials on film bears some internal relation to what are called series on television. But what I am interested in considering here is the idea of serialization generally, wishing again to leave open what the relations are between serials and series (as I wish to leave open, hence to recall, the occurrence of serialization in classical novels, in photographs, in paintings, in music, in comic strips). One might find that the closest equivalent on television to the movie serial is the soap opera, since this shares the feature of more or less endless narration across episodes, linked by crises. But in going on now to consider a little my thesis about serialization in television, I am exploring my intuition that the repetitions and recurrences of soap operas bear a significant relation with those of series, in which the narrative comes to a classical ending each time, and indeed that these repetitions and recurrences are modes of a requirement that the medium of television exacts in all its formats. A program such as *Hill Street Blues* seems to be questioning the feature of a series that demands a classical ending for each instance, hence questioning the distinction between soap opera and series. Similarly, or oppositely, the projected sequence of movies instanced by *Star Wars* and *The Empire Strikes Back* seems to be questioning the distinction between a serial and a cycle by questioning the demand of a serial (a narrative that continues over an indefinite number of episodes) *not* to come to a classical ending before the final episode. This would bring the sequence closer in structure to literary forms such as (depending on individual taste) the King Arthur legends, the Shakespeare Henry plays (perhaps in a Lamb-like retelling), or Tolkien's *Lord of the Rings* trilogy.

A genre, as I use the notion in *Pursuits of Happiness*, and which I am here calling genre-as-medium, behaves according to two basic "laws" (or "principles"), one internal, the other external. Internally, a genre is constituted by members, about which it can be said that they share what you might picture as every feature in common. In practice, this means that, where a given member diverges, as it must, from the rest, it must "compensate" for this divergence. The genre undergoes continuous definition or redefinition as new members introduce new points of compensation. Externally, a genre is distinguished from other genres, in particular from what I call "adjacent" genres, when one feature shared by its members "negates" a feature shared by the members of another. Here, a feature of a genre will develop new lines of refinement. If genres form a system (which is part of the faith that for me keeps alive an interest in the concept), then in principle it would seem possible to be able to move by negation from one genre through adjacent genres, until all the genres of film are derived. Hitchcock's corpus provides convenient examples: his *North by Northwest* shares an indefinitely long list of features with remarriage comedies, which implies, according to my work on the subject, that it is about the legitimizing of marriage. In this film, as in other adventures, by Hitchcock and by others, legitimacy is conferred by a pair's survival together of a nation-saving adventure.[8] But that film can further be understood as negating the feature of the remarriage genre according to which the woman has to undergo something like death and revival. When this happens in Hitchcock, as in *Vertigo*, the Hitchcock film immediately preceding *North by Northwest*, it causes catastrophe. In *North by Northwest* it is the man who undergoes death and revival (and for a reason, I claim, having to do with the structure of the remarriage form). A dozen years earlier, in *Notorious*, Hitchcock compensates for the feature of the woman's death and revival (hence, maintaining the happiness of a remarriage ending) by emphasizing that her death and revival are not the condition of the man's loving her, but the effect of his failure to acknowledge her (as happens, seminally, according to my discussion of the genre, in *The Winter's Tale*).

The operations of compensation and negation are meant to specify the idea of a genre in *Pursuits of Happiness*, in contrast to what I take to be the structuralist idea of a genre as a form characterized by features, as an object is characterized by its properties, an idea that seems to me to underlie, for example, Todorov's work on the fantastic tale. I put it this way:

> An alternative idea ... is that the members of a genre share the inheritance of certain conditions, procedures, and subjects and goals of composition, and that in primary art each member of such a genre represents a study of these conditions, something I think of as bearing the responsibility of the inheritance. There is, on this picture, nothing one is tempted to *call* the features of a genre which all its members have in common (28).

Such operations as compensation and negation are not invoked either in genre-as-cycle or in serial-episode procedure. So I am saying that they are made by serialization as opposed to the generation in genre-as-medium. But in neither sense of genre are the members of a genre episodes of a continuing story or situation or setting. It is not the same narrative matter for Frankenstein to get a bride as for Rhoda (in a popular television series of a few years ago bearing her name) to get a husband. The former is a drama on its own; the latter serves a history, a before and after.

In speaking of a procedure of serialization, I wish to capture what seems to me right in the intuition of what are called narrative "formulas." When theorists of structural or formal matters speak of "formulas" of composition, they are thinking, I believe, of genre-as-cycle or of serial-episode construction, in which each instance is a perfect exemplification of the format, as each solution of an equation, or each step in a mathematical series, is a perfect instance of the formula that "generates" it. The instances do not compete with one another for depth of participation, nor comment upon one another for mutual revelation; and whether an instance "belongs" to the formula is as settled by the formula as is the identity of the instance. (Such remarks are really recipes—most untested—for what a formula would look like; hence, for what would count as "generation" in this context. I am taking it that no item of plot need be common to all the episodes of, say, *Rhoda* so that the formula that does the generating is sufficiently specified by designating the continuing characters and their relations with one another (characters and relations whose recurrent traits are themselves specifiable in definite ways). This is the situation in the situation comedy. A certain description of the situation would constitute the formula of the comedy. Then the substitution of the unknown new element to initiate the generation, the element of difference, can be any event that alters the situation comically—Rhoda develops a rash; her sister is being followed by the office lothario; her mother's first boyfriend has just showed up; and so on. A minimum amount of talent is all it takes to write out the results of the generation competently—which of course does not necessarily mean salably; a much higher order is required to invent the characters and relations, and cast them, in such a way as to allow new generations readily and consistently to be funny. Whereas in genre-as-medium, none of this is so. In what I call the genre of remarriage comedy, the presence or absence of even the title of the genre does not insure that an instance does or does not belong to the genre. Belonging has to be won, earned, as by an argument of the members with one another; as adjacency of genre must be proved, something irrelevant to the existence of multiple series, which, further, raise no issue of the definition and refinement a genre undergoes. ("Belonging has to be won, as by an argument...." Here is an allegory of the relation of the principal pair in such comedies. In their adventures of conversation, the pair are forever taking each other by surprise, forever interesting each other anew. To dream up these surprises and interests demands an exercise of talent that differs not only, or primarily, in its degree of energy from the energies I imagine in connection with developing a series, but differs in its order of deployment: here, the initiating idea is next to nothing compared with the details of the working out, which is what one would expect where the rule of format is, so to speak, overthrown. Here, what you might call the formula, or what in *Pursuits of Happiness* I call the myth, is itself under investigation, or generation, by the instances.)

What difference does any of this make? I expect no simple or direct answer to the question of the difference between generation and serialization. Perhaps they name incompatible ways of looking at human activities generally, or texts. It might be thought, for example, that a series and its formulas specify the construction of the popular arts, whereas genre-as-medium and its arguments specify the construction of the higher arts. John G. Cawelti's *Adventures, Mystery, and Romance: Formula Stories as Art and Popular Culture* perhaps suggests this. Charles Rosen's *The Classical Style* states a related distinction within high art, between the great and the mediocre, or between the original and the academic.[9] Vladimir Propp's classical analysis of the fairy tale virtually declares that you would not expect a sophisticated work of art to obey formulas in that way.[10] But this merely transfers the question: What is "that way"?

One wants to answer by saying something like, "Mechanically or automatically (or formulaically?)." But maybe this is specific to fairy tales, not to all forms you might call popular. Are black-figure and red-figure vase paintings less formulaic? And are they less than high art? American quilts of the nineteenth century are surely not less formulaic, yet the effect of certain of them is breathtaking, not unlike the directness of certain non-objective paintings. Like those paintings (I think of certain works of Rothko, Louis, Noland, Olitski, Stella), these examples exist essentially as items of a series. It would follow that the concept of existence in a series, of being composed according to a serial-episode principle, does not distinguish popular from high art, only if, for instance, one accepts such paintings as high art, something not everyone does. And it would follow only if the concept of a series in painting (or quilts) captures the same thought as the concept of a serial in film and a series in television. So far as the thought is one of establishing a formulaic relation between instances, the relation between paintings in a series certainly seems at least as strong (as, so to speak, mechanical) as the relation of episodes to one another. In fact, the relation between the paintings seems *too* strong to yield works of art: here, the instances seem purely generated, or determined, by a format with finite features, each of which can be specified and varied to yield new items. (I think here of Stella's Z-forms, or Noland's Chevrons or Ribbons, or Louis' Unfurleds.) The relation between members is exhaustively constituted, one may say, by their mutual differences, as if to illustrate a linguist's vision, or that of the more advanced of today's textualists, according to which language, and meaning, and hence whatever replaces or precedes art, is constituted not by signs (inherently) possessing or containing meaning, but by the weave of the relation of difference among them (say their synthesis of distinctive features). But at the same time, the idea of the series can be taken to dispute the linguistic or textualist appeal to difference, since this appeal generally accompanies, even grounds, a claim that the sensuous properties of the signs themselves are arbitrary. What painting in series argues is rather the absolute *non*-arbitrariness of format, because the artistic discovery is precisely that *this* synthesis of features generates instances, each of which maintains itself as a proposal of beauty. The achievement may be felt as something like an empirical discovery of the *a priori*—not unlike a certain aspiration of philosophy. (The implications of the fact of series for modern painting's disputing of received ideas of craft and style and medium, and its proposal of surprising consequences for thinking about the relation of painting and photography, is the subject of a pivotal chapter, "Excursus: Some Modern Painting," in *The World Viewed*.)

> Stanley Cavell, "The Fact of Television" (1982), *Themes Out of School: Effects and Causes* (San Francisco: North Point Press, 1984), 241–9.

* * * *

Every true work of art has violated some established kind and upset the ideas of the critics, who have thus been obliged to broaden the kinds, until finally even the broadened kind has proved too narrow, owing to the appearance of new works of art, naturally followed by new scandals, new upsettings and—new broadenings.

> Benedetto Croce, "Criticism of the Theory of Artistic and Literary Kinds," *Modern Genre Theory*, trans. Douglas Ainslie, ed. David Duff (London and New York: Routledge, 2014), 27.

Nevertheless, genre resisted. It resisted first in the "New Criticism," which postulated that any text is a structure of meaning in which aesthetic form and discursive content are inseparable. In this perspective, genre is fundamental, as proven by the "heresy of paraphrase," to quote Cleanth Brooks—that is, the impossibility of the rendition in prose of a poetic work.[11]

> Roger Chartier, "Genre between Literature and History" (2006), 130.

By participating in a genre, the text marks itself as a made object that occupies a position—quite possibly a temporary position—rather than exemplifies a class. The performance of genre membership opens space for reflection on genres, on textuality, on words as written marks rather than frictionless highways, a readerly reflection that potentially overwrites the overt content of the text.

> Susan Wells, "Genres as Species and Spaces" (2014), 131–2.

Let us consider the most general concept of genre, from the minimal trait or predicate delineating it permanently through the modulations of its types and the regimens of its history: it rends and defends itself by mustering all its energy against a simple opposition that from nature and from history, as from nature and the vast lineage others (*technè, nomos, thesis,* then *spirit, society, freedom, history,* etc.). Between *physis* and its others, *genos* certainly locates one of the privileged scenes of the process and, no doubt, sheds the greatest obscurity on it. One need not mobilize etymology to this end and could just as well equate *genos* with birth, and birth in turn with the generous force of engenderment or generation—*physis*, in fact— as with race, familial membership, classificatory genealogy or class, age class (generation), or social class; it comes as no surprise that, in nature and art, genre, a concept that is essentially classificatory and genealogico-taxonomic, itself engenders so many classificatory vertigines when it goes about classifying itself and situating the classificatory principle or instrument within a set.

Jacques Derrida, "The Law of Genre" (1980), 60–1.

Rhetorical genres have always been understood as nested and seen as multiplying in response to the complexities of specific situations. Quintilian speculated that there might be any number of genres, although he opted for the canonic Aristotelian three. But literary genres were stable "kinds" of texts, determined either by their formal features, especially meter, or by the ethos of the writer: serious writers, for example, produce tragedies. For Greek and Latin antiquity, poetic genres were never indeterminate: each poem belonged to one and only one genre, whatever the complexities of actual poetic genre performances.

Susan Wells, "Genres as Species and Spaces" (2014), 116.

We are already alerted by the idea of what I am calling a genre that the members of it will emphasize, or discover, different or further features of the genre. I say the members are in argument with the genre, by which I mean that some feature or features of one member will quite inevitably seem at first not to fit with the features of others, hence that each is in argument over what defines the genre. (This is not true of all useful ideas of what constitutes a genre. Argument marks what I call genre-as-medium, which I contrast with the idea I call genre-as-cycle, which used to characterize Hollywood films under the titles of westerns, gangster films, musicals, women's films, screwball comedies, and which still characterize the episodic and serial continuities of character and situation essential to television sitcoms, detective and hospital soap operas, and so on.) In the case of

It Happened One Night, the earliest member of the genre of remarriage comedy I propose (1934), at least two features are clearly at variance with what we have derived or predicted from the members of the genre we have considered so far, *The Philadelphia Story* and *Adam's Rib*. First, and most obviously, the pair in *It Happened One Night* are not officially married until the final sequence, so this sequence cannot strictly speaking be understood as their remarriage, nor, it should follow, can the film as a whole be called a comedy of remarriage; second, remarriage comedies end in a place Shakespeare calls the green world, a place of spiritual perspective, a mythical Connecticut, hardly represented by an undistinguished motel.

Such "variances" require, according to the laws of genre-as-medium, compensations, or what amount to additional revelations of genre. [...]

> Stanley Cavell, "*It Happened One Night*," *Cities of Words: Pedagogical Letters on a Register of the Moral Life* (Cambridge: The Belknap Press of Harvard University Press, 2004), 150–1.

Law and counter-law form a coequal pair. A specific genre demands, at once, purity and impurity from each of its instances: each instance must be like the others and also different from them. If there were no impurity the genre would collapse into self-identity. If there were no purity the genre would cease to function.

> Jonathan Crimmins, "Gender, Genre, and the Near Future in Derrida's 'The Law of Genre'" (2009), 50.

But the whole enigma of genre springs perhaps most closely from within this limit between the two genres of genre which, neither separable nor inseparable, form an odd couple of one without the other in which each evenly serves the other a citation to appear in the figure of the other, simultaneously and indiscernibly saying "I" and "we," me the genre, we genres, without it being possible to think that the "I" is a species of the genre "we." For who would have us believe that we, we two, for example, would form a genre or belong to one?

> Jacques Derrida, "The Law of Genre" (1980), 56–7.

We could speak of adjacency, overlapping, sedimentation, nesting, embedding; of separation, isolation, invagination; of pocket genres and genre fields. In discussing genre change, we could consider such operations as assemblage, division, and budding. In such a context, we would not use genre membership to think about the text's offspring but about its partners in exchange.

> Susan Wells, "Genres as Species and Spaces" (2014), 115.

[... G]enres should not intermix. And if it should happen that they do intermix, by accident or through transgression, by mistake or through a lapse, then this should confirm, since, after all, we are speaking of "mixing," the essential purity of their identity. This purity belongs to the typical axiom: it is a law of the law of genre, whether or not the law is, as one feels justified in saying, "natural." This normative position and this evaluation are inscribed and prescribed even at the threshold of the "thing itself," if something of the genre "genre" can be so named.

Jacques Derrida, "The Law of Genre" (1980), 57.

It is clear that seeing genre as species has not done us much good.

Susan Wells, "Genres as Species and Spaces" (2014), 123.

I have often been asked why it is, or whether it is true, that remarriage comedies are no longer made, given my insistence on their preeminence among comedies in the opening two decades of the Hollywood talkie. I think it is true to say that there are many good films made that have remarriage elements in them (I'm grateful that people, strangers as well as friends, continue to let me know about certain of these films), but the genre can no longer be said to inspire a continuous series of such films, and in any case as a genre does not have the importance it once did in forming the concept of what a Hollywood film is—nothing like a genre-as-medium now plays such a role, but only something like a genre-as-cycle, such as the *Star Wars* series, or other sci-fi technological explorations such as *The Matrix* or *Men in Black*, which have much to recommend them, including philosophical interest, but nothing quite like the development of one soul's examination of another and a consequent contesting of social institutions, matters such as are featured in classical remarriage comedy. Such matters must seem like luxuries in the face of the question whether the human soul and society as such are to survive. (I do not take the case of *The Matrix* to show moral encounters between master and disciple since the master is not changed by encounters and the disciple is not enabled to live a better life in the world he had known. An understanding of its combination of religiosity with advanced technology requires a separate development of the ideas of perfectionism and of associated green and black worlds).

By films with remarriage elements in them I have in mind such films as *Moonstruck* (with Nicolas Cage and Cher), which emphasizes the incestuous intimacy underlying marital intimacy and relies on a talent for dialogue that is at once morally severe and intellectually inventive; and *Groundhog Day* (with Bill Murray and Andie MacDowell), which emphasizes the necessity of improvisation and repetition in achieving the mutuality or reality of marriage; and *Four Weddings and a Funeral* (with Andie MacDowell and Hugh Grant), which underscores the contempt for conventional marriage that nevertheless fails to still the desire for and the quest for marriage of another kind; and *Say Anything* (with John Cusack and Ione Skye), which elaborates the inevitable feature of classical remarriage comedy in which the pair become incomprehensible to (most of) the rest of the world, which may be taken as the essential moral risk perfectionism runs, since at the same time it fully recognizes the moral demand for making itself intelligible—but first, in the case of our couples, to each other.

Stanley Cavell, "*It Happened One Night*," *Cities of Words* (2004), 153.

Notes

1 Mikhail Bakhtin, "Epic and Novel," *The Dialogic Imagination: Four Essays*, trans. Caryl Emerson, ed. Michael Holquist (Austin: University of Texas Press, 1981), 3.
2 Arnold Hauser, "The Film Age," in *Film*, ed. Daniel Talbot (New York: Simon and Schuster, 1959), 74.
3 Erwin Panofsky, "Style and Medium in the Moving Pictures," in *Film*, 18.
4 Erwin Panofsky, "Style and Medium in the Moving Pictures," 24.
5 Erwin Panofsky, "Style and Medium in the Moving Pictures," 25.
6 Northrop Frye, *A Natural Perspetive* (New York: Columbia University Press, 1965); Tzvetan Todorov, *The Fantastic*, trans. Richard Howard (Ithaca: Cornell University Press, 1975).
7 See "Notes Toward a Tribute to Jacques Derrida" and "Feminism and Deconstruction."
8 I spell this out in "North by Northwest," reprinted in *Themes Out of School: Effects and Causes* (North Point Press: San Francisco, 1984), 152–72.
9 John G. Cawelti, *Adventures, Mystery, and Romance: Formula stories as Art and Popular Culture* (Chicago: The University of Chicago Press, 1976); Charles Rosen, *The Classical Style* (New York: Simon & Schuster, 1971).
10 *Morphologie du conte*, trans. Marguerite Derrida (Paris, 1970).
11 Cleanth Brooks, *The Well Wrought Urn: Studies in the Structure of Poetry* (New York: Harcourt, Brace, 1947).

Afterword: Trans-Ontology and the *Geschlecht* Complex

Emily Apter

> *A: Hey, I been meaning to ask you this:*
> *Are you a man or a woman?*
> *B: No, I'm not.*
> *A: Huh?*
> —URBAN DICTIONARY

THE LANGUAGE OF DIVERSITY AND GENDER DIFFERENCE, as it has developed and, so to speak, "diversified" in the American academy, constitutes a rich and volatile theoretical field and a particular flashpoint in the US where Trump's abusive, unconstitutional attacks on transgender communities, gays in the military, and women in politics and the media have served to reignite the culture wars. A simple question: "Are you a man or a woman?" can register as a traumatic blow to the psyche and soma of a subject who self-orientates outside gender binaries. In many situations today, "Are you a man or a woman?" is not an anodyne question. It can be a performative of social harming, a microaggression, an act of bullying or hate speech. It potentially transgresses the terms of sexual citizenship, social contract, non-coercive relation, sexual and racial self-sovereignty. It can threaten sexual freedom, itself understood in negative terms as *freedom from* heteronormative prescriptions and power imbalances resulting from the institutionalization of misogyny, sexism, homophobia, economic inequality, gender discrimination in the workplace. To answer the question "Are you a man or woman?" with "No, I'm not." can be taken as:

> I am neither man nor woman.
> I refuse the terms of the question.
> I am not born but become ...

"One is not born, but rather becomes a woman"
—Simone de Beauvoir, *The Second Sex*

"There is no gender from the start."
—Judith Butler, blogpost 2017[1]

"Sex is the stumbling block of sense. Sex becomes that which does not communicate itself, which marks the subject as unknowable."
—Joan Copjec, "Sex and the Euthanasia of Reason"

"As a gender variant visual artist I access 'technologies of gender' in order to amplify rather than erase the hermaphroditic traces of my body. *I name myself.*"
—Del LaGrace Volcano, cited in Beatriz Preciado, *Testo Junkie*

"I am genderfuck: a body that fucks with fucking."
—MacKenzie Wark

I am a unicorn, something that has a name but does not exist.
I am plassein, plasticity, a violence performed on substance.
I am the open call on how to call it.
I enlist the reserves of the neuter pronoun: Das, They, ze, hir, Mx ...
I am LGBTQI—across languages.
I am différance.
I am not, therefore I am.

My point here is that the phrase "No, I'm not," like Bartleby the Scrivener's "I would prefer not to," baffles the terms of the question and in doing so, points to the challenge—addressed in all the writings and essays included in this volume—of "saying difference" without committing the violence that inheres in category theory. How, the essays here implicitly ask, can sexual identities and ontologies be denominated without reproducing incumbent hierarchies of value or the effects of discrimination and exclusion? This question, along with the problem of translating designations for sexual preference and modes of existence, form part of what is at stake in *the Geschlecht complex*.

Geschlecht belongs to a nexus of associations familiar to German speakers, (especially those conversant with Fichte's *Addresses to the German Nation* or Heidegger's commentary on *Geschlecht*), that includes *genos, genus, gender, sex, race, kinship, lineage, stock, generation, community, species, human*. In the *Vocabulaire européen des philosophies: le dictionnaire des intraduisibles*, whose English edition I co-edited, *Geschlecht* is a select "Untranslatable" not because it has no equivalents in other languages but because it is a conceptual quilting point (Lacan's *point de capiton*), understood as an aporia or nub of conceptual opacity, as well as a historic site of what Barbara Cassin calls "philosophizing in languages." Cassin's ambition was to redo the history of philosophy through the lens of translation focusing on what happens to celebrated concepts and terms identified with distinct national cultures and languages. Examples included *Logos, Demos, Securitas, Vérité, Dasein, Monde, Sense, Praxis, Subject, Aufhebung, Pravda*. Not only did such terms have purchase on world philosophy, they were frequently subject to mistranslation, resistant to translation or simply *not translated*. A case in point, the British philosopher Jonathan Rée famously translated *Dasein* into English as *dasein*.

In my own work as a theorist of philosophical Untranslatables committed to unpacking some of the basic terms that underwrite discourses of security, gender violence, and self-defense, I have noted that terms like *Geschlecht*, in the shifting lexicography of sex and gender, register shifts of *Weltanshauung*, both small and tectonic. The translation test usually tells you something significant about what sex "is," and how its infrapolitics and choreographies register (or fail to) in cross-cultural contexts. Consider the term "gender," rendered as "genre" in Romance languages. "Genre" in English denotes first and foremost a category or canon of art, music and literature; a style or aesthetic manner. This sense of the word interfered with the translation of Judith Butler's landmark *Gender Trouble*, first published in 1990. The book's 2005 French translation *Trouble dans le genre*, literally "trouble in genre," prompts the question: "What genre are you? In English this sounds wrong, but in fact it may be the right question to ask because it articulates a symptomatic naming trouble that speaks very much to the larger problem of gender's untranslatability."[2] Unlike "gender," or the American idea of "gender identity," "genre" brings out the connection to the root *genos* (sex, kind, species-being), foregrounded in the German *Geschlecht*, which encompasses the meanings of sex, gender, kin, human, species, human, or people. Ironically, as *Geschlecht* is edged out in Germany in favor of "gender" (as in "Genderstudieren" in the place of "Geschlechtstudieren"), critics outside of Germany are increasingly turning to *Geschlecht* as a term that better navigates *sexus* and *genus* (the former inclusive of grammatical genders that do not coincide with sex [as in *das Mädchen*], the latter inclusive of inanimate things classifiable according to kind but not sex). *Geschlecht*, as I will argue in more detail, is particularly well-suited to contemporary debates over the intersectional regionalism of categories like "human," "animal," "living thing," "species," "kind," or "kinship." It also challenges the sex/gender divide as it has been politically manipulated in the American courts. Former Attorney General Jeff Sessions, we recall, ordered the Justice department to take the position that transgender people are no longer protected by civil rights laws against workplace discrimination based on sex. His reasoning: "The word 'sex' means biologically male or female so the Civil Rights act does not ban discrimination based on gender identity per se, including transgender status." Here "sex" was split off from "gender" with the express aim of legalizing gender discrimination, something that could not have happened with the word *Geschlecht*. In Canada, by contrast, the cause of gender justice and sexual civil rights motivated passage of bill C-279 in 2012, that equates *mis*gendering, such as calling someone by a pronoun they expressly reject, with discrimination and hate crimes.

In what's been billed as "the Epicene" era of common pronouns—Facebook currently registers a menu of seventy-one self-identifying options ranging across "agender," "cisgender," "genderqueer," "fluid," "Neutrois," "Trans"[3]—the process of naming, claiming and translating sex and gender has become constitutive of the public sphere.[4] Germany recently saw the controversial introduction of *Gendersternchen*—*Sternschen* meaning star or asterisk—where the star signals nonbinarism.[5] This orthography produces gender-neutral personal and professional designations like *Freund*in* (friend or partner) or *Mülllader*in* (garbage collector). The asterisk is commonly used as shorthand for repeated items or sets of possible variants, so one could also say it functions like an abbreviation for English indefinite pronouns: one, someone, anyone; singular "They" (in place of he/she), newly minted personal nominatives like *hir*, *ze*, *Mx*, and *thon*, or French endeavors to de-genderize grammar through postbinary pronouns or dropped accords:

Cissexisme
Ol/es est lo
"Je sol a demandé"
Lae, se, leur
Elle est courageuse becomes os est courageuil (end with il)
Ille/iel/lae/aël

Gendersternchen, in this lexicographically plastic frame, arguably refers to *all ways of calling gender* or any kind of sexed being. French philosopher Jean-Luc Nancy devised his own grammatical construction in this spirit when he coined the term *sexistence* (sexistence), for the metaphysics of sex, for a sexual ontology that conjugates itself in the verb "to sexist": *s'exister: je s'existe, tu s'existes, il/elle s'existe.*

Geschlecht might well be the most difficult Untranslatable in the German language by virtue of the sheer volume of meanings embedded in its philology. Here we will borrow David Krell's synthetic definition, matching historical semantics and salient ideas:

Geschlecht: noun, neuter, deriving from the Old High German *gislahti*, from which the English words slay and slaughter are formed. [...] The prefix *gi-*, today *Ge-*, refers to a collectivity, and means "all things involving or surrounding the root in question." The root of *Geschlecht*, that is, *slahti*, derives from early forms of the verb *schlagen*, "to beat," "strike," "smite," "stamp," "coin," but also to "play a stringed instrument," "strike up a tune," or, if the musician is a blackbird, "warble." The oldest sense of *Geschlecht*, according to Hermann Paul's *Deutsches Wörterbuch*, is equivalent to the Latin word *genus*, that is, a group of persons who share a common ancestry, especially if that group or family belongs to the Patrician class. *Schlagen* in this case means as much as "to cause to resemble," or "to imprint or coin," with particular reference to the passing on of family likenesses. Such a family might also expand to form a clan, tribe, or class. The Grimm Brothers emphasize that the blood relations and the clan ties of a *Geschlecht* found the state. *Geschlecht* and even *Schlag* might also indicate a species of animal, more properly designated by the German *Gattung*, or even a particular herd of animals, say, of magnificent horses. Furthermore, the community of persons may expand to include all of humanity, das *Menschengeschlecht*, "the human race." It later comes to mean the entire assemblage of human beings who are alive for an identical period or era, a "generation." At the same time, it refers to the genus *masculinum* and genus *femininum*, the two genders that, one might speculate, are somehow already implicated in all the other meanings. Thus the "sexual" sense of *Geschlecht* is as archaic as all the others, such that the word serves as the root for an entire series of words involving sexuality and reproduction: *Geschlechtglied, -teil,* or *-organ*, the genitalia; *Geschlechtlichkeit*, the erotic and the sexual in general; *Geschlechtstrieb*, the sex drive; *Geschlechtsverkehr*, sexual congress or intercourse, and so on. Finally, the "natural" *Geschlechter*, male and female, masculine and feminine, come to be applied to matters grammatical, namely, the masculine, feminine, and neuter genders of nouns and pronouns. The neuter gender poses a special problem to be sure, and it is referred to in various ways, early on as das *unbenahmte Geschlecht*, the "undeclared" or "unnamed" gender, *or das sächliche Geschlecht*, the gender having to do with "things" or "states of affairs," and later simply as *geschlechtlos*, "genderless." When, late in the history of this word, Heidegger notes that *das Dasein*, a neuter noun, is *geschlechtlos*, he may merely be following the guidelines of grammar. Or he may be thinking something else, something more archaic than grammar; it is difficult to say.[6]

Krell's emphasis on *Schlag*, following Derrida's dilation on Heidegger's *rechte Schlag* [righteous strike] in *Geschlecht* III, *sexe, race, nation, humanité*, testifies to the widening gyre of the Derridean *Geschlecht* complex, which spans his early essay on *différance*, the magisterial *Glas, The Politics of Friendship* and *Of Spirit: Heidegger and the Question*. In *Geschlecht* III Derrida glosses the verb "*verschlagen*" as: "at once separated, divided, compartmentalized (*cloisonnée*) and run aground (*échouée*)." These associations resonate in *différance* and *dissemination*, the Derridean keywords that register the high impact of Heideggerian *Zerstreuung*, interpolated as a strike of malediction, a rending dissension, the fatal installation of the two in the dual sexes.

In his dissection of Heidegger's reading (in *Die Sprache im Gedicht*) of Georg Trakl's poetry (particularly "Heiterer Frühling" [Spring Light], "Verklärung" [Transfiguration] and "Grodek"), the shattering force of *Schlag* embarks Being on a journey to recuperate a sexuality that may have existed prior to the agonistic, oppositional one. Derrida employs a French neologism—*désêtre*, "to unbe," for Trakl's *das Ungeborene*. Here is the relevant passage from Trakl's searing war poem "Grodek":

> *Alle Straßen münden in schwarze Verwesung.*
> *Unter goldnem Gezweig der Nacht und Sternen*
> *Es schwankt der Schwester Schatten durch den schweigenden Hain,*
> *Zu grüßen die Geister der Helden, die blutenden Häupter;*
> *Und leise tönen im Rohr die dunklen Flöten des Herbstes.*
> *O stolzere Trauer! ihr ehernen Altäre,*
> *Die heiße Flamme des Geistes nährt heute ein gewaltiger Schmerz,*
> *Die ungebornen Enkel.*
>
> All roads end in black decay
> The sister's shadow sways through the silent grove
> To greet the ghosts of heroes, the bleeding heads;
> And the dark flutes of autumn play quietly in the reeds.
> O prouder grief! You brazen altars
> Today the hot flame of the spirit is fed by a violent pain,
> The grandchildren—unborn.
>
> (trans. Christian Hawkey)

The sexual expectancy harbored in *das Ungeborene* would seem here to rejoin the prequel of undivided sex; an unexported generativity [*l'ingénéré*]. This "ingenerate sex sprung from *Geschlecht's* monstrous essence" ("le sexe ingénéré *des verwesenden Geschlecht*"[7]) arguably sets the terms for Nancy's "trans-ontology," which is in fact a "transitology," a permanent condition of transitioning which is a general ontology of the trans:

> on en vient à penser à une "*trans-ontologie*" voire à une transitologie, voire encore à aucune "*logie*" et à une espèce de *transe* générale, générique et génésique de "*etre*"

This genericity of the trans, spun out of *Geschlecht*, brings us, as well, to the problem of transgenre understood as a question of what it means "to be" in genera (human, animal, living order of nature).[8]

And this in turn brings us back to *Geschlecht*'s etymological history as a byword of kin and kind. In the *Dictionary of Untranslatables*, Marc Crépon foregrounds several distinct strands of reference: paternal or maternal lineage; the larger community or collection of individuals belonging to the same generation; sex in general (*das Männliche Geschlecht*), each sex in particular (*das weibliche Geschlecht*); and genus: both the genera of natural history and the category theory by which we typologize. Homing in on Kant's *Anthropology from a Pragmatic Point of View*, Crépon identifies race as the class "of a genus whose unity of origin remains intact," even if it is headed for sublation within broader constructions of a unified species or human differentiation. Kant's *Anthropology* is based on the assumption, still prevalent, that sexual difference (predicated on biological difference and sexual reproduction) is the guarantor of kinship, bloodlines, family trees, clans, tribes, and genealogies. But such assumptions are challenged now by what Judith Butler calls "kinship trouble," which puts kinship at odds with biological inheritance and genealogies of the genus.[9] Butler stresses that the English language fails to allow for distinctions drawn in French between *parenté* (referring to the child/parent relation, familial transmission, and property inheritance), and *filiation* (referring to blood ties or familial relations not necessarily based on conjugality). For French feminism of the 1970s, she argues, such distinctions paved the way to realizing forms of relation that were binding but not reducible to family. Butler wants to expand the ethics of kinship beyond familial norms of dependency, inheritance, and procreation, situating them instead within a realm of affinate relations, including friendship, political solidarities, and cross-species alliance. Mel Chen's notion of "animacies" adds impetus to this "kinship trouble" by projecting a nonhierarchical plane on which liveness, sentience, humanness, animality, vegetality, insectitude, and affect are coordinates.[10] These variegated orders of animacy, cutting across animal/human, inanimate/nonhuman divides make of *Geschlecht* a rubric for the difference of differences. Kinship, in this scheme, becomes a way of referring to what Nayland Blake calls "crossing objects" ("fursonas"); transitional, mutational, and transgenic.

The trans-ontology of sexual ontology implies new ways of thinking and orienting corporeality and here I would push back somewhat against Jean-Luc Nancy's rather categorical statement that "the ontological body has not yet been thought."[11] It may not have been thought or formally philosophized as such, but in a host of aesthetic practices, past and present, trans-ontologies and their bodies appear. They appear in gay, queer, and trans writing, music, art, and theory; in the way in which, for example, Kathy Acker's oeuvre forged a biography of pluri-selves transiting in volatile states between genders and sexes (as McKenzie Wark notes in a book on Acker: "there's no coherent subject, just flocks and fleets of selves that flee into sex and books").[12] They appear in the contemporary work of the Canadian artist and trans activist Cassils.[13] In *Becoming an Image*, Cassils uses their highly trained, sculpted body to battle with clay, to engage in combat with matter that both receives and obstructs human embodiment. The effect is manifold, a blurring of human agency and material resistance, a debinarization of active and passive, a staging of the encounter between a heroically singular, degendered body and formless matter. Performed in darkness, punctuated by heaves, moans, and effortful breaths, *Becoming an Image* is only fleetingly perceptible, affording flash apparitions (through the effect of a strobe light) of being as sexed becoming, or as the case may be for some viewers, of being as violent unbecoming:

> We watched—if one can call it that—the clay topple and crash to the ground only to be mounted and further assailed by the increasingly exhausted artist. [...] The lights came on and the artist and photographer were gone. What was left of the beaten body of clay lay exposed on the gym floor, mangled and molded into a sculptural sign of the assault it had undergone.[14]

Becoming an Image invites us to interrogate more fully one of the central aspects of the *Geschlecht* complex: Is there an emancipation of "to be" in the apparition of matter's generic subject-being? In Cassils' performance of the subsumption of sexual difference by matter (a Trans-sumption); in the violence acted out on gendered being we discern a creative destruction that leads to the re-regioning of differences.

Heidegger would use *die Gegend* (the "region that regions") to refer to the meaning of being in relation to the regional disciplines, or regional ontologies corresponding to a particular science or discipline: mathematics, physics, biology, theology, and so forth. But more significantly, *die Gegend* is the premier term selected to translate *chora*, to refer to "surrounding world" (*die umgebende Umgegend*), the gathering up of experience, the space in front (future) rather than against, the open clearing or countryside,[15] "the passage required in order to leave the terrain of representative thinking to which, according to Heidegger, Husserl's thinking about the transcendental horizon still belonged."[16] It connotes a process of placement and orientation—a "whithering" of being (in the sense of "whither to?")—concentrated in Derrida's use of *vers* [towards]. Nancy underscores the aleatory in ontological sexual orientation when he qualifies Heidegger's multidirectional, "transitive sense" of the "is" as "what moves being along, what traverses it and transports it, what ravishes it and what is ravished [...]."[17] Continuing in this vein, rendering *die Gegend* in English as "regioning," and affiliating it with the notion of unchained individuation, adds a specific emphasis to the definition of sexual ontology. Regioning navigates cognitive and ontological orders of sexed *différance*, emotion and affect, singular identity and transindividuation.[18] It might even bring us to the "effractive substance" where the "ça" of sex comes into the world, identified by Nancy as "*sexistence*." Taking on Lacan, specifically the famous formula "*Il n'y a pas de rapport sexuel*" [There is no sexual relation], Nancy posits a "there is" of sexual relation in the ontology of relation. This is to suggest that a happening of being occurs in the act of sex, some kind *of sexistence* that distinguishes beings without itself being or naming *Dasein*.[19] For Nancy, the oldest sense of "relation" (*rapport* as report, as naming things or qualities), opens up the question of how sex is accounted for and named in juridical discourses of intimate or sexual relations. But at the same time, "the sexual" of relation cannot be predicated because it is neither discrete substance nor thing. "The sexual [writes Nancy] is its own difference, or its own distinction. Being distinguished as sex or as sexed is what makes sex or sexed-ness." He then propounds further, moving into the territory of *Geschlecht*, with its vocabulary of species, sexes, and kind, that:

> For every living sexual being and in all regards, sex is the being's differing from itself, differing understood as differentiating itself according to multiple measures and according to all those tangled processes that go by the names *masculine/feminine, homo/hetero, active/passive*, and so on, and differing understood as the species multiplying indefinitely the singularities of its "representatives." That is to say, there is no difference of the sexes, but there is, first and always, sex differing and deferring itself.[20]

Nancy's concept of the "sexual" as "its own difference" may be difficult to grasp, but as a formula it not only subverts the Lacanian proposition that there exists "only one sexuality" (by demasculinizing sexual positions and the phallic coding of the symbolic), it also mobilizes all the stations of the fuck (licking, poking, sucking, coming).

In Nancy's book *Coming [La Jouissance]*, grammar does the grunt work: gerundives and present participles most particularly. Who and what is doing what to whom or what is being done to what are fully in play, scissiparity reigns. As McKenzie Wark maintains: "A body that fucks with fucking can be a body that fucks with gender and a writer embodied as fucking with gender can be a writer who fucks with genre, that most nucleated family of forms." Trans-ontology—which becomes thinkable within the project of the *Geschlecht* complex—points to a genre that "fucks with" the family of nucleated forms, starting with the repertory of possessive pronouns. When Wark writes (with reference to their relationship with Acker), "This body I called mine fucked myself with her dick," we discern an exercise in the rearrangement of possessive objects and ethical self-dispossession. Wark achieves something novel and significant, which is, namely, "to shock the body out of its concept."[21]

Trans-ontology, as I see it, remains alive to gendered violence, to the violence instantiated by the mark or brand of sexual difference. It channels species differentiation and gestures towards an ontology of the sexual that, in Alenka Zupancic's Lacanian terms, locates the "being" of sex in a compound sexual drive, composed of different partial drives, such as "looking, touching, sucking," actions that, as it were, re-denaturalize the "artificial naturalization of the originally denatured drives."[22] This primordial "state of the drives" resembles infantile sexuality, polymorphously perverse and not subject to the regime of the couple or the law of heteronormative sexual difference. For Shanna Carlson, this *Ursex*, a kind of *sex in common* that figures "the impasses of sexual difference," is precisely what is named by the category of "transgender."[23]

While it remains important politically to represent and protect subcultures and kinship alliances based on shared sexual practices or modes of intimate relationality, I would contend that the trans in trans-ontology exceeds categories of gender. Retaining a vital connection to ongoing struggles for recognition within identity politics, the trans is a kind of operator: the name for proliferating *Geschlecht*-effects that navigate species-being, kinship, sexual ontology (sex as an act of differing and deferring, of "relating oneself"), and practices of sexual identification that foreground the issue of nonbinary naming. Which is to say, the right to be "They" or some other variant of gender pronoun, or the obligation to answer "I'm not" to the question "Are you a man or a woman?"[24]

Notes

1 "To say gender is performative is to say that nobody really is a gender from the start. Bullying tries to keep us in our gendered place, it is important to resist the violence that is imposed by ideal gender norms, especially against those who are gender different or non-conforming in their gender presentation." Judith Butler (2017), relativesociology.blogspot.com/2017/02/judith-butler-talks-gender.html.

2 The German title of Butler's *Gender Trouble*, *Das Unbehagen der Geschlechter* distracts from "gender" through the use of the unsettling word "das Unbehagen" for trouble. Referring to states of unease, anxiety, psychic unsettledness, or the ill-fitting subject, it was marked by Freud in the title of *Civilization and its Discontents* [*Das Unbehagen in der Kultur*]. Lacan and Slavoj Žižek (among many others) have since appropriated and theoretically glossed it. The word's use in the German title is potentially misleading. Rendered literally as "the discomfort of the sexes," it suggests that the sexes are discomfited in themselves (by their nonheteronormativity, their dysphoria) rather than serving as agents that actively *make trouble* for gender categories.

3 On the prehistory of gender-neutral pronoun invention, see Dennis Baron, "The Epicene Pronouns: A Chronology of the Word that Failed," *American Speech*, vol. 56 no.2 (1981), https://doi.org/10.2307/455007

4 How the politicization of gender-naming works is, of course, language- and culture-specific. Austronesian East Asian, Quetchuan, and Uralic languages, for example, have no gender distinctions in personal pronouns.

5   It is worth noting there is strong resistance to adopting any usage for nonbinary gender in Germany. A recent poll estimated that close to 80 percent opposed statutory provisions for language neutralization, including those for names of professions and jobs. See Heike Schmoll's article on the *"ungeliebter sternschen"* [the "unloved star"] and the rejection of gender in Germany. *Frankfurter Allgemeine*, April 4, 2019. https://edition.faz.net/faz-edition/politik/2019-04 02/6dbc5478037bc37f1f63860a9e9a70d6/?GEPC=s9.
6   David Farrell Krell, *Phantoms of the Other: Four Generations of Derrida's Geschlecht"* (Albany: State University of New York Press, 2015), 1–2.
7   Jacques Derrida, *Geschlecht* III: *Sexe, race, nation, humanité*, ed. Geoffrey Bennington, Katie Chenoweth, and Rodrigo Therezo (Paris: Seuils, 2018), 92.
8   Foucault's course on "La Sexualité" (at the University of Clermont-Ferrand in 1964) and his course devoted to "Discourse on Sexuality" given at Vincennes in 1969 presciently challenge the binarism of sexuality's basic terms, underscoring that "male" and "female" are metaphors. This metaphoric status is particularly evident when applied to the sex of plants: "Notions of male and female are used metaphorically (the stronger plants called male). But the problem is to figure out why there is metaphor; or why, on the basis of this metaphoric usage, nobody arrived at more precise determination of the sexes. [...] One could say there is a dearth of concepts for life functions. Sexuality is the form taken by proliferating growth in living species. [...] The conjunction male–female is nothing but a supplement superimposed on the intangible virginity of nature." Michel Foucault, "Le discours de la sexualité," Course given at Vincennes (1969), 166, 169.
9   For Joan Copjec, psychoanalysis introduces what might be called "inheritance trouble," even if this is not her expression. Taking issue with the historicism of gender theory (in "The Inheritance of Potentiality: An Interview with Joan Copjec"), she insists that "What we inherit through the id, or as *jouissance*, is not something we have conscious access to and it does not mold us; we have to mold or express it. In his *Encore* seminar, Lacan seems to be recasting Freud's argument in different terms when he defines *jouissance* as a kind of inheritance we can use, but not use up; something that can never be titled to us. By this he means that *jouissance* is not like property (or a property of an individual), but like common property in the Communist sense. It is not ours alone even if it is the most intimate part of who we are. What every individual inherits is not an identity or identifying property, but a potentiality, a capacity, which does not prescribe in advance what it is a potential for."
10 Mel Y. Chen, *Animacies: Biopolitics, Racial Mattering, and Queer Affect* (Durham: Duke University Press, 2012).
11 Jean-Luc Nancy, *Corpus* (Paris: Editions Métailié, 2006), 17.
12 McKenzie Wark, *Philosophy for Spiders: On the Low Theory of Kathy Acker* (Durham: Duke University Press, 2020).
13 Emma Bianchi, "Becoming Mythological: Barthes with Butler and Aristotle," presented at NYU Comparative Literature Graduate Colloquium, November 2012.

14 Review of trans artist Cassils' *Becoming an Image,* passengerart.com/2013/03/20/the-agony-and-the-ecstasy-of-becoming-and-image/.
15 Thomas Sheehan, "Did Heidegger Ever Finish *Being and Time?*," in *Division III of Heidegger's* Being and Time: *The Unanswered Question of Being,* ed. Lee Braver (Cambridge: MIT Press, 2015), 275.
16 Maria Villela-Petit, "Heidegger's Conception of Space," in *Critical Heidegger,* ed. Christopher Macan (New York: Routledge, 1996), 149.
17 Nancy, *Corpus* II: *Writings on Sexuality,* trans. Anne O'Byrne (New York: Fordham University Press, 2013), 2.
18 In adopting Krell's term "region," in assigning it special (neologistic) usage as a verb, I am assigning resonant meanings to the term that Krell himself might disavow or judge to be over-extended. Certainly his use of the term is thought-provoking and bridges different conceptual contexts. In *Phantoms of the Other,* for example, we discover a "region of disclosedness" associated with the encounter with *Das Nichts,* a space of Heideggerian anxiety: "in anxiety, nothing at all threatens us, even as it—the nothing—grows near; no source of comfort or assuredness prevails in that nearness. *Das Nichts* encroaches precisely because it comes from nowhere and has nowhere else to go. The region of disclosedness that opens up in anxiety offers no solace: it is no spark of divine light, no cogito, and no transcendental unity of apperception. Rather, anxiety "is already 'there' ['*da*']—and yet nowhere; [...]." In his chapter on *Geschlecht* I, Krell again has recourse to "region" in relation to the "exemplary being for the existential analysis of *Being and Time.*" Noting that the "*Da-* of *Dasein* does not manifest sexual difference," he argues that such a difference "along with all the adventures, joys, and calamities that accompany it, Heidegger would presumably relegate to some regional ontology or to one or other constellation of the 'sciences of man,' to biology or anthropology, sociology or psychology, or perhaps even religion." Here, "region" lines up with ontologies defined by specific disciplines. This is a far cry from the earlier usage—associated with "nothing" and with anxiety. But there is a symptom at hand, in the recurrence of the word. One which suggests that to think in terms of regionalized ontology in relation to gender differences, might produce fresh approaches to epigenetic accounts of sexual difference or new ontologies of pronomial gender difference, at once unyielding to categories (in their status as "existentials"), yet recognizant of the marking of sex. See Krell, *Phantoms of the Other,* 14, 20–1.
19 Nancy, *Corpus* II, 6–8.
20 Jean-Luc Nancy, *Corpus* II, 9–11.
21 Wark, *Philosophy for Spiders,* 24.
22 Alenka Zupancic, *What IS Sex?* (Cambridge: MIT Press, 2017), 9.
23 Shanna T. Carlson, "Transgender Subjectivity and the Logic of Sexual Difference," *differences,* vol. 21 no. 2 (2010), https://doi.org/10.1215/10407391-2010-003.
24 Nancy, *Corpus* II, 11.

BIBLIOGRAPHY

I. Contending with Untranslatable Categories; or, Inducing the Nervous Condition of the *Geschlecht* Complex
OSCAR JANSSON AND DAVID LAROCCA

Appadurai, Arjun, *Modernity at Large: Cultural Dimensions of Globalization* (Minneapolis: University of Minnesota Press, 1996).

Apter, Emily, *Against World Literature: A Politics of Untranslatability* (New York: Verso, 2013).

Apter, Emily, "Lexilalia: On Translating a Dictionary of Untranslatable Philosophical Terms," *Paragraph*, vol. 48, no. 5 (2015).

Badiou, Alain, *Being and Event*, trans. Oliver Feltham (New York: Continuum, 2005).

Badiou, Alain, "French," in *Dictonary of Untranslatables: A Philosophical Lexicon*, ed. Barbara Cassin, trans. eds. Emily Apter, Jacques Lezra, and Michael Wood (Princeton: Princeton University Press, 2014).

Badiou, Alain, *Logics of Worlds: Being and Event II*, trans. Alberto Toscano (New York: Bloomsbury Academic, 2019).

Baer, Benjamin Conisbee, *Indigenous Vanguards: Education, National Liberation, and the Limits of Modernism* (New York: Columbia University Press, 2019).

Beecroft, Alexander, *An Ecology of World Literature: From Antiquity to the Present Day* (New York: Verso, 2015).

Borgmann, Dimitri, *Language on Vacation: an Olio of Orthographical Oddities* (New York: Charles Scribner's Sons, 1965).

Burke, Kenneth, *The Rhetoric of Religion: Studies in Logology* (Berkeley and Los Angeles: University of California Press, 1970).

Casanova, Pascale, *The World Republic of Letters*, trans. M. D. De Bevoise (Cambridge: Harvard University Press, 2004).

Cassin, Barbara, *L'Effet sophistique* (Paris: Gallimard, 1995).

Cassin, Barbara, ed., *Vocabulaire européen des philosophies: le dictionnaire des intraduisibles* (Paris: Seuil, 2004).

Cassin, Barbara, "Philosophizing in Languages," *Nottingham French Studies*, vol. 49, no. 2 (June 2010).

Cassin, Barbara, *Jacques le Sophiste: Lacan, Logos et Psychanalyse* (Paris: EPel, 2012).

Cassin, Barbara, "Introduction," in *Dictionary of Untranslatables: A Philosophical Lexicon*, ed. Barbara Cassin, trans. eds. Emily Apter, Jacques Lezra and Michael Wood (Princeton: Princeton University Press, 2014).

Cassin, Barbara, *Sophistical Practice: Toward a Consistent Relativism* (New York: Fordham University Press, 2014).

Cassin, Barbara and Charles T. Wolfe, "Who's Afraid of the Sophists? Against Ethical Correctness," *Hypatia*, vol. 15, no. 4 (Autumn 2000).

Chenoweth, Katie, "*Faute de frappe*: Derrida's Typos," *Research in Phenomenology*, vol. 51 (2021).

Cole, Thomas R., ed., *Medical Humanities: An Introduction* (Cambridge: Cambridge University Press, 2014).

Coxon, A. H., *The Fragments of Parmenides: A Critical Text with Introduction and Translation, The Ancient Testimonia and a Commentary*, revised edition (Las Vegas: Parmenides Publishing, 2009).

Crary, Alice and Joel De Lara, "Who's Afraid of Ordinary Language Philosophy? A Plea for Reviving a Wrongly Reviled Philosophical Tradition," *Graduate Faculty Philosophy Journal*, vol. 39, no. 2 (2019).

Cremin, Ciara, *The Future is Feminine: Capitalism and the Masculine Disorder* (New York: Bloomsbury, 2021).

Crépon, Marc, "*Geschlecht*," in *Dictionary of Untranslatables: A Philosophical Lexicon*, ed. Barbara Cassin, trans. eds. Emily Apter, Jacques Lezra, and Michael Wood (Princeton: Princeton University Press, 2014).

Dauber, Kenneth and K. L. Evans, "Revisiting Ordinary Language Criticism," in *Inheriting Stanley Cavell: Memories, Dreams, Reflections*, ed. David LaRocca (New York: Bloomsbury, 2020).

Derrida, Jacques, "The Law of Genre," trans. Avital Ronell, *Critical Inquiry*, vol. 7, no. 1 (Autumn 1980).

Derrida, Jacques, "*Geschlecht* I: Sexual Difference, Ontological Difference," trans. Ruben Bevezdivin and Elizabeth Rottenberg, in *Research in Phenomenology*, vol. 13 (1983). Reprinted in *Psyche: Inventions of the Other*, vol. II, eds. Peggy Kamuf and Elizabeth Rottenberg (Stanford: Stanford University Press, 2008).

Derrida, Jacques, "Racism's Last Word," trans. Peggy Kamuf, *Critical Inquiry*, vol. 12, no. 1 (1985).

Derrida, Jacques, "*Geschlecht* II: Heidegger's Hand," trans. John P. Leavey, Jr., in *Deconstruction and Philosophy: The Texts of Jacques Derrida*, ed. John Sallis (Chicago: The University of Chicago Press, 1987).

Derrida, Jacques, *Geschlecht III: Sex, race, nation, humanity* (Paris: Seuils, 2018).

Dolan, Brian, ed., *Humanitas: Readings in the Development of the Medical Humanities* (San Francisco: University of California Medical Humanities Press, 2015).

Halberstam, Jack, *Trans* A Quick and Quirky Account of Gender Variability* (Oakland: University of California Press, 2018).

Jakobson, Roman, "On Linguistic Aspects of Translation," in *On Translation*, ed. Reuben A. Brower (Cambridge: Harvard University Press, 1959).

Klevan, Andrew, "Ordinary Language Film Studies," *Aesthetic Investigations*, vol. 3, no. 2 (2021).

Krell, David Farrell, *Phantoms of the Other: Four Generations of Derrida's Geschlecht* (Albany: State University of New York, 2015).

LaRocca, David, "The Limits of Instruction: Pedagogical Remarks on Lars von Trier's *The Five Obstructions*," *Film and Philosophy*, vol. 13 (2009).
LaRocca, David, "Teaching without Explication: Pedagogical Lessons from Rancière's *The Ignorant Schoolmaster* in *The Grand Budapest Hotel* and *The Emperor's Club*," *Journalism, Media and Cultural Studies*, vol. 10 (2016).
LaRocca, David, "SCT: Summer Camps for Theorists," in *In Theory: The Newsletter of the School of Criticism and Theory*, Cornell University (Winter 2017).
LaRocca, David and Ricardo Miguel-Alfonso, eds., *A Power to Translate the World: New Essays on Emerson and International Culture* (Hanover: Dartmouth College Press, 2015).
Laugier, Sandra, *Why We Need Ordinary Language Philosophy*, trans. Daniela Ginsburg (Chicago: The University of Chicago Press, 2013).
Malabou, Catherine, *What Should We Do With Our Brain?*, trans. Sebastian Rand (New York: Fordham University Press, 2008).
Malabou, Catherine, *Changing Difference: The Feminine and the Question of Philosophy*, trans. Carolyn Shread (Cambridge: Polity Press, 2011).
Mandelbaum, David G., ed., *Selected Writings of Edward Sapir on Language, Culture and Personality* (Berkeley: University of California Press, 1963).
McKeane, John, "Universalism and the (un)translatable," *Translation Studies*, vol. 12, no. 1 (2019).
Moretti, Franco, *Modern Epic: The World System from Goethe to García Marquez*, trans. Quintin Hoare (New York: Verso, 1996).
Novalis, "Logological Fragments I," *Novalis: Philosophical Writings*, trans. Margaret Mahony Stoljar (Albany: State University of New York Press, 1997).
Reinhard, Kenneth, "Badiou's Sublime Translation of the *Republic*," in Alain Badious, *Plato's Republic*, trans. Susan Spitzer (Cambridge: Polity, 2012).
Ricœur, Paul, *On Translation*, trans. Eileen Brennan (New York: Routledge, 2007).
Venuti, Lawrence, *The Translator's Invisibility: A History of Translation* (New York: Routledge, 2004).

II. Antitheatricality as Critical Idiom
CARO PIRRI

"Anti-, Prefix1," *OED Online* (Oxford University Press), n.d., http://www.oed.com/view/Entry/8501.
Artaud, Antonin, *The Theater and Its Double*, trans. Mary Caroline Richards (New York: Grove Press, 1958).
Bailes, Sara Jane, *Performance Theatre and the Poetics of Failure*, first edition (New York: Routledge, 2010).
Barish, Jonas A., *The Antitheatrical Prejudice*, first edition (Berkeley: University of California Press, 1981).
Berger, Jr., Harry, *Imaginary Audition: Shakespeare on Stage and Page* (Berkeley: University of California Press, 1990).
Crane, Mary Thomas, "Optics," in *Early Modern Theatricality*, ed. Henry S. Turner, Oxford 21st Century Approaches to Literature (Oxford: Oxford University Press, 2013).

Crépon, Marc, "*Geschlecht*," in *Dictionary of Untranslatables: A Philosophical Lexicon*, ed. Barbara Cassin, trans. eds. Emily Apter, Jacques Lezra, and Michael Wood (Princeton: Princeton University Press, 2014).

Derrida, Jacques, "*Geschlecht* I: Sexual Difference, Ontological Difference," *Research in Phenomenology*, vol. 13 (1983).

Doyle, Richard, *On Beyond Living: Rhetorical Transformations of the Life Sciences* (Stanford: Stanford University Press, 1997).

Eck, Caroline Van and Stijn Bussels, "The Visual Arts and the Theatre in Early Modern Europe," *Art History*, vol. 33, no. 2 (April 1, 2010). https://doi.org/10.1111/j.1467-8365.2010.00738.x.

Eggert, Katherine, *Disknowledge: Literature, Alchemy, and the End of Humanism in Renaissance England* (Philadelphia: University of Pennsylvania Press, 2015).

Féral, Josette, "Foreword," *SubStance*, vol. 31, no. 2 (2002). https://doi.org/10.1353/sub.2002.0025.

Féral, Josette and Ronald P. Bermingham, "Theatricality: The Specificity of Theatrical Language," *SubStance*, vol. 31, no. 2 (2002). https://doi.org/10.1353/sub.2002.0026.

Frow, John, *Genre*, first edition (London and New York: Routledge, 2005).

Gosson, Stephen, 1554–1624. *The Schoole of Abuse Conteining a Plesaunt Inuectiue Against Poets, Pipers, Plaiers, Iesters, and such Like Caterpillers of a Co[m]Monwelth; Setting Vp the Hagge of Defiance to their Mischieuous Exercise, [and] Ouerthrowing their Bulwarkes, by Prophane Writers, Naturall Reason, and Common Experience: A Discourse as Pleasaunt for Gentlemen that Fauour Learning, as Profitable for all that Wyll Follow Virtue. by Stephan Gosson. Stud. Oxon London, for Thomas Woodcocke, 1579.* http://pitt.idm.oclc.org/login?url=https://www-proquest-com.pitt.idm.oclc.org/books/schoole-abuse-conteining-plesaunt-sic-inuectiue/docview/2264173271/se-2?accountid=14709.

Gosson, Stephen, *The Schoole of Abuse Contayning a Pleasaunt Inuectiue against Poets, Pipers, Players, Iesters, and Such like Caterpillers of a Common Wealth; Setting vp the Flagge of Defiance to Their Mischiuous Exercise, and Ouerthrowing Their Bulwarkes, by Prophane Writers, Naturall Reason and Common Experience. ... By Stephan Gosson Stud. Oxon*. Early English Books, 1475-1640/244:04. Imprinted at London: [By Thomas Dawson] for Thomas Woodcocke, 1587.

Greenblatt, Stephen, *Renaissance Self-Fashioning: From More to Shakespeare* (Chicago: The University of Chicago Press, 2005).

Gurr, Andrew, *Playgoing in Shakespeare's London*, third edition (Cambridge and New York: Cambridge University Press, 2004).

Helgerson, Richard, *Self-Crowned Laureates: Spenser, Jonson, Milton, and the Literary System*, first edition (Berkeley: University of California Press, 1983).

Heller-Roazen, Daniel, *No One's Ways: An Essay on Infinite Naming* (New York: Zone Books, 2017).

Hill, Tracey, "'The Cittie is in an Uproare': Staging London in *The Booke of Sir Thomas More*," *Early Modern Literary Studies*, vol. 11, no. 1 (May 2005).

Hilliard, Stephen S., "Stephen Gosson and the Elizabethan Distrust of the Effects of Drama," *English Literary Renaissance*, vol. 9, no. 2 (March 1979). https://doi.org/10.1111/j.1475-6757.1979.tb01468.x.

Hodgdon, Barbara and W. B. Worthen, "Renaissance and/or Early Modern Drama and/or Theater and/or Performance: A Dialogue," *Renaissance Drama*, vol. 40 (January 1, 2012). https://doi.org/10.1086/rd.40.41917495.

Jakobson, Roman, "On Linguistic Aspects of Translation," in *On Translation*, ed. Reuben Arthur Brower (Cambridge: Harvard University Press, 1959).

Johnston, Daniel, "Ontological Queasiness: Antitheatricality and the History of Being," *About Performance*, nos. 14 and 15 (2017).

Jowett, John, "Introduction," *Sir Thomas More*, third edition (London: Bloomsbury Arden Shakespeare, 2011).

Kinney, Arthur F., "Stephen Gosson's Art of Argumentation in *The Schoole of Abuse*," *Studies in English Literature, 1500–1900*, vol. 7, no. 1 (1967). https://doi.org/10.2307/449455.

Levine, Nina S., "Citizens' Games: Differentiating Collaboration and Sir Thomas More," *Shakespeare Quarterly*, vol. 58, no. 1 (2007). https://doi.org/10.1353/shq.2007.0014.

Lin, Erika T., *Shakespeare and the Materiality of Performance* (Basingstoke: Palgrave Macmillan, 2012).

Lopez, Jeremy, *Theatrical Convention and Audience Response in Early Modern Drama* (Cambridge: Cambridge University Press, 2007).

Lopez, Jeremy, "Dumb Show," in *Early Modern Theatricality*, ed. Henry S. Turner, Oxford 21st Century Approaches to Literature (Oxford: Oxford University Press, 2013).

Menzer, Paul, "Lines," in *Early Modern Theatricality*, ed. Henry S. Turner, Oxford 21st Century Approaches to Literature (Oxford University Press, 2013).

Muggli, Mark Z., "Ben Jonson and the Business of News," *Studies in English Literature, 1500–1900*, vol. 32, no. 2 (1992). https://doi.org/10.2307/450739.

Orgel, Stephen, "The Poetics of Incomprehensibility," *Shakespeare Quarterly*, vol. 42, no. 4 (December 1, 1991). https://doi.org/10.2307/2870462.

"Privative, Adj., Adv., and N," *OED Online* (Oxford University Press), n.d., http://www.oed.com/view/Entry/151615.

Puttenham, George, *The Arte of English Poesie. Contriued into Three Bookes: The First of Poets and Poesie, the Second of Proportion, the Third of Ornament*, Early English Books, 1475-1640/2394:02. At London: Printed by Richard Field, dwelling in the black-Friers, neere Ludgate, 1589.

Reynolds, Bryan, *Becoming Criminal: Transversal Performance and Cultural Dissidence in Early Modern England* (Baltimore: Johns Hopkins University Press, 2002).

Shakespeare, William, *Hamlet*, ed. G. R. Hibbard (Oxford: Oxford University Press, 2008).

Sidney, Philip, "The Defense of Poesy," in *English Renaissance Literary Criticism* (Oxford: Oxford University Press, 1999).

States, Bert O., *Great Reckonings in Little Rooms: On the Phenomenology of the Theater* (Berkeley: University of California Press, 1985).

Turner, Henry S., "Toward a New Theatricality?" *Renaissance Drama*, vol. 40 (January 1, 2012). https://doi.org/10.1086/rd.40.41917496.

"Under'stander, N," *OED Online* (Oxford University Press), n.d., http://www.oed.com/view/Entry/212089.
Weimann, Robert, *Author's Pen and Actor's Voice: Playing and Writing in Shakespeare's Theatre*, eds. Helen Higbee and William West (Cambridge: Cambridge University Press, 2000).
West, William, "Understanding in the Elizabethan Theaters," *Renaissance Drama*, vol. 35 (2006).
West, William, "Intertheatricality," in *Early Modern Theatricality*, ed. Henry S. Turner, Oxford 21st Century Approaches to Literature (Oxford University Press, 2013).
Wickham, Glynne, Herbert Berry, and William Ingram, *English Professional Theatre, 1530–1660* (Cambridge: Cambridge University Press, 2000).
Woods, Gillian, "'Strange Discourse': The Controversial Subject of 'Sir Thomas More,'" *Renaissance Drama*, New Series, 39 (January 1, 2011).
Yates, Julian, *Error, Misuse, Failure: Object Lessons From The English Renaissance*, first edition (Minneapolis: University of Minnesota Press, 2002).

III. The Cruel Beast: Settler Sovereignty and the Crisis of American Zoopolitics
BRIAN W. NAIL

Berlant, Lauren, *The Queen of America Goes to Washington City: Essays on Sex and Citizenship* (Durham: Duke University Press, 1997).
Brands, Hal, *American Grand Strategy in the Age of Trump* (Washington, D.C.: Brookings Institution Press, 2018).
Crépon, Marc, "Geschlecht," in *Dictonary of Untranslatables: A Philosophical Lexicon*, ed. Barbara Cassin, trans. eds. Emily Apter, Jacques Lezra, and Michael Wood (Princeton: Princeton University Press, 2014).
Dahl, Adam, *Empire of the People: Settler Colonialism and the Foundations of Modern Democratic Thought* (Lawrence: University Press of Kansas, 2018).
Derrida, Jacques, "Geschlecht I: Sexual Difference, Ontological Difference," *Research in Phenomenology*, vol. 13 (1983).
Derrida, Jacques, "Racism's Last Word," trans. Peggy Kamuf, *Critical Inquiry*, vol. 12, no. 1 (1985).
Derrida, Jacques, "Geschlecht II: Heidegger's Hand," trans. John P. Leavey, Jr., in *Deconstruction and Philosophy: The Texts of Jacques Derrida*, ed. John Sallis (Chicago: The University of Chicago Press, 1987).
Derrida, Jacques, *Given Time: I. Counterfeit Money*, trans. Peggy Kamuf (Chicago: The University of Chicago Press, 1991).
Derrida, Jacques, *Specters of Marx: The State of the Debt, the Work of Mourning, and the New International*, trans. Peggy Kamuf. Routledge Classics (New York and London: Routledge, 1994).
Derrida, Jacques, *The Gift of Death*, trans. David Wills (Chicago: The University of Chicago Press, 1996).
Derrida, Jacques, *Monolingualism of the Other: Or, The Prosthesis of Origin*, trans. Patrick Mensah, first edition (Stanford: Stanford University Press, 1998).

Derrida, Jacques, *The Animal That Therefore I Am*, trans. David Wills, ed. Marie-Louise Mallet (New York: Fordham University Press, 2009).

Derrida, Jacques, *The Beast and the Sovereign*, vol. I, trans. Geoffrey Bennington, eds. Michel Lisse, Marie-Louise Mallet, and Ginette Michaud (Chicago: The University of Chicago Press, 2010).

Derrida, Jacques, Catherine Porter, and Philip Lewis, "No Apocalypse, Not Now (Full Speed Ahead, Seven Missiles, Seven Missives)," *diacritics*, vol. 14, no. 2 (1984).

Dunbar-Ortiz, Roxanne, *Loaded: A Disarming History of the Second Amendment* (San Francisco: City Lights Books, 2018. eBook).

Esposito, Roberto, *Bíos: Biopolitics and Philosophy*, trans. Timothy Campbell (Minneapolis: University of Minnesota Press, 2008).

Esposito, Roberto, *Immunitas: The Protection and Negation of Life* (Cambridge: Polity, 2011).

Fisher, Marc, Meagan Flynn, Jessica Contrera, and Carol D. Leonnig, "The Four-Hour Insurrection: How a Trump Mob Halted American Democracy," *Washington Post*, January 7, 2021. https://www.washingtonpost.com/graphics/2021/politics/trump-insurrection-capitol/.

Foster, Sheila, "Race and Ethnicity, Rawls, Race, and Reason," *Fordham Law Review* vol. 72, no. 5 (January 1, 2004).

Fraser, Nancy, *The Old Is Dying and the New Cannot Be Born: From Progressive Neoliberalism to Trump and Beyond* (New York: Verso Books, 2019).

Freud, Sigmund, *Civilization and Its Discontents*, trans. James Strachey (New York: W. W. Norton, 1962).

Gawboy, Anna, "Horned Headdress Guy Is Not A Viking: White Supremacy's Native American Thefts," *Medium*, January 17, 2021. https://medium.com/perceive-more/horned-headdress-guy-is-not-a-viking-392777632215.

Grandin, Greg, *The End of the Myth: From the Frontier to the Border Wall in the Mind of America* (New York: Metropolitan Books, 2019).

Green, Joshua, *Devil's Bargain: Steve Bannon, Donald Trump, and the Nationalist Uprising* (New York: Penguin, 2017).

Guttentag, Lucas, "Coronavirus Border Expulsions: CDC's Assault on Asylum Seekers and Unaccompanied Minors," *Stanford Law School* (blog), April 15, 2020. https://law.stanford.edu/2020/04/15/coronavirus-border-expulsions-cdcs-assault-on-asylum-seekers-and-unaccompanied-minors/.

Hardt, Michael and Antonio Negri, *Empire* (Cambridge: Harvard University Press, 2000).

Huber, Lindsay Pérez, "Make America Great Again: Donald Trump, Racist Nativism and the Virulent Adherence to White Supremacy Amid U.S. Demographic Change," *Charleston Law Review*, vol. 10 (2016).

Kimball, A. Samuel, *The Infanticidal Logic of Evolution and Culture* (Newark: University of Delaware Press, 2007).

Kistner, Ulrike, "Translating the First Edition of Freud's *Drei Abhandlungen Zur Sexualtheorie*," in Sigmund Freud, *Three Essays on the Theory of Sexuality: The 1905 Edition*, trans. Ulrike Kistner (New York: Verso Books, 2017).

Lara, Maria Pía, *The Disclosure of Politics: Struggles Over the Semantics of Secularization* (New York: Columbia University Press, 2013).

Marin, Louis, *Food for Thought*, trans. Mette Hjort (Baltimore: Johns Hopkins University Press, 1997).

Mogelson, Luke, "Among the Insurrectionists," *The New Yorker*, January 25, 2021.

Murphy, Michael Warren, "'No Beggars amongst Them': Primitive Accumulation, Settler Colonialism, and the Dispossession of Narragansett Indian Land," *Humanity & Society*, vol. 42, no. 1 (February 1, 2018).

Naylor, Brian, "Read Trump's Jan. 6 Speech, A Key Part Of Impeachment Trial," *NPR*. https://www.npr.org/2021/02/10/966396848/read-trumps-jan-6-speech-a-key-part-of-impeachment-trial.

Press, Bill, "Donald Trump Comes Completely Unhinged," *Chicago Tribune*, August 16, 2018.

"'QAnon Shaman' claims he wasn't attacking the country in first interview since Capitol riot arrest," *CBS News*, March 5, 2021. https://www.cbsnews.com/news/qanon-shaman-capitol-riot-interview-60-minutes-plus-2021-03-04/.

"Remarks by President Trump at a California Sanctuary State Roundtable," The White House, May 16, 2018.

Roitman, Janet, "Crisis," in *Political Concepts: A Critical Lexicon*, no. 1 (2012). https://www.politicalconcepts.org/roitman-crisis/.

Rothberg, Michael, "Power," in *The Routledge Handbook of Contemporary Jewish Cultures*, eds. Nadia Valman and Laurence Roth (London: Routledge, 2017).

Schwartz, Ian, "Trump Addresses Illegal Immigration Crisis: 'We Will Not Allow Our Generosity To Be Abused,'" *RealClear Politics*, November 1, 2018.

Scott, Joan Wallach, "Trump," in *Political Concepts: A Critical Lexicon*, "The Trump Edition," no. 5.1 (2018). https://www.politicalconcepts.org/category/issue-5-1-2/.

Shahloulian, David, et al., *The Trump Administration's Family Separation Policy: Trauma, Destruction, and Chaos* (Washington DC: Subcommittee on Immigration and Citizenship. US House of Representatives, 2020). https://judiciary.house.gov/uploadedfiles/the_trump_administration_family_separation_policy_trauma_destruction_and_chaos.pdf?utm_campaign=4526–519.

Shiraev, Eric, *Personality Theories: A Global View* (London: SAGE Publications, 2016).

Singh, Nikhil Pal, *Race and America's Long War* (Berkeley: University of California Press, 2017).

Slotkin, Richard, *Regeneration Through Violence: The Mythology of the American Frontier, 1600–1860* (Norman: University of Oklahoma Press, 2000).

Vlach, Michael J., "Various Forms of Replacement Theology," *The Master's Seminary*, vol. 20, no. 1 (2009).

Ward, James F., *Heidegger's Political Thinking* (Boston: University of Massachusetts Press, 1995).

Westerink, Herman, "Freud's Discussion with Psychiatry on Sexuality, Drives and Object in Three Essays," in *Deconstructing Normativity?: Re-Reading Freud's 1905 Three Essays*, eds. Philippe Van Haute and Herman Westerink (London and New York: Routledge, 2017), 28–43.

Whitman, Walt, "Whitman's Preface," in *Walt Whitman: Selected Poems 1855–1892*, ed. Gary Schmidgall (New York: St. Martin's Press, 1999).

IV. Between the Body and Language: Narratives of the Moving Subject in Okwui Okpokwasili's *Bronx Gothic*
LAUREN DIGIULIO

Altman, Janet, *Epistolarity: Approaches to a Form* (Columbus: Ohio State University Press, 1982).
Aristotle, "Poeticsm," in *Aristotle on the Art of Poetry*, trans. Ingram Bywater (Oxford: Clarendon Press, 1920).
Armstrong, Nancy, *Desire and Domestic Fiction: A Political History of the Novel* (Oxford: Oxford University Press, 1990).
Bower, Anne, *Epistolary Responses: The Letter in 20th Century American Fiction and Criticism* (Tuscaloosa and London: The University of Alabama Press, 1997).
DuBois, W. E. B., *The Souls of Black Folk*, ed. Brent Hayes Edwards (Oxford: Oxford University Press, 2007).
Evans, Dylan, *An Introductory Dictionary of Lacanian Psychoanalysis* (London: Routledge, 1996).
Gates Jr., Henry Louis, *Signifying Monkey: A Theory of African-American Literary Criticism* (Oxford: Oxford University Press, 2011. eBook).
Habermas, Jürgen, *The Structural Transformation of the Public Sphere: An Inquiry into a Category of Bourgeois Society*, trans. Thomas Burger (Cambridge: MIT Press, 1989).
Hale, Thomas A., *Griots and Griottes: Master of Words and Music* (Bloomington: Indiana University Press, 1998).
Hartman, Saidiya V., *Scenes of Subjection: Terror, Slavery, and Self-Making in Nineteenth-Century America* (New York: Oxford University Press, 1997).
Heckendorn Cook, Elizabeth, *Epistolary Bodies: Gender and Genre in the Eighteenth-Century Republic of Letters* (Stanford: Stanford University Press, 1996).
Henderson, Mae G., "Speaking in Tongues: Dialogics, Dialectics, and the Black Woman Writer's Literary Tradition," in *African American Literary Theory: A Reader*, ed. Winston Napier (New York: New York University Press, 2000).
Irigaray, Luce, *To Be Two*, trans. Monique M. Rhodes and Marco F. Cocito-Monoc (New York: Routledge, 2001).
Lacan, Jacques, "The Seminar on 'The Purloined Letter,'" *Yale French Studies*, no. 48 (1972).
Lacan, Jacques, "The Signification of the Phallus," in *Ecrits: A Selection*, trans. Alan Sheridan (London: Routledge, 1977).
Kosofsky Sedgwick, Eve, *Touching Feeling* (Durham: Duke University Press, 2003).
Kristeva, Julia, *Powers of Horror: An Essay on Abjection*, trans. Leon S. Roudiez (New York: Columbia University Press, 1982).
MacLean, Gerald, "Re-siting the Subject," in *Epistolary Histories: Letters, Fiction, Culture*, eds. Amanda Gilroy and W. M. Verhoeven (Charlottesville: University Press of Virginia, 2000).
Okpokwasili, Okwui, *Bronx Gothic*, video, ontheboards.tv, 2014.
Okpokwasili, Okwui, Artist in Residence talk for Artists at the Crossroads, Times Square, New York City, February 1, 2016. https://www.youtube.com/watch?v=DkmY1BF4eZI&app=desktop.

Okpokwasili, Okwui, "Artist Statement" for *Bronx Gothic.* http://mappinternational.org/blocks/view/477/.
Patterson, Orlando, *Slavery and Social Death: A Comparative Study* (Cambridge: Harvard University Press, 1982).
Punter, David, *The Literature of Terror: A History of Gothic Fictions from 1765 to the Present Day,* Vol. 1: *The Gothic Tradition* (New York: Routledge, 2013).
Roach, Joseph, *Cities of the Dead: Circum-Atlantic Performance* (New York: Columbia University Press, 1996).
Scarry, Elaine, *The Body in Pain: The Making and Unmaking of the World* (Oxford: Oxford University Press, 1985).
Schechner, Richard, *Between Theater and Anthropology* (Philadelphia: University of Pennsylvania Press, 1985).
Smith, Andrew, *Gothic Literature* (Edinburgh: Edinburgh University Press, 2013).
Spillers, Hortense J., "Culture and Countermemory: The 'American' Connection," *diacritics,* vol. 17, no. 2 (Summer 1987).
Tennyson, G. B., "The Bildungsroman in Nineteenth-Century English Literature," in *Medieval Epic to the Epic Theater of Brecht: Essays in Comparative Literature,* eds. Rosario Armato and John M. Spalek (Los Angeles: University of Southern California Press, 1968).
Watt, Ian, *The Rise of the Novel: Studies in Defoe, Richardson and Fielding* (Berkeley: University of California Press, 1959).

V. Collapsing the Gender/Genre Distinction: On Transgressions of Category in Woolf's *Orlando*
OSCAR JANSSON

Auerbach, Erich, *Mimesis: The Representation of Reality in Western Literature,* trans. Willard R. Trask (Princeton: Princeton University Press, 1971 [1946]).
Bakhtin, Mikhail, "Epic and Novel," trans. Caryl Emerson and Michael Holquist, in *The Dialogic Imagination: Four Essays,* ed. Michael Holquist (Austin: University of Texas Press, 1981).
Batchelor, John, *Virginia Woolf: The Major Novels* (Cambridge: Cambridge University Press, 1991).
Bell, Quentin, *Virginia Woolf: A Biography,* vol. II (London: The Hogarth Press, 1990 [1972]).
Bennett, Arnold, "A Woman's High-Brow Lark," *Evening Standard,* November 8, 1928. Reprinted in *Virginia Woolf: The Critical Heritage,* eds. Robin Madjumdar and Allen McLaurin (London: Routledge & Kegan Paul, 1975).
Booker, M. Keith, "What's the Difference? Carnivalization of Gender in Virginia Woolf's *Orlando*," in *Techniques of Subversion in Modern Literature: Transgression, Abjection and the Carnivalesque,* ed. M. Keith Booker (Gainsville: University of Florida Press, 1991).

Caughie, Pamela L., "Virginia Woolf's Double Discourse," *Discontented Discourses: Feminism/Textual Intervention/Psychoanalysis*, eds. Marleen S. Barr and Richard Feldstein (Urbana: University of Illinois Press, 1989).
Caughie, Pamela L., "The Temporality of Modernist Life Writing in the Era of Transsexualism: Virginia Woolf's *Orlando* and Einar Wegener's *Man Into Woman*," *Modern Fiction Studies*, vol. 59, no. 3 (2013).
Ciecko, Anne, "Transgender, Transgenre, and the Transnational: Sally Potter's *Orlando*," *The Velvet Light Trap*, vol. 41 (1998).
Crawford, Lucas, "Woolf's *Einfühlung*: An Alternative Theory of Transgender Affect," *Mosaic*, vol. 48, no. 1 (2015).
Cuddy-Keane, Melba, *Virginia Woolf, The Intellectual, and The Public Sphere* (Cambridge: Cambridge University Press, 2003).
Eagleton, Terry, *The English Novel* (Malden: Blackwell Publishing, 2005).
Forster, E. M., *Aspects of the Novel* (London: Edward Arnold & Co., 1928).
Fowler, Alastair, *Kinds of Literature: Introduction to the Theory of Genres and Modes* (Oxford: Clarendon Press, 2002 [1982]).
de Gay, Jane, "Virginia Woolf's Feminist Historiography in *Orlando*," *Critical Survey*, vol. 19, no. 1 (2007).
Genette, Gérard, *Paratexts: Thresholds of Interpretation* (New York: Cambridge University Press, 2001 [1987]).
Gilbert, Sandra, "*Orlando*: Introduction," in *Virginia Woolf: Introduction to the Major Works*, ed. Julia Briggs (London: Virago Press, 1994).
Goldman, Jane, *The Cambridge Introduction to Virginia Woolf* (New York: Cambridge University Press, 2006).
Hankins, Leslie Kathleen, "Orlando: 'A Precipice Marked V' Between 'A Miracle of Discretion' and 'Lovemaking Unbelievable: Indiscretions Incredible,'" in *Virginia Woolf: Lesbian Readings*, eds. Eileen Barrett and Patricia Cramer (New York: New York University Press, 1997).
Jameson, Fredric, *Antinomies of Realism* (New York: Verso, 2013).
Kalmár, György, "Parler-Entre-Elles: Possibilities of a Less Phallocentric Symbolic Economy in Virginia Woolf's *Orlando*," *The AnaChronisT*, vol. 16 (2011).
Knopp, Sherron E., "'If I Saw You Would You Kiss Me?': Sapphism and the Subversiveness of Virginia Woolf's *Orlando*," *PMLA*, vol. 103, no. 1 (1988).
Kristeva, Julia, *Revolution in Poetic Language*, trans. Margaret Waller (New York: Columbia University Press, 1984).
Kristeva, Julia, "A New Type of Intellectual: The Dissident," trans. Seán Hand, in *The Kristeva Reader*, ed. Toril Moi (Oxford: Basil Blackwell, 1986).
Leaska, Mitchell A., *The Novels of Virginia Woolf: From Beginning to End* (London: Weidenfeld and Nicolson, 1977).
Levý, Jiří, "Translation as a Decision Process," in *The Translation Studies Reader*, ed. Lawrence Venuti (London and New York: Routledge, 2004).
Lukács, Georg, *The Theory of the Novel*, trans. Ana Bostock (London: Merlin Press, 2006 [1920]).
Malabou, Catherine, *Changing Difference: The Feminine and the Question of Philosophy*, trans. Carolyn Shread (Cambridge: Polity Press, 2011 [2009]).
Malabou, Catherine, "Plasticity," in *Dictionary of Untraslatables: A Philosophical Lexicon*, ed. Barbara Cassin, trans. eds. Emily Apter, Jaqcues Lezra, and Michael Wood (Princeton: Princeton University Press, 2014).

Mao, Douglas and Rebecca Walkowitz, eds. *Bad Modernisms* (Durham: Duke University Press, 2006).

Marcus, Laura, *Virginia Woolf* (Plymouth: Northcote House Publishers, 1997).

Mazzoni, Guido, *Theory of the Novel*, trans. Zakhia Hanafi (Cambridge: Harvard University Press, 2017).

Melita, Maureen M., "Gender Identity and Androgyny in Ludovico Ariosto's *Orlando Furioso* and Virginia Woolf's *Orlando: A Biography*," *Romance Notes*, vol. 53, no. 2 (2013).

Micir, Melanie, "The Queer Timing of *Orlando: A Biography*," *Virginia Woolf Miscellany*, vol. 82 (2012).

Moi, Toril, *Sexual/Textual Politics: Feminist Literary Theory*, second edition (London: Routledge, 2002).

Nicolson, Nigel, *A Portrait of a Marriage: V. Sackville-West and Harold Nicolson* (New York: Atheneum, 1974).

Olin-Hitt, Michael R., "Desire, Death, and Plot: The Subversive Play of *Orlando*," *Women's Studies*, vol. 24, no. 5 (1995).

Reviron-Piégay, Floriane, "Translating Generic Liberties: *Orlando* on Page and Screen," *Biography*, vol. 32, no. 2 (2009).

Riatt, Suzanne, *Vita and Virginia: The Work and Friendship of V. Sackville-West and Virginia Woolf* (Oxford: Clarendon Press, 1993).

Ryan, Derek, "*Orlando*'s Queer Animals," in *A Companion to Virginia Woolf*, ed. Jessica Berman (Hoboken: John Wiley & Sons, 2016).

Sánchez-Pardo González, Esther, "'What Phantasmagoria the Mind is': Reading Virginia Woolf's Parody of Gender," *Atlantis*, vol. 26, no. 2 (2004).

Scott, Pauline, "The Modernist Orlando: Virginia Woolf's Refashioning of Ariosto's *Orlando Furioso*," *Modern Retellings of Chivalric Texts*, ed. Gloria Allaire (Farnham: Ashgate, 1999).

Showalter, Elaine, *A Literature of their Own: From Charlotte Brontë to Doris Lessing* (London: Virago, 2011 [1977]).

Southworth, Helen, "Virginia Woolf's *Orlando* Preface, the Modernist Writer, and Networks of Cultural, Financial and Social Capital," *Woolf Studies Annual*, vol. 18 (2012).

Spater, George and Ian Parsons, *A Marriage of True Minds: An Intimate Portrait of Leonard and Virginia Woolf* (London: Jonathan Cape & Hogarth Press, 1977).

Wilson, J. J., "Why is *Orlando* Difficult?" *New Feminist Essays on Virginia Woolf*, ed. Jane Marcus (London: MacMillan, 1981).

Woolf, Virginia, *A Room of One's Own* (London: The Hogarth Press, 1959 [1929]).

Woolf, Virginia, *A Writer's Diary* (London: The Hogarth Press, 1959 [1953]).

Woolf, Virginia, *The Letters of Virginia Woolf. Volume 3: 1923–1928. A Change of Perspective*, eds. Nigel Nicolson and Joanne Trautmann (London: The Hogarth Press 1977).

Woolf, Virginia, "The New Biography," *The Essays of Virginia Woolf. Volume IV: 1925–1928*, ed. Andrews McNeillie (London: The Hogarth Press, 1994).

Woolf, Virginia, "What is a Novel?" in *The Essays of Virginia Woolf. Volume IV: 1925–1928*, ed. Andrews McNeillie (London: The Hogarth Press, 1994).

Woolf, Virginia, *Orlando: A Biography* (London: Vintage Classics, 2016 [1928]).

VI. Gazing at the Untranslatable Subject: From Velázquez's *Las Meninas* to Ellison's *Invisible Man*
RICHARD HAJARIZADEH

Agamben, Giorgio, "Epilogue: Toward a Theory of Destituent Potential," in *The Use of Bodies: Homo Sacer IV, 2*, trans. Adam Kotsko (Stanford: Stanford University Press, 2015).

Bolt, Marvin, *Glass: The Eye of Science* (New York: Corning Museum of Glass, 2016).

Brockelman, Thomas, "The Other Side of the Canvas: Lacan Flips Foucault over Velázquez," *Continental Philosophy Review*, vol. 46, no. 2 (2013).

Copjec, Joan, *Read My Desire: Lacan Against the Historicists*, second edition (New York: Verso, 2015).

de Man, Paul, "Metaphor: Second Discourse," in *Allegories of Reading: Figural Language in Rousseau, Nietzsche, Rilke, and Proust* (New Haven: Yale University Press, 1979).

Derrida, Jacques, "*Geschlecht* I: Sexual Difference, Ontological Difference," in *Psyche: Inventions of the Other*, vol. II, eds. Peggy Kamuf and Elizabeth Rottenburg (Stanford: Stanford University Press, 2008).

Derrida, Jacques, *Geschlecht* II: "Heidegger's Hand," in *Psyche: Inventions of the Other*, vol. II, eds. Peggy Kamuf and Elizabeth Rottenburg (Stanford: Stanford University Press, 2008).

Ellison, Ralph, *Invisible Man*, second edition (New York: Vintage, 1995).

Foucault, Michel, "Governmentality," in *The Foucault Effect: Studies in Governmentality*, eds. Graham Burchell et al. (Chicago: The University of Chicago Press, 1991).

Foucault, Michel, *The Order of Things: An Archaeology of the Human Sciences* (New York: Vintage Books, 1994).

Foucault, Michel, *Abnormal: Lectures at the Collège de France 1974–1975*, trans. Graham Burchell, ed. Arnold I. Davidson (New York: Picador, 2003).

Foucault, Michel, *History of Madness*, trans. Jonathan Murphy and Jean Khalfa (New York: Routledge, 2009).

Lacan, Jacques, *Le Séminaire. Livre XIII: L'objet de la psychanalyse (1965–1966)*, ed. Michel Roussan, unpublished. http://www.valas.fr/IMG/pdf/s13_objet.pdf.

Lacan, Jacques, *The Object of Psychoanalysis*, trans. Cormac Gallagher (2010). www.lacaninireland.com/web/wp-content/uploads/2010/06/13-The-Object-of-Psychoanalysis1.pdf.

Leroi-Gourhan, André, "Introduction to a Paleontology of Symbols," in *Gesture and Speech*, trans. Anna Berger (Cambridge: MIT Press, 1993).

Velázquez, Diego, *Las Meninas* (1656), oil on canvas, Museo del Prado, Madrid.

Žižek, Slavoj, "Class Struggle or Postmodernism? Yes, Please!" in *Contingency, Hegemony, Universality: Contemporary Dialogues on the Left*, second edition (New York: Verso, 2011).

VII. From Lectiocentrism to Gramophonology: Listening to Cinema and Writing Sound Criticism
DAVID LAROCCA

Abbott, Mathew, "On Film in Reality: Cavellian Reflections on Skepticism, Belief, and Documentary," in *The Thought of Stanley Cavell and Cinema: Turning Anew to the Ontology of Film a Half-Century after The World Viewed*, ed. David LaRocca (New York: Bloomsbury, 2020).

Altman, Rick, "Sound Space," in *Sound Theory/Sound Practice*, ed. Rick Altman (New York: Routledge, 1992).

Altman, Rick, "Four and a Half Film Fallacies," in *The Philosophy of Documentary Film: Image, Sound, Fiction, Truth*, ed. David LaRocca (Lanham: Lexington Books of Rowman & Littlefield, 2017).

Apter, Emily, "Untranslatable? The 'Reading' versus the 'Looking,'" *Journal of Visual Culture*, vol. 6, no. 1 (2007).

Apter, Emily, "Lexilalia: On Translating a Dictionary of Untranslatable Philosophical Terms," *Paragraph*, vol. 48, no. 5 (2015).

Balázs, Béla, "Theory of the Film: Sound," in *Film Sound: Theory and Practice*, eds. Elisabeth Weis and John Belton (New York: Columbia University Press, 1985).

Balsom, Erika, "A Cinephilic Avant-garde: The Films of Peter Tscherkassky, Martin Arnold, and Gustav Deutsch," *New Austrian Film*, eds. Robert von Dassanowsky and Oliver C. Speck (New York: Berghahn Books, 2011).

Barad, Karen, *Meeting the Universe Halfway: Quantum Physics and the Entanglement of Matter and Meaning* (Durham: Duke University Press, 2007).

Benjamin, Walter, "The Work of Art in the Age of Mechanical Reproduction," in *Illuminations*, trans. Harry Zohn, ed. Hannah Arendt (New York: Schocken Books, 1968).

Bering-Porter, David, "The Automaton in All of Us: GIFs, Cinemagraphs, and the Films of Martin Arnold," *The Moving Image Review and Art Journal*, vol. 3, no. 2 (December 2014).

Billiter, Bill, "Satanic Messages Played Back for Assembly Panel," *Los Angeles Times*, April 28, 1982, latimes.com.

Bordwell, David and Kristin Thompson, *Film Art: An Introduction*, tenth edition (New York: McGraw Hill, 2013).

Buhler, James, *Theories of the Soundtrack* (Oxford: Oxford University Press, 2019).

Butler, Rex, *Stanley Cavell and the Arts: Philosophy and Popular Culture* (New York: Bloomsbury, 2020).

Carroll, Noël, *The Philosophy of Motion Pictures* (Oxford: Blackwell, 2008).

Cavell, Stanley, *Must We Mean What We Say? A Book of Essays* (Cambridge: Cambridge University Press, 2002 [1969]).

Cavell, Stanley, *The World Viewed: Reflections on the Ontology of Film*, Enlarged Edition (Cambridge: Harvard University Press, 1979 [1971]).

Cavell, Stanley, *Pursuits of Happiness: The Hollywood Comedy of Remarriage* (Cambridge: Harvard University Press, 1981).
Cavell, Stanley, *Emerson's Transcendental Etudes*, ed. David Justin Hodge (Stanford: Stanford University Press, 2003).
Cavell, Stanley, *Cities of Words: Pedagogical Letters on a Register of the Moral Life* (Cambridge: The Belknap Press of Harvard University Press, 2004).
Cavell, Stanley, "What Photography Calls Thinking: Theoretical Considerations on the Power of the Photographic Basis of Cinema," in *The Philosophy of Documentary Film: Image, Sound, Fiction, Truth*, ed. David LaRocca (Lanham: Lexington Books of Rowman & Littlefield, 2017).
Chion, Michel, *The Voice of Cinema, La Voix au cinéma*, trans. Claudia Gorbman (New York: Columbia University Press, 1999 [1982]).
Chion, Michel, *Audio-Vision: Sound on Screen*, second edition, ed. and trans. Claudia Gorbman (New York: Columbia University Press, 2013).
Chion, Michel, *Words on Screen, L'Écrit au cinéma*, trans. Claudia Gorbman (New York: Columbia University Press, 2017 [2013]).
Clark, David, "The Discrete Charm of the Digital Image: Animation and New Media," in *The Sharpest Point: Animation at the End of Cinema*, eds. Chris Gehman and Steve Reinke (Ottawa: YYZ Books/Ottawa International Animation Festival and the Images Festival, 2005).
Corrigan, Timothy, *The Essay Film: From Montaigne, after Marker* (New York: Oxford University Press, 2011).
Crépon, Marc, "*Geschlecht*," in *Dictionary of Untranslatables: A Philosophical Lexicon*, ed. Barbara Cassin, trans. eds. Emily Apter, Jacques Lezra, and Michael Wood (Princeton: Princeton University Press, 2014).
Derrida, Jacques, *Of Grammatology*, trans. Gayatri Chakravorty Spivak (Baltimore: Johns Hopkins University Press, 2016 [1974]).
Devereaux, Leslie and Roger Hillman, eds., *Fields of Vision: Essays in Film, Visual Anthropology, and Photography* (Berkeley: University of California Press, 1995).
Dyson, George, "From Analog to Digital and Back," *OneZero*, August 18, 2020, www.onezero.medium.com.
Dyson, George, *Analogia: The Emergence of Technology Beyond Programmable Control* (New York: Farrar, Straus, and Giroux, 2020).
Emerson, Ralph Waldo, "Gifts," in *Essays: Second Series, The Complete Works of Ralph Waldo Emerson*, vol. III (Boston: Houghton, Mifflin and Company, 1903–4).
Erik, Davis, "What exactly lurks within the backward grooves of 'Stairway to Heaven'?," *Salon*, June 24, 2017, salon.com.
Everett, Wendy, ed., *The Seeing Century: Film, Vision, and Identity* (Amsterdam: Rodopi, 1994).
Freud, Sigmund, *Three Essays on the Theory of Sexuality* (Vienna: Franz Deuticke, 1905).
Gaudreault, André, "Showing and Telling: Image and Word in Early Cinema," trans. John Howe, in *Early Cinema: Space, Frame, Narrative*, ed. Thomas Elsaesser (London: BFI, 1990).
Gilbey, Ryan, "How I Trekked Across Oregon for *Meek's Cutoff* Then Returned to Teaching," *The Guardian*, April 8, 2011.

Gould, Timothy, *Hearing Things: Voice and Method in the Work of Stanley Cavell* (Chicago: The University of Chicago Press, 1998).

Greenwood, Veronique, "How the Shape of Your Ears Affects What You Hear," *The New York Times*, March 6, 2018.

Gunning, Tom, "Before Documentary: Early Nonfiction Films and the 'View' Aesthetic," in *The Philosophy of Documentary Film: Image, Sound, Fiction, Truth*, ed. David LaRocca (Lanham: Lexington Books of Rowman & Littlefield, 2017).

Habermas, Jürgen, "Beyond a Temporalized Philosophy of Origins: Jacques Derrida's Critique of Phonocentrism," *The Philosophical Discourse of Modernity: Twelve Lectures*, trans. Frederick G. Lawrence (Cambridge: MIT Press, 1987), Lecture VII.

Harman, Graham, *Art and Objects* (Cambridge: Polity, 2020).

Kirbach, Ben, "Reading for the Apparatus: An Interview with Garret Stewart," September 17, 2019. https://english.uiowa.edu/resources/news.

Ives, Lucy, "After the Afterlives of Theory," *The Baffler*, no. 39, May 2018, thebaffler.com

Kracauer, Siegfried, *Theory of Film: The Redemption of Physical Reality* (Princeton: Princeton University Press, 1997; orig. pub. Oxford University Press, 1960).

Krell, David Farrell, *Phantoms of the Other: Four Generations of Derrida's Geschlecht* (Albany: State University of New York Press, 2015).

LaRocca, David, "Review of Timothy Gould's *Hearing Things: Voice and Method in the Writing of Stanley Cavell*," *The Review of Metaphysics*, vol. LIII, no. 4 (June 2000).

LaRocca, David, "The Limits of Instruction: Pedagogical Remarks on Lars von Trier's *The Five Obstructions*," *Film and Philosophy*, vol. 13 (2009).

LaRocca, David, *Emerson's English Traits and the Natural History of Metaphor* (New York: Bloomsbury, 2013).

LaRocca, David, "Shooting for the Truth: Amateur Documentary Filmmaking, Affective Optics, and the Ethical Impulse," *Post Script: Essays in Film and the Humanities*, vol. 26, nos. 2 and 3 (Winter/Spring/Summer 2017).

LaRocca, David, "Translating Carlyle: Ruminating on the Models of Metafiction at the Emergence of an Emersonian Vernacular," *Religions*, vol. 8, no. 8 (2017).

LaRocca, David, "Acknowledgments: Thinking of and Thanking Stanley Cavell," *Conversations: The Journal of Cavellian Studies*, no. 7 (2019).

LaRocca, David, "'One of the Most Phenomenal Debut Films in the History of Movies': *The Sugarland Express* as Expression of Spielberg's 'Movie Sense' and as Contribution to a Genre Cycle," in *A Critical Companion to Steven Spielberg*, eds. Adam Barkman and Antonio Sanna (Lanham: Lexington Books, 2019).

LaRocca, David, ed., *The Philosophy of Charlie Kaufman* (Lexington: University Press of Kentucky, 2011; updated edition, 2019).

LaRocca, David, "Autophilosophy," in *Inheriting Stanley Cavell: Memories, Dreams, Reflections*, ed. David LaRocca (New York: Bloomsbury, 2020).

LaRocca, David, ed., *Inheriting Stanley Cavell: Memories, Dreams, Reflections* (New York: Bloomsbury, 2020).
LaRocca, David, "Must We Say What We Learned? Parsing the Personal and the Philosophical," in *Inheriting Stanley Cavell: Memories, Dreams, Reflections*, ed. David LaRocca (New York: Bloomsbury, 2020).
LaRocca, David, "On the Aesthetics of Amateur Filmmaking in Narrative Cinema: Negotiating Home Movies after *Adam's Rib*," in *The Thought of Stanley Cavell and Cinema: Turning Anew to the Ontology of Film a Half-Century after* The World Viewed, ed. David LaRocca (New York: Bloomsbury, 2020).
LaRocca, David, "Thinking of Film: What is Cavellian about Malick's Movies?" in *A Critical Companion to Terrence Malick*, ed. Joshua Sikora (Lanham: Lexington Books, 2020).
LaRocca, David, "*Alone.*, Again: On Martin Arnold's Metaformal Invention by Intervention," in *Metacinema: The Form and Content of Filmic Reference and Reflexivity*, ed. David LaRocca (Oxford: Oxford University Press, 2021).
LaRocca, David, "Contemplating the Sounds of Contemplative Cinema: Stanley Cavell and Kelly Reichardt," in *Movies with Stanley Cavell in Mind*, ed. David LaRocca (New York: Bloomsbury, 2021).
LaRocca, David, "Memory Translation: Rithy Panh's Provocations to the Primacy and Virtues of the Documentary Sound/Image Index," in *Everything Has a Soul: The Cinema of Rithy Panh*, eds. Leslie Barnes and Joseph Mai (New Brunswick: Rutgers University Press, 2021).
LaRocca, David, "Object Lessons: What Cyanotypes Teach Us About Digital Media," in *Photography's Materialities: Transatlantic Photographic Practices over the Long Nineteenth Century*, eds. Geoff Bender and Rasmus S. Simonsen (Leuven: Leuven University Press, 2021).
LaRocca, David, "Virtual Round Table: An Experiment," *Cinema: The Journal of Philosophy and the Moving Image*, vol. 12, Images of the Real: Philosophy and Documentary Film (2021).
LaRocca, David and Ricardo Miguel-Alfonso, eds., *A Power to Translate the World: New Essays on Emerson and International Culture*, part of the Dartmouth Series in American Studies "Re-Mapping the Transnational" from series editor Donald E. Pease (Hanover: Dartmouth College Press, 2015).
Lippit, Akira Mizuta, *Ex-Cinema: From a Theory of Experimental Film and Video* (Berkeley: University of California Press, 2012).
Littau, Karin, "Eye-Hunger: Physical Pleasure and Non-Narrative Cinema," in *Crash Cultures: Modernity, Mediation, and the Material*, eds. Jane Arthurs and Iain Grant (Bristol: Intellect, 2002).
Littau, Karin, "Silent Films and Screaming Audiences," On *Arrival of a Train at La Ciotat*, in *Film Analysis: A Norton Reader*, second edition, eds. Jeffrey Geiger and R. L. Rutsky (New York: Norton, 2013).
MacDonald, Scott, "Sp ... Sp ... Spaces of Inscription: An Interview with Martin Arnold," *Film Quarterly*, vol. 48, no. 1 (Autumn 1994).
MacDonald, Scott, *A Critical Cinema 3: Interviews with Independent Filmmakers* (Berkeley: University of California Press, 1998).

MacDonald, Scott, *Binghamton Babylon: Voices from the Cinema Department, 1967–77* (Albany: State University of New York Press, 2015).
MacDonald, Scott, "My Troubled Relationship with Stanley Cavell: In Pursuit of a Truly Cinematic Conversation," in *The Thought of Stanley Cavell and Cinema: Turning Anew to the Ontology of Film a Half-Century after The World Viewed*, ed. David LaRocca (New York: Bloomsbury, 2020).
Manovich, Lev, "What is Digital Cinema?" (1995), in *Critical Visions in Film Theory*, eds. Timothy Corrigan, Patricia White, and Meta Mazaj (New York: Bedford/St. Martin's, 2011).
Marcel, Gabriel, "Possibilités et limites de l'art cinématographique," *Revue international de filmologie*, vol. 5, nos. 18–19 (1950).
Merleau-Ponty, Maurice, *Phenomenonology of Perception*, trans. Colin Smith (Delhi: Motilal Banarsidass, 1996).
Mulhall, Stephen, "What a Genre of Film Might Be: Medium, Myth, and Morality," in *The Thought of Stanley Cavell and Cinema: Turning Anew to the Ontology of Film a Half-Century after The World Viewed*, ed. David LaRocca (New York: Bloomsbury, 2020).
Mulvey, Laura, "Visual Pleasure and Narrative Cinema," in *Visual and Other Pleasures*, second edition (New York: Palgrave Macmillan, 1989).
Mulvey, Laura, *Death 24x a Second: Stillness and the Moving Image* (London: Reaktion Books, 2006).
Petrie, Dennis and Joseph Boggs, *The Art of Watching Films*, eighth edition (New York: McGraw Hill, 2012).
Petrusich, Amanda, "Merging Lanes," *The New Yorker*, March 15, 2021.
Pinch, Trevor and Karin Bijsterveld, eds., *The Oxford Handbook of Sound Studies* (New York: Oxford University Press, 2011).
Pippin, Robert B., *Hollywood Westerns and American Myth: The Importance of Howard Hawks and John Ford for Political Philosophy* (New Haven: Yale University Press, 2012).
Radiolab, "Breaking News," July 27, 2017, http://www.radiolab.org/story/breaking-news/.
Rao, Tejal, "Will Fish Sauce and Charred Oranges Return the World Covid Took from Me?" *The New York Times*, March 2, 2021.
Ray, Robert B., *The Avant-Garde Finds Andy Hardy* (Cambridge: Harvard University Press, 1995).
Ray, Robert B., "How to Start an Avant-Garde," in *How a Film Theory Got Lost and Other Mysteries in Cultural Studies* (Bloomington: Indiana University Press, 2001).
Sacks, Oliver, *The Man Who Mistook His Wife for a Hat and Other Clinical Tales* (New York: Gerald Duckworth, 1985).
Schatz, Thomas, *Hollywood Genres: Formulas, Filmmaking, and the Studio System* (New York: McGraw-Hill, 1981).
Schaeffer, Dirk, "Alone: Life Wastes Andy Hardy," Program notes, in *Views from the Avant-Garde*, curated by Mark McElhatten and Gavin Smith, New York Film Festival, October 10–11, 1998.
Smigel, Eric, "Sights and Sounds of the Moving Mind: The Visionary Soundtracks of Stan Brakhage," in *The Music and Sound of Experimental Film*, eds. Holly Rogers and Jeremy Barham (Oxford: Oxford University Press, 2017).

Stephens, Chuck, "Exploded View: Hollis Frampton's *Critical Mass*," *CinemaScope*. http://cinema-scope.com/columns/exploded-view-hollis-framptons-critical-mass-by-chuck-stephens/.

Stevens, Kyle, "The World Heard," in *The Thought of Stanley Cavell and Cinema: Turning Anew to the Ontology of Film a Half-Century after* The World Viewed, ed. David LaRocca (New York: Bloomsbury, 2020).

Stewart, Garrett, *Reading Voices: Literature and the Phonotext* (Berkeley: University of California Press, 1990).

Stewart, Garrett, *The Deed of Reading: Literature * Writing * Language * Philosophy* (Ithaca: Cornell University Press, 2015).

Stewart, Garrett, "'Assertions in Technique': Tracking the Medial 'Thread' in Cavell's Filmic Ontology," in *The Thought of Stanley Cavell and Cinema: Turning Anew to the Ontology of Film a Half-Century after* The World Viewed, ed. David LaRocca (New York: Bloomsbury, 2020).

Stewart, Garrett, *Book, Text, Medium: Cross-Sectional Reading for a Digital Age* (Cambridge: Cambridge University Press, 2020).

Stewart, Garrett, "A Metacinematic Spectrum: Technique through Text to Context," in *Metacinema: The Form and Content of Filmic Reference and Reflexivity*, ed. David LaRocca (Oxford: Oxford University Press, 2021).

Teuber, Andreas, "Cavell's Ear for Things," in *Inheriting Stanley Cavell: Memories, Dreams, Reflections*, ed. David LaRocca (New York: Bloomsbury, 2020).

Turvey, Malcolm, *Doubting Vision: Film and the Revelationist Tradition* (Oxford: Oxford University Press, 2008).

Villarejo, Amy, *Film Studies: The Basics*, second edition (New York: Routledge, 2013).

Warren, Charles, "Cavell, Altman, Cassavetes: The Melodrama of the Unknown Woman in *A Woman Under the Influence* and *Nashville*," in *Movies with Stanley Cavell in Mind*, ed. David LaRocca (New York: Bloomsbury, 2021).

West, Cornel, *The Brian Lehrer Show*, WNYC Studios, April 4, 2018.

Wheatley, Catherine, *Stanley Cavell and Film: Scepticism and Self-Reliance at the Cinema* (New York: Bloomsbury, 2019).

Wheatley, Catherine, "Passionate Utterances: Cavell, Film, and the Female Voice," in *Movies with Stanley Cavell in Mind*, ed. David LaRocca (New York: Bloomsbury, 2021).

Whittington, William, "The Sonic Playpen: Sound Design and Technology in Pixar's Animated Shorts," in *The Oxford Handbook of Sound Studies*, eds. Trevor Pinch and Karin Bijsterveld (New York: Oxford University Press, 2011).

Williams, Linda, *Hard Core: Power, Pleasure, and the "Frenzy of the Visible"* (Berkeley: University of California Press, 1989).

Williams, William Carlos, "A Statement by William Carlos Williams about the poem Paterson," in *Paterson*, revised edition prepared by Christopher MacGowan (New York: New Directions, 1992).

Wittgenstein, Ludwig, *Philosophical Investigations*, trans. G. E. M. Anscombe (Englewood Cliffs: Prentice Hall, 1953).

Wittgenstein, Ludwig, *Culture and Value*, trans. Peter Winch, ed. G. H. Von Wright (Chicago: The Univerity of Chicago Press, 1980).

Wollen, Peter, *Singin' in the Rain* (London: BFI and Palgrave Macmillan, 1992).

Wood, James, *Serious Noticing: Selected Essays* (New York: Farrar, Straus and Giroux, 2019).
Zeilinger, Martin J., "Sampling as Analysis, Sampling as Symptom: Found Footage and Repetition in Martin Arnold's *Alone. Life Wastes Andy Hardy*," in *Sampling Media*, eds. David Laderman and Laurel Westrup (New York: Oxford University Press, 2014).
Zryd, Michael, "Alone: Life Wastes Andy Hardy," *Cinémathèque Annotations on Film, Senses of Cinema* no. 32 (July 2004), sensesofcinema.com.

Afterword: Trans-Ontology and the *Geschlecht* Complex
EMILY APTER

Baron, Dennis, "The Epicene Pronouns: A Chronology of the Word that Failed," *American Speech*, vol. 56 no. 2 (1981). https://doi.org/10.2307/455007.
Bianchi, Emma, "Becoming Mythological: Barthes with Butler and Aristotle," presented at NYU Comparative Literature Graduate Colloquium, November 2012.
Carlson, Shanna T., "Transgender Subjectivity and the Logic of Sexual Difference," *differences*, vol. 21 no. 2 (2010). https://doi.org/10.1215/10407391-2010-003.
Chen, Mel Y., *Animacies: Biopolitics, Racial Mattering, and Queer Affect* (Durham: Duke University Press, 2012).
Copjec, Joan, "The Inheritance of Potentiality: An Interview with Joan Copjec," *Revue électronique d'études sur led monde anglophone*, vol. 12, no. 1 (2014). https://doi.org/10.4000/erea.4102.
Foucault Michel, "*Le discours de la sexualité*," course given at Vincennes (1969).
Krell, David Farrell, *Phantoms of the Other: Four Generations of Derrida's Geschlecht* (Albany: SUNY Press, 2015).
Nancy, Jean-Luc, *Corpus* (Paris: Editions Métailié, 2006).
Nancy, Jean-Luc, *Corpus II: Writings on Sexuality*, trans. Anne O'Byrne (New York: Fordham University Press, 2013).
Review of trans artist Cassils' "Becoming an Image," passengerart.com/2013/03/20/the-agony-and-the-ecstasy-of-becoming-and-image/.
Schmoll, Von Heike "*Ungeliebter Sternschen*," *Frankfurter Allgemeine*, April 4, 2019. https://www.faz.net/aktuell/politik/inland/mehrheit-der-deutschen-lehnt-gendergerechte-sprache-ab-16119532.html.
Sheehan, Thomas, "Did Heidegger Ever Finish *Being and Time*?" in *Division III of Heidegger's* Being and Time: *The Unanswered Question of Being*, ed. Lee Braver (Cambridge: MIT Press, 2015).
Villela-Petit, Maria, "Heidegger's Conception of Space," in *Critical Heidegger*, ed. Christopher Macan (New York: Routledge, 1996).
Wark, McKenzie, *Philosophy for Spiders: On the Low Theory of Kathy Acker* (Durham: Duke University Press, 2020).
Zupanic, Alenka, *What IS Sex?* (Cambridge: MIT Press, 2017).

Appendices I–III: Unfinished Definitions | Indefiniteness, *Geschlechtslosigkeit*, Undoing, Unknowing, Unlearning | Genre Unlimited/ Genre Ungenred

OSCAR JANSSON AND DAVID LAROCCA

Alexander of Aphrodisias, *On Aristotle's Metaphysics* IV, trans. Arthur Madigan (Ithaca: Cornell University Press, 1993).
Apter, Emily, "Untranslatable? The 'Reading' versus the 'Looking,'" *Journal of Visual Culture*, vol. 6, no. 1 (2007).
Apter, Emily, "Lexilalia: On Translating a Dictionary of Untranslatable Philosophical Terms," *Paragraph*, vol. 48, no. 5 (2015).
Ammonius, *In Aristotelem "De Interpretatione" Commentarius*, ed. Adolf Busse (Berlin: Reimber, 1897).
Ammonius, *On Aristotle's "On Interpretation,"* ed. David Blank (Ithaca: Cornell University Press, 1996).
Arendt, Hannah, "What remains? The language remains: an interview with Günter Gaus," in *Hannah Arendt, Essays in Understanding*, ed. Jerome Kohn (New York: Schocken Books, 2005).
Aristotle, *The Complete Works: The Revised Oxford Translation*, ed. Jonathan Barnes (Princeton: Princeton University Press, 1984).
Aristotle, *De interpretatione*, ed. Hermann Weidemann (Berlin/Boston: De Gruyter, 2014).
Bäck, Allan T., *Aristotle's Theory of Predication* (Leiden/Bostion/Cologne, E.J. Brill, 2000).
Bakhtin, Mikhail, "Epic and Novel," *The Dialogic Imagination: Four Essays*, trans. Caryl Emerson, ed. Michael Holquist (Austin: University of Texas Press, 1981).
Barthes, Roland, *The Pleasure of the Text*, trans. Richard Miller (New York: Hill and Wang, 1975).
Beauvoir, Simone de, *The Second Sex*, trans. Constance Borde and Sheila Malovany-Chevallier (New York: Vintage Books, 2011).
Boethius, Anicius Manlius Severinus, *Commentarii in librum Aristotelis Peri hermeneias*, ed. Karl Meiser (Leipzig: Teubner, 1887–80).
Braidotti, Rosi, *Nomadic Subjects: Embodiment and Sexual Difference in Contemporary Feminist Theory* (New York: Columbia University Press, 1994).
Brooks, Cleanth, *The Well Wrought Urn: Studies in the Structure of Poetry* (New York: Harcourt, Brace, 1947).
Browne, June, ed., *The Future of Gender* (Cambridge: Cambridge University Press, 2007).
Butler, Judith, *Gender Trouble: Feminism and the Subversion of Identity* (New York: Routledge, 1990).
Butler, Judith, *Bodies That Matter: On the Discursive Limits of Sex* (New York: Routledge, 1993).
Butler, Judith, "Gender and gender trouble," in *Dictionary of Untranslatables: A Philosophical Lexicon*, ed. Barbara Cassin, trans. eds. Emily Apter, Jacques Lezra, and Michael Wood (Princeton: Princeton University Press, 2014).

Cassin, Barbara, *L'Effet sophistique* (Paris: Gallimard, 1995).
Cassin, Barbara, *La Décision du sens, le livre* Gamma *de la* Métaphysique *d'Aristote* (Paris: Vrin, 2000).
Cassin, Barbara, "Philosophizing in Languages," *Nottingham French Studies*, vol. 49, no. 2 (June 2010).
Cassin, Barbara, *Sophistical Practice: Toward a Consistent Relativism* (New York: Fordham University Press, 2014).
Cavell, Stanley, *The World Viewed: Reflections on the Ontology of Film*, enlarged edition (Cambridge: Harvard University Press, 1979 [1971]).
Cavell, Stanley, "The Fact of Television" (1982), in *Themes Out of School: Effects and Causes* (San Francisco: North Point Press, 1984).
Cavell, Stanley, "Beginning to Read Barbara Cassin," *Hypatia*, vol. 15. no. 4 (Fall 2000).
Cavell, Stanley, *Cities of Words: Pedagogical Letters on a Register of the Moral Life* (Cambridge: The Belknap Press of Harvard University Press, 2004).
Cawelti, John G., *Adventures, Mystery, and Romance: Formula Stories as Art and Popular Culture* (Chicago: The University of Chicago Press, 1976).
Chartier, Roger, "Genre between Literature and History," *Modern Language Quarterly*, vol. 67, no. 1 (March 2006).
Clarey, Christopher, "Gender Test after a Gold-Medal Finish," *The New York Times*, August 19, 2009, http://www.nytimes.com/2009/08/20/sports/20runner.html.
Courtine-Denamy, Sylvie, "Postface," in Hannah Arendt, *Journal de pensée: 1950–1973*, vol. II (Paris: Seuil, 2005).
Crépon, Marc, "*Geschlecht*," in *Dictionary of Untranslatables: A Philosophical Lexicon*, ed. Barbara Cassin, trans. eds. Emily Apter, Jacques Lezra, and Michael Wood (Princeton: Princeton University Press, 2014).
Crimmins, Jonathan, "Gender, Genre, and the Near Future in Derrida's 'The Law of Genre,'" *diacritics*, vol. 39, no. 1 (2009).
Croce, Benedetto, "Criticism of the Theory of Artistic and Literary Kinds," in *Modern Genre Theory*, trans. Douglas Ainslie, ed. David Duff (London and New York: Routledge, 2014).
David-Menard, Monique, *Hysteria from Freud to Lacan: Body and Language in Psychoanalysis*, trans. Catherine Porter (Ithaca: Cornell University Press, 1989).
David-Menard, Monique, "Sexual Alterity and the Alterity of the Real for Thought," trans. Diane Morgan, *Angelaki*, vol. 8, no. 2 (2003).
David-Ménard, Monique and Penelope Deutscher, "Gender," in *Dictionary of Untranslatables: A Philosophical Lexicon*, ed. Barbara Cassin, trans. eds. Emily Apter, Jacques Lezra, and Michael Wood (Princeton: Princeton University Press, 2014).
Delphy, Christine, "Penser le genre. Quels Problème?" in *Sexe et genre: de la hiérarchie entre les sexes*, eds. Marie-Claude Hurtig et al. (Paris: Éditions du CNRS, 1991).
Derrida, Jacques, "The Law of Genre," trans. Avital Ronell, *Critical Inquiry*, vol. 7, no. 1 (Autumn 1980).
Derrida, Jacques, "*Geschlecht* I: Sexual Difference, Ontological Difference," trans. Ruben Bevezdivin and Elizabeth Rottenberg, in *Psyche: Inventions of the*

Other, vol. II, eds. Peggy Kamuf and Elizabeth Rottenberg (Stanford: Stanford University Press, 2008).

Descartes, René, *Passions of the Soul*, trans. Stephen Voss (Indianapolis: Hackett Publishing Company, 1989).

Deutscher, Penelope, *Yielding Gender: Feminism, Deconstruction and the History of Philosophy* (London: Routledge, 1997).

Dorlin, Elsa, *Sexe, genre et sexualités* (Paris: Presses Universitaires de France, 2008).

Fraisse, Geneviève, *Reason's Muse: Sexual Difference and the Birth of Democracy*, trans. Jane Marie Todd (Chicago: The University of Chicago Press, 1994).

Fraisse, Geneviève, *La Différence des sexes* (Paris: Presses Universitaires de France, 1996).

Fletcher, John, "The Letter in the Unconscious: The Enigmatic Signifier in Jean Laplanche," in *Jean Laplanche: Seduction, Translation and the Drives*, eds. John Fletcher and Martin Stanton, ICA Documents, no. 11 (London: Institute of Contemporary Arts, 1992).

Foucault, Michel, *History of Sexuality*, vol. I (New York: Vintage Books, 1990).

Freud, Sigmund, "Triebe und Triebschicksale," in *Gesammelte Werke, Chronologish Geordnet*, vol. 10, eds. Anna Freud et al. (London: Imago Publishing Co., 1913–17).

Freud, Sigmund, "Instincts and Their Vicissitudes," in *The Standard Edition of the Complete Works of Sigmund Freud*, vol. 14, ed. James Strachey (London: Hogarth Press, 1957).

Frye, Northrop, *A Natural Perspective* (New York: Columbia University Press, 1965).

Gatens, Moira, "A Critic of the Sex/Gender Distinction," in *Imaginary Bodies: Ethics, Power and Corporeality* (New York: Routledge, 1995).

Genette, Gérard, *Bardadrac* (Paris: Seuil, 2006).

Gorgias, *Encomium of Helen* (414 B.C.E.), reprinted in *The Norton Anthology of Theory and Criticism*, eds. Vincent B. Leitch et al. (New York: W.W. Norton & Company, 2001).

Grosz, Elizabeth, *Volatile Bodies: Toward a Corporeal Feminism* (Bloomington: Indiana University Press, 1994).

Guattari, Félix, "Microphysics of Power/Micropolitics of Desire," in *The Guattari Reader*, trans. John Caruana, ed. Gary Genosko (Oxford: Blackwell, 1996).

Haraway, Donna, *Simians, Cyborgs, and Women: The Reinvention of Nature* (New York: Routledge, 1991).

Hauser, Arnold, "The Film Age," in *Film*, ed. Daniel Talbot (New York: Simon and Schuster, 1959).

Heidegger, Martin, "Vom Wesen und Begriff der Φυσις," *Gemsatausgabe* I, vol. 9: *Wegmarken* (Frankfurt am Main: V. Klostermann, 1976).

Heidegger, Martin, *Unterwegs zur Sprache. Gesamtausgabe*, vol. 12, ed. Friedrich-Wilhelm von Herrmann (Frankfurt am Main: Klostermann, 1985).

Heller-Roazen, Daniel, *No One's Ways: An Essay on Infinite Naming* (New York: Zone Books, 2017).

Herder, Johann Gottfried, *Ideen zur Philosophie der Geschichte der Menschheit*, vol. 13, in *Sämmtliche Werke*, ed. B. Suphan (Berlin: Weidmann, 1877–1913).

Herder, Johann Gottfried, *Reflections on the Philosophy of the History of Mankind*, trans. Frank E. Manuel (Chicago: The University of Chicago Press, 1968).

Humboldt, W. von, *Über die Verschiedenheiten des menschlichen Sprachbaues, Gesammelte Schriften*, vol. VI, ed. A. Leitzmann (Berlin: B. Behr, 1907).
Irigaray, Luce, *Ethics of Sexual Difference*, trans. Carolyn Burke and Gillian C. Gill (Ithaca NY: Cornell University Press, 1984).
Irigaray, Luce, *To Be Two*, trans. Monique M. Rhodes and Marco F. Cocito-Monoc (New York: Routledge and The Athlone Press, 2001).
Jauss, Hans Robert, "Theory of Genres and Medieval Literature," in *Modern Genre Theory*, trans. Timothy Bahti, ed. David Duff (London and New York: Routledge, 2014).
Kant, Immanuel, *Anthropologie in pragmatischer Hinsicht*, in *Gesammelte Schriften*, vol. 7, ed. Königlich Preussischen Akademie der Wissenschaften (Berlin: De Gruyter, 1902).
Kant, Immanuel, *Observations on the Feeling of the Beautiful and Sublime*, trans. John T. Goldthwait (Berkeley: University of California Press, 1960).
Kant, Immanuel, *Anthropology from a Pragmatic Point of View*, trans. Robert B. Louden (Cambridge: Cambridge University Press, 2006).
Kant, Immanuel, *Bestimmung des Begriffs einer Menschen Passe, Gesamtausgabe*, vol. 8, *Determination of the Concept of a Human Race*. §6 in *Anthropology, History and Education*, eds. R. Louden and G. Zöller (Cambridge: Cambridge University Press, 2011).
Krell, David Farrell, "One, Two, Four—Yet Where Is the Third? A Note on Derrida's Series," *Epoché*, vol. 10 (2006).
Lacan, Jacques, "*L'Etourdit*," *Scilicet*, vol. 4 (Paris: Le Seuil, 1973).
Lacan, Jacques, "The Four Fundamental Concepts of Psychoanalysis, 1964," *The Seminar*, vol. 11, ed. Alan Sheridan (London: Hogarth Press and Institute of Psychoanalysis, 1977).
Lacan, Jacques, *Écrits: The First Complete Edition in English*, trans. Bruce Fink (New York: W. W. Norton, 2002).
Laplanche, Jean, "The Drive and the Object-Source: Its Fate in the Transference," *Jean Laplanche: Seduction, Translation, and the Drives*, eds. John Fletcher and Martin Stanton, ICA Documents, no. 11 (London: Institute of Contemporary Arts, 1992).
Laplanche, Jean and Susan Fairfield, "Gender, Sex and the Sexual," *Studies in Gender and Sexuality*, vol. 8, no. 2 (2007).
Laqueur, Thomas, *Making Sex: Body and Gender from the Greeks to Freud* (Cambridge: Harvard University Press, 1990).
Longino, Helen E., *Science as Social Knowledge: Values and Objectivity in Scientific Inquiry* (Princeton: Princeton University Press, 1990).
Malabou, Catherine, *Changing Difference: The Feminine and the Question of Philosophy*, trans. Carolyn Shread (Cambridge: Polity Press, 2011).
Merleau-Ponty, Maurice, *Phenomenology of Perception*, trans. Colin Smith (New York: Routledge, 2002).
Momigliano, Arnaldo, "The Fault of the Greeks," *Essays in Ancient and Modern Historiography* (Middletown: Wesleyan University Press, 1977).
Nancy, Jean-Luc, *L'intrus*, trans. Susan Hanson (East Lansing: Michigan State University Press, 2002). https://www.jstor.org/stable/41949352.
Novalis, "Monologue," in *German Aesthetic and Literary Criticism: The Romantic Ironists and Goethe*, ed. Kathleen Wheeler (Cambridge: Cambridge University Press, 1984).

Nietzsche, Friedrich, "*Fragments sur le langage*" (*note de travail pour Homére el la philologie classique*), trans. J-L. Nancy and P. Lacoue-Labarthe, *Poétique*, vol. 5 (1971).
Oakley, Ann, *Sex, Gender, and Society* (London: Temple Smith, 1972).
Ortner, Sherry B., "Is Female to Male as Nature Is to Culture?" in *Woman, Culture and Society*, eds. Michelle Zimbalist Rosaldo and Louise Lamphere (Stanford: Stanford University Press, 1974).
Panofsky, Erwin, "Style and Medium in the Moving Pictures," in *Film*, ed. Daniel Talbot (New York: Simon and Schuster, 1959).
Parménide, *Sur la nature ou sur l'éant. La langue de l'être* (Paris: Seuil/Points-bilingue, 1998).
Perlin, Ross, "Philosophers of Babel," *The New Inquiry*, May 4, 2014, thenewinquiry.com/essays/philosophers-of-babel-2.
Petrilli, Raffaella, *Temps et détermination dans la grammaire et la philosophie anciennes* (Munster: Nodus Publikationen, 1997).
Plato, *Cratylus, Complete Works*, eds. J. M. Cooper and D. S. Hutchinson (Indianapolis: Hackett, 1997).
Preciado, Paul Beatriz, *Testo Junkie: Sex, Drugs, and Biopolitics in the Pharmacopornographic Era*, trans. Bruce Benderson (New York: The Feminist Press at the City University of New York, 2013).
Propp, Vladimir, *Morphologie du conte*, trans. Marguerite Derrida (Paris: Seuil 1970).
Rijk, L. M. De, "The Logic of Indefinite Names in Boethius, Abelard, Duns Scotus and Radulphus Brito," in *Aristotle's Peri hermeneias in the Latin Middle Ages: Essays on the Commentary Tradition*, eds. H. A. G. Braakhuis and C. H. Kneepkens (Groningen: Ingenium Publishers, 2003).
Rosen, Charles, *The Classical Style* (New York: Simon & Schuster, 1971).
Rubin, Gayle S., "The Traffic in Women: Notes on the 'Political Economy' of Sex," in *Toward an Anthropology of Women*, ed. Rayna R. Reiter (New York: Monthly Review Press, 1975).
Sandford, Stella, *Plato and Sex* (Cambridge: Polity Press, 2010).
Sandford, Stella, "'Sex' and 'Sexual Difference,'" in *Dictionary of Untranslatables: A Philosophical Lexicon*, ed. Barbara Cassin, trans. eds. Emily Apter, Jacques Lezra, and Michael Wood (Princeton: Princeton University Press, 2014).
Schleiermacher, Friedrich, *Des differentes méthodes de traduire et autre texte*, trans. A. Berman and C. Berner (Paris: Seuil, 1999).
Schleiermacher, Friedrich, "On the different methods of translating," in *The Translation Studies Reader*, trans. Susan Bernovsky, ed. Lawrence Venuti (London: Routledge, 2004).
Schor, Naomi and Elizabeth Weed, eds., *The Essential Difference* (Bloomington: Indiana University Press, 1994).
Scott, Joan W., "Gender: A Useful Category of Historical Analysis," in *Gender and the Politics of History*, eds. Carolyn G. Heilbrun and Nancy K. Miller (New York: Columbia University Press, 1988).
Scott, Joan W., *Only Paradoxes to Offer: French Feminists and the Rights of Man* (Cambridge: Harvard University Press, 1996).
Shepherdson, Charles, *Vital Signs: Nature, Culture, Psychoanalysis* (New York: Routledge, 2000).

Shiel, James, "Boethius's Commentaries on Aristotle," *Mediaeval and Renaissance Studies*, vol. 4 (1958).

Spillers, Hortense J., "Mama's Baby, Papa's Maybe: An American Grammar Book," *diacritics*, vol. 17, no. 2 (Summer 1987).

Stoller, Robert, *Sex and Gender: On the Development of Masculinity and Femininity* (New York: Science House, 1968).

Todorov, Tzvetan, *The Fantastic*, trans. Richard Howard (Ithaca: Cornell University Press, 1975).

Weheliye, Alexander G., *Habeas Viscus: Racializing Assemblages, Biopolitics, and Black Feminist Theories of the Human* (Durham: Duke University Press, 2014).

Wells, Susan, "Genres as Species and Spaces: Literary and Rhetorical Genre in *The Anatomy of Melancholy*," *Philosophy and Rhetoric*, vol. 47, no. 2 (2014).

Winterson, Jeanette, *Written on the Body* (London: Jonathan Cape, 1992).

Wittgenstein, Ludwig, *Philosophical Investigations*, trans. G. E. M. Anscombe (Oxford: Blackwell, 1974).

Wittig, Monique, *Les guérillères* (Paris: Éditions de Minuit, 1969).

Wittig, Monique, "The Category of Sex," in *The Straight Mind and Other Essays* (Boston: Beacon Press, 1992).

Wolfson, Harry Austryn, "Infinite and Privative Judgments in Aristotle, Averroes and Kant," *Philosophy and Phenomenological Research*, vol. 8, no. 2 (1947). Reprinted in *Studies in the History of Philosophy and Religion*, eds. Isadore Twersky and George H. Williams (Cambridge: Harvard University Press, 1973–7).

ACKNOWLEDGMENTS

From the Editors

IN THE INTRODUCTION, while shaping the contours of our imagined campus novel in brief sketches, we kept anonymous the specific people, places, programs, and institutions that gave rise to such a conjuring of *The Geschlecht Complex*. Here, in a space better suited to the occasion of praising and thanking, we supply further details of our gratitude—making more explicit those who informed the gestation of the volume.

A reader coming to *The Geschlecht Complex* can measure our debts to Emily Apter on each page; to be sure, though, given our license, we editors are alone responsible for the ways in which her work and her pedagogy have come to endow the present volume and propel it forward. As a teacher and scholar one never knows the true extent of one's impact, and sometimes the effects can be surprising—drawing interest or hoping for distance! That said, along with a few signal inspirations—Barbara Cassin and Stanley Cavell come immediately to mind—Apter's framing and filling-in of possibilities for "thinking in untranslatables" proved a transformative gift, and we are duly, deeply grateful to her.

Looking around the shared table a few summers back, we wish to thank each individual participant in Apter's "Thinking in Untranslatables" seminar, which convened in the summer of 2017 as part of the School of Theory and Criticism at Cornell University, Ithaca, New York. They arrived from around the country and the globe and made a home, for a brief season, in this little hamlet of the Finger Lakes, ancestral homelands and waters of the Gayogo̱hó:nǫ' (the Cayuga Nation), members of the Haudenosaunee Confederacy. In particular, and apart from the contributors to this volume who participated in the seminar—heralding here our brilliant, magnanimous collaborators, Caro Pirri and Lauren DiGiulio—we are thinking of Emily Antenucci, Swayam Bagaria, Tanja Beljanski, John Casey, Kris Conner, Miguel Lizada, Prathna Lor, Kelly Morgan, Shoshana Olidort, Phillipe Panizzon, Nitin Patil, Fernanda Righi, Ami Scheiss, Dylan Shaul, Javier Suarez, Di Wu, and Victor Zhang. We hope you recognize portions of our in-person conversations as they have been embodied and transformed in this collection, and call to mind, like us, those aspects that remain, fittingly, untranslatable.

We offer special thanks to Richard Hajarizadeh, who contributed to the first sparks of the collection and introduced us to Brian W. Nail. Given our wide-ranging discussions with him, we are very pleased to see how our three chapters gathered here—5, 6, and 7—found a favorable sequencing and interactive harmony, a complementarity in keeping with the pleasures of our in-person dialogues and long-distance exchanges.

As part of the School of Criticism and Theory (SCT) community of participants and visitors, we are keen to highlight our affection for and admiration of Hent de Vries, capable director of the operation. Whether in his formal talks or in after-session conversations, Hent epitomizes the capacious, polyglot, and syncretic intellect necessary for attempting the best interdisciplinary research in the humanities.

In the wider community that summer, and in surrounding summers, we benefited from conversations in the A. D. White House, Goldwin Smith Hall, and elsewhere on campus and by the lake with Amanda Anderson, Branka Arsić, Robert Brandom, Warren Breckman, Susan Buck-Morss, Cathy Caruth, Jonathan Culler, Veena Das, Philippe Descola, Faisal Devji, Frances Ferguson, Neil Hertz, Renate Ferro, Philip Lewis, Heather Love, Avishai Margalit, W. J. T. Mitchell, Timothy Murray, Catherine Porter, Michael Puett, Carolyn Rouse, Shirley Samuels, Anthony Vidler, and Mariët Westermann. Jim Utz was our adept program coordinator.

During the development of the manuscript, we were very fortunate to have the input and collegial cheer of Brian James Baer, founding editor of *Translation and Interpretation Studies* and coeditor with Michelle Woods of the Bloomsbury series "Literatures, Cultures, Translation." Anonymous referees for the press rounded out our sense of what was working and what might be possible for the collection, and we remain grateful for the range and depth of informed remarks sent our way.

At Bloomsbury, working with Haaris Naqvi and Rachel Moore, once again—including the capable team of editors, production assistants, designers, and more—proved invigorating. Along with project management by Joanne Rippin, Zeba Talkhani, and Rachel Walker, and copyediting by Sara Brunton, we are grateful, indeed, for your sage counsel and your savvy direction.

From Oscar

Speaking for the Swedish and, at times, Belgian portion of the collective and collaborative labors that have gone into bringing forth this volume, I must first give thanks to David LaRocca—my wonderful coeditor and valued *cicerone* of all things American (including the finer workings of its publishing practices). From the very beginning, his ingenuity and inquisitiveness have both plotted our course to unknown terrains and kept us clear of numerous pitfalls. For that, and all else, I am forever grateful.

I would also attest that many colleagues at the department of Literary Studies at Lund University have shaped my research in one way or another, and further that the Centre for Languages and Literature will always be a benchmark for my views of the possibilities of interdisciplinary research—even if the cohabitation of philology and philosophy is sometimes turbulent. More specifically, the numerous talks and presentations and the Komplitt-seminar must be mentioned, alongside its founders and steering committee: Paul Tenngart, Alexander Bareis, Chistian Claesson, Annika Mörte Alling, and Shuangyi Li. I would also like to express my gratitude to friends and colleagues in Lund who have kept asking questions, and kept encouraging me to go beyond local contexts and readily definable perspectives on any literary or linguistic category; among them Torbjörn Forslid, Ann Steiner, and Eva Hættner Aurelius. And a special mention must be made of Anna Hultman and Magdalena Malmfors, who kept open minds, read drafts, and always asked questions to push ideas further.

Beyond the halls of Lund University, I am also grateful for the productively inquisitive Centre for Reception Study and its surrounding intellectual environments at the University of Leuven. A heartfelt thanks to Tom Toremans, Ortwin de Graef, Elke Brems, Pieter Vermeulen, Núria Codina, Jack McMartin, Ernest de Clerck, and Laura Cernat, and all others at the Center for Reception Study (CERES) and the Center for Translation Study (CETRA) who are ever curious and keen on understanding both the new and the old of literature, language, and philosophy.

Last but not least, I want to extend my everlasting affection and gratitude to Jonna Jansson, who once, long ago, taught me how Paris works, and who has remained my most important teacher ever since.

From David

In addition to the foregoing lines of influence drawing our appreciation, there are several salient experiences with amiable accomplices that informed the development of my chapter and approach to *The Geschlecht Complex* more generally. Thus, continuing from our shared notes of gratitude above, I extend my personal thanks to these others, appropriately beginning with my esteemed coeditor, Oscar Jansson.

Luck plays a significant role in our lives—maybe it's all luck. If so, then once again, I reaffirm *amor fati*. As it happened, our kindred sense for texts and topics was initially cultivated during *fika* on the Arts & Humanities Quad and around the seminar table, first in Ithaca, then in Lund. Oscar's instigation of the present collection—rightly sensing the vitality of the subject matter and the promise of issuing new reflections on it—created conditions for discovering his generosity, talent as a bibliophile and language scholar, and willingness to experiment, all of which helped, in turn, to precipitate and complete these labors. A tremendous collaborator—not just by contributing relevant ideas and the sentences that hold them, but inspiring me to attempt the same—Oscar exemplified the best traits of that mysterious activity, shared authorship.

Time as Visiting Scholar in the Department of English at Cornell University aided research and writing that culminated first in *A Power to Translate the World: New Essays on Emerson and International Culture*, which I coedited with another dear collaborator, Ricardo Miguel-Alfonso, a volume that is part of the Dartmouth Series in American Studies "Re-Mapping the Transnational" from series editor Donald E. Pease. Later some contributors to the volume convened on campus to celebrate and share their work at the symposium "Global/Emerson: Transmission, Translation, Transnational." Another project defined by a trans function was also completed while in residence: *The Bloomsbury Anthology of Transcendental Thought: From Antiquity to the Anthropocene*. Over seasons of research, it was my good fortune to discuss these projects with and benefit from the input of Kevin Attell, Susan Buck-Morss, Hent de Vries, Andrew Galloway, Roger Gilbert, Neil Hertz, John Lachs, Masha Raskolnikov, and many visitors to the Society for the Humanities. Other Cornellians have been generous with their time and critical acumen, among them Caroline Levine, Roger Gilbert, and Thomas Campanella. Thomas Elsaesser's memorable visit to campus was made possible, and further enriched, by Amy Villarejo, Nick Salvato, Jeremy Braddock, Patrizia McBride, Erik Born, Leslie Adelson, Paul Fleming, Kizer Walker, and at Cornell Cinema, Mary Fessenden. And I recall salutary visits to Ithaca from Samuel A. Chambers, Curtis Brown, Rebecca Brown, Paul Cronin, William Day, M. Jane Evans, Gil Even-Tsur, David and Stephanie Insley Hershinow, Todd May, John Opera, Adria Pecora, Kristen Steslow, and Alessandro Subrizi. Prior to both of these trans-centric endeavors, editing *Emerson's Transcendental Etudes* provided occasion to discuss with Stanley Cavell ever-evolving interactions between the transcendental and the ordinary, the momentous and the uneventful, the quixotic and the demotic—and along the way, glean more about his marvelous, coruscate sentences in that collection, and elsewhere.

In the context of preparing this volume, a certain set of formative influences, other than Cavell—first, in the classroom, then later, beyond it—made their effects known by turns and degrees, among them J. M. Bernstein, Giuliana Bruno, Anthony Cascardi, Kay-Kyung Cho, Kenneth Dauber, Newton Garver, Stephen Jay Gould, Elizabeth Grosz, Peter H. Hare, Gregg Horowitz, Despina Kakoudaki, Gordon D. Kaufman, Helmut Koester, Michael Mascuch, Stephanie Paulsell, Peggy Phelan, Barry Smith, Cornel

West, and David Wood. Richard Lanham's advice still tracks all critical and editorial essaying.

Deliberations on the presence of sound in film—as part of the development of *The Philosophy of Documentary Film: Image, Sound, Fiction, Truth* and sustained in *Movies with Stanley Cavell in Mind*—underwrote the exploration here of genres of sound in experimental and avant-garde cinemas. A series of appointments placed me (again, with good fortune) in communities filled with talented agents of these arts and knowing pedagogues of these fields, who expanded for me the possibilities for approaching such dynamic realms of cinematic experience. In particular, there were appointments as visiting assistant professor in the Cinema Department at Binghamton University; visiting assistant professor in the Department of Philosophy at the State University of New York College at Cortland; lecturer in Screen Studies in the Department of Cinema, Photography, and Media Arts at the Roy H. Park School of Communications at Ithaca College; and visiting lecturer at the School of Visual Arts. Points of edification and inspiration include sharing conversations or classrooms with Ariana T. Gerstein, Vincent Grenier, Matthew Holtmeier, Scott MacDonald, Tomonari Nishikawa, Chantal Rodais, Daïchi Saïto, J. P. Sniadecki, Andrew Utterson, Brian K. Wall, Chelsea Wessels, and Patricia R. Zimmermann.

Research for Chapter 7 benefitted immensely from institutional knowledge, or more precisely, the generosity of those who possess it. Teaching at Ithaca College featured memorable screenings of Martin Arnold's *The Cineseizure* in Patricia Zimmermann's canonical "Film Aesthetics and Analysis" course. Teaching at Binghamton, home to a pantheon of experimental filmmakers, once and ongoing (including the residencies of Hollis Frampton and Martin Arnold), much was gleaned about the history of cinema at Harpur College. Talking with Larry Gottheim, who crewed as sound recordist on *Critical Mass*, was a special highlight. Vincent Grenier, as he was for *Metacinema*, proved a significant ally in deliberating over some lessons of Frampton and Arnold's work (often in conversation with Grenier's own accomplished films).

When I took this research on the road, tuitions were gratefully received from many directions and disparate communities. Let me thank those who occasioned conversations with the most conspicuous impact on the present research. Emily Thomas offered an invitation to the New Directions conference at the University of Arizona in Tucson, where I was delighted by the collegial reception of the work. In the same season, Shai Biderman, Dan Geva, and Ohad Landesman dispatched an invitation to the Docusophia: Documentary Film and Philosophy conference, sponsored by the Steve Tisch School of Film and Television, convened at Tel Aviv University; at that gathering, Linda Williams' direct commentary on an earlier version of what became chapter seven helped me clarify the stakes of the investigation, and lent credence to viable methodological approaches for making them evident to others. Also while in Israel, Dan Geva and Avner Faingulernt shared reflections on documentary film production and pedagogy. Oscar Jansson's invitation to Lund, Sweden, precipitated a generative visit with him, including time with his colleagues at the Centre for Languages and Literatures and the Department of Comparative Literature at Lund University; Oscar's hospitality coupled with critical notes from those gathered enriched the scope of these investigations of *Geschlecht*. Most recently, and arriving from the University of Ottawa, Arnaud Petit and Patrice Philie's invitation to present at "Inheriting Cavell"—an exploratory, synchronous, transnational forum on the inheritance of the thought of Stanley Cavell—provided an opportunity to solicit commentary on a range of enduring topics (including the work of acknowledgment, here attempted), and for learning from them as well as from fellow participants Richard Eldridge, Simon Glendenning, Russell Goodman, Sandra Laugier, David Macarthur, and Andrew Norris.

Co-teaching with Paul Cronin at the School of Visual Arts has provided an invigorating context in which to experiment with and explore what is possible in film pedagogy; in several classes, over as many semesters, our attention to genre proved a fecund field in which to engage multiple histories of cinema. Conversations in recent years with Diana Allan and J. P. Sniadecki have been especially helpful for better understanding the outlook from Harvard's Sensory Ethnography Lab, and those who are innovating in and beyond that community. Discussions with Scott MacDonald about the history of experimental and avant-garde filmmaking have decisively shaped my appreciation of selected films and figures as well as their once and ongoing significance. Corresponding with Garrett Stewart about genre, metacinema, interpretive method, the sounds of writing and cinema, the uncoupled achievements of Barbra Streisand and Stanley Cavell, and much else, has consistently illuminated and inspired; his readings—both in the spirit *and* the letter, and the spirt *of* the letter—have become edifying gifts that shore up scholarly ventures; indeed, I often learn from him what it is I am doing, or should be, or want to be; such effects summon heady feelings, but in just the right ways. Likewise, Robert Pippin's encouragement and comments stand out for modeling collegiality of an especially rare and precious sort. My debts to Stanley Cavell mount even now, after his death, for in his writing he continues, as he did in life, to give graciously and generously.

Loving family who make such efforts possible and worthwhile include Sheldon and Lorna K. Hershinow, Ian M. Evans and Luanna H. Meyer, Frances LaRocca and Roselle Sweeney, and David N. and Hi-jin Hodge. Although we share a time, our dispersal in space has made for memorable and continual efforts to reconcile distance.

In all matters intellectual and domestic, my thoughts turn to K. L. Evans. She remains the *sine qua non* for any such endeavors—a keen mind, the brilliance of her casual remarks often outstripping my most deliberate ones; a proximate, sometimes involutary audience for this work under development, and a fellow alumnus of the School of Criticism and Theory, her impactful comments prompted much productive revision. Ruby, a German and Latin scholar in her own right, sets a new standard for the resident etymologist, lexicographer, and linguist. Star's ethereal offerings—seemingly the precipitate of a curious mind making contact with the potencies of language—gratifyingly and reliably stagger.

* * * *

On each new occasion of writing Acknowledgments, one is invited (compelled?) anew to consider what it would mean to acknowledge others, in particular, to speak to their influence on the work at hand, and to find measures of thanks for such beneficent consequences. And yet, are we equipped to properly identify the one and articulate the other—to discern cause and perceive effect? Such a rhetorical question leaves us surprised to discover that Acknowledgments too—that most familiar and standard paratext—is yet another genre of the untranslatable.

In writing Acknowledgments for this volume, I have, as it seems one must, once again brushed up against the latent frustration constituting this mode of address—one more akin to the impressionism of memoir than the systematicity and completeness of the *curriculum vitae*: first, there is a haunting sense of forgetfulness (that one has difficulty recalling who has helped, perhaps especially those who may have genuinely aided an endeavor, yet precisely because their effects have been so deeply impactful or thoroughly incorporated—in a word, are so near—they cannot be seen); and second, there arises the perplexing sense of not being sure, in fact, how one has been helped, or to what degree or extent (so that tangential, if still pertinent, aids may be cited while central, absolutely essential ones are insufficiently recognized, or simply, that is, with chagrin, overlooked). In the attempted translation of thanks, thoughts and sentiments can be distorted or lost. Acknowledgments are always already some portion of mourning and apology, constituted by them—a bid against necessary impairments and dispossessions. For how could we say precisely when influence begins—and when it ends? If a collaborator or teacher lives (on) in one's mind—a voice still in conversation, still offering counsel (as the another's death is the end of the relationship for only one of us)—why not go on thanking through thinking further with them (even as apparitions), or in casting about for a quantum of memorialization?[1]

Acknowledgment is, in some measure, an attempt to account for influence, for the reception of an inheritance—how they are received, processed, and subsequently manifested; as such, the form assumes one is poised to trace how experience radiates, how context informs the creation of texts.[2] "If [Plato] had lover, wife, or children, we hear nothing of them," wrote Emerson. "He ground them all into paint." No acknowledgment necessary, then? ("As a good chimney burns its smoke, so a philosopher converts the value of all his fortunes into his intellectual performances."[3]) It appears so. The work itself *is* the acknowledgment. And yet, at this juncture, for this undertaking on the very conditions for the possibility of translation, we want to give names, or further phrasing, to what present as structural aspects of the genre—noting that part of the effort to acknowledge others in Acknowledgments requires a confrontation with the dual frontiers of forgetfulness and blindness. Are these fated too, like the optic blind spot that endures though rarely, if ever, recognized—a feature persistently unacknowledged? If so, then these are regretful and disagreeable existential facts—ones that contribute a fitting gesture of the untranslatable to the proceedings of acknowledgment, here and elsewhere; yet when admitted, perhaps such limitations liberate us from the task—or, as a certain temperament would have it, provide us license to go on trying to thank.

As we ask "What of the translatability of thanks? How does one thank; how can one? If one can thank, does one?," we wonder about proportionality and purpose. The genre suggests we thank the right people in the right order (a rightness that is arbitrary, perspectival), but those we thank may be placeholders for others we cannot thank, proxies for those we would thank, if we knew ourselves and our work better. Must we personally know those we thank—and thus appoint embodied contact a criterion for membership in the catalog—or can we cast wider to influences that may, as it were, enrich an understanding of the work itself (as if Acknowledgments *want* to be at times a subgenre of literary memoir or private journal and at other times a mode of criticism[4]—when an author is given license to make debts known without regard to time and place, fraternity or disciplinary field, prior proclamations or institutional sanctions and affiliations)? Consider as a reply that Acknowledgments parallel Cavell's sense of acknowledgment in so far as thanks are not facts but gestures—and thus phenomenological rather than epistemological. Like readings of texts, they are not conclusive but ever onwardly propulsive; and like apologies, there is no guarantee that in being made they will be received as intended: they may misfire, backfire, or have no effect at all. The statement of acknowledgment (as thanks) is an interpretation of a text (or experience); it is conjectural, speculative, indeed, at times, a mere sharing of private impressions, perhaps still inchoate or in development; in this sense, they are akin to an Emersonian "spiritual fact"—expressible but not verifiable.

In the final lines of *Philosophy the Day after Tomorrow*, Cavell asked and answered: "Why do we put things together as we do? Why do we put ourselves together with just these things to make a world? What choices have we said farewell to? To put things together differently, so that they quicken the heart, would demand their recollecting."[5] Acknowledgments may be regarded as a genre of inheritance that demands a recollection, a remembering, and a productive synthesis of "things" (memories, dreams, and our reflections on them in the present). If philosophy, as Cavell understood it, is fundamentally a function of responsiveness to others and the world we share—and moreover, a responsiveness to the human need for acknowledgment (praise, reception, gratitude), there may be "the other side" of this relationship, namely, the human need to let others know they are acknowledged. From one strain of approach, thinking becomes a form of reception—a mode of receiving, of "bearing the responsibility of the inheritance" we are said to receive, belong to, or find ourselves constituted by—that, in turn, compels us to respond (to speak back, to say something).[6] Reception and response are entwined helixes. Yet, there is more to adduce, another valence to consider, as Derrida declared helpfully in *Specters of Marx*, with his emphases intact:

> Inheritance is never a *given*, it is always a task. [...] That we *are* heirs does not mean that we *have* or that we *receive* this or that, some inheritance that enriches us one day with this or that, but that the *being* of what we are is first of all inheritance, whether we like it or know it or not.[7]

We face the strange, bottomless need to acknowledge and to be acknowledged. Perversely, neither type of need is ever met, because the "task" of acknowledgment always falls short, always fails because no one knows the standards or criteria for the giving or the receiving of acknowledgment. From one side, what would it mean to fully thank, or to thank fittingly? From the other side, what would it mean to feel properly thanked? The questions as much as the shared condition suggest that the giving—and the receiving—of acknowledgment, like the giving of gratitude or the making of apologies, fundamentally involves the work of mourning. How much is thinking of past times (of texts, of events, of the living and the dead) a meditation on loss as much as on bounty? Acknowledgments gather effects up to the point of publication; they create a border between the book's birth and the entire sweep of its prehistory—again, after Derrida, all that we are as inheritances-unto-ourselves up to this fraught present.

Thanking as acknowledging, then, involves a narration of mourning along with an incantation of apology—for one is dismayed by conditions that leave us unsure about our debts, and instinctively seeking to set things right: to give due where it is deserved, to account for gifts received, and to expiate our liabilities accordingly; in many cases, curiously, we certify gifts that may not, in an empirical sense, have been given at all. Acknowledgments presume a logic of exchange; the genre expects that gifts, in fact (real or imagined), have been given—and thus stand in need of public confession; a response seems a responsibility. And yet, gifts and debts are intimate, often overlapping categories. As Emerson wrote, "It is not the office of a man to receive gifts. How dare you give them? [...] We do not quite forgive a giver."[8] Let us bracket talk of self-sufficiency here, so the resistance or anxiety elicited is not predicated on a wish to be self-giving, endogeneous; rather, in a more germane moment, Emerson suggests that "He is a good man who can receive a gift well." Yes, that sense is much preferable—so, then, what characterizes such a capacity for reception? Perhaps it is the entire labor of Acknowledgments to find out—to hazard such a discovery, and perhaps, time and again, to fail in finding, in short, to allow for living in the impasse between reception and response. "We are either glad or sorry at a gift, and both emotions are unbecoming. Some violence I think is done, some denegration borne, when I rejoice or grieve at a gift."[9] To avoid these extremes, Emerson seeks an equilibrium, a state of reciprocity: "the flowing of the giver unto me, correspondent to my flowing unto him."[10] We are left to ask and explore how the genre known as Acknowledgments achieves such displacement of grief and gift, of mourning and apology, availing, at last, a thanks and a thinking that gets the level right.

If Acknowledgments is a genre, it is also a ritual—a durable imposition that we are called to invent for a specific occasion; still, the genre may allow or encourage the generic, a repetition of testimony from book to book, or indeed, the registration of belated thanks (as time affords the appreciation of new candidates and categories). Yet, what do we as readers want from such faithfully rendered (spiritual?) exercises, and what do authors want from performing them? Do we write acknowledgments for an (anticipated) audience, even if it (likely) does not include those we thank? Creating and maintaining a ritual space can go unnoticed, its repeated use no guarantee that practitioners have been shown what it is for, what it can do, or might. The purposes of title and contents pages remain essential, and their meaning would appear mainly utilitarian, yet innovation is possible even within a book's vestibule. Meanwhile, without warning, Acknowledgments flip from front matter to back matter, a first sign of a logic unarticulated or of significance under debate. How is one's reading affected, if at all, by such inverted placements? Still, the theater of thanks abides: the question is whether the ritual is perfunctory (indeed, a kind of rehearsal), or sincerely mounted as an expression of the titular gesture, acknowledgment.

Placed here as an outro-excursus, these notes cast an eye about at those volumes arriving without Acknowledgments. Emerson gives us Plato, but there are many others. Should one aspire to write a work without Acknowledgments? Would such an absence, paradoxically, actualize Emerson's sought-for balance, because no apology, no mourning, no grieving, no gratitude is admitted—or do they all remain: suppressed and hidden from writer and reader alike? In such cases, the reader, of course, is deprived of an author's attempt at accounting for her work (and accounting always encodes apology and the rest). Despite the apparent liberation implied by a book without Acknowledgments, better, we may come to think, that an author—even out-of-sorts in her accounting—dares to sketch, because a book (without Acknowledgments) may give the impression of "uncaused" creation. To front that peculiar thought, Acknowledgments. A counter peril arises: "thou dost thank too much"—and yet no state of sufficiency, no resting place, will emerge despite the extent. Can one think without thanks? Acknowledgments as a genre, then, has us aim toward the revelation—the admission, the truth, yes, even the apology, etc.—that such enterprises are not made alone, in isolation[11]; and, as thoughts continue to arise, and as a work lives on in us past its publication, so are such thoughts of thanks also endless.

Given the vexing aliveness of such fundamental human issues and questions, ones that lie at the heart of any attempt to acknowledge another through responsive recollection, can one help but be been caught up with, captivated by, the genre of Acknowledgments, where two needs (to thank, to be thanked) appear to perpetually, that is, unresolvedly interact? Again, a gifted dispatch from Derrida, with his italics and disarming assessment of the fraught undertaking that befalls us, that is us:

> An inheritance is never gathered together, it is never one with itself. Its presumed unity, if there is one, can consist only in the *injunction* to *reaffirm by choosing*. "One must" means *one must* filter, sift, criticize, one must sort out several different possibles that inhabit the same injunction. And inhabit it in a contradictory fashion around a secret. If the readability of a legacy were given, natural, transparent, univocal, if it did not call for and at the same time defy interpretation, we would never have anything to inherit from it. We would be affected by it as by a cause—natural or genetic. One always inherits from a secret—which says "read me, will you ever be able to do so?" The critical choice called for by any reaffirmation of the inheritance is also, like memory itself, the condition of finitude.[12]

If Acknowledgments demand simultaneously "bearing the responsibility" for acknowledging and yet also assure a certain degree of the untranslatable (e.g., that thanking cannot be achieved, that a legacy may "call for and at the same time defy interpretation"), then the genre itself appears structurally, constitutionally compromised. This too is an inheritance. In such a faulty forum (modeled by others, learned from them, imitated by us), and in these "last words," the author finds an appropriate place to front the obstacles and risk thinking thanks—doing so in a mood fit for a *Gedankenschrift*[13]; in turn, the reader may inadvertently discover herself to be the subject of such tidings. At last, we cannot be sure who is giving and who is receiving—an ambiguity that tethers us, one to another.

Notes

1. See also my "Acknowledgments: Thinking of and Thanking Stanley Cavell," in *Conversations: The Journal of Cavellian Studies*, no. 7 (2019), 248–67.
2. See *Inheriting Stanley Cavell: Memories, Dreams, Reflections*, ed. David LaRocca (New York: Bloomsbury, 2020), and my introduction, "Must We Say What We Learned? Parsing the Personal and the Philosophical," 1–48.
3. Ralph Waldo Emerson, "Plato; or, the Philosopher," in *Representative Men, The Complete Works of Ralph Waldo Emerson*, vol. IV (Boston: Houghton, Mifflin and Company, 1903–4), 43.
4. See my "Autophilosophy," in *Inheriting Stanley Cavell*, 275–320.
5. Stanley Cavell, "The World as Things," in *Philosophy the Day after Tomorrow* (Cambridge: The Belknap Press of Harvard University Press, 2005), 280.
6. Stanley Cavell, *Pursuits of Happiness: The Hollywood Comedy of Remarriage* (Cambridge: Harvard University Press, 1981), 28.
7. Jacques Derrida, *Specters of Marx: The State of Debt, the Work of Mourning, and the New International*, trans. Peggy Kamuf (New York: Routledge, 1994), 67–68.
8. Ralph Waldo Emerson, "Gifts," in *Essays: Second Series, The Complete Works of Ralph Waldo Emerson*, vol. III (Boston: Houghton, Mifflin and Company, 1903–4), 162.
9. Emerson, "Gifts," *Essays: Second Series*, 162.
10. Emerson, "Gifts," *Essays: Second Series*, 163.
11. Notice that even when the topic of a work is solitude—famously in Thoreau's *Walden*, and in moments of Emerson—the apparatus of society, of community is on offer, in one's hands, in the ink and pulp of the book's own haptic existence.
12. Derrida, *Specters of Marx*, 18.
13. For more on *Gedankenschrift*, see my "Must We Say What We Learned? Parsing the Personal and the Philosophical," in *Inheriting Stanley Cavell*, 1–48, esp. 2–13.

CONTRIBUTORS

Emily Apter is Julius Silver Professor of French and Comparative Literature at New York University, and Remarque-École Normale Supérieure Visiting Professor in Paris, France; she has also taught at the University of California, Los Angeles; University of California, Davis; Cornell University; and Williams College. Apter was president of the American Comparative Literature Association in 2017–18. She is editor of the book series "Translation/Transnation" from Princeton University Press, and serves on the editorial boards of *Publications of the Modern Languages Association of America*, *Comparative Literature*, *October*, *diacritics*, *Sites*, and *Signs*. A Guggenheim Fellow in 2003, Apter was awarded, with Jacques Lezra, a two-year Mellon Grant in 2011–12 for a seminar on "The Problem of Translation." With Jacques Lezra and Michael Wood, she translated Barbara Cassin's *Dictionary of Untranslatables: A Philosophical Lexicon* (Princeton, 2014). In fall 2014, she was a Humanities Council Fellow at Princeton University. Her books include *Unexceptional Politics: On Obstruction, Impasse, and the Impolitic* (Verso, 2018), *Against World Literature: On the Politics of Untranslatability* (Verso, 2013), and *The Translation Zone: A New Comparative Literature* (Princeton, 2006). She has also published extensively in *Third Text*, *e-flux*, *October*, *boundary 2*, *New Literary History*, *Littérature*, *Artforum*, *Critical Inquiry*, *Translation Studies*, *Cabinet*, *The Global South*, *Grey Room*, *Boston Review*, *differences*, and *Public Culture*.

Lauren DiGiulio is an art historian and curator. Her research focuses on contemporary visual art and performance, with a particular emphasis on the way these fields intersect with feminist and queer theory, genre, and critical race theory. Her writing has been published in *PAJ: A Journal of Performance and Art*, *Momus*, *Lateral Addition*, *In/Visible Culture*, *The Huffington Post*, and *Idiom* magazine. She has written commissioned texts for numerous museums and galleries, including the Institute for Contemporary Art at UPenn, the Barbican Centre, and the Kunstverein Langenhagen. From 2019 to 2021, she was the Andrew W. Mellon Postdoctoral Fellow at Carolina Performing Arts at the University of North Carolina-Chapel Hill. She received her PhD from the Program in Visual and Cultural Studies at the University of Rochester, her MA with Distinction from the Department of French at King's College London, and her BA in Art History and French from Vassar College.

Richard Hajarizadeh is a doctoral candidate in English Literature at Binghamton University, State University of New York. Encompassing critical practices of deconstruction, biopolitics, and Trans* theories of representation, his recent work explores entangled forms of institutional power, language, and identity in modernist literature. He is currently authoring a genealogy of the modernist subject, highlighting the exercise of power across symbolic and material forces that enjoin bodies to inhabit identity in relation to normalizing knowledges. Specifically, he is examining modernist knowledge structures of race and gender, and the forms of embodiment they demand, as represented in the literary works of Nella Larsen and Virginia Woolf. He has also written on biopolitical theories of social belonging in connection to race, gender, and their representation in law.

Oscar Jansson is the author of *Graham Greene and the Conditions of 20th Century Literature* and a handful of articles on modern literature and media, ranging from the aesthetics of national romanticism in J. L. Runeberg's *The Tales of Ensign Stål* to pandemic media assemblages in *The Last of Us: Remastered*. He studied literature, languages, and history at Lund University and Linneaus University, Sweden, and participated in the School of Criticism and Theory at Cornell University. In 2019 he was International Doctoral Research Fellow at Center for Reception Studies at the University of Leuven, Belgium, with support from the Royal Academy of Arts and Letters. He is currently a lecturer and postdoctoral research fellow at Lund University, and an editor of the literary review *TFL*.

David LaRocca is the author, editor, or coeditor of more than a dozen books. He edited two previous volumes that explore the potencies of the trans function in language and culture: *A Power to Translate the World: New Essays on Emerson and International Culture*, with Ricardo Miguel-Alfonso, and *The Bloomsbury Anthology of Transcendental Thought: From Antiquity to the Anthropocene*. Another prefix that has declared its independence—meta—is the subject of a volume from Oxford University Press, *Metacinema: The Form and Content of Filmic Reference and Reflexivity*. He edited a suite of volumes on Stanley Cavell: *The Thought of Stanley Cavell and Cinema*, *Inheriting Stanley Cavell*, and *Movies with Stanley Cavell in Mind*; and a triad in film philosophy: *The Philosophy of Charlie Kaufman*, *The Philosophy of War Films*, and *The Philosophy of Documentary Film: Image, Sound, Fiction, Truth*. He is the author of *On Emerson*, *Emerson's English Traits and the Natural History of Metaphor*, and editor of *Estimating Emerson: An Anthology of Criticism from Carlyle to Cavell* and Stanley Cavell's *Emerson's Transcendental Etudes*. His articles have appeared in journals such as *Afterimage*, *Cinema*, *Epoché*, *Estetica*, *Liminalities*, *Post Script*, *Transactions*, *Film and Philosophy*, *The Senses and Society*, *The Midwest Quarterly*, *Journalism, Media and Cultural Studies*,

The Journal of Aesthetic Education, and *The Journal of Aesthetics and Art Criticism*, and he has served as guest editor of a commemorative issue of *Conversations: The Journal of Cavellian Studies* entitled Acknowledging Stanley Cavell (no. 7). As a documentary filmmaker, he produced and edited six features in *The Intellectual Portrait Series*, directed *Brunello Cucinelli: A New Philosophy of Clothes*, and codirected *New York Photographer: Jill Freedman in the City*. He studied in the Rhetoric department at Berkeley, conducted research as Harvard's Sinclair Kennedy Traveling Fellow in the United Kingdom, and participated in an NEH Institute, a workshop with Abbas Kiarostami, Werner Herzog's Rogue Film School, and the School of Criticism and Theory at Cornell. He has taught philosophy, rhetoric, and cinema and held visiting research or teaching positions at Binghamton, Cornell, Cortland, Harvard, Ithaca College, the School of Visual Arts, and Vanderbilt. www.DavidLaRocca.org, DavidLaRocca@Post.Harvard.Edu.

Brian W. Nail is an instructional designer at Unity College in Maine. As a writer and scholar, he specializes in religion and literature, legal philosophy, and theories of sacrifice and sociopolitical crisis. After completing his doctorate in Literature and Theology at the University of Glasgow, Scotland, he was awarded an AFR-Marie Curie Cofund Fellowship in the Legal Philosophy Research Unit at the University of Luxembourg. In addition to his published journal articles and book chapters, he is a coeditor and contributor to *Law's Sacrifice: Approaching the Problem of Sacrifice in Law, Literature, and Philosophy* (Routledge, 2020). He is currently working on a monograph exploring the sacrificial legacies of settler colonialism in American culture.

Caro Pirri is Assistant Professor of English at the University of Pittsburgh. She is currently working on her first book, *Settlement Aesthetics: Theatricality, Form, and Failure in Early Modern England*, which shows how English dramatists were turning to the early accounts of England's New World conquests to solve theatrical problems, recognizing in them a set of formal techniques for representing crisis that could help them respond to changes in their own dramatic medium. Her research and teaching interests include Renaissance Literature and Culture, art and aesthetics, settler colonial studies, early theater history, and performance theory. Her published work has most recently appeared in *Exemplaria* and *Renaissance Drama*.

INDEX

Acker, Kathy 299, 301
  See also autobiography; biography
Acknowledgments, as genre 340–1
  See also Stanley Cavell:
    acknowledgement, concept of
acoustics 205, 208–9, 214–16, 233,
    251
  unconscious 208
  See also sound
adaptation 103
  film 169 n25, 275
  literary 103, 111
  as translation 33 n33
  See also genre
Adorno, Theodore 235
Agamben, Giorgio 78, 190
alienation 135–6, 190–1
  natal 122
  as defamiliarization 246
Alone. Life Wastes Andy Hardy
  (Arnold) 234–52
  See also Martin Arnold
Altman, Rick 205, 225, 234–5
Altman, Robert 226
Anatomy of Abuses (Stubbe) 52
Andy Hardy Meets Debutante (Seitz)
  237–9, 242–3, 249–51
androgyny 146–8, 154, 160, 162–3
  See also gender; genre
antitheatricality 47–69
  as anti-visuality (Fried) 66 n19
  See also theater, theatrics
Appandurai, Arjun 17
Apter, Emily 11, 13, 17, 22, 26, 31
    nn4–5, 32 n23, 36, 204, 219,
    224–5, 227, 233–4
  on gender 293–304
  on *Geschlecht* 293–304

  on lectiocentrism 280
  on lexilalia 31 n4, 37, 39, 43, 204
  on looking and reading 219, 224,
    280–1
  seminar with 14, 18–19, 35, 331–4
  on trans-ontology 293–304
  untranslatability, approach to 11,
    17, 32 n23
  "Untranslatable?" 281
Aristotle 5, 27, 37, 41–2, 105, 123 n6,
    128–9, 132, 138–9, 154
Arnheim, Rudolph 234–5
Arnold, Martin 234–55, 258, 266
    n110, 335
Arrival of a Train at La Ciotat
    (Lumière) 214
Auerbach, Erich 144
autobiography and autobiographical
    38, 158, 222, 239
  See also biography
avant-garde film (and experimental
    cinema) 229, 237–42, 246–9,
    251, 254–6, 258, 335–6
  See also film

Babe in Arms (Berkeley) 237–9, 242
Badiou, Alain 5–6, 17, 31 n12
Baer, Benjamin Conisbee 17
Bakhtin, Mikhail 145, 164, 272
Balázs, Béla 220, 235, 245
Balsom, Erika 248–9
Bardadrac (Genette) 38–9
Barish, Jonas 50
Barthes, Roland 38, 211, 219, 274
  The Pleasure of the Text 274
Batchelor, John 144
Bazin, André 275
de Beauvoir, Simone 294

Becoming an Image (Cassils) 299–300
Beecroft, Alexander 17
Bell, Quentin 143, 147, 168 n21
Bennet, Arnold 150, 153
Bennington, Geoffrey 10
Benjamin, Walter 44, 208, 245–6, 248, 262 n41, 263 n46
Bering-Porter, David 244–6
Berkeley, Busby 238
Bildungsroman 102–3, 111–13
biography and biographical 143–53, 156, 158–64, 166–7, 168 n21,168 n24, 299
   intellectual 13, 38
   See also autobiography; Virginia Woolf: *Orlando*
biopolitics 187, 194, 196
Blake, Nayland 299
Bloom, Harold 225, 281
body politic 74–5, 87–8
   See also embodiment; human body
Bolt, Marvin 180
Bordwell, David 217–18
Borgmann, Dimitri 7
Born, Peter 101
boundaries 8, 16–21, 26–30, 47, 80, 85, 107, 113, 116, 252–8
   binaries and 254
   borders and 252
   generic 148, 158, 194, 197, 258
   linguistic 17, 252–3, 281, 287–8
   See also borders; migration
borders 16, 18–19, 72–4, 117–18, 149, 252, 257
   crossing 30, 78, 128
   cultural 73
   death and 95
   form and 111
   genre 252–60
   security 77, 80, 87, 91, 93
   See also boundaries; migration
Bower, Anne 109
Breaking Point (Curtiz) 278
Brakhage, Stan 218, 220, 249
Brecht, Bertolt 169 n29, 246
Brockelman, Thomas 175–6, 185
Brontë, Charlotte 111, 160
Bronx Gothic (Okpokwasili) 101–25

Buber, Martin 85–6
Burke, Kenneth 7
Butler, Judith 9–10, 131, 133–4, 187–8, 281, 294–5, 299, 302 n1–2
   "Gender and Gender Trouble" 131, 133–4
   Gender Trouble 9–10, 295, 302 n2
Butoh 103

Cagney, James 279
Capitol Riot 89–91
Carlson, Shanna 302
Casanova, Pascale 17
Cassils 299–300
Cassin, Barbara 2–8, 11, 13, 22, 27, 29, 30 n4, 36–40, 43–4, 129, 130–1, 224–7, 233–4, 295, 331
   Vocabulaire européen des philosophies 3–4, 30 n4, 31 n12, 39, 43, 226–7, 294–5
   L'Effet Sophistique 4
   Jacques le Sophiste 4
   "Philosophizing in Languages" 36–8, 43–4
   Sophistical Practice 129, 131
category problems 2, 8, 15, 20, 61, 128, 148, 153, 163–4
   categorization and 161–7
   category and 2, 10, 256, 294–5
Caughie, Pamela L. 148, 164
Cavell, Stanley 38, 40, 205, 208, 210, 218, 220–4, 233–4, 237, 246, 258, 262 n27, 265 n86, 272, 280, 288, 290, 292, 331, 334, 336, 338–9
   acknowledgement, concept of 336, 338–9
   "Beginning to Read Barbara Cassin" 38, 40
   on cycles 279, 282–6, 289, 291
   on film as medium 221–4, 233, 262 n26, 280, 288, 290
   on genre 275, 279, 282–95
   inheritance of 336–41
   on inheritance 285
   "It Happened One Night" 290, 292
   on photography 265 n86, 276, 280, 284, 288

on television 282–9, 291
on types 277–80
"Types; Cycles as Genres" 280
See also Acknowledgments
Chansley, Jacob (Jake Angeli) 90–2
QAnon Shaman 90
Chaplin, Charlie 275, 280
Chartier, Roger
"Genre between Literature and History" 274, 288
Chion, Michel 205, 206, 210, 213, 215, 217, 219–20, 230, 244, 263 n43
Chen, Mel 299
Chenoweth, Katie 10, 28–9
cinegraphia 224
cinema
aroma-haptic 230
avant-garde 229, 237–8, 246, 248–9, 256, 258, 335–6
of de-marriage (MacDonald) 237
experimental 16, 203, 212, 215, 229, 237–42, 246, 251, 253, 254–5
medium of 221–4, 233, 261 n26, 275–80, 288, 290
metacinema and 212, 215–17, 235, 237, 239, 248, 255, 335–6, 344
psychoanalysis and 238–40, 245, 247, 250
of remarriage (Cavell) 220–1, 237, 246, 282, 285, 290–2
sound and 26, 203–69
See also film
cinema studies See film studies
cinematograph 214, 228
cinephilia 214
The Cineseizure (Arnold) 237–43, 247, 249, 252
See also Martin Arnold
Clark, David 242–3
cognitive film theory 205, 239
colonialism (settler) 74, 76, 90–4
See also hegemony; sovereignty; zoopolitics
The Color Purple (Walker) 109
comedy of remarriage (Cavell) 220–1, 237, 246, 282, 285, 290–2

complex
Geschlecht as 1–33, 48, 63, 64, 74–6, 85–7, 92–4, 239, 294, 300
nervous condition as 8, 12–13, 19–20, 28, 30, 247–8
Oedipus 187
scholarly-industrial 10
computer-generated imagery (CGI) 212
concert recordings (audio) 218
concert film 218
Cook, Elizabeth Heckendorn 106
Cooper, Gary 279
Copjec, Joan 187, 294, 303 n9
Corrigan, Timothy 214, 216, 263 n46
Covid-19 (coronavirus pandemic) 13, 206, 259
Cremin, Ciara 10
Crépon, Marc 9, 36, 40, 81, 85–6, 132, 226–8, 298–9
Geschlecht (definition) 36, 39–40, 86, 131–2, 226–8, 298–9
Crimmins, Jonathan
"Gender, Genre and the Near Future in Derrida's 'The Law of Genre'" 273, 281, 290
Critical Mass (Frampton) 234–7
See also avant-garde film
crisis 71–99
of liberalism 73–4
of neoliberalism 72
critical vocabulary 2, 7
criticism
sound 203–69
theatrical 66 n13
See also film criticism
Croce, Benedetto
"Criticism of the Theory of Artistic and Literary Kinds" 288
Cuddy-Keane, Melba 155, 157, 166

Dahl, Adam 94
Danto, Arthur 222
Dasein
Geschlecht and 36, 60–1, 82–3, 134, 295
neutrality of 11, 133–4, 190–1, 296–7
sexistence and 300–1

sexual difference and 304 n18
thereness of 10
See also body politic; embodiment
(and the linguistic); human body
David-Ménard, Monique
"Gender" 130-2
Davis, Wendy 88
death drive 84-5, 95
deepfake 212, 230, 258
de Gay, Jane 158
Deleuze, Gilles 214, 216, 218-19, 228
de Man, Paul 196, 219, 281
democracy 76, 90-1, 94
Derber, Charles 74
Derrida, Jacques 10-12, 22, 28-9, 38,
   60-1, 76-80, 82-4, 86-9, 92,
   94-5, 131-2, 165, 173-4, 190-1,
   216, 226-7, 262 n27, 263 n58,
   280-2, 289-91, 297-8, 300,
   339, 341
  The Beast and the Sovereign 71,
   78-9, 85, 89
  The Gift of Death 78, 95
  "*Geschlecht* I: Sexual Difference,
   Ontological Difference" 10-11,
   129, 134-5, 173-4, 191
  "*Geschlecht* II: Heidegger's Hand"
   82
  "*Geschlecht* III: Sex, Race, Nation,
   Humanity," 297
  "*Geschlecht* IV: Heidegger's Ear—
   Philopolemology," 10
  Of Grammatology 209, 211, 243,
   261 n21
  Krell, David Farrell and 10-11,
   296-7
  "The Law of Genre" 12, 273-5,
   281-2, 289-91
  Monolingualism of the Other 92
  "Racism's Last Word" 79
  Specters of Marx 96 n21, 339, 342
   n7
Descartes, René 5, 137, 141 n8, 165,
   263 n58
Deutscher, Penelope
  "Gender" 130-2
Dickens, Charles 111, 275
digesture (Lippit) 243-4, 249

documentary
  filmmaking 16-17, 258, 262 n32
  index 212, 262 n32
Driver, Adam 204-5
DuBois, W. E. B. 111, 131

Eagleton, Terry 144, 164
Early English Theater 47-68
  See also theater
Edison, Thomas 228
Eisler, Hans 235
Eggert, Katherine 63
Ellison, Ralph 26, 174, 191, 194-8
  Invisible Man 26, 174, 196-8
Elsaesser, Thomas 229, 334
embodiment (and the linguistic) 25,
   102-3, 107, 113, 115, 118, 122,
   233, 241, 253, 255
  See also body politic; *Dasein*;
   human body
Emerson, Ralph Waldo 33 n32, 260
   n7, 265 n88, 268 n166, 334,
   337-8, 340, 342 n11, 344
epistolary
  form 104-6, 108-9
  literature 106
  narrative 102-3, 105-9, 115, 120-2
  novel 105, 109, 111, 123 n5, 124
   n19
  mode 107-13
Epstein, Jean 219, 245
Eros 84
Esposito, Roberto 74-5, 84, 87-9
  autoimmunity 75, 88-9, 93
  body politic 74-5, 88
  Immunitas 95 n12
Eurochronology Problem 17

fable 79-80
Fichte, J. G. 294
Fields, W. C. 280
film 8, 13, 17, 21-2, 101, 204-58,
   275-87, 289-91
  adaptation 169 n25, 275
  citationality of 221
  cognitive film theory and 205, 239
  criticism 210, 212, 224, 246-7, 259
  criticism as translation 237

documentary 16–17, 258, 262 n32
experimental 28
Hollywood 215–16, 220, 231–2, 236, 239–40, 242, 248–52, 256, 258
medium of 221–4, 233, 261 n26, 275–80, 288, 290
ontology of 20, 207, 212, 221, 229–30, 235–6
ordinary language film studies 20
reading 26, 208, 210, 217–24, 234, 238–41, 247, 251–2, 255, 277, 280–1, 283
sound on 26, 203–69
See also avant-garde; cinema
film studies 20, 22, 205–6, 218–19, 221, 232, 234–5, 238, 256
film theory 23
First Cow (Reichardt) 233
Fontaine, Jean de la 79–80
Ford, John 232–3
Forster, E. M. 144
Foucault, Michel 26, 36, 174–84, 186–90, 192–4, 196, 198 n11, 198 n16, 199 n21, 199 n48, 263 n58, 303 n8
history 176–7, 183–9
History of Madness 178–9, 198 n11, 198 n16, 199 n48
The Order of Things 175–6, 180, 183, 199 n21
representation and 177–81, 189
and the subject 182–4, 186–90
Velázquez, *Las Meninas*, and 174–86, 189
See also psychoanalysis
Fowler, Alistair 145
Frampton, Hollis 234–7, 254–5, 265 n99, 335
See also avant-garde film
Fraser, Nancy 72
Freska, Friedrich 214
Freud, Sigmund 41, 83–4, 96 n40, 125 n37, 187, 238–40, 246, 262 n41, 302 n2, 303 n9
Beyond the Pleasure Principle 84
cinema and 238, 240–1, 246, 262 n41, 302 n2

Civilization and Its Discontents 84
Oedipus complex 187
Psychopathology of Everyday Life 246
Three Essays on the Theory of Sexuality 83
See also psychoanalysis

Garfield, John 278
Garland, Judy 237–8, 241–2
Gates, Jr., Henry Louis 109
Gedankenschrift 341, 342 n13
See also Acknowledgments; Stanley Cavell: acknowledgment, concept of; translatability of thanks
Gehr, Ernie 265 n98
See also avant-garde film
gender 2, 9, 10, 17, 20, 28, 146, 148, 153, 155, 159–60, 162–3, 165–6, 293–7, 300–2
binaries 135, 145–6, 149, 163, 230, 293, 296, 300, 302, 303 n5
difference 9–10, 25, 134–7, 148, 164–5, 174, 281, 293, 294, 299–302, 304 n18
discrimination 293–6
gendered being and 106, 160, 300–2, 302 n1
geschlechtlos and 297
naming 1, 10, 12, 106–7, 174, 295–6, 302
of sound 205
violence 165, 295, 300–2, 302 n1
See also *Dasein*; embodiment; genre; *Geschlecht*; human body
general adversarial network (GAN) 212, 230
Genesis 24, 85, 260 n7
See also ontogenesis
genre 10, 17, 20, 26, 28, 145, 148–50, 152–5, 158–66, 295, 301
as cycle 222, 232, 256, 268 n176, 279, 282–6, 289, 291
as medium 222, 232, 279, 282–7, 289, 291
ontology and/of 60, 174, 207, 221, 225, 229–30, 235, 257, 301

post- 20–1, 253, 257
remarriage (Cavell) 220–1, 237, 246, 282, 285–6, 290–2
transgenre 146, 148, 169 n25, 298
See also borders; boundaries; gender; *Geschlecht*; migration
generic
  contest 156, 254
  conventions 145, 150, 152–3, 156–7, 159–62, 164, 167, 231
  designations 163
  disorder 10
  identity 144–6, 149, 153, 159
  instability 161, 164
  See also genre
Genette, Gérard 38, 149, 274
Geschlecht 1–3, 8–12, 15, 20, 22, 24–6, 33 n33, 36, 39–40, 60–1, 74–5, 82–3, 127–8, 131, 149, 169 n29, 173–4, 227, 257, 294–9, 301
  Dasein and 36, 60–1, 82–3, 133–4, 295
  multivocality/multivocity of 9, 20, 40, 48, 85, 131, 227, 271
  polysemy of 1, 8–9, 25, 40, 61, 82–3, 86, 94, 230, 271
  as untranslatable 3, 7–11, 19–20, 36–7, 39, 227, 230, 295
  See also Dasein; gender; genre
geschlechtlos 297
  See also human body: degendered
Geschlechtslosigkeit 25, 128, 134–5
glossolalia 112
Goethe, von J. W. 111
Goldman, Jane 146, 148
Gone with the Wind (Fleming) 278
Gorgias 5, 37–8
Gosson, Stephen 24, 52–9, 62, 64, 66 n17, 67 n28
Gothic literature 103–4, 111
Gottheim, Larry 236, 335
  See also avant-garde film
graphics interchange format (GIF) 212
grammatology 209–11, 261 n21
  of the unconscious 243
  See also Jacques Derrida; metagrammatology

gramophone 209
gramophonology 26, 203–69
Great Expectations (Dickens) 111
griot 102–3, 121–2

Hagan, Jean 217
Halberstam, Jack 11
Hapax Legomena (Frampton) 234, 265 n99
  See also avant-garde film
Hartman, Geoffrey 210
Hauser, Arnold 275
Hegel, G. W. F. 5, 42–3, 164
hegemony
  American 72–4
  cultural 81
  crisis 72–5
  genre 145
  heteropatriarchal 89
  narrative 113, 124 n28
  political 88
  See also settler colonialism; sovereignty
Heidegger, Martin 5, 8, 10–11, 37, 43, 61, 79–83, 129, 131–2, 134–5, 173–4, 186, 190, 226–7, 294, 297–8, 300, 304 n18
  See also Dasein
Heller-Roazen, Daniel 58, 128, 130, 132, 140
  "Varieties of Indefiniteness" 128–30, 132, 138–40
Henderson, Mae G. 111–12
Heraclitus 2
Herzog, Werner 225–6, 258, 269 n181, 345
Hilliard, Stephen 53
Histrio-mastix (Prynne) 52
Hobbes, Thomas 84
Hollywood *See* film: Hollywood
the Holocaust 87
Homer 5
Huber, Lindsay Perez 75
human body
  Blackness and the 25, 101, 103–4, 108–13, 118–22
  as degendered 300
  dissolution of the 107–8, 116

geschlechtlos 297
language and the 25, 101–4, 106, 116–17, 120–2
pain and the 108, 110–11, 118–21
See also Dasein; gender; genre; embodiment
humanism 2, 22, 82, 111, 199 n48, 253
Humboldt, Wilhelm von 3
Hurston, Zora Neale 109
Husserl, Edmund 300

immigration 25, 72–82, 93
See also borders; boundaries; migration
inheritance 17, 152, 257, 285, 299, 303 n9, 336–7, 339, 341
Cavell, Stanley and 336–9
Copjec, Joan on 303 n9
Derrida, Jacques on 339, 341
inclusive-exclusive 73, 76, 80, 82–3, 88, 90
intersemiotic (translation) 21, 25, 64
See also semiotics
Invisible Man (Ellison), 26, 174, 196–8
Irigaray, Luce 108, 136, 141 n8, 165, 263 n58, 281
To Be Two 108, 124 n15, 136
Ives, Lucy 211

Jakobson, Roman 21, 64
James, Henry 280
Jane Eyre (Brontë) 111
Jarmusch, Jim 204–5
Jauss, Hans Robert
"Theory of Genres and Medieval Literature" 273
Johnston, Daniel 50

Kant, Immanuel 43, 85, 258, 299
Kaufman, Charlie 258, 269 n181
Keaton, Buster 280
kinetograph 228
kinship trouble (Chen) 299
Kistner, Ulrike 83–4
Kracauer, Siegfried 208, 245
Krell, David Farrell 10–11, 296–7, 304 n18
Kristeva, Julia 146–7, 162–4

Lacan, Jacques 4, 26, 41, 108, 117, 125 n37, 173–7, 184–90, 199 n36, 199 n40, 295, 300–1, 302 n2, 303 n9
The Object of Psychoanalysis 173, 200 n49
"The Purloined Letter" and 108
and the subject 108, 117, 173–7, 185–90, 200 nn48–49
Velázquez, *Las Meninas* and 176, 184–6, 189
See also psychoanalysis
Laclau, Ernesto 187
Las Meninas (Velázquez), 26, 173–86, 189
law of non-contradiction 9, 27–8
Leaska, Mitchell A. 144, 149
lectiocentrism 26, 203–69, 280
Leigh, Vivian 278
Leroi-Gourhan, André 192, 193, 196
lexilalia 31 n4, 36–9, 43, 224, 234
liberalism 73–4, 76, 92–4
See also neoliberalism
Life of an American Fireman (Porter) 215
Lin, Erika 49, 68 n66
linguistics
attunement 20
boundaries 17, 252–3, 281, 287–8
description 16, 20–1, 107, 140, 255
displacement 3
embodiment and the 25, 103, 107, 113, 115, 118, 122, 231, 237, 252, 255
expression 24, 115, 118, 122
intra- 39
modern 2
negation 25
non- 64, 211, 224
pre- 230–1
recreational 7
signifier 108, 125 n37, 135
trans- 27
translation 2, 4, 113, 169 n29
turn 5
Littau, Karin 208, 214, 262 n41
Lippit, Akira Mizuta 243–4
Loesser, Frank 275

logology 5–7, 37, 41, 131
Lopez, Jeremy 49, 68 n65
Lumière brothers 214–15, 219, 228
Lukács, Georg 144, 164
Luther, Martin 85–6
Lyly, John 53
Lynch, David 251

MacLean, Gerald 108
MacDonald, Scott 236–7, 248, 251, 336
Make America Great Again (MAGA) 73–4, 87, 89–90, 93
Malabou, Catherine 11, 17, 135–7, 164–6
  Changing Difference 135–7, 164–5
Malick, Terrence 226, 232, 258
Manovich, Lev 256
Marcel, Gabriel 207–8
Marcus, Laura 147, 149, 152
Marin, Louis 79
Marlowe, Christopher 53
medieval period
  epistemology of 63
  literature and the 155, 273
  logic of the 36–7
  See also antitheatricality
Meek's Cutoff (Reichardt) 233
Melita, Maureen M. 154
Melville, Herman 219
memory 195, 229
  history and 121
  inheritance and 341
  personal 103, 119–21
  See also inheritance
Merleau-Ponty, Maurice 205–6, 230
messianism 85, 95
metacinema 212, 215–17, 235, 237, 239, 248, 255, 335–6, 344
  sound and 212, 215–17, 235, 255, 336
  See also cinema
metacognition, nondual 254
metacognitive subvocalization 211
metacriticism 20–2, 109, 114, 220
metadocumentary 272
metadrama 49, 64
metaformalism 239, 246

metagrammatology 209–10
metalepsis 155–8, 166
metaphilology 206
metaphilosophy 12, 206, 239, 248, 252
metaphor 19, 38–9, 77, 194–7, 203, 217–19, 224, 234, 260 n2, 265 n88, 274–5, 303 n8
metapoetics 144–5, 149, 151, 157–61
Metro-Goldwyn Mayer (MGM) 215
migration/the migratory 19, 78, 95
  See also borders; boundaries; gender; genre; immigration
Moi, Toril 146–7, 162, 166
Moretti, Franco 17
MS-13 77–8
multivocality/multivocity 9, 20, 40, 48, 85, 131, 227, 271
  See also univocity
Mulvey, Laura 231–2, 242–4
Muybridge, Eadweard 214, 228, 245

Nancy, Jean-Luc 130, 136–7, 296, 298–301
  L'Intrus 130, 136–7
neoliberalism 72–6
  See also liberalism
New Criticism 288
New Formalism 62
New Historicism 62
Nicolson, Harold 152–3
Nicolson, Nigel 144
Nietzsche, Friedrich 45 n8, 280–1
Novalis 6–7, 44 n6
novel 143–5, 150, 155–6, 160–1, 163–4
  anti-novel 145
  epistolary form and the 105, 109

ocularcentrism 210, 214
Okpokwasili, Okwui 101–26
Olin-Hitt, Micheal R. 160–1
ontogenesis 26, 174, 260 n7
ontology
  of film 20, 206–7, 212, 221–5, 229–30, 235–6
  and/of genre 60, 174, 205–7, 222–3, 225, 229–30, 235, 257, 301

sexual 25, 162, 164–5, 174, 228, 296–302
   of sound on/in/as film 203–69
   trans- 2, 298–302
Ordinary Language Philosophy (OLP) 20
Ordinary Language Film Studies (OLFS) 20
Ordinary Literary Criticism (OLC) 20
Orlando Furioso (Ariosto) 154–5, 160
ostranenie 246

Padgett, Ron 205
Palance, Jack 277
Pamela (Richardson) 105, 124 n19
Panh, Rithy 258
Panofsky, Erwin 275–7
paratext 149–53, 161, 166
Parmenides 1–2
Passage à l'acte (Arnold) 237, 244, 266 n113
   See also Martin Arnold
Paterson (Jarmusch) 204–5
Paterson (Williams) 203–7
Patterson, Orlando 122
Petrusich, Amanda 256–8
philology 2–4, 7–8, 12, 22, 45 n8, 206, 211, 213, 216, 296–7, 333
philosophizing in languages 3, 7, 36–8, 41–4, 295
   See also Barbara Cassin
phonocentrism 209–10, 261 n21
phonograph 209, 228
phonophobia 209, 219
photographs 90, 150–1, 284
   projecting 276
   ontology of 280
photography 214, 227–8, 262 n32, 265 n86, 288, 300
   painting and 288
   time-lapse 245
   trick 248
Pièce touchée (Arnold) 237, 266 n113
   See also Martin Arnold
Pinch, Trevor 205
Pinky (Kazan) 279
Pixar 220

Plato 5, 37, 43, 44 n3, 44 n4, 193, 209, 253, 337–8, 340
plasticity 164–6
plurality (semantic) 74, 75, 82
   See also multivocality
Poe, Edgar Allan 108
Pollock, Jackson 222, 276
Porter, Edwin S. 215
Preciado, Paul Beatriz 294
   Testo Junkie 133–4
Proust, Marcel 161, 280
Prynne, William 52
psychoanalysis 96 n40, 131, 162, 208, 303 n9
   Arnold, Martin and 237–40, 245, 247–8, 250–1
   cinema and 235–6
   Foucault and 175–6
   Gothic literature and 103–4
   Lacan and 4, 117, 173, 175–6, 199 n35, 199 n40
   semiotics and 216
   See also Sigmund Freud; Jacques Lacan
"The Purloined Letter" (Poe) 108

racist nativism 75–6, 86, 89, 92
A Raisin in the Sun (Petrie) 279
reality
   augmented (AR) 230
   dream and 153, 155
   illusion and 63, 68 n65
   mixed (MR) 230
   social 50, 165, 167, 245
   of sound 219, 228, 256
   text 161
   virtual (VR) 230
reception 232, 235, 237–41
   audience 256
   histories 19, 61
   of images 217
   practices 231, 235, 238, 241
   of sound 212, 237
   studies 232
Rée, Jonathan 295
Reichardt, Kelly 226, 233, 255, 258, 260 n8

Removed (Uman) 249
Renaissance 154–5, 158–60, 345
repetition compulsion 247, 251
revelationism (film) 245–6, 248, 250
Reynolds, Debbie 217
Richardson, Samuel 105–6, 124 n19, 159
Ricoeur, Paul 21
Roach, Joseph 121
Rooney, Mickey 237–8, 241–2
Rosenzweig, Franz 85–6
Rouch, Jean 17

Sacks, Oliver 206, 228
Sackville-West, Vita 143–5, 148, 150–1, 156, 159
Sandford, Stella
  "'Sex' and 'Sexual Difference'" 132–3
Sapir-Whorf hypothesis 2
Scarry, Elaine 118
Schaefer, Dirk 240, 251
Schatz, Thomas 225, 256
The Schoole of Abuse (Gosson) 24, 52–9, 67 n26, 67 n28
scopocentrism 211, 214, 227
scopophilia 211, 214, 262 n41
  fetishistic 232
The Searchers (Ford) 232–3
Sensory Ethnography Lab 17
Seitz, George B. 237–8
self-identification (gender) 293, 296
Sensory Ethnography Lab (SEL) 17, 32 n27, 336
semiotics 16, 19, 21, 25, 27, 60, 64, 216
Serene Velocity (Gehr) 265 n98
settler colonialism 74, 76, 90–4
  See also hegemony; sovereignty; zoopolitics
sex 1–2, 9–11, 13, 25, 36, 40, 81, 83–6, 89, 110–11, 127, 129–35, 146–8, 152, 157, 164–6, 174, 227, 241, 293–5, 298–301, 302 n2
sexed becoming 11, 296, 300–1
sexism/sexist 73, 88, 293, 296, 300–1
sexistence (Nancy) 296, 300–1

sexual
  difference 10–11, 25, 40, 60, 82, 89, 129, 134–7, 174, 281, 295, 300–1
  hierarchies 75, 84, 89
  identity 183, 188, 194, 294
  ontology 25, 162, 164–6, 174, 228, 296–302
  violence 105, 165, 294–5, 300–2, 302 n1
  relation 11, 85, 129, 165, 293, 301
  See also sex
Shakespeare, William 53, 159–60, 284, 290
  Hamlet 63–4
Showalter, Elaine 146–7
silence
  cinematic 208, 210, 215, 225–7
  sound and 189, 205, 215, 227
  worldly 205, 226, 254, 257
  See also film; sound
Silverman, Kaja 205
Singin' in the Rain (Donen and Kelly) 215–17, 235
Sophists (ancient Greek) 4–6, 8–9, 24, 31 n12, 37–8, 41, 43, 45 n7, 193
  See also Barbara Cassin
sound
  cinema and 26, 203–69
  genres 22, 26, 102, 203–69
  as index 212–13, 217, 262 n32
  reading 26, 209–11, 217–21, 223–5, 237, 251–2, 255, 262 n27
  sync 205, 215, 218, 225–6, 229, 235–6, 255
  See also criticism; film; silence
sound-image (and sound/image) 219, 221, 230, 235–6
  See also sound
sound studies 205, 219, 235
  on film 203–69
sovereignty 25, 72–4, 79–80, 84, 86–8, 92–5
  American 72
  settler 74, 92–5
  See also hegemony; settler colonialism; zoopolitics

Spillers, Hortense J.
  "Mama's Baby, Papa's Maybe" 112, 130–1, 137
Stagecoach (Ford) 232–3
Stevens, Kyle 205, 260 n8
Stewart, Garrett 205, 209–11, 221, 261 n26, 262 n27, 336
  metagrammatology 209
  phonophobia 209, 219
  subvocal literary enunciation 210–11, 255
Strachey, James 83
Stubbe, Philip 52
style 159–61
subjectivity
  split 108, 111, 120–2

Tarantino, Quentin 232
television 258, 282–90
  See also Stanley Cavell: on television
Thanatos 84
theater 8, 24, 26, 28, 47–69, 114, 275
  as spectacle 54–6, 61
  conventions 48–51, 56–7, 61–2, 68 n65
  community 47–8
  epic (Brecht) 246
  genre(s) of 47–69
  Hollywood as 280
  reflexiveness of 62–3
  See also antitheatricality; Early English Theater
theatricality, 24–5, 47–69
  in criticism, 24, 49–50, 59–62, 64
  as style 57, 59
  See also antitheatricality; theater
theatrics
  of vision 216
theatron 47
Their Eyes Were Watching God (Hurston) 109
Therezo, Rodrigo 10
Thompson, Kristin 217–18
Trakl, Georg 298
transdisciplinarity 2, 15–17
  border-crossings and 19, 29–30
  boundaries and 16–19, 27–8
  See also borders; boundaries; genre; migration
transgender 146, 151–2, 154, 293–5, 302
translatability
  of thanks 337–41 *See also* *Gedankenschrift*
translation 1–4, 6–12, 14–15, 18–29, 33 n33, 36–9, 42, 47, 60–2, 64, 79, 83–6, 127–8, 174, 207–8, 220, 237–9, 295, 337–8
  conceptual 2–4, 8, 11–12, 19–21, 26–7, 29, 127–8, 131, 174, 191, 205, 220, 271
  corporeality and 102, 128
  intergeneric 48, 50, 58, 60, 159
  media and 203–6, 212, 222–3, 252, 255, 257
  plurality of languages and 36–7, 43–4
  problems 6–9, 19–20, 24, 36, 40, 61, 79, 191, 206, 224–5, 255, 281, 295
  See also borders; boundaries; gender; genre; migration; untranslatability
translational hermeneutics 21, 26, 203, 217, 253, 255
translator, the 3–4, 13, 39, 45 n14, 83, 227, 271
  invisibility of 3–4
trans-ontology 298–302
transsexuality 26, 146, 162, 168 n15
transvestism 11–12, 33 n33
Trakl, Georg 80, 82–3, 298
trouble
  gender (Butler) 9–10, 131, 133–4, 295, 302 n2
  inheritance (Copjec) 303 n9
  kinship (Chen) 299
Trump, Donald J. 25, 28, 70, 77, 80–1, 86, 88–93, 293
  2016 Presidential election 72–3, 76
  Trumpism 72–4, 93
  See also hegemony; sovereignty; zoopolitics
Turvey, Malcolm 245

Uman, Naomi 249
univocality/univocity 41, 85, 271, 341
  See also multivocality/multivocity; plurality (semantic)
untranslatability 2–3, 8–9, 11, 17, 19–22, 26–7, 203, 224–5, 230, 295
  See also translation
untranslatable, concept of the 5–6, 8–20, 24, 27, 36–7, 39, 41, 43, 58, 64, 175, 224, 227, 234, 237, 253–4, 257, 295–6
U.S. Immigration and Customs Enforcement (ICE) 72, 77

Velázquez, Diego 173–4, 175–82, 183–6, 189
  Las Meninas 173–4, 175–82, 182–6, 189
Venuti, Lawrence 3–4
Verdi, Giuseppe 275
Verfremdungseffekt 246
Vertov, Dziga 245
Villarejo, Amy 231–4
vococentrism 210
voyeurism 214, 232

Walker, Alice 109
Wark, MacKenzie 294, 299, 301
Watt, Ian 105
Wayne, John 233
Weheliye, Alexander G.
  Habeas Viscus 132
Wells, Susan
  "Genres as Species and Spaces" 273–5, 282, 288–90

West, Cornel 213
West, Will 48, 67 n33
Whitman, Walt 82
Wilson, J. J. 145
Wittgenstein, Ludwig 38, 238, 246, 253
Wood, James 255
Woolf, Virginia 1, 25, 28, 143–71
  The Letters of 145
  To the Lighthouse 143–5, 158
  "The New Biography" 152–3
  Orlando: A Biography 143–71
  A Room of One's Own 146–7
  "What is a Novel?" 147
  A Writer's Diary 143
  See also biography
Wollen, Peter 216–17
Wilhelm Meister's Apprenticeship (Goethe) 111
Williams, Linda 215, 335
Williams, William Carlos 203–7

Yates, Julian 63

Zeilinger, Martin J. 247
Žižek, Slavoj 187–8, 302 n2
zoopraxography 214, 228
zoopolitics 25, 74–81, 86–8, 91–3
  See also settler colonialism; sovereignty
Zryd, Michael 238, 240, 244–5, 247, 251
Zunshine, Lisa 205
Zupancic, Alenka 301–2